Malory's *Morte Darthur*

Malory's
Morte Darthur

LARRY D. BENSON

Harvard University Press
Cambridge, Massachusetts
and London, England

Second printing 1977

Publication of this volume has been aided by a grant from the
Hyder Edward Rollins Fund

Printed in the United States of America

Library of Congress Cataloging in Publication Data

Benson, Larry Dean, 1929-
    Malory's Morte Darthur.

    Bibliography: p.
    Includes index.
    1. Malory, Thomas, Sir, 15th cent. Morte d'Arthur.
I. Title.
PR2045.B45   823'.2   75-19233
ISBN 0-674-54393-9

For Amanda and Geoffrey

Preface

Sir Thomas Malory's *Le Morte Darthur* has delighted readers of English literature for over five hundred years, and it remains today the only literary work written between the times of Chaucer and Shakespeare that is still read for pleasure by the general public. It is most often known in "translation" or adaptation, but Malory's work survives even that, and rare indeed is the cultivated reader who has not encountered, in some form, the *Morte Darthur*; it is a part of almost everyone's youth. Consequently, few literary works have so powerfully affected the imagination of the English-speaking peoples. Our idea of King Arthur and his knights depends on Malory, for to most readers, Malory's history of the Round Table is *the* history, and our images of chivalry, of knight-errantry, of adventure in King Arthur's time, and of love in "the lusty month of May" have been shaped by Malory's work.

So popular and influential a work is not much in need of literary criticism; Malory's book did quite well for many years without, sometimes in spite of, the ministrations of literary critics. In the past three decades there has been a great deal of criticism, more than in all the preceding centuries combined, and though this has been unnecessary to the maintenance of Malory's general popularity, it has been necessary to his academic reputation. The old idea of Malory as a genial but usually bungling translator has been changed by this criticism, which has demonstrated clearly that Malory is an artist of skill and imagination, worthy of academic respect as well as general popularity. Perhaps even some nonacademic readers have been shown a new dimension of pleasure in the *Morte Darthur*, which not too long ago was regarded as mainly a work for boys and girls and which is now more widely respected as a serious work of art.

Too serious, I believe. One of the prices we have paid for modern criticism has been an increasingly gloomy interpretation, so that what once seemed a joyous celebration of Arthurian chivalry has become a dark, even "existential" tragedy which reveals the moral degeneration of Arthur's Round Table and ends with dark despair. One wonders if the book the Elizabethan critic Roger Ascham condemned—a work of "open manslaughter and bold bawdry"—would not be more healthy for boys and girls than the hopeless tragedy the *Morte Darthur* appears to be in much modern criticism.

Yet both the idea that the *Morte Darthur* is a children's book and the assumption that it is a tragedy are modern interpretations, arising primarily from the fact that we read the book in isolation from its own time and place. When we think of Malory's book as an Arthurian work, we tend to think of it in relation to the thirteenth-century French romances rather than in a fifteenth-century context, and consequently we assume, with R. W. Chambers, that Malory "held firmly to the old ways" and "at the eleventh hour" looked back nostalgically to a world that was gone forever. When we think of his work as a chivalric romance, we think of the supposedly great days of chivalry in the twelfth century, pay little attention to the actual state of affairs in the fifteenth century, and assume that Malory either mourned the passing of his ideal or bitterly condemned its degeneracy. And, when we think of Malory's work as narrative, we too often assume that he was trying (and failing) to write modern fiction rather than fifteenth-century romance, and we fail to appreciate some of the most delightful parts of the *Morte Darthur*, such as *The Book of Sir Tristram*, which in most modern adaptations is mercilessly cut or omitted altogether.

The study that follows is an attempt to consider the *Morte Darthur* in the context of its own time, and it is based on the assumption that Malory's work can best be appreciated and understood in the light of the traditions on which the author drew and in the literary and historical context in which he wrote. My study is divided into four parts. The first attempts to define the genre of the *Morte Darthur* by considering it in relation to the Arthurian prose cycles as they developed from the thirteenth to the fifteenth centuries and in relation to fifteenth-century, mainly Continental romance. The second part considers Malory's work in relation to the English romance tradition and attempts to explicate his methods of adaptation in the light of the practices of his English predecessors and contemporaries, concentrating primarily on the problem of narrative structure, since that is the main problem for modern readers. Here, as throughout the early chapters of the book, I attempt to trace Malory's general development as a writer by showing the ways in which he applies his narrative techniques with increasing skill from the early tales to his first completely successful works, *The Tale of Sir Gareth* and *The Book of Sir Tristram.*

Just as the *Morte Darthur* seems to go back to the beginning and start anew with *The Book of Sir Tristram,* so my study may seem to start over again in its third major division, in which I consider Malory's relation to chivalry in fifteenth-century life and therefore shift the focus from purely literary to more historical concerns. This section must sometimes move rather far afield from the *Morte Darthur,* but such a move is necessary, for perhaps no aspect of Malory's work has suffered more from our failure to consider the work in the cultural context of its own time, since many modern interpretations of the work are based upon assumptions about the state of chivalry in Malory's time. Interpretation is the principal concern of the fourth part, which concentrates on the last three tales of the *Morte Darthur* in the light of its literary and historical context.

I have tried to avoid making any assumptions about Malory's life, though I suspect that he was advanced in years when he wrote this book, and that suspicion may sometimes be apparent. We know that Malory was a knight, that he was imprisoned, and that he delighted in hunting, in chivalric practices, and in Arthurian literature. William Matthews has shown that we cannot go beyond that. Our Sir Thomas Malory was almost certainly not the colorful jailbird who enlivened so many classroom lectures on the *Morte Darthur,* but as yet none of the other fifteenth-century Thomas Malorys has been proven our author.

I discuss the tales in the *Morte Darthur* as if they were written in roughly the order in which they appear in Eugène Vinaver's edition. Though I realize that Malory perhaps did not write them in this exact order, the first two tales do seem less accomplished than the later ones, and we can trace what seems to be an increasing mastery of narrative technique from *The Tale of King Arthur* to *The Tale of Sir Gareth.* Whether *Gareth* was written before, after, or during the composition of *Sir Tristram* is more difficult, perhaps impossible, to decide, as is the question of when the last three tales were composed. My discussion of *The Tale of King Arthur, Arthur and Lucius, Sir Lancelot,* and *Gareth* is based on the assumption that these four tales were written in roughly that order (though *Arthur and Lucius* may be earlier than *King Arthur* and parts of *Sir Tristram* may have intervened between *Sir Lancelot* and *Gareth*). In the rest of my study, the order in which I consider the tales is simply a matter of convenience.

In studying Malory's use of his sources, I have usually proceeded as if I assumed that the versions he knew are in all essentials the same as those we know. I realize that this is rarely the case, but my interest is generally in relatively large matters, such as the narrative structures, which I do assume are fairly represented by most of the surviving versions.

I have adopted the convention of printing the titles of the eight tales in italics, not because I think they are independent works but because this practice allows me to use quotation marks for the titles supplied by Vinaver for the internal divisions of the tales, such as "La Cote Mal Tayle" or "The Great Tournament." I am not always convinced that Vinaver's internal divisions of the tales are justified (as will appear in my discussion of *King Arthur*), but they supply a convenient form of reference.

I have translated all quotations from foreign languages into modern English and, to save space, I have not usually quoted the original along with the translation, though of course the original is cited in the notes (or in the bibliography in the case of primary sources). I have also regularized the spellings in most Middle English prose quotations, especially those from nonliterary sources, for the spelling variations of late Middle English texts are of minimal interest even to most specialists (including the variations in the Winchester and Caxton versions of Malory; it is a pity we do not have a good regularized edition of the whole *Morte Darthur*).

All quotations of the *Morte Darthur*, aside from a few references directly to the manuscript, are from the second edition of Eugène Vinaver's *Works of Sir Thomas Malory* (1967). This is one of four editions by Vinaver (the first and second three-volume editions and the first and second one-volume editions), all of which differ in pagination and are recent enough that they may still be found in personal libraries. For the benefit of readers who may have a different edition from mine, or may even prefer some edition of Caxton, I have cited references to Malory not by page number but by Caxton's book and chapter divisions (e.g., x.21), which are included in all the available editions.

This study of Malory began some years ago, when a Guggenheim Fellowship allowed me the leisure to begin the reading of Continental prose romances, and my initial debt is therefore to the Guggenheim Foundation. In the years that followed I fitfully pursued this study, often setting it aside for other projects. An invitation from Robert Lumiansky and Herschel Baker to participate in an English I section of the MLA allowed me to organize part of my thinking about Malory, and my chapter on Malory in the book that resulted from that section has been frequently plundered for the present study. Some of the ideas underlying this study have been tried out as lectures over the past few years—a lecture on the *Morte Darthur* as tragedy for the Medieval Guild of Chestnut Hill, on *Sir Tristram* at the University of Toronto, and on chivalry at the University of Arkansas. These occasions allowed me an opportunity to clarify my thoughts about these matters, and if surviving members of those audiences fail to recognize in the following pages the ideas I held when I lectured, this is largely because of the valuable discussions to which the talks led and the helpful suggestions and criticisms that I received. I have discussed Malory privately with so many people over the past few years that I can only offer general thanks to my friends for saving me from more absurdities than this book now may contain. I am especially indebted to my colleagues David Staines and Theodore M. Andersson for reading drafts of the manuscript and offering valuable suggestions and needed encouragement.

I benefited from a careful reading of my manuscript by Robert Lumiansky, who saved me from many stylistic blunders. Luann McCarty typed and retyped the manuscript with patient good cheer.

I owe thanks to Oxford University Press for permission to quote from *The Works of Sir Thomas Malory*, edited by Eugène Vinaver, 2d ed. (1967), 3 vols. (as reprinted with corrections in 1971), and to G. D. Macrae-Gibson for generously supplying me with material to be included in volume II (forthcoming) of his Early English Text Society edition of *Arthour and Merlin*.

I hope that my debt to previous scholars is adequately recorded in the notes, but anyone who writes on Malory owes a special debt to Eugène Vinaver, whose studies and editions of Malory have made all our later work possible.

Contents

I

Malory and Arthurian Romance

1

Malory and the Prose Cycles

Sir Thomas Malory's *Morte Darthur* is a product of the most vigorous and creative literary movement in fifteenth-century Europe, the widespread cultivation of prose romance. Far from dying in the fifteenth century, the genre of romance burst into flourishing new life. In Spain works such as *Amadís de Gaula* engendered scores of imitations that fed the fire of Don Quixote's curate two centuries later. In France writers such as David Aubert produced works such as *Perceforest*, one of the most elaborate fifteenth-century romances and one that remained popular well into the Renaissance. In Germany prose romance had its beginnings in this period, as it did in England, where Malory was among the first practitioners of the new genre. Caxton's press bears witness to the popularity of the fifteenth-century prose romances which set the fashion followed by English writers of aristocratic fiction from Lord Berners to Sir Philip Sidney. It was a general European phenomenon; a work such as *Ponthus et la belle Sidoine* was translated into German, Icelandic, Spanish, and English within a few years of its composition, and the new heroes of fifteenth-century romance, such as Palmerin of England and Amadís of Gaul, quickly gained international fame.

At the same time, the older Arthurian prose romances remained very popular, gaining new readers because of the new interest in prose romance and often being recast into forms more to the taste of the time for brief compilations such as Malory's own work. The *Morte Darthur* belongs both to this older, continuing tradition of Arthurian romance and to the new genre of fifteenth-century prose romance. This fact has seldom been appreciated in Malory studies, where the argument over whether Malory wrote one book rather like a modern novel or eight separate tales has been fiercely debated with little or no attention to the tradition on which Malory drew or the genre in which he worked. The old idea was that Malory inherited a "jumble of stories about Arthur" and, as George Saintsbury wrote, Malory, "and he only in any language, makes of this vast assemblage of stories one story, one book."[1] The discovery of the Winchester Manuscript with its "explicits" dividing the work into eight tales convinced Eugène Vinaver that the *Morte Darthur* was actually eight stories and eight books—*The Works of Sir Thomas Malory.*

The arguments for and against the eight-tale theory have been based largely on the assumption that if Malory's work is "one story, one book," it must resemble a modern novel: internal contradictions, digressions, and temporal inconsistencies prove that the eight tales lack the unity we demand of modern fictional narrative; yet, the opponents reply, consistency of characterization, the use of foreshadowings, and a continuing concern with the history of the Round Table prove that the *Morte Darthur* is a continuous narrative.[2] The *Morte Darthur* is both eight separate tales and one continuous narrative, for it is a brief prose cycle. The tradition on which Malory drew was not a "jumble of stories" but a tradition of cyclic narrative, and all the romances he knew were parts of "one story, one book," though not in our sense of those words. At the time Malory wrote it would have been surprising if he had written anything but a *Morte Darthur* organized as one continuous narrative. Malory moreover wrote a peculiarly fifteenth-century Arthurian work, for his book belongs to the genre of one-volume prose histories that were popular at the time, a genre in which the old cycles were reduced to brief continuous narratives but in which, of course, there are few traces of our ideas of prose fiction. That Malory's book is still read and those of his contemporaries largely forgotten is not because of the originality, much less the modernity, of what he did, but because he did it so much better than anyone else.

Conclusion

The most important influences on Malory's work were the thirteenth-century prose romances. They not only supplied much of the material for his book, they taught him what a "book of King Arthur" should be and how it should be made.[3] So far as we can tell, Malory knew no French verse romances. In England native verse romances remained popular, but in France the older verse romances had fallen out of favor, and most readers knew Arthurian romance mainly as a genre of prose literature. When modern readers think of medieval romance, they think first of verse romances and of writers such as Chrétien de Troyes, and there is therefore a tendency to regard the *Morte Darthur* as part of the tradition to which Chrétien belongs. This is unfortunate, for it leads readers to condemn Malory for not having virtues to which he never pretended, just as the French prose romances seem to those who judge them by the standards of Chrétien "mere rubble left over from some statelier building."[4] Yet Malory and the authors of his French prose sources have virtues of their own quite different from those of twelfth-century verse romance. For most fifteenth-century readers the earlier verse romances simply did not exist. When they thought of the Grail quest or the love of Lancelot and Guenevere, they thought not of Chrétien, if indeed they knew the name, but of Walter Map, the supposed author of the Vulgate prose *Lancelot* and *Queste del Saint Graal*. And when they thought of the virtues of romance, they thought not of the lightness and sophistication of a work like *Le chevalier de la charette* but of the graver historical qualities of the cyclic prose romances.

These cyclic romances—and almost all Arthurian prose romances are cyclic—are not distinct and independent tales in the manner of earlier verse romances; each is part of a larger and coherent "history" that comprehends all stories of Arthur and his knights. The thirteenth-century cyclic romances are apparently a by-product of the general thirteenth-century tendency toward the organization of all knowledge, history, and stories into *summae, encyclopediae*, universal chronicles, and vast cycles of the tales of Charlemagne and his peers or of Arthur and his knights. Even in Chrétien's romances there is a hint of cyclic composition, and in the verse romances of Robert de Boron, *Joseph d'Arimathea* and *Merlin*, we have the beginning of a true cycle.[5] Perhaps Robert's work itself, or that of the adapter who turned Robert's works into prose and combined them with the Didot *Perceval*, provided the model for the earliest of the cycles known to Malory, the Vulgate Cycle. However that may be, it is clear that the author (or "architect," as Jean Frappier calls him) of the Book of Lancelot was the first and in some ways the best of the prose cyclic romancers. His cycle consists of the prose *Lancelot* ("Lancelot proper"), the *Queste del Saint Graal*, and the *Mort Artu*. The first part to be composed was the *Lancelot*, a huge and elaborately organized collection of all the adventures of Lancelot and his fellow knights. To this was added the *Queste del Saint Graal* and the *Mort Artu*, each by a different author, in order to bring the story of Lancelot and the Round Table to a conclusion. Thus was formed the three-part Book of Lancelot, which was the most popular of all the cycles and enjoyed a wide readership well into the sixteenth and seventeenth centuries.[6]

The impulse to add a suitable conclusion to the prose *Lancelot*, to provide a larger historical framework into which it might fit, is similar to that which led so many thirteenth-century romancers to supply "elucidations" and "enfances" to other popular romances, so that no hero was left without the "enfances" that precede his principal adventures or the glorious death that ends them. Sometimes the "enfances" would extend into a full account of the hero's father's adventures, and if the hero had a son, his adventures had to be told, with the result that some cycles are carried through generation after generation in order to tell the "whole history." The whole history of the Round Table was lacking in the Book of Lancelot, which told the end of the Round Table but not its beginning. And so a later writer composed a "retrospective sequel," recounting the beginnings of the Round Table and of the Grail quest, the principal adventure of Arthur's knights.[7] These additions, the *Estoire del Saint Graal* and the *Estoire de Merlin*, were based on the prose redactions of Robert de Boron's *Joseph d'Arimathea* and *Merlin*, to which was added a long sequel, comprising most of the *Estoire de Merlin*. Thus was formed a two-part prose cycle which was then attached to the Book of Lancelot to make the full five-part narrative that we now call the Vulgate Cycle. The resulting structure is not altogether graceful. The Vulgate Cycle is clearly unified at the beginning and end but unskillfully joined at the middle, where the *Merlin* ends and the *Lancelot* begins almost as if the cycle were beginning anew, just as Malory's work seems to begin afresh with *The Book of Sir Tristram*. But the author of the first two parts of the Vulgate Cycle was probably not bothered by such considerations; apparently elegance of structure was less important to him than the necessity to comprehend the whole history of Arthur in one coherent historical framework.

The prose *Tristan* was in its own time the most popular of all the Arthurian romances.[8] It was based on the old verse romances of Tristan, which were not widely circulated in the Middle Ages, judging from the number of manuscripts that have survived. The verse romances had little to do with Arthurian history, but when the prose romance was written, Tristan became a member of the Round Table, and the story became a tale of Arthurian adventure. The prose romance was so popular that it exists in a great many versions, and it is difficult to speak of *a* prose *Tristan;* there seem to be almost as many prose *Tristans* as there are manuscripts. Two redactions can be distinguished, however, a relatively short version (the "Luces de Gast" version) and a longer "cyclic" version (whose author claims to be Helie de Boron, a friend and companion-in-arms to Robert de Boron). It was the latter, cyclic version that Malory knew and used. In the cyclic version the *Tristan* often serves as a sort of alternative to the prose *Lancelot,* so that in effect a new cycle was created, consisting of a *Tristan,* a *Queste,* and a *Mort Artu,* with the adventures of Tristan serving, as in Malory, as a long introduction to the Grail story.[9] Malory evidently knew *Tristan* in a defective manuscript, but, as I shall show, he probably regarded it as part of such a cycle.

The *Suite du Merlin* (also called the Huth *Merlin*), which Malory used as the basis of the first tale in the *Morte Darthur,* is part of yet another cycle, one which Fanni Bogdanow has taught us to call the *Roman du Graal.*[10] The whole of this cycle has not survived, but according to Bogdanow it consisted of the Vulgate *Estoire del Saint Graal,* the *Suite du Merlin* (which is the same as the Vulgate *Merlin* up to the coronation of Arthur and then diverges widely), a *Queste,* and a *Mort Artu.* The author of this cycle had a clear sense of literary form, and he had explicit ideas about how such a long work should be written. Yet his work never enjoyed the popularity accorded to the older Vulgate Cycle, and it survives only in fragments. The *Roman du Graal* did have a great influence on the literature of the Iberian peninsula, where, as the ultimate source of both the Portuguese *Demanda do Santo Grial* and the Spanish *Demanda del Sancto Grial,* it shaped the dominant tradition.[11] And, of course, the *Suite du Merlin* is far better known to English readers than the corresponding section of the Vulgate Cycle, since Malory used the *Suite* as the source of his *Tale of King Arthur.*

Malory therefore knew parts of at least four cycles—the Book of Lancelot (*Lancelot-Queste-Mort Artu*), the expansion of that cycle which we call the Vulgate Cycle, the cyclic version of *Tristan,* and the *Roman du Graal,* and he also knew *Perlesvaus,* which, though part of no existing cycle, ends with the author's promise of a continuation, presumably cyclic. So far as we can tell, these were the only French prose romances that he knew. In short, all of his known experience with French romance was with works that were—or at least claimed to be—parts of "one story, one book." In the light of this fact, there is nothing very remarkable in Malory's decision to combine his "diverse stories" into a "whole book of King Arthur." In doing so, he was simply following what must have seemed to him the universal practice of his French authorities.

Some readers may find this statement difficult to accept because, though these romances all claimed to be parts of cycles, most of them circulated in manuscripts containing only one or two of the parts, and it must have been a rare reader indeed who was able to know the whole of any one of these cycles. In the fifteenth century, when the custom of collecting romances for personal (usually noblemen's) libraries seems to have become fashionable, there were probably more readers who knew more parts of these cycles than ever before, and Malory seems to have been such a reader. Yet, so far as we can tell, Malory knew only the first branch of the *Roman du Graal*, the *Suite du Merlin*; he probably knew the *Tristan* in a manuscript containing that romance alone (perhaps only a part of it) rather than a cycle of which it was a part; though he may have known the Vulgate *Merlin*, there is no evidence that he knew the *Estoire del Saint Graal*, and we therefore cannot assume that he knew the whole Vulgate Cycle as we now have it. We cannot even be sure that Malory knew the whole Book of Lancelot, since though he used all of the *Queste* and *Mort Artu* he used only parts of the prose *Lancelot* for his *Noble Tale of Sir Lancelot du Lake*, and there is at least the slight possibility that he knew these parts from some condensed or fragmentary version of that work. And there is, of course, no "Frensshe booke" that supplied the pattern of Malory's narrative; it combines parts of the Vulgate Cycle, the *Roman du Graal*, and *Perlesvaus* along with some matter (*The Tale of Sir Gareth*, for example) of Malory's own invention.

Yet a medieval reader did not have to read all the parts of a cycle to know that a cycle existed or even to know what it and the "livre du latin" that all claimed to be translating contained. The authors of the prose romances lost no opportunity to establish the "cyclic" character of their works and to specify the exact relation between their individual romances and the whole works of which they were parts. This is a convention of Arthurian prose romance, and only rarely does one encounter a prose Arthurian romance (such as *Le chevalier du papagao*) that is not explicitly fitted into one of the cycles. This is because the prose romances were presented as "true histories." The use of prose itself was a signal that the authors were dealing with "facts,"[12] and the prose writers took elaborate pains to authenticate their narratives: the original source, we are customarily told, is a "livre du latin" which contains the true history of the Round Table. The truth of that history is established by the fact that the original Latin book was written by eyewitnesses, such as Nascien (*Estoire del Saint Graal*), Merlin, who tells the adventures to Blaise (*Estoire de Merlin*), and Arthur himself, who has the adventures of his knights carefully recorded (*Queste, Mort Artu*). Then, we are told, this original Latin book was faithfully translated by those who had access to the original—Robert de Boron (*Estoire del Saint Graal, Estoire de Merlin, Roman du Graal*), his friend Helie de Boron (*Tristan*, the cyclic version), Walter Map (the Book of Lancelot). We are thus assured of a proper scribal tradition, for the authors do not allow us to doubt that the Latin book has been handed down exactly as it was written.

A writer of a prose romance may decide to omit some parts of that "livre du latin"—though in this case it is safest to assure his readers that he does indeed know the true history and is leaving something out for good reason, as the author of the *Roman du Graal* does—but he cannot, so he pretends, add anything to the book. By this convention, each new adventure is a part of the original work, and its relation to that true history must be shown very clearly. That is why each branch of these cycles is explicitly linked to the other branches and carefully fitted into the overall framework of that history. Such explicit connections are the basic means of establishing the "authenticity" of the individual romance.

When that author who claimed to be Robert de Boron wrote the *Estoire del Saint Graal* and the *Estoire de Merlin* as retrospective sequels to the Book of Lancelot, he therefore had to establish the clear relation of his work to the rest of Arthurian history as it had been defined in the work of Walter Map. He does this by establishing the claim that his work is the authentic beginning of the history of the Arthurian court, "li commencemens de lestoire del saint graal." This claim is made in the explicit at the end of the *Estoire del Saint Graal*, which also establishes the relation between that work and the *Estoire de Merlin*: "Here ends ('explicit') the beginning of the History of the Holy Grail and after this comes the History of Merlin. God bring us all to a good end! Amen" (Sommer, I, 296). Here the "explicit" and the "amen" clearly mark the end of a major division in the Vulgate Cycle, but just as clearly the "explicit" serves notice to the reader that more is to follow, that what is finished is only the necessary first part of a larger work, of which the "History of Merlin" is the next branch. And at the end of the *Estoire de Merlin*, the author uses a somewhat similar linking device, placing the link not in the explicit itself but in a brief résumé of what "li contes" will tell next: "And he [Bans] had a

seneschal whom he had raised from infancy and to whom he had
entrusted all his land after the death of Gracien; and it was he who
betrayed him and through whom he lost the Castle of Trebes, just as
will be told to you in the tale that follows. Here ends ('explicit') the
Imprisonment of Merlin. God bring us all to a good end!" (Sommer,
II, 466).

These linking explicits are found in manuscripts in which the *Estoire
del Saint Graal* or *Estoire de Merlin* are the only items, for phrases like
"just as will be told to you in the tale that follows" are assurances that
what we are reading is part of the true history, whether the next
branch does or does not follow in any one manuscript. These explicits
are very brief and relatively unimportant, and they may even be
scribal additions (as are similar passages in the Book of Lancelot), but
they seemed both important and authentic to later romancers, who
tended to write more and more elaborate explicits and even prologues.[13] Malory's older contemporary, the London leather merchant
Henry Lovelich, ends his translation of *The History of the Holy Grail*
with a long passage in which he names his source, explains why he is
translating it, and then asks his readers:

> And þerfore Atte the Ende of this storye
> A pater noster ʒe wolden for me preye,
> For me that herry Lonelich hyhte;
> And greteth Oure lady ful of Myghte,
> Herteliche with an Ave that ʒe hire bede,
> This processe the bettere I myghte procede
> And bringen this book to A Good Ende.
>   Now therto Jesu Crist grace me sende;
> And that an end there-offen myghte be,
> Now, goode lord, graunt me for Charyte.   (56. 531-540)

Lovelich uses his explicit to show that he is at the "Ende of this storye"
but that he has by no means finished the task of bringing "this book to
A Good Ende." And, in the only surviving manuscript of Lovelich's
work, that task is continued on the next folio with Lovelich's translation of the *Estoire de Merlin*. So much thought, and ink, has been
expended on Malory's explicits, and so common is the assumption
that a passage of this sort is "the mediaeval equivalent of THE
END,"[14] that we should take special note of the fact that the writer of
these French romances as well as their English translator, Lovelich,
used explicits in the way Malory did, as a means of linking, rather
than separating, parts of a larger narrative.

The author of the Book of Lancelot provided more significant transitions between the branches of his work by writing the links into the opening and closing scenes of the tales themselves. As we have noted, scribes sometimes added explicits of the sort we have been examining, as in a fifteenth-century English manuscript of the prose *Lancelot* (Harley 5342): "Thus Master Walter Map finishes here his book of Lancelot and begins the book of the Holy Grail, and first he begins to speak of Galahad, the son of Lancelot. Here after follows the *Queste del Saint Graal*" (Sommer, V, 409). But such an explicit is not needed, since the last events in *Lancelot* lead directly to the opening scene in the *Queste*. Arthur, in the forest, meets a hermit,

And he said to him, "King Arthur, I tell you truly that at the next Day of Pentecost there will come a new knight who will bring the adventures of the Holy Grail to an end. And he will come to your court on that day and will accomplish the adventure of the Siege Perilous. Therefore see that you summon all your barons so that they will be at Camelot that day to see the marvels which will happen there" . . . And when he was returned to Camelot he sent through all the realm of Logres and commanded all the barons who held his lands to come to court on the Day of Pentecost. (Sommer, V, 409)

The following tale, the *Queste*, begins "On the Eve of Pentecost, when all the fellowship of the Round Table had come to Camelot" (VI, 3). That same evening a mysterious damsel summons Lancelot to knight Galahad, who comes the next day to occupy the Siege Perilous and to begin the accomplishment of the adventures of the Holy Grail.

The *Queste del Saint Graal* is bound to the *Mort Artu* in much the same way. The *Queste* ends with the return of Bors to Camelot, where he recounts his adventures to the king, who orders that the adventures be written down:

Thus they were put in writing and placed in the Abbey of Salisbury, from which Master Walter Map took them to make his Book of the Holy Grail for the love of King Henry, who had it translated from Latin into French. Now he is silent, for the tale says no more of the Adventures of the Holy Grail.
  Here end ("explicit") the Adventures of the Holy Grail. (Sommer, VI, 199)

The *Mort Artu* takes up at the point where King Henry tells his faithful servant Walter (despite the apparent "finality" of the above explicit) that "what he had written would not suffice if he did not recount the end of those whom he had mentioned and of how those whose prowess he had described in his book had died." Walter obeys the command and begins the "final part." This "final part" begins with exactly the same scene that concluded the *Queste*, at the point "When Bors had come to the court in this same city of Camelot" (Sommer, VI, 203). The linking of scenes in this way is, of course, more important than the account of the supposed composition of the work. As the reader knows, Malory wisely suppresses the passages about Walter and King Henry, but he joins his version of the *Queste* to the tale that follows by retaining these linking scenes. Perhaps profiting by this example, he uses similar links between his first and second tales and between *The Book of Sir Tristram* and *The Tale of the Sancgreal*.

The Vulgate is the cycle that Malory knew in its most nearly complete form, and it is therefore likely that his own practice of establishing such "links" between his tales was modeled on the sorts of explicits and linking scenes that he knew from this work. But the relations between the different parts of a cycle, like those between the tales in the *Morte Darthur*, are obvious in more important features than such nearly external details as the beginnings and endings of the branches. Though only the unknown genius who was the "architect" of the Lancelot trilogy (the prose *Lancelot-Queste-Mort Artu*) was completely successful, all the authors of the various parts of the cycles aimed at producing works that were thoroughly integrated with the cycles to which they belonged. One did not simply write independent romances and then join them together into cycles by writing the sorts of links that we have examined above. If the reader was to accept a romance as an integral part of the true history of the Arthurian court, he had to be shown the many ways in which each individual romance was related to the whole cycle, and the writers of the prose romances showed such relationships by establishing networks of references to other parts of the cycle and by frequent statements of exactly how the episodes in the particular branch were related to events in the rest of the cycle.

That is why a reader who knew only one part of a cycle—as Malory knew only the *Suite du Merlin* of the *Roman du Graal*—would nevertheless have a very clear idea of what the rest contained. As an example, let us take the Vulgate *Merlin*, since it was very popular in England (we have three separate English versions of it, including two made in Malory's own lifetime).[15] The English prose *Merlin*, a very close translation of the French, exists independently, and so far as we know its author had no intention of translating any other parts of the Vulgate Cycle. But it is rich in references to other parts of the cycle, not only in thematic allusions (e.g., p. 341) but in the author's explicit statements of what will later be told in the "whole book." We learn, for example, that the adventures of Lancelot are a part of this "book"; when Agravain is cursed we are told that the affliction cannot be healed, "but yef it were be tweyne of the beste knyghtes of the worlde to whom she sette terme of garison, as the booke shall yow devyse here-after, how that it was warisshed by Gaweain his brother, and by launcelot de lak that was so noble a knyght" (p. 527).

We are told that the story will deal with the False Guenevere section of the prose *Lancelot* (p. 466) and with the engendering of Galahad (p. 326). The cycle will also include the quest of the Holy Grail: "This mayden was the feirest lady that euer was in eny londe . . . but at this tyme cesseth the storye of hir, but it shall here-after be declared how that she was discesed of the seynt Graal and wherefore, and how the adventures of the seynt Graal were brought to fin" (p. 229). And the author frequently assures us that his whole history of King Arthur will include a *Mort Artu* (cf. p. 393), as he does when he tells us of the name Logres: "This Logryn a-mended gretly the citee and . . . chaunged the name and cleped it Logres . . . and this name dured unto the deth of kynge Arthur but affter his deth, and the deth of his barouns that thourgh Mordred and Agravain eche slow other an the playn of Salisberi, as the boke shall reherse her-after" (p. 147). The word "boke" is used here, as it was by Lovelich, in the same way the French writers used "livre du latin," meaning "the whole of the authentic narrative," however many parts it might have or however many separate volumes might be required to contain it. Malory was not violating normal usage when he called his work the "whole book of King Arthur."

Any of the French prose romances that Malory knew would have given him the same sort of indications of what branches were related to it. We have Malory's own word that he had only the first two books of the French prose *Tristan*, and therefore he could not have read any version of the cycle to which this romance belongs. But Malory probably did know the prologue that is preserved in MSS B.N. frs. 103, 334, and 99 (these are the manuscripts containing what Vinaver says is Malory's immediate source),[16] which announces that what follows is a translation from "the great Latin book, the same which relates completely the History of the Holy Grail . . . And this same Latin History of the Holy Grail tells clearly that in the time of King Arthur there were only three knights who excelled in chivalric undertakings, and they were Galahad, Lancelot, and Tristan . . . And because I know well what was the truth, I should like to begin here the History of Tristan in this manner" (Löseth, *Tristan*, pp. 1-2). After reading this, Malory could have no doubt that the whole "livre du latin" would include the adventures not only of Tristan but of Galahad and Lancelot (the three principal knights of his own work), and he knew that the whole book would include a *Queste* (in his own reading he got at least as far as the events preliminary to the Grail adventures), and later in his reading he learned that it would end with an account of the death of Arthur brought on by the treason of Mordred, "as we shall tell toward the end of our book."[17]

In the *Suite du Merlin* Malory read not only about what would be in the cycle to which it belonged but why these materials were selected. From this work he learned how a cycle should be made. The cyclic method has necessarily a loose structure. This, of course, is one of its pleasures for the reader who prizes copiousness and variety. But the cyclic form is always in danger of collapsing into a merely incoherent collection—perhaps especially in the later cycles, as the number of romances that were part of the "whole book of Arthur" increased. The author of the *Suite*, who claimed to be Robert de Boron, solved this problem by observing the principle of proportion:

Let all those who want to hear the history written by my Lord de Boron know that he divides his book in three parts, one part as long as the other, the first part as long as the second, and the second as long as the third. The first part ends at the beginning of this quest, the second at the beginning of the Grail, and the third ends after the death of Lancelot at the same point where he tells of the death of King Mark. (I, 280)

In order to maintain these proportions, the author of the *Suite* must omit materials freely. Like Malory, he excludes the whole of the prose *Lancelot:*

The Lady of the Lake had given him this ring, as the great History of Lancelot tells it—that same history that must be omitted from my book, not because it is not relevant to it and should not be told, but because it is desirable that the three parts of my book be equal, each as long as the other, and if I were to add this long history, the middle of my book would be three times as long as the other two parts. Therefore it is necessary that I leave out this long History which tells of the deeds of Lancelot and his birth, and I shall tell of the nine generations of Nascien, exactly as it pertains to the *Noble Record of the Holy Grail*. Nor shall I tell any more than I should, but rather I shall tell much less than I find written in "l'estoire dou latin." (II, 57)

The author maintains the air of authenticity, for his reader cannot doubt that Robert has access to the great "estoire dou latin" that contains the complete authentic record. Yet, as he explains, aesthetic criteria are more important than completeness, and the cyclic author is obligated to tell only as much as is necessary for his purposes.

In order to maintain the proportion between the three parts of his cycle, Robert consciously violates the natural chronological order of the whole history: "While the two knights were thus speaking to the dwarf, King Mark came out of the forest. He was then married to Iseult la Blonde, as this same tale will fully relate, since it is an adventure of which the *Grail* tells" (I, 230). The appearance of Mark already married at this point in the narrative shows that "Robert de Boron" planned to introduce at least part of the *Roman de Tristan* into his work by a "loop in time" such as Malory himself later used;[18] it also shows that although the author of the *Suite* was keenly aware of the problems of literary structure, he was, like Malory, not bothered by what seem to us annoying chronological inconsistencies, such as the fact that Mark is here already married to Iseult although Tristan, who is to fetch her from Ireland, has not yet been born.

Malory may have felt a special regard for "Robert de Boron," not only because he claimed to be, like himself, a knight now getting along in years (*Suite*, II, 57), but because Robert encountered in his composition, and discusses his solution to, the same sorts of problems that Malory faced. Robert taught him that a cycle must have an aesthetically satisfying structure. The tales within this larger structure remain independent entities; Robert even assigns to his friend and companion-in-arms Helie de Boron the task of translating one of the branches of his book, the "Conte del brait" (II, 58). But each of these parts must be organized, Robert maintains, in a coherent whole.

Malory must have taken these lessons to heart, for he uses the same sort of loop in time to organize his book that Robert used in the *Roman du Graal*, and Malory's book also shows traces of a balanced three-part structure. Malory likewise includes a version of the prose *Tristan* instead of the *Lancelot*, which, perhaps on Robert's authority, he felt free to omit along with such matters as Arthur's war with King Royn. These were all matters of the "true history," but they did not pertain to his own purposes, which, Robert de Boron held, a cyclic romancer was free to define for himself.

The most important lesson about Arthurian romance could have been gained from almost any of the works that Malory read: each of his tales had to be fitted into a "whole book of King Arthur," for, as we have seen, the authenticity of any Arthurian prose romance depends upon its demonstrated relationship to the whole book that is its reputed source and into which each branch must fit. Even the

English verse romances on which Malory drew, the alliterative *Morte Arthure* and the stanzaic *Morte Arthur*, which are not parts of cycles, are specifically fitted into a larger history. The alliterative poem begins just after the completion of Arthur's conquest of France and refers frequently to Arthur's victory over the French champion Flollo. The stanzaic poem begins with the statement that the adventures it contains take place after the completion of the Grail quest.

Therefore, Saintsbury was simply wrong in his assumption that Malory and Malory alone made of the diverse stories "one story, one book." A distinguished series of romancers, claiming such authoritative names as Walter Map and Robert de Boron, had done just that. Indeed, Malory would probably have found it difficult to conceive of an Arthurian prose romance that was not part of a "whole book," and when we debate the question of whether Malory wrote one book or several, we should remember that the whole weight of authority and of his own literary experience impelled him to make a single "book of King Arthur."

2

Fifteenth-Century
Prose Romance

S ince modern scholarship has taught us that the prose cycles are products of the thirteenth century, Malory's interest in these works seems definitely old-fashioned, for he was, as critics have emphasized, separated by two centuries from his ultimate sources. Neither Malory nor his readers realized this, however, for the old prose romances were recopied and recirculated throughout the fourteenth and fifteenth centuries. Judging from the number of fifteenth-century manuscripts and early printed editions that have survived, the vogue of Arthurian prose romance was even stronger in the late Middle Ages than it had been in the thirteenth century, and old romances were read as eagerly as new ones by the most sophisticated readers of the time. On the Continent, the most brilliant center of artistic patronage was the court of the dukes of Burgundy, and in the fifteenth century England's most important foreign relations, both political and cultural, were with the house of Burgundy.[1] Every sort of literature was richly supported in this court; Laurent de Premierfait (whose translations of Boccaccio were used by Lydgate) wrote for the Burgundian court, as did Christine de Pisan (whose *Livre de faits d'armes et de chevalrie* was translated by Caxton), Raoul Lefèvre (whose *Recueil des histoires de Troyes* and *Istoire de Jason* were translated by Caxton), David Aubert (the author of *Perceforest*, which was written for Margaret of York, and who was probably the author of *The Three Kings' Sons*, translated into English around 1500), and many others. Scribes and artists in the employ of the ducal household pro-

17

duced the most beautiful fifteenth-century manuscripts in northern Europe, including a good number that by way of intermarriage between the noble families of Burgundy and England found their way across the Channel.

The manuscripts acquired by the dukes of Burgundy range from works of classical antiquity to books of devotion; they also include a large number of Arthurian romances. According to the catalog of his library drawn up in 1467, Philip the Good of Burgundy acquired, in addition to a good many Arthurian works already in the ducal library, "a *Grand Saint Graal* or *Joseph of Arimithea*, two copies of *Lancelot du Lac* or *Queste du Saint Graal* (the second including a short *Mort Artu*), three copies of the prose *Tristan*, a *Guiron le Cortois*, an *Ysaie le Triste*, and a *Meraugis de Portlesguez*."[2] Georges Doutrepont notes that in the catalog of 1467 all these works are classified as "histories," all but one (*Ysaie*) are on parchment, and one (*Meraugis*) is characterized as "un volume de luxe."[3]

It was perhaps inevitable that Caxton, who lived and worked in the Flemish domain of the dukes of Burgundy, should have drawn so heavily on the works of writers employed by the dukes for the books that he printed. Indeed, in the preface to his *History of Jason* he tells of visiting the castle at Hesdin, one of the favorite residences of Philip the Good, and, as noted above, this work was translated from the French of Raoul Lefèvre, one of Philip's writers. Even before Caxton became a printer he translated the same author's *Recueil des histoires de Troyes*, which he began in 1469 and finished in 1471, though he did not print it until about 1474 (two years before the first French edition, printed in Bruges about 1476).[4] Many critics have considered such works evidence that Caxton, like Malory, was retrospective in his tastes, that he "purveyed to his aristocratic English public a selection of works, French or English, from a former generation."[5] But Caxton translated the *Recueil* at the "dreadfull commandment" of Margaret of York, sister of Edward IV and wife of Duke Charles the Bold of Burgundy. Margaret, patroness of both the English writer Caxton and the French writer David Aubert, personifies the close cultural and political ties between the English and Burgundian aristocracy in the fifteenth century, and Caxton's work reflects the taste of the English nobility for Burgundian culture. That is as true of the *Morte Darthur* as of works such as the *Recueil* or *Paris and Vienne*, for the taste for prose romance was strong in Burgundy, and, as we shall see, the Burgundian court encouraged new compilations, like Malory's, as well as the older versions of the prose romances.

There is ample evidence that the aristocracy in England shared this taste for Arthurian romance, as indeed did most noble readers throughout fifteenth-century Europe. British Museum MS Royal 14.E.iii is, according to Henry L.D. Ward, an early fourteenth-century manuscript containing a *Histoire del Saint Graal*, a *Queste du Saint Graal*, and a *Mort d'Artus*: "On the first fly-leaf of this volume are the autographs of 'Elysabeth the kyngys dowther' (afterwards queen of Henry VII) and her sister 'Cecyl the kyngys dowther' (afterwards married to John, Viscount Welles) and also that of 'Jane Grey' (f. 1.). On the next leaf is written in a hand of the fifteenth cent.: 'Ceste liure est a moy Richard Roos cheualier.' On the last fly-leaf are the following entries: 'E. Wydevyll' (afterwards queen of Edward IV, and mother of the two princesses above-mentioned), 'This boke ys myne dame Alynor Haute,' and 'Jane Grey.' "[6] The inscriptions show us some of the readership this one volume enjoyed in the fifteenth and early sixteenth centuries—the noble family of the Woodvilles, the Lancastrian poet Sir Richard Roos, and queens of England from the wife of Edward IV to Henry VIII's unfortunate Lady Jane Grey. A similar example, with an even later readership, is MS Harley 49, an imperfect copy of the prose *Tristan*: "On the last fly-leaf (f. 155) is written 'Iste liber constat duci Gloucestre' and at the bottom of the same page 'Sans r . . . yr. Elyzabeth' (Elizabeth of York). At f. 148b. is the autograph of George Turbervyle, the poet (died about 1595), with a distich, and at f. 154b. is the autograph inscription of his daughter, Judith Turbervyle."[7]

As readers of Malory know, Caxton himself published the *Morte Darthur* at the insistence of "many noble and diverse gentylemen of this royame of England," and Roger Ascham, writing in 1570, was notoriously scandalized to report: "Yet I know when Gods Bible was banished the Court, and *Morte Arthure* received into the Princes chamber."[8] Though by the end of the sixteenth century the Arthurian romances were condemned by critics such as Meres and Nash, Sir Philip Sidney himself avowed, "I dare vndertake *Orlando Furioso* or honest *King Arthur* will never displease a souldier."[9] The reader of the fine chapter on romance in Rosamund Tuve's *Allegorical Imagery* needs no further proof that Arthurian romance was far from dead in the sixteenth year of Edward IV, when Malory completed his *Morte Darthur*.[10]

As I have said, the fifteenth century witnessed a new birth of romance—a great outburst of creative activity in the relatively new genre of prose romance. Of course, in England verse romance remained popular; in Germany Ulrich Füetrer produced an Arthurian verse cycle of over 80,000 lines; and in the year Malory finished the *Morte Darthur* Boiardo began his *Orlando innamorato*. But for history (and the Arthurian romances were regarded as such) the fifteenth century was an age of prose.[11] As Léon Gautier wrote of the Charlemagne cycle, "In the fifteenth century, there is a frenzy, there is a rage against verse and in favor of prose."[12] The same is true of the Alexander romances, which gained new popularity in fifteenth-century prose redactions.[13] And this is preeminently true of Arthurian romance, as shown not only in the survival and continued popularity of the older prose romances but in the production of new redactions of the older prose versions and of new prosifications of originally verse romances.[14]

The new interest in prose romance, it should be noted, was an aristocratic concern. The fact that Malory chose prose for his *Morte Darthur* is sometimes taken as evidence of his essentially "bourgeois" outlook (whatever that may mean when applied to the fifteenth century), and the idea that Malory is a "middle-class" writer still lurks in the background of much of our thinking about his work, especially his use of "realism." But as long ago as the 1860s Gautier laid to rest the idea that the nobility continued to cultivate the "aristocratic" verse romances while the cloddish bourgeoisie encouraged prose: "The truth is that many of these romances in prose were composed at the express order of the nobility, were *commanded* by powerful lords."[15] The author of a history of *Charles Martel* (1448) explains that he uses prose "because today the great princes and other lords prefer prose to verse."[16] He describes what seems to have been a general European phenomenon. In Germany the tradition of prose romance began in the mid-fifteenth century (if we set aside the much earlier translation of *Lancelot*) with the noble authoresses Elisabeth von Nassau-Saarbrücken and Eleanor of Tyrol (daughter of James I of Scotland), who translated *Ponthus et la belle Sidoine* into German in 1448, and Ulrich Füetrer's prose *Lantzelot* was written under the patronage of Albrecht, count of the Palatinate of the Rhine and duke of Upper and Lower Bavaria. In England, as we have seen, the highest nobility owned and read French Arthurian prose romances; Henry L.D. Ward describes a French prose version of the brief *Historia de proeliis*, the Latin history of Alexander, which was "presented by the first Earl of Shrewsbury (killed in France in 1452) to Margaret of Anjou, wife of Henry VI of England (married in 1445)," and another manuscript "probably executed at Bruges for Edward IV about 1470-80" of the prose *Recueil des histoires de Troyes*.[17] Caxton diligently cultivated this genre for his aristocratic patrons; the late Middle English verse romances that did achieve print had to wait for Caxton's successors, who discovered a lower class of readers eager for cheap, usually short, editions.

Malory's choice of this new, still imperfect instrument—prose narrative—shows that he shared the taste for prose that characterized European literature in the fifteenth century. Especially in England, this was a new taste. The idea that Malory was one of those who "here and there" held "firmly to the old ways" is very misleading. The "old way" of writing Arthurian narrative in English was to use verse, as Lovelich did, and Malory had very few predecessors in the new way of using English prose for secular fiction. This is not to say that he had none at all; I have already mentioned the English prose *Merlin*, written around 1450, and before Malory wrote there were also the English prose versions of *Ipomedon, King Ponthus* (a version of *Ponthus et la belle Sidoine*), a prose *Alexander*, and the very brief epitomes, the prose *Siege of Troy* and the prose *Siege of Thebes*, both of which are so condensed they are hardly narratives. This handful of works hardly established a tradition of English secular prose on which Malory could draw for his style, but it does show that he was not alone and that "here and there" throughout England there were writers who were experimenting with this new and promising way of composing narrative.

Malory reveals his close relation to the literary temper of the fifteenth century not only in his choice of prose but in his treatment of his materials. Both of his fifteenth-century English predecessors, the author of the prose *Merlin* and Lovelich, simply translated their French sources, reproducing their exemplars as faithfully as possible. Lovelich's choice of verse shows that he was perhaps more old-fashioned in outlook than the unknown author of the prose *Merlin*, but both treated their materials in exactly the same way, working more as scribes than as authors. Because the old romances never lost their popularity in the fifteenth century, these writers were by no means cultivating a dead form when they faithfully turned their French originals into English. Yet Arthurian romance did change in a variety of ways in the Middle Ages, and the fifteenth century witnessed the development of a new form of Arthurian romance, that which authors such as Malory cultivated.

The changes in the narrative forms from the twelfth to the fifteenth century were partly a result of the composition of new cycles. We have noticed how in the thirteenth century the Vulgate Cycle was developed from a Lancelot trilogy into a five-part cycle, and how the *Roman du Graal* and a separate *Tristan* cycle were developed within decades after the completion of the Vulgate. The romance of *Palamède* followed soon after the *Tristan*, and around 1270 the Italian Rusticiano da Pisa, writing in French, produced his new compilation for the pleasure of Edward I of England.[18] Early in the fourteenth century the Italian *Tavola ritonda* was written, and it exercised considerable influence on Italian literature in the next two centuries.[19] In Spain, Juan Vivas, writing in the early fourteenth century, produced a new version of the *Roman du Graal* that helped define the shape of the Arthurian history on the Iberian peninsula, and new redactions of Vivas's work were written in the fifteenth century.[20] In the Netherlands a new Lancelot cycle, considerably different from the Vulgate, was produced in the fourteenth century, and this was followed a few years later by a new Merlin cycle.[21] In France the scribe Jean de Vaillant, writing at the command of the duc de Bourbon in 1391, produced a new compilation of the Arthurian histories, and Cedric Pickford reports the existence of two new cyclic redactions of *Palamède*.[22]

The works listed above are all in some sense new cycles of romance, but actually the number of "cycles" is much larger than this, and the form even of the established cycles was always subject to change, since any scribe could in effect make his own "cycle" simply by rearranging the old materials. I mentioned above the British Museum MS Royal 14.E.iii, which contains the *Estoire del Saint Graal*, the *Queste del Saint Graal*, and the *Mort Artu*. This is not what we think of as one of the usual cycles of Arthurian romance; it is a complete cycle nevertheless, a sort of shortened "Livre du Saint Graal" that was probably quite satisfying to its readers. Likewise, there are manuscripts of *Tristan* which include that romance and a version of the "post-Vulgate" *Queste*, others that contain these two items and then the whole Vulgate *Mort Artu*, and still another that has the *Tristan*, the *Queste*, and then ends with only a brief summary of the *Mort Artu*.[23] Even the Lancelot trilogy appears in some manuscripts with large omissions from one or another of the branches.

None of these scribal rearrangements gained any sort of authority, probably because the ultimate shape of a cycle rested on internal correspondences between the branches rather than their arrangement, and the cycle that had the most carefully established internal artistic structure, the Book of Lancelot (the prose *Lancelot*, the *Queste*, and the *Mort Artu*), easily survived such scribal alterations. However, the very existence of differing cycles and of differing versions of these various cycles meant that fifteenth-century readers were confronted with a rich and sometimes confusing number of Arthurian histories. Moreover, at this period, when for the first time even country gentry like the Pastons could afford to hire scribes,[24] more readers than ever before were able to read such a great number of tales. It is difficult to think of a reader much before the fifteenth century who could exclaim, as Caxton did, "O blessed lord, when I remember the grete and many volumes of seynt graal, ghalehot, & launcelott de lake, Gaweyn, perceual, Lyonel, trystram, and many other, of whom were ouer longe to reherse and also to me vnknowen!"[25]

The very riches of which Caxton exclaims created a problem. Confronted with so many different versions of the Arthurian story, all claiming to be part of the "true history," fifteenth-century readers were naturally led to demand books in which these conflicting histories would be combined and harmonized into the one "true history" all claimed to be. Caxton's friend, Henry Bolymer, encountered this problem in his reading of the Charlemagne romances; he found "this matter and the hystoryes disioyned withoute order" and he turned to Caxton and begged him to "reduce" them into a single book, properly "ordeyned" and "autentyke."[26] Readers of the other matters of romance encountered the same problem and created a general demand for one-volume histories, containing "all of a *geste*, an entire collection of histories in prose or a brief compilation of several narratives in one redaction."[27] In response to this demand, fifteenth-century writers developed what is almost a distinct genre of one-volume histories that were produced by combining, condensing, and reordering the materials of several older volumes in order to produce a single volume shaped to the taste of the time. The anonymous *Charles Martel* is such a work; its author explains that he has drawn his material from several ancient histories and "reduced" them to prose ("I have taken ancient histories written in rime and translated and reduced them in this prose work").[28] Jean Wauquelin's *Histoire du bon Alexandre* (1440-1448) is a condensed combination of the *Roman d'Alexandre* with the French prose *Alexandre* ("An attempt," writes George Cary, "that leads the author into many morasses of textual contradictions").[29] In 1460 David Aubert did much the same in his *Conquestes de Charlemagne*, as did Raoul Lefèvre in his *Istoire de Jason* (1445) and his *Recueil des histoires de Troyes* (1464); the author of *Guillaume d'Orange*, written for Jacques d'Armagnac before 1477, produced his compilation by condensing and combining no less than thirteen different romances into one. In Germany, Füetrer used the same technique of composition,[30] and in England Caxton himself used this method in his *Charles the Grete*, for he tells us in his epilogue that he produced that volume by combining material from Vincent of Beauvais's *Speculum historiale* with material taken from a French romance.[31] Apparently Caxton regarded the *Morte Darthur* as a work belonging to this same genre, for he was aware that there were "many noble volumes" concerning Arthur and that Malory's work was a "book of the noble hystories of the sayd kyng Arthur," "which copy Sir Thomas Malory did take out of certeyn bokes of French and reduced it into English." Caxton therefore classified Malory's work as one of a series of books, all belonging to this genre, that dealt with the Christian Worthies: "The second was Charlemayn, or Charles the Grete, of whom thystorye is had in many places, bothe in Frensshe and in Englysshe; and the third and last was Godefroy of Boloyn, of whose actes and lyf I made a book unto th'excellent prynce and kyng of noble memorye, King Edward the Fourth."

Caxton's use of the word "history" is a reminder of how important history was to fifteenth-century readers of romance. They are distinguished from their predecessors not only by their generally wider literary experience but by their more critical and historical attitude toward the materials. Of course, earlier readers of romance were also interested in true history, and they too demanded "authentication" for the works they heard, but in the fifteenth century the demand became more insistent. It is reflected in the fact that even works that must have seemed obviously fictional to contemporary readers, such as *Perceforest* or *Huon of Bordeaux*, were given the air of chronicles by a careful citation of sources, by an attention to exactness in matters of time and place, and by the use of realistic details.[32] This is even more apparent in the elaborate pains that Caxton took to establish the authenticity of the Arthurian legend; as the reader will recall, Caxton adduces what he considers sound archaeological evidence to refute those cynics who had already appeared in this more historically sophisticated time.

A one-volume history of Arthur, like all of the works in this genre, was possible only at the expense of great condensation, and to fifteenth-century readers condensation was not only necessary but desirable. In one of his prologues Wauquelin assures his readers that he will "sincoper et retranchier les prolangacions" of his sources, just as

Caxton, in the preface to *Charles the Grete*, assures his audience that they will have the matter "without grete atedacyon."[33] Often the writers of fifteenth-century prose compilations specify that they have chosen prose because of its greater brevity, and their desire for brevity and their interest in history usually lead to a pronounced emphasis on action at the expense of the mysticism, psychologizing, and symbolism that we prize in the older romances. The result is a generally more matter-of-fact treatment of the older materials. In *The Medieval Alexander* George Cary notes how in the late Middle Ages "the historical bent of the times" led to an Alexander greatly simplified from the hero of earlier centuries, a hero "stripped of feast and frolics and jousts and love affairs; he is again the warrior and man of action."[34] Gautier likewise describes how the *remanieurs* of the matter of France tended to omit the symbolic and spiritual and even the amatory and to stress the actions—both in battles and in jousts—of their heroes, so that Roland and Oliver become fifteenth-century Burgundian noblemen rather than the heroes of Roncesvalles.[35] The same tendency is apparent in fifteenth-century treatments of Arthur, and critics have often noted in Malory's own work a preference for action over spiritualization.

Given the existence of this genre, if I may call it such, and the widespread demand for one-volume compilations of the older materials, it is not surprising to find that Malory was not the only European writer to handle the Arthurian legend in this way. In France, Michel Gonnot completed his one-volume compilation, *Le livre de Lancelot*, for Jacques d'Armagnac, duc de Namours, on July 4, 1470, just fifteen months to the day after Malory finished his work. In Germany, Ulrich Füetrer completed his prose *Lantzelot* in 1467 and wrote his *Buch der Abenteuer* sometime between 1481 and 1484 and then added his verse version of *Lantzelot* in 1487. Critics of French and German literature have noted the resemblances between these writers and Malory, but in general critics of English literature have paid them little attention.

We have ignored these writers for the good reason that only Füetrer's prose *Lantzelot* is easily available in print. There has never been a complete edition of the *Buch der Abenteuer*, and to read it one must assemble a variety of editions of the different parts. Most of Gonnot's work, which is contained in MS B.N. fr. 112, is likewise unavailable in print, though at least one section of this manuscript is well known to students of Malory, since it contains a portion of the *Suite du Merlin* that is missing from the Huth Manuscript and that was, until the recent discovery of the Cambridge Manuscript, the only known analogue for the last section of Malory's *Tale of King Arthur*. That part of Gonnot's work was printed by Sommer, and several other sections of the manuscript were printed by Cedric Pickford as a prose *Erec*.[36] Aside from these portions, the work remains generally unavailable.

However, we do have an excellent account of Gonnot's work in Pickford's *L'évolution du roman arthurien*, a full critical study of Gonnot's *Livre de Lancelot*. As Pickford tells us, the manuscript contains all of the prose *Lancelot*, a version of the prose *Tristan*, a redaction of the *Queste del Saint Graal*, the entire *Mort Artu*, and fragments of the *Suite du Merlin* and *Palamède*. By abridgment and rearrangement of the "plusiers livres anciennes"[37] Gonnot produced a volume of 870 large vellum pages divided into four "livres," each with its prologue and each divided into chapters. Gonnot, in short, "attempted in French what Malory at the same time carried out more successfully in England."[38] Pickford notes that there are important differences between Malory's *Morte Darthur* and Gonnot's *Livre de Lancelot*, but Gonnot and Malory nevertheless encountered the same sort of problem: to reduce the romance matter in such a way that all the tales could be contained in a single volume of a manageable size.[39] Consequently, their works suffer from much the same sort of errors, such as occasional internal contradictions; they present the material in much the same way, for example, supplying names for characters left anonymous in their sources; and they produce rather similar narratives, marked by far less interweaving than in the older cycles, with the result that in each case, though a good deal of interweaving remains, we have "an anthology of Arthurian narratives rather than a tapestry of the same type as the prose *Lancelot*."[40] The tendency in both authors seems to be to combine in a single volume "a collection of tales which he did not himself invent but which he gathered together and which he attempted to make into one book."[41]

More interesting perhaps than these external similarities are the similarities in spirit and tone. In Gonnot's work, Pickford tells us, "the adventure ceases to be spiritual and becomes purely chivalric."[42] In characterizing Gonnot, Pickford writes: "He was interested in the practice rather than the theory of chivalry . . . He chooses two principal heroes, Tristan and Lancelot, and depicts them to us with more concern for prowess than the doctrines of chivalry or even love. Micheau Gonnot places in relief the type of Arthurian knight who seeks adventures and prefers the active life to the idle life of the court."[43] Nevertheless, the adventure remains on a firm (and typically fifteenth-century) moral basis, and Gonnot's statement of this, in one of his prologues, recalls both Malory's tone and Caxton's words: "For the evil deeds are written in this book to be fled from and avoided, and the good deeds to be followed and emulated, each with good will."[44] There is, of course, no possibility of Malory's and Gonnot's knowing one another's works; the similarities in tone between the two books simply show how much both authors were affected by the common currents of fifteenth-century literature.

Füetrer took up much the same sort of task at almost the same time as Gonnot and Malory were at work. In his prose *Lantzelot* (1467) he reduced the whole of the Lancelot cycle into one brief volume. He explains his technique in the dedicatory prologue: "For the distinguished and high-born prince and Lord, Lord Albricht . . . I Ulrich Füetrer, a painter of Munich, have collected with a simple German pen from several books the *gestes* or deeds of Lord Lancelot of the Lake, in brief sense yet with no omission of adventures that belong to the book." The impulse toward condensing and simplifying is even more apparent in his somewhat later verse cycle, the *Buch der Abenteuer* (1481-1484), which, though it is in verse, is nevertheless of interest to the student of Malory, since in it Füetrer attempted to "weld all the Arthurian romances into one vast, all-embracing cycle."[45] Vast as it is, the 41,500 verses of the *Buch der Abenteuer* (plus a 38,000 verse version of *Lantzelot*) represent a high degree of condensation, and the cycle consists of a series of brief romances, each produced by reducing several longer works, and each existing as a separable unit, with an elaborate prologue and epilogue. James Boyd describes Füetrer's method: "One is rather left with the impression that he reproduced in their entirety those episodes that held for him the greatest measure of interest, i.e., those containing definite action; the others, reflective, philosophic, didactic, he contracted accordingly."[46] The result is a work much closer in tone to Malory's work than to the romances that were Füetrer's sources. The same might be said of the prose *Lantzelot*, though in general he carries the compression much further than Malory. The last section of *Lantzelot*, which deals with the same events as Malory's *Death of Arthur*, runs to only thirty-four pages, and yet Füetrer omits no important incident. His omissions remove almost all the spirit and tone of the older romances while leaving the bare bones of the narrative intact. The result is not bad, but—as Karl Brogsitter has emphasized—Füetrer's work compares only in intention to Malory's greater achievement.[47]

In fact, none of the fifteenth-century works that I have mentioned in this chapter is as good as Malory's. These works are worth considering, for they show us that Malory was not an isolated writer, cultivating a worn-out genre. The *Morte Darthur* belongs in the general movement of European literature that favored the production of one-volume versions of the old matters of romance and that encouraged the duc de Namours and the duke of Bavaria to patronize the works of Gonnot and Füetrer. Malory's work is remembered and theirs forgotten not because Malory was the only man of his time to write such a book but because his work succeeds as theirs did not.

One of the most important reasons for Malory's success was that he, unlike his contemporaries on the Continent, profited fully from the older cyclic tradition. Gonnot's work, like most of the one-volume compilations written in the fifteenth century, is learned in tone, complete with book and chapter divisions, with prologues marking the books. This was the fashion in one-volume compilations, and doubtless Caxton was justified in imposing book and chapter divisions on Malory's work, though his chapter divisions often simply break the flow of the narrative and the book divisions do not always correspond to the underlying narrative units, especially within *The Book of Sir Tristram*. Füetrer's work, on the other hand, consists of a series of almost completely independent tales, with almost no overall coherence (a fact that justifies the piecemeal publication it has received). Malory wrote neither a learned history, in which book divisions impose an artificial unity on the diverse materials, nor a collection of brief romances, in which none has much relation to the others. Instead he profited fully from both of the traditions we have considered; the *Morte Darthur* clearly belongs in the genre of one-volume compilations characteristic of the fifteenth century, but the main organizing principle of the work remains that of the older cyclic romances. Malory learned well the lessons the older cycles taught him, and he succeeded in the difficult task of writing not simply a condensation of previous cycles but a true brief cycle of his own invention.

The fact that the *Morte Darthur* is Malory's own invention shows that he had learned from Robert de Boron the most significant lesson his predecessors could offer—the freedom of an author to control his materials, to select or omit as he chooses in accord with his own ideas of relevance and proportion while remaining true to the "history."

This was a most important lesson, for, as we have seen, in Malory's day more readers knew more versions of Arthurian history than ever before. Malory knew that in the Vulgate version the adventures of Lancelot precede the quest of the Grail whereas in the *Roman du Graal* the adventures of Tristan precede the quest. He knew at least two different versions of the events following Arthur's coronation—those in the *Estoire de Merlin* and those in the *Suite du Merlin*—and he knew two quite different versions of the Grail quest, the *Queste del Saint Graal* and *Perlesvaus*. If we add Malory's English sources to the French, we see he knew even more alternate versions of the same events. He knew three accounts of Arthur's death (*Mort Artu*, the alliterative *Morte Arthure*, and the stanzaic *Morte Arthur*) and three of the Roman campaign (*Estoire de Merlin*, *Mort Artu*, and the alliterative *Morte Arthure*), and he knew at least one alternative chronicle version of the whole history (Hardyng's *Chronicle*). Faced with such richness, most compilers of one-volume histories fell back on simple condensation. Malory followed the example of Robert de Boron. He selected among his sources (choosing, for example, to use the *Suite du Merlin* instead of the *Estoire* for his first tale), omitted some materials (such as the war with King Royn), and added others to shape his cycle in accord with his own ideas of coherence and proportion.

Apparently Malory experimented with this form before he attempted it on the larger scale of the whole *Morte Darthur*. *The Tale of King Arthur* seems to have been Malory's first attempt to "reduce" a complicated narrative into a brief, coherent work. Vinaver may be right in regarding the adaptation of the alliterative *Morte Arthure* as Malory's first composition, but, if so, the experience he gained was mainly a matter of handling a relatively straightforward narrative.[48] The *Suite du Merlin*, the main source of *The Tale of King Arthur*, is a far more complicated work, containing a great variety of materials narrated in an often elaborately interwoven manner. As Vinaver has shown, Malory works carefully to disentangle the interwoven narratives "in accordance with a wholly different architectural design . . . to him a story was, above all, a well-circumscribed set of incidents."[49] This is certainly true, and in the next chapter I shall examine how Malory goes about turning such complicated narratives into series of well-circumscribed episodes. The resulting episodes in *The Tale of King Arthur* are relatively self-contained, and yet Malory knew that they are necessary parts of a larger whole, a history of events, as he says in the explicit, "fro the Maryage of Kynge Uther unto Kyng

Arthur that regned after hym and ded many batayles" (iv.29). Malory's solution to the problem raised by his own preference for self-contained narratives and his responsibility to the "whole book" was to turn the *Suite du Merlin* into a brief cycle.

There are four branches in this cycle, corresponding to the first four books of Caxton's edition. Vinaver's edition unfortunately obscures this organization, for he follows the manuscript in the first three divisions of the tale—"Merlin," "Balin," and what he labels "Tor and Pellinor" (though Malory calls it "The Wedding of King Arthur"). Then, without manuscript justification, he divides the fourth section (Caxton's book iv) into three units: "The Death of Merlin and the War with the Five Kings," "Arthur and Accalon," and "Gawain, Ywain, and Marhalt." Vinaver apparently regarded the manuscript divisions as purely scribal and therefore felt justified in making new divisions of his own. However, Caxton's manuscript, which obviously was not identical with the Winchester, contained exactly the same major divisions as the Winchester (as shown by the book divisions in this section), and it is therefore most probable that the divisions are Malory's own.

These divisions are marked by explicits. The first is clear enough; it ends, "But whan the messenger com to kynge Royns than was he woode out of mesure, and purveyde hym for a grete oste, as hit rehersith aftir in the BOOKE OF BALYNE LE SALVEAGE that folowith nexte aftir: that was the adventure how Balyn gat the swerde" (fol. 22r). There is no precedent for this in the *Suite du Merlin*; it is rather the same device that the French author uses at the end of the *Suite* in order to establish the relation between the *Suite* and the next branch of the cycle: "Now the tale ceases to speak more of the damsel and the king and the whole life of Merlin and instead will relate another matter which speaks of the Grail, for that is the beginning of this book." As we have seen, every branch of the Arthurian cycle ends in about this way. The Vulgate *Estoire de Merlin* uses almost the same phrasing as Malory—"si comme li contes le vous devisera cha avant," "as hit rehersith aftir in the BOOKE . . . that folowith nexte aftir."

In order to establish the independence of "Balin" and at the same time to emphasize its relation to the preceding part of his brief cycle, Malory begins with a summary of the preceding branch (for which there is, again, no precedent in the *Suite*): "After the deth of Uther regned Arthure, hys son, which had grete warre in his days for to get all Inglonde into his hande; for there were many kingis within the realme of Inglonde, and of Scotlande, Walys, and Cornuwayle" (fol.

22r). This sort of summary, marking as it does a fresh beginning, sets off a new branch even more clearly than the explicit that ends "The Tale of Balin": "Thus endith the tale of Balyn and Balan, two brethirne that were borne in Northumbirlonde that were two passiynge good knyghtes as ever were in tho dayes. EXPLICIT" (fol. 34r).

Yet "Balin" is tightly connected with the preceding "Merlin." That division ended with a broad hint that this tale would narrate an invasion by King Royn: the penultimate episode in "Merlin" was a brief scene in which King Royn sent an insulting message to King Arthur, who vowed, "I shall ordeyne for hym in shorte tyme" (i.26). Consequently, after the brief summarizing introduction just quoted, "Balin" begins with: "So hit befelle on a tyme whan kynge Arthure was at London, ther com a knyght and tolde the kynge tydingis how the kynge Royns of Northe Walis had rered a grete nombir of peple and were entred in the londe and brente and slew the kyngis trew lyege people . . . 'Well,' seyde the kynge, 'I shall ordayne to wythstonde hys malice' " (ii.1). This is the same sort of linking episode that binds *Lancelot* to the *Queste* or the *Queste* to the *Mort Artu*.

The third section of *The Tale of King Arthur*—"The Wedding of King Arthur"—is even more clearly distinct from the second ("Balin"), than the second was from the first. The scribe has left a blank page between "Balin" and "The Wedding" (34v) and begins "The Wedding" with a large (seven-line), flourished capital. The break here, we might note, is even more distinct than that between the *Tale of Sir Lancelot* and *The Tale of Sir Gareth* (113r-v). There is one subdivision within the "Wedding" section; Gawain's adventure is set off by "Here begynneth the Fyrst batayle that ever Sir Gawayne ded after he was made knyght" (37v) and "thus endith the adventure of Sir Gawayne that he dud at the mariage of Arthure." I doubt that these are to be taken as in any sense equivalent to the major divisions; the episode lacks the sort of introduction we have noted, beginning only "Syr Gawayne rode more than a pace," and is clearly one of a series of subordinate adventures, each of which is set off in the manuscript (possibly the line beginning "Here begynneth" is a gloss that crept into the text).

At the end of "The Wedding of King Arthur" there is a distinct explicit: "Explicit the Weddyng of kyng Arthure" (44v). The rest of the folio—this occurs about a quarter of the way from the top—is blank, and the next major division begins with a large capital and the usual summarizing introduction: "SO AFTIR THESE QUESTIS OF SIR GAWAYNE SIR Tor and kynge Pellinor, then hit befelle" (44v). This

final division is linked with the preceding by much the same device as
we saw binding the first and second tales. The next-to-the-last episode
in "The Wedding" is a brief scene in which Pellinor overhears two
knights discussing fresh plots by their chieftains in the north against
Arthur (iii.14); the final division, after a brief account of Merlin's
entombment, relates the invasion of the five kings from the north
(iv.2).

Hereafter—and this is the main point of this long excursus—there
are no manuscript divisions and no clear justification for Vinaver's
division of the work. The section that Vinaver calls "Arthur and
Accalon" does handle a new subject and does begin with a large
(three-line) capital, but such internal subdivisions are common (e.g.,
52r, 56r, 59r), and Caxton rightly used them as chapter divisions.
Vinaver's final division, "Gawain, Ywain, Marhalt," has not even this
justification. In the manuscript there is no break whatsoever: ". . . for
allwey she drad muche kyng Arthure. Whan the kynge had well rested
hym at the abbey he rode unto Camelot . . ." (58r). There is no reason
to insert a major division here, and it is unfortunate that Vinaver did
so. Malory's four-part division reveals a relatively solid cyclic structure; the six-part division makes it seem as if *The Tale of King Arthur*
starts out well enough and then trails off into assorted, apparently
unconnected adventures.

Most unfortunately, the six-part division obscures the main principle of construction in *King Arthur*, the principle of proportion that
Malory knew from the express concern of the author of the *Suite du
Merlin*, that the "parts of my book may be equal." Malory seems
clearly to be working toward this end; he omits much of the Merlin
material and almost all of the materials before Arthur's birth, and he
works to achieve a balance between his four divisions. He does this by
dividing his four parts into two groups. As we have seen, the first and
second divisions and the third and fourth are explicitly linked. But
there is no such link between the second and third tales. Instead, *King
Arthur* seems to make a fresh beginning at this point: "In the begynn-
yng of Arthure, aftir he was chosen kynge by adventure and by
grace, for the . . ." (iii.1). The second half of *King Arthur* could be
separated from the first without much effect on what went before,
since there is no linking episode of the sort that binds the units within
the two halves.

Nevertheless, the two halves are closely related by parallels in
action and proportion in construction. They are almost exactly equal
in length; the first fills folios 1-34v in the Winchester Manuscipt, the

second, 35r-70v (82 and 92 pages in Vinaver's one-volume edition). The divisions within the two halves are roughly balanced in a chiasmic manner; the first consists of a long, relatively varied tale (1-22r) and then a briefer, more circumscribed tale ("Balin," 22r-34r); the second begins with a brief tale ("The Wedding of King Arthur," 35r-44r) and ends with a longer, more varied section (45r-70v).

Malory was probably not counting pages as he wrote, but he was clearly aiming at this sort of balance not just on the authority of the *Suite du Merlin* but because, like most romancers, he delighted in parallels and favored a narrative technique that Thomas R. Rumble has called "development by analogy."[50] The first half begins with Uther and Ygraine, the second with Arthur and Guenevere. The first half concerns the establishment of Arthur's rule and consequent adventures, the second the establishment of the Round Table and the adventures following that. In the first half Arthur fights an indecisive duel with Pellinor to obtain Excalibur, in the second he fights another indecisive duel with Accalon to regain the sword. And just as the first half ends with prophecies of Lancelot and of the Grail, so the second half ends with prophecies of Tristram, of Lancelot, and of the Grail.

Prophecy is the means of combining the two halves of this tale as well as providing for its inclusion in the larger work. Malory's French source was heavy with prophecy, since the *Suite* was designed as an introduction to the story of the Grail and the death of Arthur. Malory retains much of this and adds to it, providing for the stories of Lancelot and Tristram as well. Within the limits of the tale, he also experiments with prophecy as a unifying device. As I have noted, there is no linking episode to hold the first part to the second; "The Wedding of King Arthur" contains no episode that was begun in the preceding "Tale of Balin." But major episodes in the second half are fulfillments of prophecies made in the first; Merlin's entombment is foretold in "Merlin" (i.21), as is Arthur's battle with Accalon (i.25). There are recurrent themes as well, such as Morgan's enmity for Arthur and Gawain's hatred of Pellinor (the main link between "Balin" and "The Wedding").

In short, if we look at *The Tale of King Arthur* as a brief four-part cycle, we can appreciate its structure. This is not to say that the work is an unqualified success; *King Arthur*, like the *Suite* itself, is too obviously a preliminary work, too dependent on what will follow, to develop an internal thematic coherence of its own. Nevertheless, writing it was a profitable experience for Malory. He used somewhat the same technique again at the end of the *Morte Darthur*, when he made another "brief cycle" by dividing the matter of the *Mort Artu* into two distinct but related tales, *Lancelot and Guenevere* and *The Death of Arthur*. Most important, he applied the same technique to his whole book of King Arthur.

So long as critics were dependent solely on Caxton's edition, the cyclic character of Malory's book was badly obscured. The virtue of the Winchester Manuscript, and thus of Vinaver's edition, is the division into eight tales, which is doubtless Malory's own device and which reveals the essential structure of his book. Each part of the whole book is a self-contained tale in the same way as "The Tale of Balin" is within *The Tale of King Arthur*. In this sense, Malory did write eight "separate" tales rather than one unified narrative. Yet each of the eight tales exists within a well-defined cycle, linked together in the same way "Balin" is linked to the other parts of *The Tale of King Arthur*. In some cases (at the ends of *Arthur and Lucius*, *Sir Tristram*, and *Lancelot and Guenevere*) one tale is bound to the next by explicits of the "here-followeth-after" variety that Malory uses to link "Merlin" with "Balin." More often, the tales are bound together by the sorts of linking episodes that are also used in *The Tale of King Arthur*. That tale itself ends when Lancelot and Tristram come to the court; the second begins with this episode. Likewise, *The Book of Sir Tristram* ends with the feast of Pentecost at which Galahad comes to court, and the next tale begins with that episode; *The Sancgreal* ends with Bors's return to the court, and the following *Lancelot and Guenevere* begins with Bors's return. The only tale that has no obvious link to what precedes and follows is *Gareth*, but here the case is similar to the problem of the two halves of *King Arthur*, and *Gareth* is linked to its context by common, repeated themes.

Within the whole *Morte Darthur* we find the same concern with a symmetrically balanced structure that we noted in *King Arthur*. Even before he finished that tale Malory had apparently decided that his cycle would include the adventures of Tristram: as the prophecies at its close imply, Tristram, Lancelot, and the Grail will be the central concerns of Arthur's knights. However, Lancelot will be the focal character throughout the book (as he is in *Gareth*, *Sir Tristram*, and *The Sancgreal*, since he has a major role in each). To establish the dominance of Lancelot, the three central tales are bracketed within two tales of Lancelot (*A Noble Tale of Sir Lancelot du Lake* and *Lancelot and Guenevere*). It looks as if Malory wrote *Gareth* in order to provide a tale with a secular hero to balance the account of the

Grail hero, for the result is a nicely symmetrical structure; Lancelot-Gareth-Tristram, then Tristram-Galahad-Lancelot. *Sir Tristram* is the center, in which we move from the purely secular concerns at its beginning to the introduction of the Grail mysteries at its end, with Perceval appearing to take his place at the right side of the Siege Perilous at the center of *Sir Tristram* and nearly at the center of the whole book (fol. 252). The result is the same sort of balanced structure that we have noted in *King Arthur*, with also the same sort of observance of "proportion." The section of the *Morte Darthur* preceding *The Book of Sir Tristram* is almost the same length (148 folios) as that which follows the book (142 folios—approximately, since the last few folios are missing).

The central position of *Sir Tristram* and its comparatively disproportionate length imply the presence of a three-part structure within the balanced overall scheme. We begin the *Morte Darthur* with a fairly straightforward narrative chronology. Then, as has often been noted, Malory seems to start all over again with *The Book of Sir Tristram*, which is a "retrospective narrative," a "loop in time" of the sort he had experimented with in *The Tale of King Arthur*.[51] Tristram and Mark had already appeared in the first four tales, and Mark is already married to Isode. Now Malory loops back to a time even before Tristram's birth and follows the history of the Round Table from this new perspective to the moment when the Tristram story and the Grail converge in the appearance of Galahad, and we move from the flowering of the Round Table to the beginning of its end. We therefore have a fairly clear beginning (*King Arthur* to *Gareth*, 148 folios), flowering (*Sir Tristram*, 198 folios), and end of the Round Table (*The Sancgreal* to end, 142 folios). Malory does not insist on this three-part scheme in any way, though it is obvious enough that Richard Stansby, the last of Malory's early printers, chose to divide the *Morte Darthur* in just that fashion.[52]

A sophisticated sense of cyclic structure is not surprising in one who read so carefully the work of the "architect" of the *Lancelot-Queste-Mort Artu* trilogy nor in one who pondered the advice of the author of the *Suite du Merlin*. It is rather surprising in the author of a one-volume history of the fifteenth-century sort, for only Malory succeeded in writing a work that was at once a brief compilation and a new cycle, worthy of a place in the tradition that includes such venerable names as Walter Map and Robert de Boron.

In this sense, there is, after all, some validity in the old idea that

Malory was the last of his line and the one writer who could make the old materials live again, for he was indeed the one writer bold enough to carry on the older tradition and not just "reduce" but also remake his sources. Others of his time and before had tried to make "one story, one book" of the old materials. Malory alone had the ability to make such a book a work of art. That ability was sharpened by a careful and profitable reading of the old cycles and by an even more profitable experience of English romance.

II

Malory and English Romance

3

Techniques of Adaptation:
The Tale of King Arthur
and
Arthur and Lucius

Malory's work is seldom considered in the light of the English romance tradition, for the good reason that Malory is in many ways a French romancer. His cyclic form, as well as most of his materials, is drawn from French romance, and his delight in an abundance of characters and actions shows his aesthetic relation to that tradition rather than to the English line of simple and brief romance narratives. Unlike most English romancers, Malory seems convinced that many stories are better than one, and even when telling one story he prefers a large cast of characters and a multiplicity of episodes. What *entrelacement* remains in his tales seems to be there for the same reason that the sixteenth-century Italian critic Geraldi Cinthio recommended the device: "There can be introduced into the composition loves, unexpected events, wrongs, vices, offenses, defenses, deceits, deeds of courtesy, justice, liberality, virtue, treachery, faith, loyalty, etc., and such other episodes, and there can be introduced such variety and delight that the poem will become most interesting."[1] The remarkable, though general, resemblance between Cinthio's catalog of delights and Caxton's preface to the *Morte Darthur* ("Herein may be seen noble chyvalrye, curtoysye, humanyte, friendliness, hardynesse, love, frendshyp, cowardyse, murdre, hate, virtue, and synne") shows that later English readers did indeed relish such copiousness and variety, but in this Malory was ahead of his time, for most English romances of his day were brief and relatively simple.

Nevertheless, Malory's narrative technique is quite distinct from that of his French predecessors and contemporaries. His tales are much briefer than his French sources, and his method of narrating episodes differs greatly from that of the old cyclic romancers. He treats episodes as self-contained units in a serial order rather than interlacing the parts of differing episodes as the old romancers did. Malory never completely rejected the technique of *entrelacement*, which he uses to good effect even in his earliest tales, but the *entrelacement* we find in the *Morte Darthur* is very simple, and the tendency is to narrate related actions in brief and complete episodes. To use Vinaver's method of notation, Malory tells two episodes (*a* and *b*) in a direct ($a^1a^2a^3$; $b^1b^2b^3$) rather than an interlaced manner ($a^1b^1a^2b^2a^3b^3$). This tendency can also be found in contemporary French prose romances, such as *Le comte d'Artois* or *Paris et Vienne*, but in those works the episodes are lengthy, characterized by elaborate descriptions and long rhetorical speeches quite foreign to Malory's style. Malory's episodes are brief, and the narrative focuses primarily upon the action. The effect is similar to that in the one-volume histories discussed in the previous chapters, but Malory adapts rather than condenses, and we seldom have the feeling that we are reading a summary of some longer work. This is because Malory worked not to "modernize" his sources but to "anglicize" them. His technique of straightforward narrative of action, his manner of constructing and organizing his episodes, and even his method of anglicizing his sources had been developed and used by English verse romancers for over two centuries before his time.

Though Malory chose to write in prose, and to this extent aligned himself with his French rather than his English predecessors, his work reveals a considerable acquaintance with and respect for English verse romance. We see little of this in the works of later English prose romancers, such as Lord Berners or even Caxton, probably because by the late fifteenth and early sixteenth centuries verse romance had become more obviously old-fashioned and had been largely displaced by prose as the medium of sophisticated fiction. In Malory's youth and early manhood, there was little or no English prose fiction, English verse romance still flourished, and an Englishman who relished Arthurian tales was necessarily a reader of verse romance. Vinaver suggests that "Malory first became familiar with the Arthurian legend not through 'French books' but through an English poem, the alliterative *Morte Arthure* . . . by the time Malory came to 'reduce' his French books into English, his attitude toward Arthurian knighthood had been fixed in his mind by the reading of native poetry."[2] Even Malory's earliest works reveal such a broad knowledge of both English and French romance that it is impossible to determine which books he read first,[3] but Vinaver is doubtless correct in his assertion that Malory's reading of native romances profoundly affected his attitudes toward his materials. This is clear not just in his idea of knighthood but in his idea of what a romance narrative should be.

Aside from the two English works that Malory used as direct sources, the alliterative *Morte Arthure* and the stanzaic *Morte Arthur*, we cannot be sure exactly which English romances he read. Vinaver believes that Malory knew *Sir Gawain and the Green Knight*, whose influence he detects in *The Tale of Sir Gareth*, and possibly *Sir Orfeo*, which provides a closer analogue to Tristram's madness than any version of the French *Tristan*.[4] In addition to these possible influences, Malory must have known other English romances that left no direct trace in his works. William Matthews argues that Malory's use of the alliterative *Morte Arthure* implies that he had considerable experience in reading alliterative verse.[5] Its "strange Inglis" was very difficult for an ordinary reader (hence Chaucer's Parson uses nonsense syllables—"rim, ram, ruf"—to characterize its style). Consequently, when Caxton published the *Morte Darthur* he took great pains to remove the difficult poetic words that Malory had carried over into his prose probably without thinking of the problems the vocabulary would pose for readers unaccustomed to alliterative verse.

However, Malory's knowledge of English romance is most obvious in his use of proper names, for he frequently prefers the English to the French form. The Galeron de Gales of the French *Tristan* becomes Galleron of Galloway (as in *The Awntyrs of Arthur*). Tristan himself becomes Tristram, and the pseudonym he adopts is therefore not the Tantris of French romance but the English Tramtrist.[6] Likewise, the Calogrenant of French romance becomes Colgrevaunce (as in *Ywain and Gawain* and *Arthour and Merlin*), Girflet becomes Gryflet (as in *Lybeaus Desconus*), and even Gaheriet becomes Gareth, much closer to the Garret of *Sir Launfal* and *The Wedding of Sir Gawain* than to the French form. More important, Malory frequently employs names that are known only in English romance—Baudewyne of Britain (*The Avowing of Arthur*), Sir Ironside, the Green Knight, Sir Petypace of Winchelsé (all in *The Carl of Carlisle*), Sir Degrevant (*Sir Degrevant*), Sir Gromer Somer Jour (*The Wedding of Sir Gawain*), as well as many names from the alliterative *Morte Arthure* which are used throughout the *Morte Darthur*. In short, just as Malory frequently supplies geographically accurate English places for actions only vaguely located in the French, so he frequently anglicizes the names of the French characters and supplies purely English names in a manner that indicates a considerable knowledge of English romance.

Sometimes it appears that Malory knew English romance better than French, or at least had it closer to his consciousness. In the final tale, for example, Malory names the twelve knights (anonymous in both the stanzaic *Morte Arthur* and the *Mort Artu*) whom Mordred and Agravain lead in the attack on Lancelot in Guenevere's bedchamber: "And thes were their names: sir Collgrevaunce, sir Mador de la Porte, sir Gyngalyne, sir Mellyot de Logris, sir Petipace of Wynchelsé, sir Galleron of Galoway, sir Melyon de la Mountayne, sir Ascomore, sir Gromore Somer Joure, sir Curselayne, sir Florence, and sir Lovell (xx.2)."[7] Of these twelve knights, five are characters known only in English romance (Petipace of Wynchelsé, Gromore Somer Joure, Aschamore, Florence, and Lovell), and three (Collgrevaunce, Gyngalyne, and Galleron of Galoway) have names with recognizably English forms. Of the other four, the character of Mellyot de Logris is largely Malory's invention, though his name came originally from *Perlesvaus*; Melyon de la Mountayne seems also to be Malory's own invention;[8] the same may be true of Curselayne, unknown outside the *Morte Darthur*; only Mador de la Porte is firmly based on a character well known in French romance (though he also appears in English romance, as in *Sir Gawain and the Green Knight*).

Malory's use of English names in this manner shows that he regarded English romance as equivalent, in "authority," to French romance, and his choice of sources—his use of the alliterative *Morte Arthure* and the stanzaic *Morte Arthur*—indicates that he regarded at least some as superior. Malory knew the account of the Roman Wars in the Vulgate *Merlin*, and he could easily have adapted that to his purposes—perhaps more easily than the English poem, since in the *Merlin* the Roman War occurs early in Arthur's career, long before his last battle, and it ends in triumph rather than tragedy.[9] Yet Malory chose to base his account on the version in the alliterative *Morte Arthure*, which, like the chronicles, puts the Roman War at the end of

Arthur's career immediately before the final encounter with Mordred, and Malory therefore had to supply a new conclusion, which he took from another English work, Hardyng's *Chronicle* (which ends the Roman Wars with Arthur's coronation as Roman emperor).[10] Malory's use of the stanzaic *Morte Arthur* for the seventh and eighth tales is similar. His principal source is the *Mort Artu*, one of the finest of the French prose romances. Yet he seems to prefer the structural plan of the English version; where the French and English versions differ, he almost always follows the English.

Malory's high regard for English romance may seem a failure in taste to some readers, for English verse romances have suffered from comparisons with their French counterparts. Aside from obvious exceptions, such as the alliterative *Morte Arthure* and *Gawain and the Green Knight*, English romance has been regarded as a derivative genre (which it is) and therefore as an inferior one (which does not necessarily follow). The English romancers' concentration on action, as contrasted to the courtly psychological subtleties of Chrétien de Troyes, their relative lack of interest in mysticism and symbolism of the sort we find in the French Grail romances, and their preference for simple, brief, relatively straightforward narrative lines in contrast to the structural complexities of French works—all have seemed flaws to many readers and critics. "Yet," as Robert W. Ackerman has written, "in their adaptations and often in their translations as well, the English writers, who were addressing a later audience, tended to create a type of romance quite distinct from the French."[11] And this genre has virtues quite distinctly its own. These virtues are primarily narrative—an emphasis on action, a relatively simple story line, a concern with morality rather than psychology—and they are the virtues of the "prose reductions" popular in the fifteenth century. Some of Malory's French contemporaries, with their impatience at the "longeurs" of older narratives, would probably have been more appreciative of the type of narrative represented by even the earliest English romances, had they known them, than many modern critics are.

The "typically English variety of romance," as Dieter Mehl points out, is the short romance, usually a condensation of a much longer French original.[12] By Malory's time English romancers were quite capable of making their own plots (usually by combining themes and motifs from earlier romances), but when English romance began—with *King Horn*, probably written around 1225—romance was strictly a French genre. As late as the first quarter of the fourteenth century, Robert Mannyng, speaking of Arthurian romance, laments that they are "written & spoken of ffraunces usage,/þat neuer was writen þorow Englischemen" (*Story of England,* vv. 10972-73). The author of *Arthour and Merlin,* writing around 1250, explains that though "Freynsch vse þis gentilman" (v.23),

> Mani noble ich haue iseiȝe
> at no Freynsche couþe seye.   (vv. 25-26)

One suspects he is flattering his audience, but the fact remains that beginning in the thirteenth century there arose a demand for English versions of French romances.

The transition from French to English at this time was a transition from a relatively learned and leisured audience to an audience of "lewed men" with neither the time nor the literary training to appreciate the sophistication of *Tristan* or *Horn et Rigmel.* For example, the Anglo-Norman *Romance of Horn* (as the work formerly known as *Horn et Rigmel* is named by its latest editor) is the work of a cleric, Mestre Thomas, who makes good use of his theological, literary, and legal learning.[13] He wrote for an audience that shared this culture, readers such as the owner of the Oxford manuscript of the poem, who was apparently connected with the law or administration in Berkshire during the thirteenth century, who added Latin annotations to the literary pieces, including *Horn,* and who was clearly a man of broad literary experience (the manuscript contains, in addition to *Horn,* legal works, *Li chasteau d'amour,* the *Fables* of Marie de France, and a bestiary). *King Horn,* on the other hand, which is the earliest surviving English romance and which was probably written a quarter of a century before this Berkshire gentleman acquired his copy of the *Romance of Horn,* seems to have been composed by a minstrel for oral delivery and for an audience of little sophistication. For such an audience, direct translation is impossible; the English poet must adapt the work. Albert Friedman and Norman Harrington's characterization of the later *Ywain and Gawain* (c. 1300-1350) could easily apply to *King Horn:* "The poem is clearly the work of a minstrel catering for the sober, realistic audience of a provincial baron's hall, an audience whose sympathies were not adjusted to Chrétien's elaborate and subtle presentations of courtly love or highflown sentiment. The elegant and dilatory court romance of Chrétien has become in the hands of the English minstrel a rapid-paced story of love and gallant adventure."[14]

Mestre Thomas's work is by no means as elegant as Chrétien's (it retains some features—including the verse form—of the older *chansons de geste*), but it is a delightful romance, leisurely and embellished, rich in descriptions of persons, materials, and objects—even the mason who built Rigmel's chamber is named and praised. It presents an idealized view of aristocratic life in the late twelfth century, with detailed descriptions of courtly amusements, such as playing chess and singing *lais* (including a *lai* of Horn and Rigmel). The richly clad characters act, speak, and feel the way a sophisticated audience would have liked to imagine itself acting, and Horn is a model of courtly deportment—"Li beaus, li gentilz, li corteis, l'alose" (v. 785). One can easily understand why the late fourteenth-century author of *Ponthus et la belle Sidoine* chose the Anglo-Norman *Horn* to reshape "along the lines of a book of courtesy," for Horn was already a model courtier.[15]

The context of Thomas's *Horn* is not only courtly but literary; this work, Thomas tells us, is part of a cycle—preceded by a romance (now lost) about Horn's father, Aälof, and to be followed by a romance about Horn's son, Hademod, which Thomas says his own son, Willemot, will write (it has also been lost, if indeed it was ever written). The poet assumes his audience knows the first part of the trilogy ("My lords, you have heard the verses written on parchment"; v. 1) and wants to hear the next. He assumes too that his audience is familiar with the works of the Charlemagne cycle and can appreciate references to Roland, Ogiers le Danois, and Gormont. Perhaps he even expects them to recognize his adaptation of scenes from another Thomas's *Tristan* and to appreciate his defense of chastity and fidelity in contrast to the celebration of adultery in the work of his more famous fellow Anglo-Norman.[16]

The English *King Horn*, on the other hand, seems to exist in isolation, as pure narrative rather than as part of a larger literary culture. None of the literary references that we find in the Anglo-Norman poem appear in the English work. This is characteristic of the other early English romances. King Arthur appears in the Anglo-Norman *Tristan* but not in the English *Sir Tristrem*; the French versions of the Havelok story (Gaimar's *Estoire des Engles* and the Anglo-Norman *Lai d'Havelok*) contain extended passages connecting the story of Havelok to the history of Arthur, but there is nothing of this in *Havelok the Dane*. The Continental French version of *Amis and Amiloun* is closely related to the cycle of Charlemagne, in whose court the action takes place, but there is nothing of this in the English version, which is set in the court of an unnamed "duke of Lombardy"; and in the French *Floire et Blancheflor,*the lovers are the parents of Berte-as-grans-pies, the mother of Charlemagne, but again there is nothing of this in the English version. The literary allusions that French romancers use to lend an air of literary and historical authenticity to their works would have meant little to the first English audiences of romance, for their literary experience must have been restricted largely to popular tales and songs.

Such an audience would have had little experience, literary or otherwise, with the elaborate costumes, rich armor, beautiful chambers, and courtly amusements that receive so much attention in works such as *The Romance of Horn.* Indeed, few if any French-speaking listeners could have experienced life on this luxurious scale, but they had heard or read of such luxury and could at least dream that they recognized the blurred outlines of their own lives in the idealized mirror of the romances. The English-speaking audience of works like *Sir Tristrem* or *King Horn* lived and dreamed on a much lower scale. They could appreciate such matters as Sir Tristrem's skill in hunting (to which the English author pays considerable attention; vv. 445-537) but apparently had little interest in "La salle aux images" (vv. 2830-49), on which the French poet lavishes such care. They could appreciate the personal beauty of Horn (vv. 1016ff) but had no interest in the rich and fashionable clothing that Mestre Thomas carefully specifies.[17] And they could appreciate feasting, but only to a point:

> Of þe mete for to telle
> Ne of the win bidde ich nougt dwelle;
> þat is þe storie for to lenge;
> It wolde anuye þis fayre genge.　　　　(*Havelok,* vv. 1732-35;
> 　　　　　　　　　　　　　　　　　cf. *Bevis,* vv. 1483-84)

This seems less rhetorically inspired *occupatio* than an earnest assurance to a restless audience.

The emphasis is upon action, stripped of all the descriptive, psychological, courtly passages that might slow the narrative and "annoy this fair gang," and the earliest English romances consequently read like brief epitomes of their French analogues. The extreme example is *Sir Tristrem,* which is but a skeleton of its original with all the action and none of the spirit. *King Horn* is likewise a narrative of bare action, packing into less than 1,600 short lines all the essential action of the 5,250 long lines of the Anglo-Norman version. *Floris and Blancheflour,* even when complete, was probably no more than a third of the length of its French original, and *Amis and Amiloun* is at least a thousand lines shorter than its closest French analogue.[18] Only *Havelok* is markedly longer than its French analogues, but this is due to the greater number of episodes in the English version—more action rather than a dilatory style of narration.

In later times English romance gained in sophistication. Around 1300 in the London area there seem to have been audiences leisured enough to appreciate much longer romances, such as *Kyng Alisaunder* and *Richard the Lion-Hearted*. *Richard* is a crude but vigorous narrative, yet it does contain references to other romances, as in the opening lines, and seems to have been written for an audience of somewhat more sophistication than works such as *Havelok* or *Sir Tristrem*. *Kyng Alisaunder* clearly is a sophisticated work, and its author was a man of some learning, though his work is intended for oral delivery and concentrates on action more than elaboration.[19] *Guy of Warwick*, written about the same time, is another long work, fairly faithful to its Anglo-Norman original. By the late fourteenth century, as English rose in social status and English audiences gained leisure and sophistication, we have romances such as *Gawain and the Green Knight* and the alliterative *Morte Arthure*, which were intended for listeners who evidently welcomed elaborate descriptions of the manners of the nobility. English romancers learned how to handle psychological characterization, and there were English audiences for long and sophisticated works, such as Hugh of Rutland's *Ipomedon*, which was translated directly into English (as "Ipomadon A") in the late fourteenth century. By the fifteenth century there were English readers even for direct translations from the French Vulgate romances (such as the English prose *Merlin*).

Nevertheless, the typical English romance remained a relatively brief and simple narrative. The social conditions that shaped the first English romances no longer obtained, but the convention seems to have been fixed, and the emphasis was on action rather than description and reflection. Brevity remained a virtue, and simplicity of setting and characterization and the dominance of action remained the guiding principles of most native romancers. Even English romances that deviated from this pattern were frequently recast in the same way as the first English romancers adapted French models. *Guy of Warwick*, too long by ordinary standards, was broken into three separate romances by the compiler of the Auchinleck Manuscript. "Ipomadon A" was reduced to about a quarter of its length and greatly simplified by the fifteenth-century author of the *Life of Ipomedon* ("Ipomadon B"). *Sir Gawain and the Green Knight* was likewise reduced and simplified by the author of the fifteenth-century *Grene Knight*, and Malory's *Arthur and Lucius* did much the same for the alliterative *Morte Arthure*.

This method of adaptation was simple, but, judging from failures such as *Sir Tristrem*, it had to be learned. The author of *Sir Tristrem* tried to include everything that was in his source, condensing rather than selecting and adapting, and his work therefore reads more like an outline for a longer narrative than a romance in its own right. The author of the alliterative *Joseph of Arimathie*, on the other hand, was far more skilled, and his task of adaptation more difficult, for, like Malory a century later, he had to deal with one of the Vulgate prose romances, the *Estoire del Saint Graal*. The author of the English *Joseph* realized that a reduction needed only preserve the main story (or "history") of the source and that all details and actions irrelevant to that main story could be omitted. He condensed some episodes (the six-page appearance of Christ in the prose, pp. 31-35, was reduced to a few lines, vv. 258-294) and omitted others, especially in the account of the battle (pp. 49-66, vv. 450-605), where many subsidiary characters and events—such as Evelak's sparing the life of Tholomer's seneschal— were left out. He omitted almost all descriptive and reflective material; Joseph's episcopal vestments are described and allegorized at great length in the French (pp. 36-39), but in the English we learn only that Christ told Joseph of "his vestimens, what þey signifyen" (v. 301). Finally, he excluded from his narrative all digressive material. In the French, Evelak's wife tells how she was converted by a miracle and then adds more miracles concerning the later adventures of her brother and mother (pp. 69-72). The English poet's theme is "miracle and conversion," but he kept the two in tight control, allowing only so much miracle as directly relates to conversion.[20] His work, in short, is no mere epitome. Instead, the author stripped the narrative to its essentials and allowed the theme to emerge from concise dialogue and rapid action of a sort foreign to the reflective and meditative technique of the ponderous *Estoire del Saint Graal*.

This alliterative poet was simply following the set practices of English romance, but his method would have earned the approval of fifteenth-century prose writers, for, as we have noted, by the fifteenth century a preference for concise narration was a widespread European phenomenon. Almost everything that might be said in praise or blame of *Joseph of Arimathie* would apply with equal force to the work of writers such as Ulrich Füetrer or Michel Gonnot, whose work is characteristically "plus bref, plus coherent, et plus clair" than his sources.[21] A similar taste for brevity, coherence, and clarity may explain why Malory seemed to admire even relatively crude fifteenth-century English romances such as *The Wedding of Sir Gawain* and *Sir Gawain and the Carl of Carlisle*.[22] Though their style is crude, they have the simple narrative virtues that we find in English romance from its very beginnings.

The best proof of Malory's admiration for this sort of narrative is his adaptation of the alliterative *Morte Arthure*; Malory's changes create a narrative that, like Gonnot's, is "plus bref, plus coherent, et plus clair," and, like the work of his English predecessors, places the emphasis on action rather than description or analysis. Vinaver's explanation of Malory's method could apply almost as well to the author of *Joseph of Arimathie* as to Malory: "Malory reduced the narrative to about half its original size, not by means of indiscriminate omission, but by a careful elimination of passages which seemed to him to delay the action: monologues, dialogues, and descriptions of scenery. He clearly aimed at a more direct narrative and in the endeavor to avoid all that was not essential to its progress did not hesitate to omit such episodes as Arthur's council of war in Luxembourg, or the adventures of King Loth, and those of the Earl of Antele."[23] Malory, like the author of *Joseph*, aimed not at simple condensation but at adaptation. His job was easier, since his source was an English romance with the characteristic English simplicity of narrative line. There were no *entrelacements* to untangle and few digressions, and the main task was simple compression.

Malory did have to adapt the work to his own purpose, which seems to have been a straightforward celebration of Arthur as a military leader rather than the morally complex theme of the alliterative poem. Malory's Arthur is a somewhat more gentle and chivalric king than the hero of the *Morte Arthure*. Arthur's stern and rather unfair rebuke of Cador, after Cador's narrow escape from the Romans' attempt to rescue the senator Peter ("Sir Cador, thy corage confoundes us all! / Cowardly thou castes out all my best knyghtes!"; vv. 1922-23) is changed to an expression of concern for Cador's well-being ("Than the kynge wepte and with a keuerchoff wyped his iyen and sayde, 'Your corrage and youre hardynesse nerehand had you destroyed' "; v.7). Likewise, during the siege of Metz, the countess of Clarysyn kneels and begs Arthur to halt the assault on her city; in Malory, but not in the alliterative poem, the king in his turn chivalrously kneels to reply. The bombardment of that city, which is narrated in some detail in the alliterative poem (vv. 3032-43), is barely mentioned in Malory's tale, in which he generally plays down "the gruesome details of the battle scenes" and adds "details of Arthur's commiseration toward women and other non-combatants."[24]

Most of Malory's efforts, however, were directed toward the creation of an uncomplicated and relatively fast-moving narrative. Descriptions of scenery (vv. 926-932) and feasts (vv. 1074-1103) are omitted. The richly grotesque description of the Giant of St. Michael's Mount (vv. 1074-1103) is reduced to its bare essentials, as is the elaborately detailed description of Arthur's armor (vv. 900-914). Such omissions and reductions, along with the consistent compression of speeches and the elimination of unnecessary episodes, such as the council at Luxembourg, help create a more simple narrative structure. Whereas the alliterative poet, like the author of *Sir Gawain*, often juxtaposes rather than explicitly connects his scenes and sometimes shifts from one to another within a single sentence, Malory carefully supplies transitions of the sort common in most English romances: "Now leve we Sir Lucius and speke we of kyng Arthure" (v.3); "Now turne we to the Emperour of Rome" (v.8); "Now leve Sir Arthour and speke we of a senatoure that ascaped from the battle" (v.8); "Now turne we to Arthure with his noble knightes" (v.9). Such emphatic transitions hardly seem necessary in so simply organized a narrative as this, but Malory, like most of his English predecessors, obviously prizes clarity even at the cost of elegance.

Malory's most significant change is his omission of the last third of the alliterative romance. The *Morte Arthure* tells of the fall of Arthur as well as his greatest military triumph, but Malory, following the Vulgate account, delays the death until long after the Roman campaign. The account of Arthur's Roman campaign in the *Estoire de Merlin* provided a suitable precedent for this procedure, and, as we have noted, there are some details in Malory's tale that show he was familiar with this part of the *Estoire*. Moreover, Malory also aimed at producing a self-contained tale, and so he supplies a new conclusion to the adventure. On the authority of Hardyng's *Chronicle*, he ends the account with Arthur's triumphant coronation as emperor of Rome, which neatly rounds off the tale and allows it to stand alone not simply as an adaptation of a part of the alliterative poem but as an independent work in its own right.

The change makes *Arthur and Lucius* a "well-circumscribed" story,

to use Vinaver's term. Malory is reluctant to leave unresolved narrative lines, even those that remained incomplete in the alliterative
poem. Gawain's adventure with Priamus is never clearly finished in
the *Morte Arthure;* Priamus wants to be baptized, but this event is
never narrated, though we assume his desire is fulfilled, and though
Priamus is a main character in one of the longest episodes in the alliterative poem, he simply disappears after his adventure with Gawain.
Malory carefully adds a brief scene after the duel in which Priamus is
baptized and then, in keeping with the convention of such duels, is
accepted as a knight of the Round Table: "Than the kynge in haste
crystynde hym fayre and lette conferme him Priamus, as he was afore,
and lyghtly lette dubbe hym a deuke with his hands and made hym
knyghte of the Round Table" (v.12). This supplies the conclusion to
the Gawain-Priamus episode, which was lacking in the alliterative
poem. Again, at the end of the tale, Malory brings Priamus into the
foreground in order to link his adventure more tightly with the whole
tale. Arthur says: "Where art thou, Priamus? Thy fee is yet behynde.
Here I make thee and gyff the dukedom of Lorraine for ever unto thee
and thine heirs" (v.12). The result of such changes is clearly not a better work of art than the alliterative *Morte Arthure,* which has a
somber nobility at which Malory does not aim. Yet the changes show
that Malory had learned well from his English predecessors. Even in
handling a work that he preferred to the Vulgate *Merlin* (which he
might justly have considered more authoritative) and that he so
admired he carried even its style over into his tale, he showed his
artistic independence, his confidence in his own conception of narrative structure, and he did not hesitate to reshape the poem to his own
purposes.

Compared to the alliterative *Morte Arthure,* the *Suite du Merlin* is a
very long and complicated work, and Malory's task of "reducing" it
was much more formidable than that presented by the alliterative
poem. The problem is more than a matter of length, for the *Suite du
Merlin* is a leisurely interlaced romance of the sort characteristic of the
prose Arthurian romances. Many of the Anglo-Norman romances
(*Horn, Ipomedon, Gui de Warewik*) have little *entrelacement;* even
Chrétien's works are comparatively straightforward, and the Vulgate
Estoire del Saint Graal seldom uses this technique (almost none in the
section adapted by the author of *Joseph of Arimathie*). But the prose
romances on which Malory drew are often incredibly complicated,

and his method of dealing with the first of them, the *Suite du Merlin*, seems to Vinaver a strikingly original literary achievement: "Malory's most successful and historically most significant contribution to the technique of the prose tale was his attempt to substitute for the method of 'interweaving' the modern 'progressive' form of exposition."[25]

However, the first Arthurian romance in English, *Arthour and Merlin*, which may have been composed as early as 1250, was also an adaptation of a relatively complicated and interlaced narrative, the Vulgate *Estoire de Merlin*, written after 1230. In order to make an English romance out of this work, the author of *Arthour and Merlin* had to solve many of the same problems that Malory faced two centuries later. First, he had to condense. He wrote for an audience without the leisure—or patience—to devote the many hours, even days, a full rehearsal of the *Estoire de Merlin* would have required, and he had to fit into less than 10,000 lines the materials that fill 243 folio pages in Sommer's edition. He accomplished this by much the same means as Malory later used: episodes are severely condensed, often stripped to the bare actions by the omission of descriptions, analyses, and anything irrelevant to the advancement of the plot. (Guenevere, described often and in detail in the French, is never described in the English.) Most episodes irrelevant to the main plot are omitted; others are "telescoped" so that two or more episodes in the French are reduced to one in the English (e.g., pp. 88-91; vv. 3133-77)—a method, Vinaver notes, that Malory also uses in his adaptation of the *Suite*.[26]

The resulting narrative is not only much briefer than its French source (less than a third its length), it is also much clearer and easier to follow. Probably it had to be, because of the difficulty his audience would have had in following a complex narrative in an orally delivered work and because this was the first Arthurian poem in English. A sophisticated French-speaking audience could probably appreciate the complexly interwoven narrative of a work like the *Estoire* because they already knew the main outlines of the story, which was therefore less important than its artful elaboration. The *Estoire de Merlin* is by no means so elaborately interlaced as the Vulgate *Lancelot*, but it does interweave two main plots—the story of Arthur and the story of Merlin—along with a number of subsidiary plots and digressions. Our poet, who was likely writing for an audience that was hearing the history of Arthur for the first time, concentrates upon but one plot, the tale of the establishment of Arthur's kingdom. He therefore begins not with the story of Merlin, as in the

Estoire, but with the account of Constance and his heirs. Merlin's history is given to the point where he comes to Vortiger's court, but thereafter he is reduced simply to a helper first of Uther and then of Arthur, and episodes relevant only to Merlin, such as his affair with Viviane (pp. 206-212), are omitted. The changes necessary to reduce Merlin's role were so drastic in the first third of the romance that Eugen Kölbing believed the poet must have used some source other than the Vulgate version, but, as K.D. Bülbring showed long ago, there is no doubt that the English author was dependent solely on the *Estoire de Merlin* and that his changes are due to his own artistic purposes.[27]

His main purpose—to produce a clear and easily followed history of Arthur—was complicated by the length even of his greatly compressed work. He had to break it into smaller units, for apparently his poem was designed to be read aloud at several sittings, possibly spread over a number of days. Evidently his manuscript of the Vulgate version was already divided into chapters, and he adopted these as the major divisions of his narrative. His divisions, usually marked by a "seasonal lyric" prologue, are much briefer than the French, but almost all of them correspond exactly to the chapter divisions in the later English prose *Merlin*, which must therefore have preserved the divisions of an earlier manuscript. The *Estoire* itself may have suggested the device of the "seasonal prologue" as a way of marking divisions, since one of the poet's prologues (vv. 4675-80) corresponds to a similar passage in the *Estoire* (Sommer, II, 134).

Though the English divisions of the narrative preserve those in the French, their character differs greatly. They are self-contained units, complete episodes in themselves, with information given in its logical place rather than delayed in the manner of interlaced French romance. Characters are named when they appear: in the English poem Ban and Bors come to England "wiþ her broþer Gvinbaut" (v. 3551); in the French Ban and Bors come to England on page 102, Guinbaut appears on page 105, but the fact that the kings are his brothers is not stated until page 238. Events are told when they occur; when Uther marries Ygerne, the English poet tells us that Ygerne's daughters married Lot (who fathered Gawain, Agravain, Guerehes, and Gaheriet), Nanters (who fathered Galescin), and Uriens (who fathered Ywain). In the French we are told on page 73 that Lot married one of the daughters at Uther's wedding, but we do not hear of Lot's sons until page 96, and his wife (Belisant in the English) is never named. We hear nothing of Nanters' wedding until page 127 and nothing of Uriens' wedding until page

167, and even then we learn of Ywain's relation to Arthur only indirectly, when he tells his mother Arthur is "vostre frere & mes oncles." The English author, like Malory, brings together material widely scattered through his source in order to produce a coherent narrative essentially sequential rather than interlaced. This method of narration helps account for the ease with which a later adapter created "die jüngere Version"; he simply lopped off everything after the accession of Uther, wrote a conclusion, and produced a satisfyingly self-contained narrative.

This procedure does not completely remove the *entrelacement*, for a certain amount is inevitable in the later part of the poem, in which three lines of action are involved: Arthur is in Carmelide, helping Leodegan in his war against Rion and wooing and winning Guenevere; his rebellious vassals are in England fighting the invading Saxons; and the sons of the rebellious kings (Gawain, Ywain, and the others) have set out to join King Arthur and thus reconcile their uncle with their fathers. But the poet changes the narrative method of his source and handles the three plots in the simplest possible way: he makes each of his units a relatively self-contained episode, and thus the necessary *entrelacement* becomes a juxtaposition of episodes rather than an interweaving of lines of narrative. For example, chapter 12 of the *Estoire* narrates the beginnings both of the rebel kings' troubles with the Saxon invaders and of their sons' departures to join Arthur:

1. The rebel kings confer and decide to fortify their cities.
2. Yder goes to Nantes.
3. Nanters goes to his city.
4. His wife is Arthur's sister. She tells her son Galescin this, and he determines to help his uncle.
5. Lot goes to Orkney.
6. He is married to another of Arthur's sisters and has fathered Gawain, Agravain, Guerehes, and Gaheriet.
7. The fifth son, Mordred, is Arthur's, engendered when neither Arthur nor Lot's wife knew they were brother and sister.
8. Lot's wife secretly favors Arthur and tells Gawain and his brothers that they should help their uncle. They resolve to do so, and she furnishes them with arms.
9. The rest of the kings go to their homes.
10. The Saxons invade.
11. Galescin sends a message to Gawain asking him to meet him.
12. They meet at the forest of Broceliande.

The English poet separates the two lines of action. First he tells about the Saxon invasion (10) and the kings' departure to fortify their cities (2, 3, 5, 9). Then, carefully explaining to his audience what he is doing, he shifts to the story of the kings' sons:

> Ac ar ich ʒou more þing
> Of paiems telle oþer king,
> Of Nanters sone & of his feren,
> Noble þing ʒe schullen yheren.   (4549-53)

Then we are told in logical order that Galescin learns Arthur is his uncle and determines to join him (4); he sends a message to Gawain (11); the messenger finds Gawain hunting; Gawain's mother says it is time he left such foolishness and became a knight to make peace between his uncle Arthur and his father, Lot (8). There is no digression on Mordred and no hint that Gawain's mother secretly favors Arthur because of their affair; Gawain and Galescin meet at the forest of Brockland (12).

The story of Ywain's joining Gawain is begun in the French in chapter 16, where the story of his determination to join Gawain and serve Arthur is interwoven with the story of the eleven kings' war with the invaders, and we are told that Ywain and his brother (Ywain li avoutres) set out. Two chapters intervene before Ywain meets Gawain. The English poet takes the material from chapter 16 and moves it to the section of his narrative corresponding to chapter 18 (vv. 7619ff), where he tells the story of Ywain's determination to join Arthur's men, his departure, and his meeting with Gawain in one uninterrupted episode. The arrival of Sagramour is handled in the same way (though that is fairly straightforward even in the French), and the English poet completely omits the story of Dodynel le Salvage, another young knight whose departure to join Gawain is told in an interlaced fashion, and simply reports that Keus and Kehedins (whose stories are also interlaced in the Estoire) come to join Gawain. The plots of the rebel kings and the young knights, interwoven in the French, are thus separated and presented as a series of discrete episodes. And these are kept distinct from the third plot, Arthur's adventures at Carmelide, by the radical condensation of Merlin's detailed reports to Arthur about events in England (e.g., pp. 178, 181), which serve in the French to interweave these events with Arthur's adventures. In the English, Merlin reports in brief and general terms (vv. 6584ff, 8577ff), only as a reminder to the audience that Arthur has not forgotten his responsibilities at home.

Within the separate episodes, the poet often had to reorder his materials to create a clear and "progressive" narrative, for the French author favored a sort of *entrelacement* even when relating a single series of events. For example, Arthur's arrival at Carmelide and meeting with Guenevere in the *Estoire* (pp. 141-160) are told in this (greatly simplified) order:

1. Arthur and his forty-two knights arrive at Carmelide.
2. They battle against Rion's army.
3. Each of Arthur's forty-two knights is named.
4. The battle continues.
5. Leodegan fathers the False Guenevere.
6. The battle ends in victory.
7. The two Gueneveres appear at a celebration.
8. The True Guenevere is compared to Helayne, mother of Galahad.
9. Leodegan desires to find a husband for Guenevere.
10. Merlin informs Arthur of events in England.

The English poet rearranges the narrative as follows (vv. 5349-6594):

1. Arthur and his forty-two knights arrive at Carmelide.
3. Each of Arthur's forty-two knights is named.
2. They battle against Rion's army.
4. The battle continues.
6. The battle ends in victory.
7. The two Gueneveres appear at a celebration.
5. Leodegan fathers the False Guenevere.
9. Leodegan desires to find a husband for Guenevere.
10. Merlin (very briefly) informs Arthur of events in England.

In this episode, as throughout his work, the English author achieves what Vinaver thought was Malory's "historically most significant contribution," the substitution of the "modern 'progressive' form of exposition" for the method of "interlacing."[28]

Obviously the author of *Arthour and Merlin* was not aiming for a more "modern" narrative technique. He was trying to adapt the *Estoire* to the simpler narrative form characteristic of English romance. Narrative was his main interest, and though he usually compressed his source, he sometimes added details that exploit the dramatic possibilities of the story, such as the fabliauxlike hairbreadth escape of the judge's adulterous father ("Vp þou schotest a windowe/ and the persone þou out lete"; vv. 1130-32), and he even invented scenes to enliven the narrative, such as the one between Leodegan and

Cleodalis, barely mentioned in the French, but effectively told in the English (vv. 9849-82). Such additions show that his interest was not simply in condensation; his aim was effective narrative, and he worked carefully toward that end.

His method is common in English romance—so common that it must reflect a commonly held idea of narrative rather than a network of "influences"—and we see its effect even in such minor details as the manner in which characters are named. English romancers are loath to leave characters anonymous, and they customarily identify characters as soon as they appear. In the English *Guy of Warwick*, Felice is named when she first appears (v. 100); in *Gui de Warewik* she is introduced (vv. 51-69) but not identified by name until over a hundred lines later, when she and Gui finally meet (v. 182). In the Anglo-Norman *Boeve de Hamtone*, Boeve, in disguise, meets an unnamed palmer who has been seeking news of him, and he tells the palmer that Boeve is dead (vv. 820-862); a thousand lines later we learn that Saber, Boeve's faithful steward, has heard of Boeve's death from his son (vv. 1939-40). The audience is left to infer the connection—that Saber's son was the nameless palmer who appeared a thousand lines earlier. In the English *Bevis of Hampton*, we are told in one complete episode how Saber (Bevis's uncle) sends his son, Terri, disguised as a palmer to seek news of Bevis, how Terri meets but fails to recognize him and is told of Bevis's supposed death, and then how he returns to tell his father this news (vv. 1263-1344).

The remodeling of episodes from an interlaced to a seqential order is also common in English romance,[29] as is the preference for a single narrative line. Of course, Malory could hardly have been aware of this fact in reading most English romances, since only a comparison of an English work to its source can reveal exactly how it was composed, and such a comparison was seldom possible (and probably almost never even considered). Malory knew the *Estoire de Merlin*, but he probably did not know the English *Arthour and Merlin*. The resemblances between this work and Malory's adaptation of the French *Merlin* (that portion in which the *Suite* and the *Estoire* agree) in his *Tale of King Arthur*, which we shall presently examine, are probably due merely to the fact that both writers worked within the English tradition. Given a clear preference for the English style of narration, the method of adapting a French romance must almost inevitably follow.

Malory, however, could have learned the English method of

adaptation more directly, for he knew intimately both the stanzaic *Morte Arthur*, the most successful English verse adaptation, and its French source, the *Mort Artu*. As R. H. Wilson has shown, Malory had read both of these works even before he began his *Tale of King Arthur*,[30] and he had already gained the experience of comparing varying versions of the same story in the act of choosing his sources for his *Tale of Arthur and Lucius*. It seems very likely that Malory's skillful adaptation of the *Suite du Merlin* is based at least partly on the knowledge of the English method of adaptation that he gained, if only unconsciously, in his reading of the stanzaic *Morte Arthur* and the *Mort Artu*.

The method of adaptation employed by the author of the stanzaic *Morte Arthur* is the same as we have seen in *Arthour and Merlin*. He greatly condenses, fitting into less than four thousand lines the material that occupies 189 pages in Sommer's edition. Descriptions, interior monologues, analyses are all sacrificed to action. The frequent references to other parts of the Vulgate Cycle are omitted, save for an opening allusion to the Grail quest that serves to establish the place of this romance in the history of Arthur. Characters left anonymous in the French are identified, and, most important, the author works toward the creation of self-contained episodes rather than an *entrelacement* of parts of the episodes.

This is most obvious in the first part of the English poem, which relates the stories of the Maid of Astolat and the poisoned apple. In the corresponding section of the *Mort Artu*, on which the English poet based his work, these narratives (chaps. 1-85) are interlaced with the continuing story of Arthur's slowly developing realization of Lancelot's affair with Guenevere: Agravain's informing the king of the adultery (chaps. 5-7), Arthur's conclusion that Lancelot's participation in the tournament at Winchester disproves the accusation (chap. 30), and Arthur's adventure in Morgan's tower, where he sees the murals Lancelot painted—in an adventure told in the Vulgate *Lancelot* (Sommer, IV, 139-153)—which reveal his love for the queen (chaps. 48-53). All this is omitted by the English poet, who tells us at the beginning only that Agravain is eager for a chance to betray the lovers. The removal of the interlacing plot, which the French writer uses to connect the two parts of the narrative, effectively separates the poem into two self-contained parts—the section dealing with the Maid of Astolat and the poisoned apple and the section dealing with the death of Arthur. That seems to have been the poet's intention, for whereas the French author makes the shift from the poisoned apple episode to Agravain's plot against Lancelot within a single paragraph (chap. 85), the English poet makes a clear new beginning when Agravain sets his plan afoot (v. 1672). The effect is the same as we noted in *Arthour and Merlin*, where the removal of *entrelacement* allows the later author of "die jungere Version" to make a separate work of the first part; here the removal of *entrelacement* allows Malory to make two tales of the material in the English romance—*The Book of Sir Lancelot and Guenevere*, based on verses 1-1671 of the English poem (though Malory's tale is much more than that), and *The Death of Arthur*, which closely follows the narrative structure of the English romance (from v. 1672 to the conclusion).

In the second part of the poem the English adapter omits unnecessary episodes (Arthur's lament for Agravain, chap. 98; the burial of Gaheriet, the council of war, the appointment of new members of the Round Table to replace Lancelot and his brothers, chaps. 103-108; the Roman campaign, chaps. 160-162), and he removes most of the *entrelacement*. For example, in the French version Mordred's treacherous rebellion is first told while the siege of Benwick is still in progress (chaps. 134-144). Then the narrative shifts back to the siege and tells of Lancelot's duel with Gawain. Then the Roman War intervenes, and only when that is over (chap. 163) does the messenger (who set out twenty chapters before) arrive to announce Mordred's treachery. Then we are told of Gawain's death and finally (chap. 168) of Mordred's preparations to march against Arthur. In the English version, this scattered material is drawn together in one connected episode (vv. 2954-3049).

The result of such changes is a leaner and more rapidly moving narrative than in the *Mort Artu*. The English poem clearly lacks the depth of the French work, which fully and effectively explores the psychology of the characters and the nature of their tragic fates. But just as clearly the English poet had little interest in such matters, and with a "considerable degree of independence and artistic refinement" worked toward the creation of a simple and straightforward tale of adventure. Whether or not Malory did compare the English and French tales to discover exactly how the English poet accomplished this, there is no doubt that Malory preferred the English to the French, for even at the end of his career, after long and close work with French romances, Malory chose to follow the narrative structure of the stanzaic *Morte Arthur* for his own *Death of Arthur*.

Malory wrote his *Tale of King Arthur* by applying to the *Suite du Merlin* the English technique of adaptation that he could observe in the stanzaic *Morte Arthur* and that had been used two centuries before by the author of *Arthour and Merlin*. As I have already stated, the Vulgate *Estoire de Merlin* and the *Suite du Merlin* are almost identical in their opening chapters, since each begins with the pseudo-Robert de Boron *Merlin*. Malory and the author of *Arthour and Merlin* therefore began with the same materials, and they adapted the French matter to English romance in much the same way.

There are some similarities between Malory's work and the earlier English poem even in small details. For example, the list of eleven kings who rebel against Arthur (*Morte Darthur*, i.12) has no exact counterpart in any French source.[31] But all eleven are listed in *Arthour and Merlin*, which also agrees with Malory in the form Cradelman instead of the Vulgate Tradelman. Likewise, the author of *Arthour and Merlin* handles the account of Arthur's "buried treasure" in much the same way as Malory does.[32] Such agreements between Malory's version and *Arthour and Merlin* may be due to similarities in the manuscripts used by the two authors,[33] but they also reflect the fact that both authors worked to achieve narrative clarity in much the same way: they supply names for characters left anonymous in their sources, substitute English place names for the mythical geography of the French, and resolutely reduce their source to its essential narrative. They tend to omit the same digressive episodes (e.g., Sommer, II, 92-93, where we learn that Rion has attacked Leodegan; 98-99, the account of the battle between Claudas and Ban and Bors) and to reduce the *entrelacement* in the same way (as shown in the treasure episode mentioned above and in the reduction of Merlin's prophecies, such as Merlin's prediction of the future of Gawain and his brethren, omitted both in *Arthour and Merlin* and Malory). This method of adaptation is apparent throughout both works, affecting not only the pseudo-Robert de Boron material, which both authors shared, but also those parts distinctive to the *Estoire* and the *Suite*.

Malory, like the author of *Arthour and Merlin*, is interested in Arthur rather than Merlin. The *Suite* is in good part a history of Merlin, "de toute la vie de Merlin," as the explicit puts it, and the events of Merlin's life from his birth in the first chapter to his entombment near the end provide a major interlaced strand in the work. Malory omits almost all of this; he leaves out the beginning of the French work (the part that precedes Arthur's birth), which accounts for about a quarter of the whole. Merlin's entombment is dismissed in a page and a half, and in general Merlin is reduced, as he was in *Arthour and Merlin*, to the role of Arthur's helper, important in the early stages of Arthur's career but easily shuffled off after the Round Table is established and Arthur's success begins to depend on his own efforts and those of his knights.

In each case the English author was unsympathetic to the double plotting, the interweaving, that Merlin's presence requires, and in each case the author worked toward the creation of a sequence of self-contained episodes. Since Vinaver's notes supply an excellent running account of this, perhaps one brief example will suffice, this drawn from a later section of *The Tale of King Arthur*, which has no parallel in *Arthour and Merlin*. The events connected with the knighting of Tor are narrated in this order in the *Suite du Merlin:*

1. Gawain asks to be knighted on Arthur's wedding day; Arthur agrees.
2. A peasant asks that his son Tor be knighted on Arthur's wedding day. Arthur agrees.
3. Arthur marries Guenevere.
4. Arthur knights Tor.
5. Merlin says that Tor is not the peasant's son.
6. Arthur knights Gawain.
7. Pellinor takes his seat at the Round Table.
8. Gawain and Gaheriet are jealous.
9. The adventure begins.
10. Gawain and Tor complete their quests.
11. At the conclusion of Tor's quest, Merlin reveals that Pellinor is his true father.

In *The Tale of King Arthur* the events are told in this order (the numbers refer to the outline above):

1. Gawain asks to be knighted on Arthur's wedding day; Arthur agrees.
2. The cowherd Aryes asks Arthur to knight his son Tor; Arthur agrees.
4. Arthur knights Tor.
5. Merlin announces that Tor is not Aryes' son, and
11. Merlin reveals that Pellinor is Tor's true father.
6. Arthur knights Gawain.
7. Pellinor takes his seat at the Round Table.

8. Gawain and Gaheriet are jealous.
3. Arthur marries Guenevere.
9. The adventure begins.
10. Gawain and Tor complete their quests.

In the French version the peasant's request that Tor be knighted (2), the knighting (4), and the revelation that Tor is not the peasant's son (5) but rather the son of King Pellinor (11) are interwoven with the other events and widely separated; Tor appears at court on page 72, but we do not learn that he is Pellinor's son until almost sixty pages later. Malory brings all this together as part of one continuously narrated episode. Here, as throughout *The Tale of King Arthur*, he reshapes his materials "in accordance with a totally different architectural design," that of English romance. To Malory, as to his English predecessors, a story was "above all a well-circumscribed set of incidents."[34]

Yet, in any narrative consisting of a number of episodes, there must be some means of holding the parts together. That is one of the main uses of *entrelacement*. English romancers seemed to prefer the "bracketing" of episodes, a very simple kind of *entrelacement* rather similar to the use of "linking episodes" of the sort we considered in the first chapter. For example, in the alliterative *Morte Arthure* (and in Malory's *Arthur and Lucius*) Gawain's adventure with Priamus is a self-contained episode that occurs within the "brackets" of the suspended action first of the siege of Metz and then of the foraging party; the siege begins; Arthur sends out his foraging party; Gawain and Priamus duel; the foragers battle the enemy and prevail; the siege is concluded. Malory carries the bracketing a step further: in order not only to complete the story of Gawain and Priamus but to integrate it with the action, he delays the baptism of Priamus until after the return of the foraging expedition, so that we have a bracket within a bracket:

1. The siege begins.
2. The foragers leave.
3. Gawain defeats Priamus, who asks for baptism.
2. The foragers return.
3. Priamus is baptized and made knight of the Round Table.
1. The siege ends.

This might be considered interweaving, but, if so, it is interweaving of a greatly simplified, English variety; the writer breaks his narrative into as few units as possible, and suspension of action ("leve we now

N. and speak we of X."), rather than the interlacing of parallel actions, is the main device.

This is the usual method in English romance. Even *Sir Gawain and the Green Knight* (in which the alternation between the hunting scenes and the temptations comes closest to true *entrelacement*) is built mainly on this principle of bracketing. The initial challenge and its fulfillment bracket the adventure at Bercilak's castle; within the castle each day's activities are bracketed by the bargains with the host, as each day's scenes between Gawain and the lady are enclosed within the frameworks of the hunts. The author of *Arthour and Merlin* uses the same sort of bracketing to combine two story lines while yet maintaining the self-contained episodes that English romancers preferred. In the second part of *Arthour and Merlin*, for example, Arthur leaves England for Birkenho on his way to Carmelide (vv. 4100-98). Then we turn to the adventure of the eleven kings and their sons, which we follow to the point where Gawain enters London in triumph after a great victory (vv. 4199-5348); then we shift to Arthur. Gawain's adventure is not finished, for we know he intends to join Arthur. But this episode is clearly complete and could almost stand on its own. The same is true of Arthur's next adventure. He journeys to Carmelide and wins a great victory over Rion (vv. 5349-6594). His adventure is not complete, for he is now in love with Guenevere, the daughter of the king of Carmelide; but the episode concerning his battle with Rion is finished, complete in itself. Next we return to England for the further adventures of Gawain and his comrades, which we follow until he rescues his mother and returns again in triumph to London (vv. 6595-8585), another completed episode, though his quest for Arthur is still incomplete, providing the bracketing for Arthur's next adventure in Carmelide (vv. 6586-end). The episodes in this work are, as D.S. Brewer described the parts of the *Morte Darthur*, rather like beads on a string; the bracketings provide the stout links that bind the beads together.[35]

The episodes in such a structure always seem in danger of "dropping away"[36] from the main structure of the history—as the first part of *Arthour and Merlin* did indeed drop away to become the "Jüngere Merlin." Malory never lets that happen, for he binds his episodes by theme (as we shall see later) as well as in this mechanical fashion. Like his English predecessors, he works to eliminate most of the *entrelacement* from his sources and to create self-contained episodes, but he is careful to retain, or create, what links are needed to contain them in his larger structures. In the account of the knighting of Tor, for example, Malory makes a self-contained episode of the scattered details in his French source, but he also carefully brackets that episode within the story of the knighting of Gawain: Gawain asks to be knighted and Arthur agrees; then comes the episode of Tor's knighting and the revelation of his true identity; then Arthur knights Gawain. Then follow the adventures of Gawain, Tor, and Pellinor. Each is a separate, continuously narrated episode, but all are contained within the bracket provided by Arthur's charge that each shall follow his adventure (the White Hart, the brachet, the knight and the lady) and return to court.

Yet bracketing alone is not enough to hold the whole *Tale of King Arthur* together, and here as elsewhere Malory also makes use of some of the other simple forms of *entrelacement*, such as prophecies and linking episodes, and, as we have noted, he develops his structure by analogy, by parallels in action and proportioning. When we compare Malory's work to the cyclic romances, we get the impression that he consciously rejected their technique of *entrelacement*, and we tend therefore to judge his tales by the amount of *entrelacement* each contains, as if the less *entrelacement* the better, the more "modern," the narrative. However, Malory modifies rather than rejects the older technique, employing native methods of "linking" and interrelating episodes and (by an interweaving of themes) often creating very complicated narratives. Simple as his narratives are when compared to the Vulgate romances, it remains true that "no one enjoys Malory's book who cannot enjoy its *ambages*, its interweavings."[37] If Malory uses little interweaving in *The Tale of Arthur and Lucius* and relatively more in *The Tale of King Arthur*, this is not because he "regressed in technique" but because the requirements of each tale were different.[38] His next two tales, *Sir Lancelot du Lake* and *Gareth*, are somewhat simpler than *King Arthur*, for in them Malory seems to have been learning the techniques of thematic organization, almost as if he were preparing himself for the complex *entrelacement* of themes in his *Book of Sir Tristram*. However, even in that work he maintains the firm and simple narrative line and the self-contained episode that characterize the English romances on which he formed his narrative technique.

4

Thematic Invention:
A Noble Tale
of Sir Lancelot

Thus far I have concentrated so closely on Malory's relation to his sources that I may have reinforced the old assumption that the *Morte Darthur* is essentially a condensed translation and that Malory's main artistic problem was to "reduce" his French sources into English. Older studies of medieval romance frequently left the impression that almost all surviving romances were faithful adaptations of "lost sources." The supposed authors of the "lost sources" were an astonishingly creative lot, freely altering, combining, inventing; the authors of the surviving texts were more timid, simply transmitting largely unchanged the materials that came their way. This idea seems to have been the basis of C. S. Lewis's comparison of the *Morte Darthur* to a medieval cathedral, with Malory but one of a series of humble workmen, each of whom makes his modest, inessential alterations: "Whatever he does, Malory's personal contribution to the total effect cannot be very great."[1] Not all medieval cathedrals were made that way, and few, if any, of the best romances were built in that fashion.

Certainly Malory's works were not. Unlike earlier romancers, Malory knew so many different versions of the Arthurian tales that he could choose not only what he would do with a source but even which source he would use. Especially in *The Tale of the Sancgreal*, which Malory adapted from the *Queste del Saint Graal* in a relatively faith-

ful fashion, critics have felt that Malory was "at the mercy of his originals."² But his use of the *Queste* version of the Grail story rather than
Perlesvaus was a conscious choice of the sort he exercised in selecting
the sources for almost every tale in his book. Likewise, the organization of the *Morte Darthur* is Malory's own design. Insofar as the *Morte
Darthur* does resemble a medieval cathedral, Malory is its architect. He
could have organized his cycle along the lines of the Vulgate version,
or those of the *Roman du Graal*, of the cyclic *Tristan*, or even those
implied in *Perlesvaus*. Instead, he chose to create a new book of King
Arthur. Like all cycles, it follows the broad outlines of Arthur's career
as it had been defined by the historical tradition; within these broad
limits, Malory's *Morte Darthur* is unique, a new combination of old
and newly created materials such as can be found in no previous cycle.

Likewise, the tales within the *Morte Darthur* are largely Malory's
own inventions—for which he must receive the blame as well as the
artistic credit. One of the disadvantages of concentrating upon sources
is that it provides so convenient a way to ignore Malory's text; we can
always blame a source or Malory's misunderstanding for whatever
does not fit easily into our idea of what he should have been doing.
Yet Malory chose to write the tales as we have them, and most of them
are, like the *Morte Darthur* itself, unique works, markedly different in
content and structure from their sources. Only *The Tale of the Sancgreal* comes close to faithful adaptation—a reduced version of almost
all the essential material in its French source (though even it contains
significant modifications in proportion and emphasis). *The Tale of
King Arthur* and *The Tale of Arthur and Lucius* are faithful only to
parts of their sources; Malory decided to omit the whole beginning of
the *Suite du Merlin* and the whole last section of the alliterative *Morte
Arthure*, just as in *The Book of Sir Tristram* he omits the entire concluding section of the inherited source (about the last third), adds new
materials, and thus produces a new history to his own design. In *The
Death of Arthur* he combines materials from two different sources
(*Mort Artu* and the stanzaic *Morte Arthur*) with matter of his own
invention. Both *Sir Lancelot* and *Lancelot and Guenevere* are new
combinations of inherited and invented materials, and *The Tale of Sir
Gareth* is entirely Malory's own invention.

"Invention" may be the wrong word for this sort of creation, for
even when Malory invents a new romance like *Gareth*, he draws upon
familiar materials, and almost every part of that tale has numerous
analogues. If we read Malory, or any traditional narrative, from the
standpoint of the analogues, we will find little or no evidence of

"pure" invention. The characters, the scenes, the episodes, and the general contours of the story itself are all familiar. The materials are old; the use to which they are put is new.

This is characteristic of romance, which is a genre in which novelty is as important as tradition. We tend to overlook this, because the convention of romance narration requires that even the novelty be made to seem old. Every romancer must claim a source even when he is being most original: "The Frensshe book maketh mencyoun—and is auctorised." Yet every reader of romance wanted to hear something new—a new tale of an old hero, a new wonder though told with "auctoritee," or, most pleasing to the sophisticated, a new treatment of an old tale.

The cultivation of both tradition and novelty is especially obvious in English romances, which are at once among the most conventional and the most original of medieval romances. Malory's inventive treatment of his sources and the narrative mode that he uses to shape his invented tales show his most significant relation to his English predecessors and contemporaries. His Continental contemporaries, such as Ulrich Füetrer and Michel Gonnot, had little interest in this sort of invention, for their aim was simply to "reduce" the older tales. Most fifteenth-century one-volume histories, such as Caxton's *Charles the Grete*, are fairly straightforward reduced compilations. Malory's careful observation of the conventions of "auctoritee" gives the impression that his book is much the same, but beneath the veneer of the fifteenth-century historian is a freely inventive late Middle English romancer.

The earliest English romances, those written before the middle of the fourteenth century, show little in the way of invention, for in England romance itself was still new and each romance was a novelty in itself. Their authors therefore had little interest in originality: *Arthour and Merlin, Sir Tristrem, Ywain and Gawain, Lybeaus Desconus, Sir Landeval,* and *Joseph of Arimathie* are all, like most non-Arthurian romances of the period, fairly straightforward adaptations of existing French works. *Sir Perceval of Galles* is the lone apparent exception (though it may indeed have a lost source). That is not to say that the early English romancers were simply translators. As we have seen in the cases of *Arthour and Merlin* and *Joseph of Arimathie*, these authors treated their sources with considerable freedom and altered the structures to suit their own ends. Nevertheless, their alterations seem mainly intended to clarify the essential "story" (that is, history) of their French sources, and, reduced and altered as they are, they yet provided a non-French-speaking audience with a good idea of what the French romances contained.

By the latter part of the fourteenth century, English romance no longer had only that function. The patrons of works like *Sir Gawain* were probably quite capable of reading French romances for themselves, and they evidently enjoyed romance as a literary genre as well as a "historical" record. They were thus prepared to welcome new romances, new stories created from old materials. Romance had become a native genre, and English romancers, so it appears, were now more confident in their own resources. Native forms—the tail-rhyme stanza and the alliterative line—were now generally preferred to the French-derived octosyllabic couplet, and few romancers in this period were content merely to reproduce the essential story of some existing French work. While maintaining the brevity and narrative simplicity of English romance, most later romancers added new materials (rather than subtracting, as their predecessors had done) and often combined two or more sources to make new structures from old. The author of the alliterative *Morte Arthure* combined some version of Wace with materials from the Alexander romances to create a strikingly individualistic treatment of the old story of Arthur's death.[3] *Sir Gawain and the Green Knight* was a brilliant new romance of Gawain based on at least two previous romances (*Le livre de Caradoc* and some version of *Yder*), neither of which had previously concerned that hero.[4] *Sir Gawain and the Carl of Carlisle* was a new creation, based on old motifs but no one existing source.[5] *The Awntyrs of Arthur* combined the theme of *The Trentals of St. Gregory* with a new combination of traditional romance materials.[6] *Sir Degrevant* presented a new Arthurian knight—Degrevant was unknown to French romance—in an adventure with many analogues (*Sir Gareth* among them) but no direct source.[7] Of the English Arthurian works written between 1350 and 1400—using the dates in Sever's *Manual* as a convenient, though admittedly approximate, guide[8]—only the stanzaic *Morte Arthur* can be regarded as an adaptation of the older, "reduced" sort. Even the author of *Sir Launfal*, unlike the more faithful adapter of the earlier *Sir Landeval*, added significant new materials to Marie's *Lai de Lanval*.[9]

Much the same was true in the fifteenth century. The older forms of adaptation remained popular (as shown by *The Grene Knight* and some of the other works in the Percy Folio Manuscript) and, as we have noted, there was now an audience for faithful translations of even very prolix French works, such as Lovelich's versions of the *Estoire del Saint Graal* and the *Estoire de Merlin*. These may indicate a sort of full circle, a new audience with little or no French, though now with some literary sophistication and leisure. Nevertheless, the majority of fifteenth-century Arthurian verse romances were still "new creations." *Sir Lancelot of the Laik* was built on but one episode from the Vulgate *Lancelot* with the addition of considerable material from the poet's own invention.[10] *Golagros and Gawain* and *The Gest of Sir Gawain* were created in a similar way; both were based on episodes taken from the *Continuations* of Chrétien's *Perceval*, and both show less a desire to transmit the "true history" than an interest in building a satisfying brief romance.[11] *The Wedding of Sir Gawain*, *The Turk and Gawain*, and *The Avowing of Arthur* were all "original" works, based on common motifs but no direct sources.[12] In this, as was the case in the late fourteenth century, fifteenth-century English Arthurian romance differed little from non-Arthurian: *Eger and Grime*, *The Squyr of Lowe Degre*, and a good many other fifteenth-century romances were also new creations of this sort.[13] One might almost say that this kind of originality had become a conventional part of the genre.

It is not surprising to find that Malory shared his contemporaries' taste for invention. Given the usual practice of English romancers in this period, the absence of such invention would be more remarkable than its presence. There is no reason to doubt, as Sommer did, that Malory himself was responsible for shaping the Tarquin portion of *Sir Lancelot*, and no basis for the assumption, shared by many students, that a lost French or English source must be the basis of *Gareth*. Nor, on the other hand, is it necessary to credit Malory with any great share of artistic "boldness" because of the originality displayed in these works. This method of composition was common in his time, and, as so many fourteenth- and fifteenth-century romances show, the mere invention of a story is no very reliable indication of genius.

Assuming that *The Tale of King Arthur* and *Arthur and Lucius* were his first works, Malory began his career mainly as an adapter. In writing *Arthur and Lucius* he freely omitted material from the alliterative poem, added a new conclusion from another source, and thus made a much different story. Nevertheless, his work remains essentially a shortening of his source, an account of Arthur's campaign quite faithful to that in the corresponding section of the alliterative *Morte Arthure*, and he had good precedent for his nontragic version of the Roman campaign in the Vulgate *Merlin* and Hardyng's *Chroni-*

cle. *The Tale of King Arthur* is also largely a shortened adaptation; Malory freely omitted, condensed, and rearranged, but he remained fairly faithful to the essential history presented in the French work. However, in the final pages of the tale he found he needed a new conclusion. The *Suite du Merlin* ends with an episode in which Gawain and Marhalt are enticed into the "Roche aux pucelles," where they remain captive until they are delivered by Gaheriet. Apparently Malory had already decided that Gaheriet was not to appear in the *Morte Darthur* until he is suitably introduced, his name anglicized to Gareth, later in *The Tale of Sir Gareth*. Malory had apparently also decided that his cycle would include *The Book of Sir Tristram*. Marhalt was to be an important figure in that work, where he is presented as a knight of the Round Table (as he is not in any of the French versions). Malory, therefore, had to omit the Gaheriet adventure and substitute some adventure for Marhalt, preferably one that would establish his character as a member of the Round Table. Moreover, Malory's fondness for symmetrical structures must have drawn his notice to the fact that the second half of his tale began with three quests (Gawain, Tor, and Pellinor) and that his source contained the hint of three parallel quests at the end (Gawain, Marhalt, and Ywain).

Malory developed that hint by inventing a set of adventures for Marhalt and Ywain, and the techniques he used are those employed in all his inventions. First, he worked toward the creation of parallels. Gawain's adventure with Pelleas and Ettard was already in his source, and he needed only to add the detail that Gawain's action led to Ettard's death (she "dyed for sorrow"; iv. 24) to reinforce the parallel between this adventure and Gawain's first quest, in which he was also the instrument of a woman's death. Then, to complete the general parallel with Gawain's first adventure, which was followed by the quests of Tor and Pellinor, Malory had to add a set of adventures for Marhalt and Ywain. Marhalt had to be established as a member of the Round Table (since this would be important to his role in *Sir Tristram*), and to accomplish this Malory drew upon the conventional pattern of action in which a knight proves himself worthy of Arthurian knighthood: at the center of the pattern is the "tournament-quest" motif. In the proof-of-knighthood, there is first a preliminary adventure as a demonstration of the knight's worthiness to undertake the following adventures. Next comes the tournament, in which the hero triumphs, and then the quest to abolish some "ill custom" (which often involves the rescue of prisoners). Finally, having proven his prowess against the enemies of the Round Table, he successfully jousts with a series of members of the Round Table. This is the pattern followed by Alexander the Orphan in *Sir Tristram* (x. 32-40): after a series of preliminary jousts, he triumphs in a tournament, defeats Sir Malagryne and abolishes his "ill custom," and finally overthrows three knights of the Round Table with a single spear. Likewise, in *Sir Lancelot*, after a preliminary duel with Belleus, Lancelot triumphs in Bagdemagus's tournament, abolishes the evil custom of Tarquin and frees his prisoners, and then overthrows four of Arthur's knights with a single spear (vi. 1-13). Marhalt follows the same pattern (iv. 25-26): after a battle with the duke of the South Marches, who hates Arthur's knights because Gawain slew one of his sons (just as Tarquin hates Arthur's knights because Lancelot slew his brother), he triumphs in a tournament and then slays the giant Taulard and frees his prisoners. Taulard is explicitly based on the giant Taulus, whom Tristram slew, but this giant is clearly of the same class as the two giants whom Lancelot kills in order to free prisoners or as the evil Sir Malagryne, whom Alexander slays. Then, with one spear, Marhalt overthrows four knights of the Round Table, which is exactly what Lancelot later does (one of the four knights—Sagramour—appears in both lists) and is quite similar to Alexander's feat.

The method of invention is simple enough: a common pattern of action—a proof-of-knighthood theme—provides the shape of the narrative, which is composed of episodes familiar from other works, such as the prose *Lancelot* or *Tristan*. Only a few of the details and the names are new; now it is Marhalt rather than Lancelot or Alexander the Orphan who overthrows a series of opponents with a single spear. Yet the result of this simple method of invention is an altogether new adventure of Marhalt.

Malory is thus enabled to achieve his own end—the establishment of Marhalt as an important knight of the Round Table—while yet meeting the aesthetic demands of his genre. This new adventure is satisfyingly old in the impression it makes, for almost any reader of romance can recognize the common motifs used here; the very conventionality of the materials has the advantage of lending the story the twice-told aura that is part of the "authentication" of romance. Moreover, the familiar pattern of action has the sort of balanced structure that we have seen in the larger contours of *The Tale of King Arthur* and that is characteristic of this mode of narrative: a battle (with the duke of the South Marches) and jousting (in the tournament) followed by a battle (with Taulard) and jousting (with Sagramour and his companions). In effect, the adventures of Ywain which next follow are simply a parallel restatement of Marhalt's adventures: first a tournament and then a battle with two evil knights who "do ayenste the hyghe Order of Knyghthode" (iv.27). Ywain's adventures, as Vinaver notes, seem to be based on Marhalt's exploits, for there are even "curious similarities of detail."[14] Again, the method of invention is simple: a familiar pattern (tournament followed by a battle to end an evil custom) is filled in with conventional details, arranged in a novel way.

The resulting narratives are well circumscribed and self-contained, and the adventures of Marhalt and Ywain have the virtues that Malory aimed at when he "reduced" the episodes in his sources. However, neither narrative seems very satisfying from a modern point of view: the actions have no very clear relation to one another. Marhalt triumphs in a tournament and then kills a giant, but there is no obvious reason why he should not have first killed a giant and then triumphed in a tournament. Likewise, there is no very clear reason for Marhalt's entering the tournament in the first place. His lady simply takes him there, and Malory does not bother to explain why: "Within two days his lady brought hym whereas was a grete tournament that the lady de Vawse had cried" (iv.25). In the account of Ywain's adventures much the same thing happens. His lady, for no apparent reason, "brought hym theras was a tournament nigh the march of Wales" (iv.26), and Ywain, like Marhalt, apparently enters the tournament simply because it is there. These episodes are so brief that few readers are bothered by this apparent looseness of structure. But Malory's larger narrative units are organized in the same manner, and their apparent looseness of organization, their lack of causal relations between the actions, and the consequent difficulty the reader experiences in following the "progress" of the story have all seemed grave flaws, proof that Malory's work "is best read for its individual scenes and not for its connected story."[15]

The narrative structure of the Marhalt episode becomes clear once we recognize its organizing theme: the tournament must come before the battle with the giant because the proof-of-knighthood theme requires a tournament and then a quest. The tournament-quest pattern likewise accounts for the order of events in the Ywain episode and for the actions of the characters. Marhalt and Ywain enter the tournaments because they must fulfill the requirements of the theme. To a reader aware of these themes, these brief narratives are aesthetically satisfying not because the action "progresses," in the manner of a modern plot, but because the action conforms to the expected pattern.

The sort of parallel structures we have already noted in the organization of the Marhalt episode are also aesthetically pleasing, and the parallels are the key to the function of these episodes in the larger unit in which they exist, the account of the three quests. The whole unit begins with a tournament in which Pelleas wins a circlet of gold and a good sword, which he presents to his lady. Then there is Marhalt's tournament, and finally Ywain's, in which the prize is again a circlet of gold. The repeated motif of the tournament is obviously intended to unite the three parallel quests, Gawain's (which concerns Pelleas), Marhalt's, and Ywain's; by analogy and contrast the three define more fully the experience of the quest than could any one of the three alone. Once we consider these episodes from the thematic point of view, their narrative function becomes clear and we can more fully appreciate the skill with which this part of the tale was made.

By "thematic" I mean what is sometimes loosely called "mythic," the conformance of a narrative to some external, preexisting pattern. Morton W. Bloomfield, in his important essay "Episodic Motivation and Marvels in Epic and Romance," shows that in romance the motivation of episodes is characteristically "vertical" (with the motive supplied by an abstract pattern outside the work) rather than "horizontal" (the explicit cause-and-effect motivation of episodes in many nonromance genres).[16] Of course, no absolute distinctions can be made. Per Nykrog has recently shown that both "realistic" (cause-and-effect) and "thematic" modes of narrative existed in romance from its earliest development in the works of Chrétien de Troyes and Gautier d'Arras, and, as might be expected, most romances include elements of both.[17] Even in the brief adventures of Marhalt and Ywain there are causes for some of the actions, though as usual in romance the causes are inadequate to their effects (Marhalt fights in the tournament "because" the lady takes him there). Likewise, "history" provides causes for many of the larger actions in the *Morte Darthur*, and the beginning and ending of Malory's cycle are cast in a predominantly historical mode, since the establishment and fall of Arthur's kingdom are matters of "history" rather than romance. Nevertheless, in most of Malory's tales, and consequently in the *Morte Darthur* as a whole, the dominant mode is thematic, and thematic necessity rather than the requirements of the "plot" characteristically shapes the narrative structures.

I have used "thematic" rather than "mythic" to characterize this mode, because mythic patterns seem always to be with us. They may inform any sort of narrative—romance, novel, or history—and, if Jungian critics are right, they can do their work without either author or audience being fully aware of their presence. "Theme," on the other hand, is a literary device—a pattern of conventionalized action that author and audience share because of their common literary experience. This is why modern readers so often find thematic narrative puzzling; they read romances without the shared knowledge of the conventionalized narrative patterns that inform their structures.

The first hearers of English romance were in much the same situation. This is illustrated by a charming passage in *King Horn:* when Rymenhild offers her love to young Horn, he cannot immediately accept it. In romance, a knight is bound by convention to prove himself worthy of his lady's hand; thus Horn, "vertically" motivated by this pattern of action, must refuse Rymenhild's offer until he has proven his merits. This is reasonable enough, if one knows the convention, and in the Anglo-Norman *Romance of Horn* the young hero simply replies to Rigmel in a noncommittal fashion and goes off to prove himself in battle. But from the standpoint of one who does not know the convention, from a nonromance and more commonsense point of view, a poor young lad like Horn would be crazy to refuse the hand of a beautiful and wealthy princess whom he obviously loves. And so the author of *King Horn* must explain this strange conduct to his audience. He does so by having Horn instruct Rymenhild in the rudiments of knightly manners.

> "Rymenhild," quath he, "beo stille!
> Ihc wulle don al þi wille.
> Also hit mot betide
> Mid spere ischal furste ride . . .
> & of ure [knights'] mestere
> so is þe manere
> Wiþ sume oþere kniȝte
> Wel for his lemman fiȝte
> Or he eni wif take."   (vv. 541–544, 549–553)

The more sophisticated audience of the Anglo-Norman *Romance of Horn* needed no such "horizontal" motivation to account for Horn's action; their knowledge of romance conventions supplied the "vertical" pattern that explains and lends meaning to it. Likewise, when Gareth asks his lady Lyones to offer her hand as the prize at Arthur's tournament (vii.27), Malory does not need to explain Gareth's conduct. Outside the conventions of romance, Gareth's act is either foolish (why take a chance on losing her?) or prideful (his conviction that he will surely win); within romance, his act is inevitable, for he must conform to the pattern imposed by the convention and must show that he is worthy of the lady.

These patterns of action not only lend motivation to episodes (such brief patterns are "motifs"), they frequently supply the organizing principle of the entire romance (the use of "theme"). Again *King Horn* may serve as an example. Like all English romances, it has suffered from the critical assumption that there is only one sort of narrative structure—that of the realistic novel—and that any deviation from this ideal form is a flaw. George Kane, for example, is eager to praise *King Horn*, which he obviously admires. But he can praise only its general tone, since, judged from the standpoint of modern fiction, it inevitably seems a rather shoddy job: "The story is loosely episodic, distorted by gratuitous duplication . . . Yet it is decidedly attractive. It engages our sympathy and affection, and thus enables an imaginative surrender despite the absurdities which arise in it out of disregard for narrative structure and out of inadequate motivation, for it possesses a pleasing ingenuousness."[18] In my jaded way, I suspect that ingenuousness charms only in a sophisticated setting, as in *Candide*; however that may be, ingenuousness is all too easily come by in early English romance. *King Horn* succeeds not because its author disregarded the principles of narrative structure but because he had a sure command of the techniques of thematic narrative, which allowed him to build a solid and satisfying structure for his work. His techniques were the same as Malory used two centuries later, and it may therefore be useful to examine this early and relatively simple example of thematic composition before turning to Malory's more complicated tales.

The author of *King Horn* owes much of his success to his source. His near contemporary, the author of *Sir Tristrem*, had to work with a complicated romance composed of themes apparently unfamiliar to both himself and his audience. He thus lacked any clear principle of adaptation and could do little more than condense his source. The French *Romance of Horn*, on the other hand, is based on the widespread theme of "exile and return," which is as common in epic and folktale as in romance and was thus easily grasped both by the author of *King Horn* and his audience.[19] They knew, at least unconsciously, the basic elements of the theme: a young man is deprived of his inheritance and driven from his homeland; he distinguishes himself in exile, winning wealth and a princess as his wife; he returns to triumph over his enemies and regains his heritage. The pattern is a favorite in early English romance; *Havelok*, *Guy of Warwick*, and *Bevis of Hampton* all make use of this theme, which is flexible enough to admit of many variations.

In *King Horn* the poet built the structure of his work on a doubling of the theme. This, too, is common in nonromance genres, and it was, of course, present in the Anglo-Norman romance. The English poet's main accomplishment was to recognize the presence of the theme and to produce his adaptation by reducing it to its essential elements:

> Horn, the rightful heir to the kingdom of Suddene, is exiled by pagan invaders. He arrives in England, where he proves his merit by fighting pagan invaders and wins the hand of the princess, Rymenhild. He is then betrayed by his faithless follower, Fikenhild, and again he is exiled. In this second exile he goes to Westernesse (Ireland), where he again saves a kingdom by battling pagan invaders and again he is offered the hand of its princess, Reynhild. He refuses and returns to England, since he has learned that Rymenhild is about to be forced into marriage by King Modi.
>
> Disguised as a palmer, Horn saves Rymenhild from marriage to King Modi. He marries her and forgives Fikenhild. He then goes to Suddene to end his first exile by recapturing his heritage. He does so, but then he is warned by a dream that the traitorous Fikenhild has seized both the kingdom and Rymenhild.
>
> He returns to England and, disguised as a harper, he rescues Rymenhild and recaptures the kingdom. Leaving England in the charge of the faithful Arnoldin, Horn returns with Rymenhild to Suddene.

From this outline one can see why a critic who assumes that a good narrative structure is equivalent to a good plot should find *King Horn* poorly made. The last set of adventures—Horn's final rescue of Rymenhild and reconquest of England—seems completely unnecessary, for the initial problem of the "plot"—Horn's exile from Suddene—has already been resolved. Clearly, however, *King Horn*, like the works of Malory and of most romancers, is built on a system of parallels:

1. Exile from Suddene; the winning of Rymenhild (vv. 1-704)
2. Exile from England; the winning of Reynhild (vv. 705-920)
3. Rescue of Rymenhild; recapture of Suddene (vv. 921-1384)
4. Rescue of Rymenhild; recapture of England (vv. 1385-1588)

The parts are not so elegantly proportioned as Malory's narrative divisions tend to be, but the parallels are obvious—a source of annoyance to modern critics, who are bothered by "gratuitous duplications," but apparently pleasing to medieval audiences.

Horn's courtship and marriage to Rymenhild serve to unite the four parts of the narrative and the doubled exiles and returns. The themes of exile-and-return and courtship fit easily together, since winning a princess is part of the exile-and-return, and they are often found in combination, as in *Guy of Warwick*. The usual pattern of the courtship theme, most obvious in works such as *Guy of Warwick*, is: proof of worthiness; declaration of mutual love; separation for further proof; marriage. Often, as in *King Horn*, there is yet another separation, which comes after the marriage and ends in a final reunion. Horn's first exile, from Suddene, allows him to prove his worthiness and thus leads to the declaration of mutual love. His second exile, from England, provides the separation necessary for the further proof that must precede the marriage. Having shown his merits, Horn returns to claim Rymenhild as his bride, and the most important and extended episode in the romance is the recognition scene when Horn and Rymenhild meet after his return. Horn and Rymenhild marry, and this ends the first part. But, as *Erec et Enide* and *Guy of Warwick* show, the married knight must also prove his merit, and the return to Suddene (necessitated by the first exile) provides the opportunity for another set of foreign adventures, after which Horn returns to reclaim Rymenhild for the second and final time. The final reunion in England is necessary not only to complete the parallel with the first part but to reunite the two lovers in the final scene. Here the English poem is superior to the French; in the Anglo-Norman version, Rigmel accompanies Horn to Suddene (Denmark), even though she has no thematic importance in that adventure. The separation of the lovers in the English poem provides for a clear conclusion first of the theme of exile and then of the motif of the separated lovers, and at the same time it allows for a satisfyingly balanced structure.

The themes of love (courtship, separation, marriage, separation, happy reunion) and exile-and-return fit well together, because the issue of loyalty is of prime importance in both. As in *Guy of Warwick*, *Bevis of Hampton*, and many other romances in which we find both themes present, the lovers are apparently motivated more by loyalty than by passion, and the separations serve as tests of their fidelity—with the knight conventionally tested by the offer of another wife or lover and the lady tested by importunate suitors or would-be husbands. Likewise, in the exile-and-return theme, the fidelity of one's friends and retainers is almost always an issue. For example, in *Sir Orfeo*, another work that unites the themes of married love and exile-and-return, the last episode is the return of Orfeo to his court. Disguised as a harper, he falsely reports his own death to the steward. The steward's reaction shows that he is loyal to the king, and Orfeo reveals his identity to the rejoicing court. From the standpoint of plot, the episode is gratuitous, for no reason is given to explain (to motivate "horizontally") Orfeo's test of the steward's loyalty. But stewards in romance are of only two sorts, "true" and "false," and a scene of this sort is a necessary part of the exile-and-return theme; from at least the time of Ulysses, the exile must return in disguise and first determine who has been true and who false in his absence. In *King Horn* the disguised hero tests Rymenhild in the same way that Orfeo tested his steward, thus nicely uniting the two themes in the common issue of loyalty: Horn returns from Westernesse in disguise, tells Rymenhild that Horn is dead, and then, having assured himself that she passes the test of loyalty, reveals his true identity.

This scene is the central part of a continuing pattern of episodes concerning loyalty and disloyalty. The pattern begins with Rymenhild's mistaking Aþulf for Horn and offering him her hand. He, loyal to Horn, refuses to take advantage of the opportunity. As the poet has said of Horn's companions, "Aþulf was the beste / & fikenylde þe wurste" (vv. 27-28). In contrast to Aþulf, the treacherous Fikenhild then betrays Horn and thus initiates the second exile (the first had been caused by pagans, whom Horn fights in every part of the romance). Horn's loyalty is tested during this exile by the offer of the hand of Reynhild, princess of Westernesse. Faithful to Rymenhild, he refuses the offer and awards her instead to the loyal Aþulf. When Horn returns to England, tests and proves Rymenhild's faith, and then marries her, the first half of the pattern of episodes concerning loyalty is ended.

However, the first theme of exile-and-return is not ended, and so Horn must sail for Suddene. When he lands, there is another episode involving loyalty. Aþulf's father, who has remained loyal, and alive, by posing as a pagan, helps Horn reconquer the kingdom. Fikenhild again provides the contrast to the loyal friend, for he betrays the absent Horn and seizes both Rymenhild and the kingdom. This completes the pattern of betrayals; Fikenhild, whose treachery had first caused Horn to leave Rymenhild, is now the instrument of their reunion. Horn returns, again disguised, and meets another faithful retainer, conventionally required for a reconquest (this is Arnoldin, Aþulf's cousin, whom Horn rewards with the kingdom of England). The kingdom is reconquered, Fikenhild punished, and the lovers reunited.

In short, what seem gratuitous duplications are integral parts of the thematic structure, and far from disregarding narrative structure, the poet worked with considerable care and skill, as if he realized that in medieval romance character and even action are less important than structure and theme. Crude as it is in many ways, *King Horn* is a good example of a work that lacks unity of action and a tight modern plot structure but nevertheless has a coherent, skillfully handled thematic structure. And the poet achieves this without in any way obscuring the simplicity of narrative line, the emphasis on action, and the preference for the self-contained episode that characterize English romance.

Probably the failure of early critics to recognize the thematic structure of works such as *King Horn* is at least partly due to their narrative style, which, compared to that of the more leisurely French romances, often seems closer to the style of the novella or the later realistic novel. But the style of a narrative is not necessarily related to its mode, which is a matter of overall organization. Compared to the French *Romance of Horn*, *King Horn* is a "realistic" work, and many of its episodes have the sort of cause-and-effect motivation that we expect in "realistic" works (such as the fabliaux). Horn returns from Westernesse to England because he hears of Modi's intention to wed Rymenhild. That is the immediate cause of his return and is thus an obvious example of "horizontal" motivation. But the necessity for some such episode, whatever its immediate cause, is "vertically" motivated by the demands of the theme—the exile must return in disguise and reclaim his heritage (in this case, Rymenhild). It is almost as if in thematic narrative, as in Thomistic logic, the "sufficient" cause of an event requires both "efficient" and "necessary" causations. The structure is controlled vertically by the themes (the "necessary" causes of the episodes), though the individual episodes may be realistic and "horizontally" motivated (the "efficient" causes) without in any way disturbing the overall structure. The same use of causal motivation is apparent in the *Morte Darthur*, in which the occasional appearance of cause and effect and the realistic tone of much of the narration have also led to the assumption that Malory is trying to write modern, well-plotted narratives.

King Horn also shows that the thematic mode of composition results in a much looser structure than the tightly unified fabliau or modern short story, and the limits of what may be included or omitted without destroying the coherence of a thematically organized work are far more flexible than "unity of action" would allow. The Anglo-Norman *Horn* has much the same thematic structure but is about four times the length of the English poem. The English poet could have made his work even shorter, for all that is required is the minimum pattern of episodes necessary for the audience to recognize the theme; to an experienced audience merely a part of the conventional pattern is often enough to suggest the whole. Or the English poet could have added a good deal more, for the maximum limits of what a thematically organized tale may include are determined mainly by the structure of symmetries that characterizes thematic composition. The author of *Havelok*, for example, was free to expand the brief *Lai d'Havelok* in any way he chose so long as he fitted his parts into the pattern of complementary structures that reinforce the central theme of exile-and-return. As we have seen, Malory uses much the same thematic pattern for the brief account of Marhalt and the comparatively long account of Alexander the Orphan.

In the abstract, this sounds like a very subtle mode of composition. It can be both subtle and complex, but it is also an essentially simple device, well suited to oral delivery. Tightly plotted works require continuous close attention, for the progress of their narratives depends on the hearers' perceptions of the causal relation of each action to the next. If a hearer misses the connections between the actions, he loses the thread of the story. I suspect that this is why in medieval times tight plots were generally restricted to brief, easily grasped narratives, such as the fabliaux. Thematically organized narratives, on the other hand, turn not on small narrative details but on broad contours of action that can be grasped even by relatively inattentive hearers. This suggests a principle we should keep in mind when analyzing thematically organized narratives: the "meanings" of such works will seldom be found in isolated lines and passages.

This long digression has taken us some distance from Malory's *Morte Darthur*, but an understanding of the thematic mode of English romance is a necessary preliminary to an understanding of Malory's techniques of invention and to an appreciation of the narrative structure of his tales. I chose to discuss *King Horn* because it is the earliest surviving English romance, but many other English works would have served as well. So too would many French romances, both verse romances, such as those of Chrétien, and prose, such as the *Mort Artu*. Malory could have learned this method of composition in many ways (and doubtless did), but the most important sources of his knowledge were probably English romances. He had learned how to narrate episodes from English romances, and it seems most likely that the same works taught him how to organize these episodes in thematic structures. Whatever the sources of his knowledge, the flexible thematic mode of narrative organization provided a way to combine his English narrative style with his French taste for a multiplicity of episodes and characters. By using the thematic mode of composition, Malory could create new tales that were at once copious and coherent.

A Noble Tale of Sir Lancelot du Lake was apparently Malory's first experiment with the invention of an entire new tale. He needed a tale of this sort, because, as the Marhalt episode in *The Tale of King Arthur* shows, he had already decided that his cycle was to include a *Book of Sir Tristram.* Yet he had apparently also decided that Lancelot was to be his major character, since in *Arthur and Lucius* he assigns Lancelot a far more important role than he had in the alliterative poem and shows him doing such deeds "That there was never knyght dud more worshyp in his dayes" (v.8). Lancelot is a major character even in the French *Tristan* and *Queste del Saint Graal*, and Malory is well justified in saying at the end of *Sir Lancelot*, "Here followeth after many tales of Sir Launcelot du Lake." However, his role in those works depends on the establishment of his character in the Vulgate *Lancelot*, and if proportion was to be maintained in the *Morte Darthur*, Malory had no room for a *Sir Lancelot* as long as *Sir Tristram*.

His solution was to invent a new tale of Lancelot, one that would in brief compass raise him from the relatively minor role that he plays even in *Arthur and Lucius* and establish him as the greatest of knights and best of lovers, the model by which all others would be judged. Such a tale would prepare the reader for the tales of Tristram and Galahad, and, in conjunction with the other tale of Lancelot that Malory invented to end this group of tales, *The Book of Sir Lancelot and Guenevere*, it would establish the centrality of Lancelot's character in this whole section of the book.[20]

Malory goes at the task of establishing Lancelot's preeminence in as direct a manner as possible. He announces at the beginning of the tale that Lancelot is Arthur's greatest knight: "In all turnementes, justys, and dedys of armes, both for lyff and deth, he passed all other knyghtes . . . and he loved the queen agayne aboven all other ladyes" (vi.1). This functions almost like a logical proposition. Malory states this, and Lancelot sets out to prove himself in "straunge adventures." In the strange adventures that follow, he shows he is indeed the best of knights in all manner of deeds of arms and proves himself true to the queen above all other ladies. He returns to the court to be hailed as the knight that "had the grettiste name of any knighte of the worlde, and moste he was honoured of hyghe and lowe." Q.E.D.; the method is anything but subtle.

The deeds that Lancelot must perform to prove his merits are fairly well set by the tradition. To prove his prowess, a knight must do as Marhalt did—succeed in a preliminary adventure, triumph in a tournament, overcome a dangerous enemy and thus abolish an evil custom, and then out-joust his fellow knights (in disguise if he is already a member of the Round Table). To prove his merits as a lover, a knight must conventionally do his lady service (as Lancelot sends his captives to Guenevere, partly as tribute, partly as proof that he merits her love), and he must resist temptation by other ladies, as Lancelot does first in the case of Morgan and the three queens and then at the Chapel Perilous.

Malory's problem was to build a tale that would combine the two themes. There were many models at hand, since love and adventure are usually combined in Arthurian romance; Malory's own *Tale of Sir Gareth* combines the usual proof of prowess with the winning of a lady. The difficulty is that Lancelot never wins the lady. He can fully possess Guenevere only at the end of the *Morte Darthur*, when he completely breaks with Arthur, and even then he and the queen can be united only for a short time. Moreover, the usual tale of a knight's proof of prowess concerns the *enfances* of the hero, and Malory had decided (again probably to maintain proportion) that Lancelot would be presented as a mature knight, even though he had a clear idea of the shape of Lancelot's early career (cf. ix.1, 4).

Malory found an adventure in the prose *Lancelot* that would suit his purposes, the story of Lancelot's battle with Terrican (Tarquin), which contains most of the necessary elements of the proof-of-knighthood theme. Lancelot begins in a low position (captured by Morgan) and redeems himself first in the necessary preliminary duel (Belleus), then in a tournament, and finally in a battle with the evil Terrican, which ends his ill custom and frees his prisoners. Moreover, the French Terrican episode contained a sort of test of Lancelot's love for Guenevere in the initial captivity by Morgan and the three queens, who offer Lancelot their love. In the French, Lancelot's love for Guenevere had not been an issue, since the Terrican story is part of a long series of adventures in which no one can recognize Lancelot, who had lost all his hair in a previous adventure (an effect of poison; Sommer, V, 75). Morgan tempts Lancelot not because she knows he is Guenevere's lover but simply because of her habitually evil nature. Since Malory extracted the adventure from its context in the prose *Lancelot*, it was no problem to leave Lancelot with his hair, allow Morgan to recognize him, and thus turn the temptation into an explicit trial of his loyalty to Guenevere.

The first step in creating a new tale of Lancelot was to extract the Terrican adventure from its setting; Malory goes about this in much the same way as the Scottish author of *Sir Lancelot of the Laik* extracted a single episode (the Arthur and Galiot adventure) from the prose *Lancelot*, added material of his own invention, and thus created a new tale. The process was slightly more complicated in the case of the Terrican adventure, since its parts were scattered in an interlaced fashion over a long stretch of prose narrative (Sommer, V, 87-102, 204-214) and Malory not only had to separate the adventure from its context but to gather the scattered parts in order to make a single coherent episode. This was no great problem. Malory had already learned from his previous work how to make a self-contained episode from scattered materials, and his method is about the same as that used by the author of *The Gest of Sir Gawain*, who also combined materials widely separated in his source in order to "write a short romance with a well-defined conclusion."[21]

Malory thus begins his tale with the Tarquin adventure, presented as one continuous episode:

Lancelot decides to prove himself in "straunge adventures," and he and Lionel set out from court. While Lancelot sleeps beneath a tree, Lionel is captured by Tarquin. Then Ector, who is seeking Lancelot, is also captured, and he and Lionel languish in Tarquin's prison, wishing Lancelot were there to help them (vi.1-2).

Meanwhile, Lancelot is captured by Morgan and three other queens. They imprison him and declare that he must choose one of the four as his paramour or die in captivity. He refuses (vi.3-4).

King Bagdemagus's daughter frees Lancelot on condition that he help her father in a tournament. Lancelot, after a brief adventure with Belleus, whom he defeats and then promises a place at the Round Table, disguises himself (because some of the knights he will fight are members of the Round Table) and triumphs in the tournament. Then, guided by another maiden, he goes to Tarquin's castle, where he rescues Gaheris and kills Tarquin. Then he rides off, leaving Gaheris to free Lionel, Ector, and many other knights. Gaheris declares: "This day I say you are the best knight in the world" (vi.5-9).

Malory reduces the French in his usual manner and adapts it to his purposes—making Morgan's temptation an explicit test of his love for Guenevere, as we have noted, and substituting Gaheris (Guerehes) for Gareth (Gaheriet), who has a prominent role in the French but whom Malory intends to introduce in the next tale. He also works carefully to link the parts of this adventure together, in the manner of English romances (though much of this linking was present in the French). The captivity of Lionel by Tarquin is the bracket of the whole adventure, which ends only with his rescue. Then Lancelot himself is captured. When he wakes in Morgan's prison, a maiden appears to tell him that she will have news the next day. When he has heard and refused the temptation by Morgan and the three queens, the Morgan episode is complete, and the maiden reappears as she promised. She offers to free Lancelot if he will help her father, King Bagdemagus, in a tournament, and this provides a link to the next episode (in the French the maiden who frees Lancelot and Bagdemagus's daughter are two distinct characters). On his way to Bagdemagus's castle, Lancelot encounters Belleus. Then, with that episode finished, he continues to the tournament. When that is ended, the bracket provided by Lionel's captivity must be completed, and Lancelot therefore proceeds to Tarquin's castle to end the evil custom and free his fellow knights.

Had *A Noble Tale of Sir Lancelot du Lake* ended here, we would have a unified, almost novella-like tale with little in it to puzzle the modern critic. We would also have a fairly typical late Middle English romance, for most English romances are restricted to one, or at most two, major episodes. The author of *The Gest of Sir Gawain*, as I have remarked, uses much the same technique of composition as Malory employed in creating his Tarquin episode: he extracts a single line of action from its interlaced context. But for the author of *The Gest* that single episode suffices for the whole romance. For Malory, the Tarquin episode is just the beginning, and the pages that follow contain enough material for a dozen brief English romances. Yet the episodes form a coherent whole, for they are controlled by the themes. First there is the thematic necessity to prove Lancelot's chivalry. His rescue of Lionel and the others from Tarquin has already shown that Lancelot is the best of warriors, but the High Order of Knighthood also requires that a knight do special service to ladies, and so, by means of a linking episode, Lancelot moves to yet another battle. The maiden who guided Lancelot to Tarquin's castle did so on the condition that he would next battle a "false knight," and when the duel with Tarquin is finished Lancelot sets out immediately to face this knight, Perys de Foreste Savage. Malory (who supplies the name Perys) adapts the episode that immediately follows the Tarquin episode in *Lancelot*, but he completely changes its import. In the French Perys is just another evil knight. Malory makes him an infamous persecutor of ladies, shocking to Lancelot ("What . . . is he a theff and a knyght? And a ravyssher of women? He doth shame unto the Order of Knyghthode and contrary unto his oth. Hit is pyté that he lyveth!"; vi.10).

Malory also creates a parallel between Lancelot's duel with Perys and his fight with Tarquin. This is stated in almost too heavy-handed a manner. When Lancelot has defeated Perys, the maiden announces: "Lyke as Terquyn wacched to dystresse good knyghtes, so dud this knyght attende to destroy and dystresse ladyes, damesels, and jantyllwomen." And she hails Lancelot as a paragon of courtesy: "For the curteyst knyght thou arte and the mekyste unto all ladyes and jantylwomen that now lyvyth" (vi.10). Again we cannot miss the parallel (which Malory also invented); Gaheris had praised Lancelot as a warrior, the lady now praises him for his courtly virtues—the two major aspects of Lancelot's ideal knighthood that are the basis of Ector's moving threnody at the end of the *Morte Darthur* (xxi. 13). There had already been an indication that courtesy is a necessary part of Lancelot's ideal knighthood in the Belleus episode, in which Lancelot offers generous amends (as the lady had asked, "of your courtesy") to a defeated foe (whom he simply killed in the French version). And Lancelot's courtesy is further developed in the conversation between Lancelot and the damsel that occurs after she has praised his courtesy (again, Malory's invention). She speaks of his fame for faithfulness to Guenevere, and Lancelot explains that he rejects both marriage and the use of "paramours." This is, of course, not a rejection of Guenevere (the word "paramours" is almost never used for lovers such as

Guenevere or Isode) but an affirmation of his faithful service to her.[22]

On this high note the tale could again end, and this is the end of the first half, for the adventure that follows is not explicitly linked to anything that has gone before. The first half of the tale has established Lancelot as a faithful lover (the Morgan episode) and an ideal knight, generous to his foes (Belleus), skilled in jousts (deeds of arms"for lyff" at Bagdemagus's tournament) and battles ("for deth" in the fight with Tarquin), and one who uses his prowess to serve his fellows (rescue of Lionel and the others) and to punish an oppressor of ladies (the Perys episode).

However, the tale is still incomplete at this point. As we saw in the Marhalt episode of *The Tale of King Arthur*, the proof-of-knighthood theme requires not only success in a tournament and the defeat of an evil adversary but also a series of successful jousts with Arthur's knights. Until these jousts occur, the tale remains unfinished. Thus, if he so chooses, an author can expand the "evil adversary" section, with the audience's expectation of the required jousts serving as a "bracket" that contains the added adventures. The added adventures—in this case Perys and the Castle Tintagel section—are also united with the rest of the "evil adversary" section (that is, with the Tarquin adventure) by parallel contrasts of the sort we have noted in the account of Lancelot's duel with Perys. The parallel between Perys and Tarquin is obvious enough, since Malory so insists upon it, but it is incomplete, for Perys has no prisoners to provide a counterpart to the knights Lancelot frees after his victory over Tarquin. However, the next section of the Vulgate *Lancelot* contained an adventure that could be adapted to this purpose: Lancelot renews his quest for Hector, not realizing he was one of Terrican's prisoners. He stops at a "house of converts" (*maison rendu*) to inquire about Hector and, having learned nothing helpful, travels on to a castle where despite warnings he battles with a porter and two giants, overcoming all three. As a result, he frees the many ladies and gentlemen whom the giants have held prisoner (Sommer, V, 212-214).

The business about Hector—a important source of irony in the French, in which Hector and Lancelot are each in search of the other and constantly cross one another's paths—is of no interest to Malory, but the freeing of the prisoners at the castle (to which Malory supplies the name Tintagel) offers an opportunity to complete the parallel with Tarquin. Malory has changed Perys from a merely evil knight to an explicit oppressor of ladies, and he now changes the Tintagel episode in much the same way. The rescued prisoners are altered from a group of ladies and gentlemen to an all-female contingent: "three score of ladyes and damesels . . . al grete jentylwomen borne" (vi.11). And the adventure is changed from a merely chance encounter to one that is, like the duel with Tarquin, destined for Lancelot alone. The ladies, like the knights in Tarquin's castle (cf. vi.2), had long "wysshed aftir" Lancelot, for they knew that only he could rescue them: the giants "dredde never knyght but you" (vi.11).

These parallels—all Malory's addition to his sources—help hold the Tarquin, Perys, and Castle Tintagel adventures together in an obviously coherent whole:

Tarquin	Perys	Porter and giants
enemy of good knights	enemy of ladies	
freeing of knights		freeing of ladies

The parallels are pleasing in themselves, but they also provide a sort of "vertical" link, holding the Castle Tintagel episode (which has no explicit link of the sort that joins Tarquin and Perys) in a coherent unit that is one extended "evil adversary" episode in the proof-of-knighthood theme. In this way Malory achieves the variety of incident that he prizes without losing the thematic coherence of his tale.

The next set of episodes, the joustings, have no obvious connection with what went before, though they are slightly parallel to Bagdemagus's tournament, in which Lancelot, disguised, overthrew three fellow knights of the Round Table. These jousts occur only after Lancelot "rode into many strange countreys and thorow many watyrs and valeys," a journey that clearly marks a new stage in the action. Malory himself has to move far forward in the Vulgate *Lancelot* for this set of adventures: long after the Tintagel episode, Lancelot happens upon Kay, whom he rescues from two knights whom he sends as prisoners to Arthur. Then, by mistake, he dons Kay's armor, and so disguised he first overcomes four unnamed knights, whom he sends as prisoners to Guenevere, and then he unhorses Sagramour, Hector, Gawain, and Ywain with a single lance (Sommer, V, 306-310).

Malory makes a number of minor changes to fit this adventure to his themes. In *Sir Lancelot*, Lancelot sends Kay's attackers to surrender to Guenevere rather than to the king; Lancelot apparently takes Kay's armor by design rather than error, since his purpose is to prove himself by jousting with his own fellows and for this a disguise is necessary. Evidently this is why Malory included the Kay episode, though it also serves to reassert Lancelot's function as a rescuer of his fellow knights. Then Malory doubles the adventure in order to link the Kay episode more closely with the jousting required by the theme: immediately after leaving the castle in Kay's armor Lancelot meets three more knights whom he overcomes and sends to Guenevere as captives. Unlike the three anonymous knights from whom he rescues Kay, these are specifically named: Gautere, Gylmere, and Raynold; they appear again, and this adventure is recalled, in "The Healing of Sir Urry" (xix.11). Thus, instead of the Vulgate's anonymous knights divided into groups of two and four, with two sent to the queen and four to the king, Malory balances the groups—three in each, with both groups sent to the queen. Finally, naming the second group and specifying their membership in the Round Table suggests a relation between this group and the next group of four knights of the Round Table whom Lancelot overcomes with a single spear (these are not taken prisoner since this is the "friendly" joust required in the proof-of-knighthood). Malory's changes are small but significant: they create a coherent and balanced unit that unites Lancelot's service to Guenevere with his proof of prowess.

Lancelot's faith to the queen has been reasserted more or less incidentally through the proof-of-knighthood episodes, but it was the major concern of the first episode in the tale, Morgan's temptation of Lancelot. Of course, that episode served other purposes as well. The proof-of-knighthood theme customarily begins with the hero in a lowly position—an orphan (like Alexander), a kitchen knave (like Gareth), or, as in this case, a captive. Lancelot's captivity is in effect a blot on his knightly character, which must be removed by proof of his prowess. Now, with Lancelot's knighthood established, Malory returns to the theme of Lancelot's devotion to Guenevere, and he adds another episode, at the Chapel Perilous, which, like the Morgan episode, turns on Lancelot's faith to Guenevere. For this he draws upon *Perlesvaus*, where Lancelot encounters first an evil enchantress (whom Malory names Hallewes) who is intent upon murdering him, and then a young damsel hopelessly in love with him. By telescoping the two characters, Malory produces an evil enchantress who, like Morgan at the tale's beginning, is determined to have Lancelot's love despite his faith to Guenevere.

The Chapel Perilous episode involves more than this. It concerns an astonishing supernatural healing and thus provides a suitable culmination of Lancelot's feats, like the healing of Sir Urry in *Lancelot and*

Guenevere. Conventionally such a healing can be effected only by the greatest knight in the world ("And yf you spede not I know no knyght lyvyng that may encheve that adventure"), and it is especially appropriate in this tale, since it also involves Lancelot's role as a servant of distressed ladies (he undertakes the adventure at the plea of Melyot's sister) and as a helper of his fellow knights: "He is a felow of the Table Rounde and to his helpe I woll do my power" (vi.14).

The Chapel Perilous also combines a test of prowess with a test of faith to Guenevere and thus unites the two major themes of the tale. When Lancelot takes the sword from the chapel, thirty giant knights tell him to let it be, and a fair damsel, Hallewes, tells him he will die if he does not return the sword. This seems only a test of bravery, but, as she explains, "And thou dyddest leve that swerde quene Gwenyuere sholde thou never se" (vi.15). Then the lady begs him for a kiss, and this seems merely a sexual temptation. But, as she tells him, it is really a matter of his life: "And thou haddyst kyssed me thy lyff dayes had be done." Hallewes confides her problem (invented by Malory): she suffers from necrophilia and, knowing that Lancelot would never leave Guenevere, she hoped to kill him, preserve his body, "and dayly I sholde have clypped the and kyssed the, dyspyte of Quene Gwenyuere."

This sensational incident forcefully reasserts the theme of Lancelot's faith to Guenevere. The two final episodes, the encounters with Phelot and Pedyvere, seem designed to reassert the other concerns of the tale. Both are largely Malory's own invention. The Phelot episode, in which Lancelot disarms to retrieve a lady's hawk and is then attacked by her husband, may have been suggested by one of the several incidents in the Vulgate *Lancelot* in which knights retrieve ladies' hawks (though none of them lead to an unfair attack like this).[23] The Pedyvere episode may also have been suggested by the *Lancelot* (Sommer, V, 160-162, 167-168):

> Lancelot comes to a pavilion where a knight is unmercifully beating a lady. He asks the knight to desist, but the knight strikes off the lady's head. Lancelot pursues him and beats him to the ground. Reluctantly he spares the knight's life on condition that he carry the lady to Camelot and beg Guenevere's mercy. If he obtains that he must go successively to the courts of Bagdemagus and Norgales, begging forgiveness in each. The knight does so and obtains the necessary forgivenesses. The damsel is buried, and he returns to his own country.

Most likely this is the source of the Pedyvere episode. Malory turns it
into one continuous narrative, adds an amusing touch of realism
(Pedyvere's telling Lancelot to look behind him and then quickly
chopping off the lady's head), makes Guenevere alone the instrument
of Pedyvere's reform (she sends him to Rome and he ends his days as a
hermit), and plays up the trial of Lancelot's courtesy involved in his
reluctant sparing of Pedyvere's life.

Phelot, who takes advantage of the unarmed Lancelot in a manner
in sharp contrast to Lancelot's refusal to strike the prostrate Pedyvere,
seems to be intended as a vague parallel to Tarquin, just as Pedyvere is
reminiscent of Perys. Phelot is dishonorable toward knights, and
Pedyvere an enemy of ladies. And they are appropriately dealt
with—Phelot dies at the hands of a good knight, Pedyvere is reformed
by a great lady. However, these episodes function mainly as a sort of
coda to a narrative that is built upon an *entrelacement* of themes
rather than plots, and they help establish the complexly balanced
structure which thematic narrators prized: an adventure with an
enchantress (Morgan), a proof-of-knighthood which features two evil
adversaries (Tarquin and Perys), an adventure with an enchantress
(Hallewes), and two more evil adversaries (Phelot and Pedyvere).
This balance is reinforced by the chiasmic order of the major episodes.
The major episodes of the first part involve temptation (Morgan), disguise (Bagdemagus), and rescue (the knights held by Tarquin). The
second part reverses the order: a rescue (the ladies at Castle Tintagel),
disguise (jousts with Arthur's knights), and temptation (Hallewes).
There are, of course, other ways of looking at the structure. The point
is that the tale does indeed have a structure, a thematic coherence that
Malory created by the episodes he selected from his sources and by the
manner in which he altered them to make his themes clear.

Far from being "puzzling," *A Noble Tale of Sir Lancelot* is almost
too clear.[24] Its purpose is obviously to establish Lancelot as the best
knight in the world. It defines his noble character, brings his relation
to Guenevere to the center of the action, and shows in action the ideal
of knighthood that had been abstractly stated in the oath required of
Arthur's knights at the founding of the Round Table (iii.15): Lancelot,
as that oath requires, never does outrage or murder (unlike his French
counterpart, he spares Belleus); he flees treason (keeping his word and
punishing traitors such as Phelot), gives mercy to those who ask it
(even the despicable Pedyvere), succors ladies, damsels, and gentlewomen (at Castle Tintagel), and far from "enforcing them" he even

abjures the use of paramours. He fights in no wrongful causes and seeks no wordly goods (explicitly telling the prisoners he rescues from Tarquin to "take suche stuff there as they fynde"; vi.9). The tale not only shows Lancelot observing this basic code, required of all good knights, it also shows him achieving, and thus defining, the higher form of knighthood required of one who "had the grettyste name of ony knyght of the worlde" (vi.18).

Considered from the standpoint of thematic narrative, *Sir Lancelot* is a better and clearer narrative than many critics have thought. Nevertheless, perhaps because Malory was so intent upon exemplifying and defining Lancelot's chivalry, the tale is not a complete success. The themes are sometimes too obviously forced on the material (as in the Chapel Perilous episode), the parallels are too mechanically established (as in the case of Perys), and parts of the tale are developed by simple repetition of theme. We can recognize the thematic function of the duels with Phelot and Pedyvere but not their thematic necessity, for the themes do not so completely control the structure as they do in even so simple a work as *King Horn*. This is not to say that *Sir Lancelot* is an artistic failure, for its faults are not grave, and we would perhaps be inclined to ignore them were it not that Malory's next experiment with invention, *The Tale of Sir Gareth*, shows him in complete mastery of the thematic mode of composition. In *Gareth*, Malory invents far more freely and creates an original romance (that is, one with many analogues but no one source), and he manages to use theme as a means of shaping the structure of the work itself. *Gareth*, which was apparently written in the same period as *Sir Tristram*, shows Malory with a mature command of the art of romance narrative.

5

The Tale of Sir Gareth

Malory's method of invention in *The Tale of Sir Gareth* is the same as that which we examined in the Marhalt episode of *The Tale of King Arthur* and in *Sir Lancelot*, though in *Gareth* he is much more successful. In each case he begins with a basic pattern of action—a common theme or a thematically organized set of episodes drawn from an existing romance. In *Gareth* the basic theme is that of the "Fair Unknown," one of the most widespread of romance themes. It is found not only in the "Fair Unknown" romances, such as Renaut de Beaujeau's *Li biaus descouneüs* and the English *Lybeaus Desconus*, but in the stories of the *enfances* of romance heroes such as Perceval and Lancelot, in tales of young knights such as La Cote Mal Tayle and Alexander the Orphan, and—in the form of the "male Cinderella"—it is common not only in romance (as part of the three-day-tournament theme and sometimes of the theme of exile) but in folktale and nonromance genres as well (it appears even in *Beowulf*).[1] It seems to have been a favorite with Malory, for at least four of his knights begin their careers as "Fair Unknowns"—La Cote, Alexander, Gareth, and Lancelot himself.

The first part of *Gareth*—from the beginning to Gareth's battle with the Red Knight of the Red Lands—is so close to the pattern of the "Fair Unknown" romances that Malory's tale is frequently classed with this group (Renaut's *Li biaus descouneüs*, the English *Lybeaus Desconus*, the German *Wigalois*, and the Italian *Carduino* being the most important), and R. H. Wilson has shown the close affinities of *Gareth* to

92

these works.[2] But *Gareth* does not fit comfortably with these romances. As the most recent editor of *Lybeaus* notes, Malory's tale clearly has "a more synthetic look about it" than any of the other works in this group.[3] There are, for example, clear indications of the influence of *Tristan*, and Malory himself reminds the reader of the parallel between Gareth and La Cote Mal Tayle. At the beginning of the tale, Kay scornfully nicknames Gareth "Beaumains":

"Yett beware," seyde sir Launcelot, "So ye gaff the good knyght Brunor, sir Dynadans brother, a name, and ye called him La Cote Mal Tayle and that turned you to anger aftirwarde." (vii.2)

This, and other details, led Vinaver to conclude that *Gareth* must have been adapted from a lost "Romance of Gaheriet," which was based directly on the prose *Tristan*.[4]

However, the influence of other romances is also apparent in *Gareth*. The hero's encounter with Sir Ironside, the Red Knight, was apparently influenced by the "Joie de la cort" episode of Chrétien's *Erec et Enide*, and Vinaver has noted possible traces of Chrétien's other works.[5] Thomas L. Wright has found some resemblances between *Gareth* and the *Suite du Merlin*, and, as Wilfred L. Guerin has noted, almost every detail in this work can be traced to other romances.[6] In this sense it is, as Roger S. Loomis once wrote, "a pastiche."[7] In this sense, too, it differs from Malory's other tales, for obviously Malory drew not from one or two sources (as he usually did) but from a great variety of works, and his method was not adaptation but invention. As Guerin puts it, "So far as we know, Malory had before him in the writing of the 'Tale [of Gareth]' no 'source,' at least in the sense that we use in considering other segments of *Le Morte Darthur*."[8] Vinaver finds this an "astonishing statement": "If there is something we do know about this 'Tale' it is that in writing it Malory had before him a *source*, in precisely the sense that we use in considering the other segments of *Le Morte Darthur*. How else could the numerous other traits that he has in common with a wide range of earlier texts have reached him?"[9] They reached him in the same manner, one must assume, as they would have reached an earlier author of a "lost source," by way of his literary experience. Malory's knowledge of romances, as we know, was remarkably broad. If anyone could have created this "conflation of end products," that person was most likely Sir Thomas Malory.

Yet Vinaver may be right in his insistence that Malory did have some specific source as a starting point, probably a romance of the

"Fair Unknown" variety. Malory apparently knew the English *Lybeaus Desconus*; this is implied by his use elsewhere of the English name Gynglaine (the hero of *Lybeaus*) and by the appearance of a "Pas Perilous" in both *Gareth* (vii.9) and *Lybeaus*. He also obviously knew the story of La Cote Mal Tayle. I doubt, however, that either of these tales provided the pattern of action for the first part of *Gareth*. A much more likely candidate, first mentioned in this connection by Henry Weber in 1810 but seldom considered in recent years, is the twelfth-century Anglo-Norman romance *Ipomedon*, by Hugh of Rutland.[10] This work was very popular in the later Middle English period; it was translated into English three different times, a tail-rhyme version, a later brief adaptation in couplets, and a somewhat reduced prose version, and it directly influenced at least one other late romance, the Scottish *Roswall and Lillian*.[11]

Hugh's *Ipomedon* is a long and leisurely romance built around three major themes: the three-days tournament, the "Fair Unknown," and the combat between brothers—all three of which are important in *Gareth*. The "Fair Unknown" episode (which Hugh based on Renaut's *Li biaus desconeüs*)[12] resembles Malory's version far more closely than do either "La Cote Mal Tayle" or *Lybeaus Desconus*. Since the problem of the source of *Gareth* has never been settled and since doubt still exists about whether Malory drew on "La Cote Mal Tayle" (by way of a "Romance of Gaheriet") or on *Lybeaus Desconus* (or some similar romance of the "Fair Unknown" group), it may be useful at this point briefly to summarize all three—Malory's "La Cote," the English *Lybeaus*, and the English *Ipomadon*—so that the reader can form some idea of how these works compare with one another and to *Gareth*. I use the English versions for my summaries in each case, since they are fairly representative of their sources and are the versions that were most easily accessible to Malory:

"La Cote Mal Tayle." A young man comes to Camelot, wearing an ill-fitting coat over his rich garments. He wears the coat because he has sworn to avenge his father, who was wearing it when he was killed. He tells Arthur his name, Brunor le Noire, but he conceals his pedigree, though he assures Arthur that he is well born. Kay mockingly labels him La Cote Mal Tayle. On the urging of Lamerok and Gaheris (who remind Arthur that Lancelot's circumstances were similar), Arthur agrees to knight Brunor. The next day La Cote saves Guenevere from a lion. Arthur knights him. A damsel appears and asks for a champion to finish an unspecified quest, begun by a knight now dead. La Cote, over the damsel's objections, takes on the adventure. He outjousts Dagonet, the king's fool, but is unhorsed first by Bleoberis and then by Palomides. Then he saves Mordred from captivity and slays twelve knights at the Castle Orgullus. Still the Damsel Maldisaunt berates him. At Castle Pendragon, La Cote is captured when five knights attack him. Lancelot rescues him and makes the lady stop abusing La Cote. La Cote defeats two brothers at a village in Surluse but is so exhausted he cannot overcome a third, Sir Pleynorous, who takes La Cote prisoner. Lancelot defeats Pleynorous and rescues him and many others. Lancelot gives rich lands to La Cote, who marries the damsel, now called not Maldisaunt but Beau-vivante.

Lybeaus Desconus. Gawain's bastard son, Gynglaine, is raised in the forest by his mother. He does not know his own name; his mother calls him only Beaufitz. In the forest he comes upon a dead knight, whose armor he takes. He goes to Arthur's court and asks to be knighted. Arthur names him Lybeaus Desconus and knights him. Lybeaus asks for the boon of the first adventure. At dinner time a maiden enters, accompanied by a dwarf. She asks for a knight to rescue her lady, Synadown. Lybeaus is granted the adventure, over the vociferous protests of the maiden and her dwarf. Gawain and other knights richly arm Lybeaus, and he departs with the damsel and her dwarf. The maiden insults him. They arrive at Chapel Auntours, where Lybeaus fights and overcomes Sir William Cole-bronche, whom he sends as a prisoner to Arthur. William's three nephews swear to avenge him. The maiden begs Lybeaus's mercy and ceases her insults. Lybeaus defeats the three nephews and sends them as prisoners to Arthur. He next encounters two giants, a red and a black, who hold a maiden captive. He slays them and sends their heads to Arthur. He then comes upon a rich park, held by Sir Gyfron le Fludous, who will give a white hawk to any knight whose lady is fairer than his; if the knight's lady is not as beautiful as Gyfron's Gyfron does battle and beheads all the losers, placing the heads on the battlements of his castle. Lybeaus's damsel guide, Elene, loses the beauty contest, and Gyfron and Lybeaus fight. Gyfron's back is broken, and Lybeaus sends the white hawk to Arthur. Next Lybeaus comes upon a beautiful hound, which he takes with him despite the protests of its owner, Sir Otes de Lyle. Otes and his men attack, but Lybeaus overcomes all and sends Otes as a prisoner to King Arthur. Then Lybeaus comes to the Yle d'Or, whose bridge is guarded by the black giant Maugis, whom Lybeaus kills. He is entertained by the Dame d'Amours, who offers him herself and the castle. Lybeaus accepts and stays with her a full year, forgetting the maid Elene and the lady Synadown, since the Dame d'Amours is a sorceress. By chance he meets Elene, who reminds him of his duty, and he leaves the castle. They ride directly to Synadown. Lybeaus must fight Sir Lambarde, the steward, whom he defeats and then befriends. He then rescues the lady Synadown from the evil clerks Yrayn and Maboun, whom he slays. Then he disenchants Synadown, whom the evil clerks have transformed into a serpent. He marries Synadown and returns in triumph to Camelot, where (according to some manuscripts) his mother reveals his identity to Gawain, who commands all henceforth to call Lybeaus by his rightful name: Gynglaine.

Ipomadon.[13] Ipomadon is in love with the Lady of Calabria and, hearing that she is besieged, he goes to the court of King Meleager, her uncle, where he appears disguised as a fool and extracts from Meleager the joking promise that he shall have the first adventure that may appear. Later that day, after Ipomadon has been scorned and mistreated by all the court, a richly dressed maiden appears, accompanied by a dwarf. She asks for a champion to rescue her sister, the Lady of Calabria, who is besieged by the hideous Sir Lyolyne of Inde Major. Ipomadon demands the adventure. The lady scorns him and angrily leaves. Ipomadon rides after the lady. She scornfully tells him to turn back. A knight named Maugis, armed in black (cousin of Lyolyne), rides up and demands that the damsel, Emane, come with him. Ipomadon fights and defeats him, takes Maugis's black armor, and gives his horse to the dwarf. Emane says this was just luck, and she refuses to eat with Ipomadon; the dwarf is shocked, and he dines with him. The next day Maugis's cousin, Greon, who won great fame in India and Palestine, demands the lady. Emane urges Ipomadon not to fight, but he battles and defeats him. Emane repents of her behavior, and that night she goes to his bed and offers him her love. He acts like a madman and thus discourages the attempt. The next day Ipomadon encounters and kills Lyander, the brother of Lyolyne, the besieger of Calabria. That night Emane again tempts him, convinced now he is no fool. He gently dissuades her and sends her away with two kisses. The next day, wearing Lyander's armor, he defeats and kills Lyolyne. The lady of Calabria, whose castle is on the sea, thinks that Lyolyne has won, and she flees by ship. Capaneus, the heir of Meleager, then appears to give battle to Ipomadon, whom Capaneus thinks is Lyolyne, but during the duel they recognize one another, and

Ipomadon learns that Capaneus is his long-lost brother. They embrace, Ipomadon is united in marriage with his love, Capaneus marries Emane, and the tale ends in general rejoicing.

The three romances show in what strikingly different ways the same basic situation can be employed, and *Gareth* is yet a fourth. All four share the essential elements of the theme: a young man, either concealing or not knowing his parentage, undertakes an adventure to which he is guided by a scornful damsel, who heaps abuse on him until finally he proves himself worthy of the climactic adventure. It is clear from the summaries that the resemblances between "La Cote" and *Gareth* end here, since in "La Cote" the adventure is unspecified (and never, apparently, completed), whereas in *Gareth*, as in *Lybeaus* and *Ipomadon*, the hero rescues a besieged lady whom he wins as a wife.

It is also clear from the summaries that *Gareth* is in some ways closer to *Lybeaus* than to *Ipomadon*, since both Gareth and Lybeaus are young men engaged in their first adventures, whereas in *Ipomadon* the hero has already succeeded in a good many adventures and has already won the love of his besieged lady. Both Lybeaus and Gareth are therefore engaged in a serious quest for knighthood, a lady, and, most important, the discovery or vindication of their own identities. In *Ipomadon* the whole business is much less solemn. Though the summary obscures this, Hugh's romance is a lighthearted work, and Ipomadon's adopting the character of a fool as a disguise seems intended largely as the excuse for a number of jokes, occasionally risqué. In *Ipomadon*, when the damsel appears in Meleager's court, his knights see this not as the solemn beginning of an "adventure" but as the occasion for nudging one another and remarking what fun it would be to sleep with her. (This is all done much more elegantly in the twelfth-century French than in the fourteenth-century English verse version, and it is omitted altogether in the fifteenth-century prose adaptation.)

Nevertheless, the summaries also show that generally *Gareth* is much closer to *Ipomadon* than to *Lybeaus Desconus*. Most of the details that Malory does share with *Lybeaus* also appear in *Ipomadon*, since Hugh based his work on Renaut's *Li biaus descouneüs*, the source of *Lybeaus*, and there are many features that appear only in *Ipomadon* and *Gareth*. Only in these two works does the hero disguise himself as a menial—a fool or a kitchen knave. Only in these works is the damsel guide the sister of the besieged lady. Only here does the hero fight a series of antagonists who are kinsmen, including at least one brother of the besieger, and proceed directly through these battles to the final battle against the besieger. Both Ipomadon and Gareth successfully resist a sexual temptation before the climactic battle (there is no temptation in "La Cote," and Lybeaus succumbs rather too easily to the blandishments of the Dame d'Amours). Only *Ipomadon* and *Gareth* end with the hero fighting and then recognizing his own brother, and then with the marriage not only of the hero and his besieged lady but of his brother to the damsel guide (Gaheris marries Lyonet, just as Capaneus marries Emane in *Ipomadon*). There are other details peculiar to these two versions—the scornful maiden's refusal to eat with the hero, the Black Knight's demand that the hero surrender his damsel guide, her claim that his victories are due to luck, and the fact that the besieged lady's castle is explicitly located at the sea (which has a function in *Ipomadon* but not in *Gareth*).

Almost all these details can be found in other sources, for both Hugh and Malory, like Renaut de Beaujeu before them, drew freely on the stock conventions of romance. Murray A. Potter's study *Sohrab and Rustem* lists from folklore and romance no less than twenty-seven instances of the battle between brothers, and many romances of the "Fair Unknown" sort end with a battle between relatives, usually father and son.[14] *Sir Degare*, a romance in the "Fair Unknown" tradition of the *Perceval* rather than the *Li biaus descouneüs* variety, ends in exactly this way, with Degare and his father fighting and then recognizing one another. Malory could easily have chosen the duel-between-relatives motif as a way of concluding his romance for the same reasons that Hugh did, because he recognized the issue of identity implicit within the "Fair Unknown" theme. Likewise, the tournament in which Gareth fights for his lady disguised in various colors is suggestive of the three-day tournament in an earlier part of *Ipomadon*, but could have been drawn from any one of a great number of romances, since, as Jesse L. Weston showed long ago, this is one of the oldest and most common motifs in romance.[15]

Certainly Malory did draw many details from other works. The business of Gareth's nickname, scornfully bestowed by Kay, was obviously suggested by La Cote Mal Tayle, though its form, Beaumains, is reminiscent of the Beaufitz common in "Fair Unknown" romances; Perceval, Degare, and the hero of Renaut's *Li biaus descouneüs* are all known by this name, though Arthur gives Renaut's

hero the nickname Bel Inconnu. The "Joie de la cort" episode in Chrétien's *Erec et Enide* seems to have supplied (probably at some
remove) much of the shape of Gareth's battle with the Red Knight of
the Red Lands, but typically other sources are also drawn upon: the
Red Knight has an English name, Sir Ironside, and he does not behead
his opponents as Chrétien's Mabinograins and his cogeners in the "Fair
Unknown" tradition do; rather he hangs them, a punishment faintly
suggestive of the English *Sir Landeval*.[16] However, despite the stock
character of many of the incidents common to Malory's and Hugh's
works, and despite the fact that Malory drew freely from other works,
there seems little room to doubt that Malory knew and drew directly
upon *Ipomedon*, either in its original or in one of its English adaptations.

There is therefore justice in both Vinaver's and Guerin's positions:
Malory did have a source for *Gareth*, and that was *Ipomadon*; but
Ipomadon is not a "source" in the sense we use that term in discussing the other tales, for here Malory is not adapting and reshaping.
Rather he uses *Ipomadon* only for the basic pattern of the first part of
his tale, and even in that part he freely draws on other works and his
own invention, thus producing a unique, original, version of the "Fair
Unknown" theme. We can see this, and we can almost observe Malory
in the act of composition, from the following summary of the major
actions of the first part of the tale and their possible sources. I have
indented those details peculiar to Malory's version.

> A young man arrives at Arthur's court accompanied by two
> men and a dwarf (in all other versions the damsel has a dwarf).
> He serves as a menial (a fool in *Ipomadon*).
> He is unrecognized even by members of his own family
> (*Lybeaus*).
> Kay scornfully nicknames him ("La Cote").
> A maiden asks for a champion (common to all versions) to rescue
> her besieged lady (*Ipomadon*, *Lybeaus*; quest unspecified in "La
> Cote").
> Gareth demands and receives the adventure (common).
> Damsel, insulted, leaves (*Ipomadon*; she is accompanied by hero
> in *Lybeaus* and "La Cote").
> Gareth outjousts Kay (cf. Dagonet in "La Cote").
> Gareth fights Lancelot to a draw; he reveals his name and

receives knighthood (Lybeaus and La Cote are knighted by Arthur before the damsel arrives).

Gareth overtakes the damsel, who rudely orders him to turn back (*Ipomadon*).

Gareth rescues a knight from six attackers.

The damsel tells him to go back (repetition of above).

She refuses to eat with the hero (see below).

Gareth kills two knights at a ford.

The damsel says it is luck (see below).

Gareth defeats the Black Knight, brother to the besieger, who demanded that he surrender the lady (*Ipomadon*, where the attacker is the black-clad Maugis, the besieger's cousin).

The damsel says the hero won by luck (*Ipomadon*).

Gareth defeats the Green Knight, brother of the Black Knight (*Ipomadon*, where attacker is again a cousin).

Gareth spares the Green Knight's life (in *Ipomadon* all the early opponents are granted their lives).

The damsel refuses to eat with Gareth; the host, embarrassed, goes to sit with him (*Ipomadon*, where the dwarf, embarrassed, goes to sit with him).

The damsel says that Gareth will never get by the Pas Perilous (*Lybeaus*).

Gareth defeats the Red Knight, another brother of the besieger (repetition of preceding).

The damsel repents of her ill treatment (common to all versions).

Gareth defeats Sir Persaunt of Inde, brother to the besieger (*Ipomadon*; Sir Lyander, brother to the besieger, Lyolyne of Inde), whose life he spares (kills him in *Ipomadon*).

Gareth is sexually tempted by Persaunt's daughter (by Emane in *Ipomadon*, once before and once after the battle with Lyander).

Gareth reveals his name to Persaunt and the damsel Lyonet.

Gareth lodges in a hermitage near the lady's castle (*Ipomadon*).

Sir Ironside, the Red Knight, hangs all the knights he defeats (a modification of Mergier's practice in Renaut's *Li beaus descouneüs* and, ultimately, of Mabinograin's in *Erec et Enide*).

Gareth battles the Red Knight, is almost overcome, but, encouraged by the damsel and the lady, defeats and spares him (*Ipomadon*).

The Red Knight explains that his strength increases every day until noon (suggested by Gawain's trait, in *Estoire de Merlin* and elsewhere)

And that his ill custom was adopted at a lady's command (*Erec et Enide*).

Gareth is told by Lyones that he must labor a year to earn her love, but she learns his identity, and later they meet and plight their troth.

In Malory's hands the leisurely narrative of *Ipomadon*, with its elaborate descriptions and psychological analyses, becomes a rapidly moving, incident-filled story. As usual, he will not settle for one action where many can be used. Ipomadon faces only three opponents before he meets the besieger, and of these three he kills but one. Gareth fights a total of fourteen knights before he encounters Sir Ironside, and he kills an even half dozen. Nevertheless, the narrative holds together quite well, for here, as in *A Noble Tale of Sir Lancelot*, Malory makes good use of brackets, parallels, and links. The jousting with Kay and Lancelot, for example, occurs within the bracket provided by the damsel's departure and the hero's overtaking her. The battles that occur next—when Gareth rescues a knight from six attackers and then battles two knights at a ford—are united with what follows by the repetition of the damsel's claim that his victory was merely a matter of luck and by her refusal to eat with the hero. And the next series of opponents (Black, Green, and Red Knights) are obviously linked to one another by the parallel use of colors and the fact that all are brothers.

Such mechanical devices are relatively unimportant in this tale, however, for whereas in *Sir Lancelot* Malory depended mainly on the parallels themselves to provide his structure, he now makes a far more skillful use of theme as a means of shaping the narrative, and his most important additions to Hugh's tale are designed to clarify the developing theme. That seems to be the purpose of the reference to La Cote at the beginning of the tale. Lancelot's warning to Kay that the scornful nickname is similar to the one he gave La Cote is a clear signal to the audience that the hero of this tale is also a "Fair Unknown," and the nickname Kay gives Gareth, Beaumains, seems obviously reminiscent of the Beau fils that is a favored nickname of "Fair Unknowns." Moreover, the relatively important role played by Gareth's mother is an easily recognized feature of "Fair Unknown" romances. Usually the mother appears at the end to reveal the father and son to one another. Here the mother's appearance is part of a series of continuing revelations of Gareth's name, with each revelation marking the end of an important stage of the action as a kind of signal that one set of tests had been successfully passed and that the hero is ready for the next.

The usual "Fair Unknown" romance has but one discovery of the hero's name, for conventionally the hero is unknown even to himself. Raised in isolation, he knows only his nickname, and his quest is not just a quest for knighthood and chivalric love and adventure. It is rather a search for his own identity, a quest to discover his name and his parentage. Gareth, like Ipomadon, knows his own name: his quest is to prove himself worthy of that name, to show himself, King Arthur, and his brother Gawain that he is worthy of his lady, his place at the Round Table, and membership in his own family.

This is, of course, not peculiar to Gareth. To a knight his name is his renown, his *status*, and he must constantly prove his worthiness of his name and good fame. That is one of the main problems faced by Gawain in *Sir Gawain and the Green Knight*; it is the problem confronted by Lancelot in *A Noble Tale of Sir Lancelot*; and it is a recurring concern throughout the *Morte Darthur*. For Gareth the problem has the added dimension of an initiation into the knightly life. To prove his worthiness of his name, Gareth must adopt a disguise, as Lancelot did in *Sir Lancelot*. To undergo the necessary initiation into knighthood, a disguise as a "Fair Unknown" is almost inevitable, for he must start in a low position, even lower than Ipomadon, and, like any knight engaged in proving his merits, he must not reveal his true identity to any save those to whom he has visibly demonstrated his worth.[17]

The first stage of this process is Gareth's servitude in Arthur's court as a despised kitchen worker. Conventionally, the hero who is to win fortune and a princess must start off in a lowly position—an exile (Horn), a prisoner (Lancelot), a foreigner (Tristram), or a fool or kitchen knave. Gareth's servitude is ended when the damsel appears to ask for a champion and he takes up the adventure. Gareth, unlike Ipomadon, is not yet a knight, and unlike La Cote and Lybeaus he does not ask for knighthood from Arthur. But he must be knighted before the adventures begin, and so Malory adds the duels with Kay and Lancelot. First he fights and defeats the scornful Kay, and then he battles to a draw with Lancelot. The great hero assures Beaumains that he is a worthy opponent for any knight in the world. Gareth, having proven himself worthy of knighthood, can now reveal his identity to Lancelot, and he begs him for the accolade. Lancelot then knights Gareth, thus forging the close relation between them that will be so important in the later tales. (There is always a special tie between an Arthurian knight and the one who gave him the Order of

Knighthood.) More immediately important, Gareth's achievement of knighthood and the revelation of his identity to Lancelot mark the end of the first stage of his development as a knight and as an individual. This is not so extended as Perceval's, but it is more clearly developed and marked than in most "Fair Unknown" stories.

In the next stage Gareth passes the test posed by the damsel guide's abuse of him—an extension of his humiliation as a kitchen knave. Simultaneously he is tested by the foes he must overcome on his way to the lady's castle. As usual in the "Fair Unknown" romances, especially those of the Perceval variety, the young man is undergoing an education at the same time he is proving his fighting abilities; though Gareth kills his first opponents, he grants mercy to the last three at the maiden's request (an improvement on *Ipomadon*, in which the hero grants mercy to the first two and then kills the third). He is learning noble manners, especially chivalric self-control, which he shows both in suffering the lady's abuse (he tells her "a knyght may lytyll do that may not suffer a jantyllwoman"; vii.11) and in granting mercy to his defeated opponents. He shows self-control too in resisting the sexual temptation that occurs after the last of these preliminary duels. When Gareth spares the life of Sir Persaunt, that former opponent sends his daughter to Gareth's bed, and Gareth, in a line reminiscent of *Sir Gawain and the Green Knight*, gently puts aside her offer: "I were a shamefull knyght and I wolde do youre fadir ony disworshyp" (vii.12). When Sir Persaunt hears this, he concludes that truly Gareth "is com of ful noble blod." Having proven this, Gareth now learns the name of the damsel who guided him, Lyonet, and of her besieged sister, Lyones. In turn he reveals his name to Lyonet and Sir Persaunt—those to whom he has proven himself at this stage of his adventure.

Gareth's success in this second stage qualifies him to seek a much higher status than simple knighthood. Sir Persaunt tells him that the next adventure, for which he has now proven himself worthy, is one suitable for a Lancelot, a Tristram, or a Lamerok. There are many noble knights of the sort Gareth has proven himself to be in the second stage of his career, Persaunt says, but "There be none that bere the name but thes three . . . and ye macche that Rede Knyght ye shall be called the fourth of the worlde" (vii.13). The temporarily evil Sir Ironside believes that the four best knights of the world are Lancelot, Tristram, Lamerok, and Gawain, for he thinks only they are suitable opponents for him. As he later tells Gareth, his evil custom was designed specifically to lure Lancelot or Gawain to his castle. Gareth is thus displacing Gawain, taking his brother's rank among the four best knights of the world and achieving an adventure designed for Gawain. Gareth will not surpass Gawain in prowess, for he remains a younger knight, and in the following tale Palomides assumes the place now held by Gareth alongside Lamerok, Tristram, and Lancelot. But Gareth does become Gawain's moral superior, a kind of antitype of his brother, whose company, we learn at the end of the tale, Gareth will henceforth shun. This marks the separation of Gawain from the rank of noble knights, a position he held throughout *Arthur and Lucius* and *Sir Lancelot*, despite the rather unpromising character he had displayed in the first tale. Throughout the rest of the *Morte Darthur* Gawain is a member of another, more sinister group of four—Gawain, Agravain, Gaheris, and Mordred.

Gareth's qualifying himself for his high position—which adds to the final battle with Gawain a dimension of significance beyond the usual "Fair Unknown" duel between relatives—is the main justification for the extension of the story beyond the winning of the lady. One battle, even with so formidable an opponent as Ironside, is hardly enough for the exalted position for which Gareth next proves he is eligible. He now goes directly to his battle with the Red Knight. The battle is long and difficult (since the Red Knight has supernatural strength),[18] but Gareth finally defeats his opponent and spares his life, despite Ironside's evil ways (thus showing the virtue of mercy that he learned on his journey). Gareth has proved himself worthy of Lyones, and she now learns his name. Moreover, captive after captive has come to surrender to Arthur, and the king and his court have thus received ample proof of Gareth's merits.

"Jesu mercy!" seyde knyge Arthur and sir Gawayne, "We mervayle muche of what blood he is com, for he is a noble knyght."   (vii.18)

Lancelot knows Beaumains' identity, but he keeps it secret. When the last of the captives surrenders to Arthur and the whole Dame Lyones adventure is successfully ended, the court can now know who Beaumains is. The queen of Orkney therefore arrives to announce Beaumains' identity to Arthur and his knights, just as, at the conclusion of a "Fair Unknown" romance, the hero's mother usually appears to unravel the mystery of his identity.

The story cannot end here, however, for Gareth has yet to prove himself in the physical presence of Arthur and, most important, of Gawain. The identity theme remains incomplete until Gareth meets and fights to a draw a member of his own family. Moreover, Gareth's victory over the Red Knight was but the first of the proofs of his worthiness to displace Gawain as one of the four best knights in the world. To provide further evidence, Malory introduces the proof-of-knighthood theme, which requires, after a preliminary battle (here the whole Red Knight adventure), success in a tournament, then a quest in which an evil custom is abolished (and usually prisoners are freed and some enemy of Arthur's is punished), and finally the jousting of the hero, unrecognized, with some of Arthur's knights. This is the pattern of the rest of the tale, with Gawain functioning in place of the knights of the Round Table whom the hero must duel in his final adventure. By this means, the tale is extended within the limits of the "Fair Unknown" theme, since the duel with Gawain is a culmination of that theme as well as of the proof-of-knighthood theme.

Yet one other subsidiary theme is introduced, the courtship of Gareth and Lyones. As we have seen, courtship in romance requires first a set of successful adventures that qualify the hero for the lady's hand; then a declaration of love; then another adventure as proof that the hero is worthy of the lady whose love he has won. The form that Malory uses is an adaptation of the three-day tournament, in which, as in *Ipomadon*, the hero appears in disguise (wearing various colors on succeeding days—though it lasts but a single day in *Gareth*) and triumphs in a tournament in which the lady's hand is offered as a prize. In *Ipomadon*, as in *Gareth*, this is followed immediately by a separation of the lovers, who are reunited only after the battle between brothers. This must have appealed to Malory, since it allowed him to delay the final union of the lovers until the duel between Gareth and Gawain, so that all three themes can reach a simultaneous conclusion.

The disguise necessitated by the three-day tournament also meshes very neatly with the continuing "Fair Unknown" theme, since Gareth thus has the occasion to prove himself in the physical presence of King Arthur and his knights. Moreover, the courtship theme is neatly interlocked with the proof-of-knighthood, since it motivates the necessary tournament. The proof-of-knighthood, in turn, separates the lovers and holds them apart until their final reunion, since in this theme the hero must immediately leave the tournament to launch his quest to free captives, abolish an ill custom, and punish the king's enemies.

The introduction of a courtship theme into this pattern of the "Fair Unknown" story is natural enough, since conventionally the hero in this theme wins a princess, and Malory had before him the example of *Ipomadon*, and perhaps other early romances in which the theme of exile, which is similar in many ways to the "Fair Unknown," is combined with courtship. But Malory so insists upon the correctness of Gareth's and Lyones' relations, one wonders if he did not also intend to draw a contrast between Gareth's chastity, however forced, and Gawain's celebrated incontinence. We have already noted that the temptation by Persaunt's daughter was probably suggested by the parallel temptations in *Ipomadon*, but Gareth's manner of dealing with the problem is reminiscent rather of *Sir Gawain and the Green Knight*. The second temptation scene, if that is what it should be called, occurs when Lyones and Gareth decide to forgo both the proof of worthiness required by the courtship theme and the rites of marriage. They agree to meet at night in the great hall of the castle. Just as the crucial point is reached, Gareth is attacked by a strange axe-wielding knight who wounds him, though the hero succeeds in beheading his attacker. When Gareth's wound is healed, he and his lady try again. The same knight attacks, and Gareth again beheads him, though he is again gravely wounded. Then Lyonet in the sight of all revives the knight and replaces his head. The whole incident is reminiscent of *Gawain and the Green Knight*, and we can at least speculate that Malory intended Gareth to have the virtues of that earlier, idealized Gawain. However that may be, it is clear that Gareth does not have the vices of the Gawain who appears in the rest of the *Morte Darthur*. He treats Persaunt's daughter in the most correct fashion, and no more than a healthy youthful desire accounts for his attempted misconduct with Lyones. Lyonet (in the damsel guide's usual role as teacher) forestalls them: "She lete ordeyne by her subtyle craufftes that they had nat theire intentys neyther with othir as in her delytes untyll they were maryed" (vii.22).

This episode provides the link between the first and second parts of the tale. Gareth is left wounded in Lyones' castle while the scene shifts to Camelot for the queen of Orkney's arrival. Then the narrative moves back to Lyones' castle, where Gareth, still wounded, but now knowing the value of patience, asks his lady to offer her hand as the prize at Arthur's tournament. The tournament thus functions not only as part of both the themes of courtship and proof-of-knighthood but also as a sort of necessary penance for Gareth and Lyones' "overhasty" behavior, and the attempted sin itself thus serves as a symbolic lowly position from which Gareth will rise by means of the proof-of-knighthood theme that informs the second half of the tale.

This skillful interweaving of thematic structures so that each supports and enriches the others shows how far Malory has progressed as a writer beyond the stage represented by *Sir Lancelot*. He is still concerned with balance and proportion, and he gives *Gareth* a carefully wrought pyramidal structure, with the center marked by the queen of Orkney's arrival and the two halves linked by the suspended episode that brackets that scene. Each half has its scene at court (Gareth's abasement at the beginning, his elaborate triumph at the end), a quest, and an elaborately narrated battle ("for deth," the battle with the Red Knight in the first half; and "for lyff," the tournament in the second). Moreover, the whole is nicely proportioned between the dominant theme—the "Fair Unknown," which is the major concern of the first seventeen folios—and the two subsidiary themes—the major concerns of the next seventeen (Caxton assigned exactly eighteen chapters to each half). However, in *Gareth* the obvious parallels serve only to add a pleasing dimension to the structure. In *Sir Lancelot* the parallels alone carry the major structural burden of the work, and, as we have noted, Malory sometimes had to insist too obviously on the existence of the parallel and had to force the thematic meaning upon his episodes. In *Gareth* the themes themselves supply the essential structure of the tale, and though it is even richer in incident than *Lancelot* it is a more coherent work, a tale unified in the thematic and well-proportioned manner of the best romances.

Gareth is not only satisfying in itself; it also functions well in the larger economy of the *Morte Darthur*. Like all the tales in the central part of the *Morte Darthur*, *Gareth* is concerned mainly with defining, by way of example, the High Order of Knighthood. The tales of Lancelot, Gareth, Tristram, and Galahad define the various levels comprehended by the High Order. Clearly Gareth represents the lowest level. As we have noted, though he becomes one of the four best knights in the world, he is displaced by Palomides in the following tale and remains a young knight who attains only the first stage of greatness. His tale ends not with a miraculous healing, such as Lancelot achieved in the preceding tale, but with a great display of material possessions—riches, a powerful retinue formed by his captives, and, perhaps most important to Gareth, a wife: "And there the kynge asked his nevew, sir Gareth, whether he wolde have this lady as peramour other ellys to have hir to his wyff" (vii.35).

Gareth chooses marriage. This may show his moral superiority to Gawain, who makes enthusiastic use of paramours, but it also symbolizes a lower order of knighthood than that of Lancelot, who refuses both marriage and paramours, or that of Galahad, who remains a pure virgin. Yet Gareth's knighthood is admirable, and it is a necessary part of the total spectrum that extends from young knights like Gareth through the four heroes of *The Book of Sir Tristram*—Lamerok, Palomides, Tristram, and Lancelot—to the four knights of the Grail—Lancelot, Bors, Perceval, and Galahad. Galahad, who achieves the Grail, represents the furthest extreme of impracticality, just as Gareth, who achieves all a gentleman needs to found a noble fifteenth-century family, seems to represent the nearest one could come to practicality and still remain within the limits of romance knighthood. Probably Malory's early readers found Gareth's more modest form of knighthood the most congenial of all. Riches, a noble wife, and a mighty retinue of the sort so necessary to the great households of Malory's time are an almost possible dream for fifteenth-century gentlemen who could never hope to see the Grail or love a Guenevere.

This is all part of the charm of *The Tale of Sir Gareth*, which is one of Malory's most satisfactory works. It succeeds at least partly because Malory, dependent mainly on his own invention, was fully in control of his materials. Most important, at this stage of his career he was fully in control of the thematic method of composition, which allowed him to solve the problem raised by his own taste for copiousness and variety and the demands of his genre for proportion and thematic coherence. It is pleasant to speculate—though impossible to prove—that Malory himself was pleased with his success in *Gareth* and was thereby emboldened to undertake his most ambitious thematically structured work, *The Book of Sir Tristram de Lyones*.

6

The Book of Sir Tristram

The Book of Sir Tristram de Lyones is the centerpiece of the Morte Darthur, a third of the entire work given over to a lively and leisurely account of Arthurian chivalry in all its variety, from the evil Breunys sanz Pité to the saintly Galahad. Its pages are crowded with knights, good and evil, with lovers, true and false, with "noble chyualrye, curteysye, cowardys, murdre, hate, virtue, and synne," and the effect is less of a stately tapestry than of a dazzling kaleidoscope of the color, sounds, and emotions of the chivalric life. Yet all is controlled in a solidly coherent, even elegant, thematic structure. It is true that Sir Tristram has had few official admirers. Some critics prefer the old poetic romances of Tristan (which are altogether different and which neither Malory nor the great majority of his readers knew anyway), and even Malory's admirers are apt to deplore the structural "failures" of Sir Tristram. The tale is a failure only from the standpoint of modern ideas of plot, and we must therefore give most of our attention to its thematic structure. However, Sir Tristram has had such a bad press that we should, simply to redress the balance, begin by noting some of the pleasures it offers any reader, whatever his expectations about narrative structure. The tale has many, and it is hard to believe that even the critics who think that "Malory would have done better to have left the Tristan alone" could fail to delight in this work.[1]

Malory himself obviously delighted in writing it. The prose Tristan, despite its length and complexity, is closer in spirit to his own work than any of the Vulgate romances, and he seems to have found it more congenial to his tastes than any of the French works he had previously used. It is a straightforward tale of chivalric adventure, spiced with humor and realism and very nearly devoid of the supernatural. Even the famous magic potion is of little importance in this version of the story and serves simply to reinforce a love that has already begun in the more human and naturalistic manner that Malory apparently preferred to the "faery" aspects of earlier romance.[2] Moreover, the prose *Tristan* had a hero whom Malory warmly admired. Tristram is, even more than Lancelot has yet been shown to be, Malory's ideal gentleman, the originator of the noble arts of the chase. Malory adds to his French source admiring comments on Tristram's invention of the "termes" of hunting (a purely English tradition),[3] and at one point he cannot resist breaking into the narrative in his own person to applaud the hero: "For, as bookis reporte, of sir Trystram cam all the good termys of venery and of huntynge . . . that all maner jantylmen hath cause to the worldes ende to prayse sir Trystram and to pray for his soule. AMEN SAYDE SIR THOMAS MALLEORRE" (x.52).[4]

When Tristram is imprisoned, Malory—who knew from personal experience what prison was like—is deeply moved. He expands on his source in a manner that shows his sympathetic understanding of his hero's situation (and that is also the closest we come to an autobiographical passage in the whole book):

So sir Trystram endured there grete payne, for syknes had undirtake hym, and that is the grettist payne a presoner may have. For all the whyle a presoner may have his helth of body, he may endure undir the mercy of God and in hope of good delyveraunce; but whan syknes towchith a presoners body, than may a presoner say all welth ys hym berauffte, and than hath he cause to wayle and wepe. Ryght so did sir Trystram whan syknes had undirtake hym, for than he toke such sorow that he had allmoste slayne hymselff. (ix.37)[5]

Lancelot's imprisonment in *A Noble Tale of Sir Lancelot* had not affected Malory this way. Certainly his own situation was on his mind when he wrote the earlier tales, for he prays earnestly for deliverance at the conclusions of both *The Tale of King Arthur* and *The Tale of Sir Gareth*. But he seems to have felt that Tristram, more than any of his previous characters, was an actual fellow man, whose sorrows were real and whose soul can benefit from our prayers.

Malory feels Tristram's joys as deeply as his sorrows. He becomes almost poetic (in a Chaucerian manner quite foreign to his usual narrative tone) in protesting his inability to describe the reunion of Tristram and Isode: "And to telle the joyes that were betwyxte La Beall Isode and sir Trystramys, there ys no maker can make hit, nothir no harte can thynke hit, nother no penne can wryte hit, nother no mowth can speke hit" (ix.17). And he becomes almost realistic when he turns aside from his tale to explain how it can happen that Tristram is overthrown, as if he fears that his readers might otherwise scorn his hero: "Here men may undirstonde that bene men of worshyp that man was never fourmed that all tymes mught attayne, but somtyme he was put to the worse by malefortune and at som tyme the wayker knyght put the byggar knyght to a rebuke" (ix.12). The confiding, slightly flattering address to the readers—"that bene men of worship"—helps to engage our sympathy with the hero and helps us to share at least some of the personal involvement Malory feels in this tale; he is not again so emotionally engaged with his narrative until he reaches the "most piteous" death of Arthur himself.

The idea that a major character sometimes suffers defeat might have seemed out of place in Malory's previous tales, but not in *Sir Tristram*. In this book even the best of knights grow tired during jousts and the greatest of champions are sometimes overthrown by lesser but freshly mounted men. In *Gareth* we saw the more usual romance hero, the young man who, apparently without any training, takes up arms and steadily triumphs from that day on. In the analogous tale of "La Cote Mal Tayle," which is intercalated in an early part of *Sir Tristram*, we are shown that chivalric combat is a skill that must be acquired by painful experience. Poor La Cote is knocked off his horse time and again, to the increasingly derisive comments of the Damsel Maldisaunt. Lest the reader share her scorn, Mordred lectures her on the facts of knightly life (ix.4). Young knights, he says, are at a disadvantage in mounted combat, for they lack experience; even Lancelot was often unhorsed when he first began to joust. On the other hand, he continues, young knights have an advantage on foot, for here strength and endurance are more important, and young knights are generally "better winded" than older men; hence, he concludes, the lady should note that though several older knights have overthrown La Cote, they have all carefully avoided fighting him on foot. All this strikes us moderns, who no longer joust, as obviously true, and it must have struck fifteenth-century readers, accustomed to romances that seldom made such concessions, with even more force. One can easily imagine Malory's gentlemanly readers, many of whom must themselves have jousted, murmuring "hear! hear!" They must have been delighted at this evidence that the great adventures of *Sir Tristram* happened in a real world rather like their own.

This is not to say that *Sir Tristram* is a "realistic" work. Mordred's lecture on the facts of knightly combat comes in the midst of a conventional "Fair Unknown" situation. The same is true of the other realistic details that so frequently appear in this work. The specification of the exact amount of money that Guenevere spent in her search for Lancelot—20,000 pounds—is a much-admired touch of Malory's "realism." But the search is caused by Lancelot's running mad for love in a most conventional and unrealistic way. The realistic details therefore do not make *Sir Tristram* a realistic novel, but they do help give its portrayal of knighthood a solid and lifelike texture, strong enough to survive even the commonsense objections of Sir Dinadan.

Dinadan, the comic antagonist of lovers and knights, serves much the same function as the realistic details; he brings a commonsense perspective to the action, voicing—and thus anticipating and setting aside—the objections that even a sympathetic reader might sometimes wish to raise to the endlessly jousting knights and bedazzled lovers that populate this tale. Dinadan shares Theseus's opinions of lovers ("Who may be a fool but if he love?"; *Knight's Tale*, v. 1797), and so far as he is concerned those who run mad for love, as both Tristram and Lancelot do, have merely made fools of themselves. In a well-known speech he tells Tristram, "Suche a folyshe knyght as ye ar . . . I saw but late this day lyynge by a welle, and he fared as he slepte. And there he lay lyke a fole grennynge and wolde nat speke . . . and well I wote he was a lovear" (x.55).

Dinadan has much the same opinion of overenthusiastic jousters. When he falls into the company of Tristram, he is dragged into joust after joust. No sooner do they win lodging at a castle by this means than Tristram tells him they must joust again, for two knights have come demanding "the custom of this castle." " 'What aray ys thys?' seyde sir Dynadan. 'I wolde fayne have my reste' " (ix.24). Tristram drags him out and forces him to joust. Then, while lacing poor Dinadan's helmet back on—he has just taken a painful fall—Tristram insists that they continue the fight on foot. " 'Ye fare,' seyde sir Dynadan, 'as a man that were oute of hys mynde that wold cast hymselff away. And I may curse the tyme that ever I sye you, for in all the worlde ar nat two such knyghts that ar so wood as ys sir Lancelot and ye, sir Trystram!' " (ix.24). Yet Dinadan, who mocks the higher forms of knighthood, true love and knight-errantry, simultaneously affirms their value. As we are told several times over, he is a friend to good knights and an enemy to evil ones, thus by his actions showing that he shares the system of values that he comically attacks. He takes part in tournaments, detests King Mark, is a true friend to Tristram, and finally shares the fate of so many good knights, for he is killed by Gawain and his brothers.[6] Dinadan allows the reader to smile at the excesses of chivalry from within the system and thus to admire the chivalric heroes even while conscious of the commonsense objections to which he gives voice.

Dinadan's merry japes are not always as amusing as the other characters seem to think (Mark Twain, in *A Connecticut Yankee*, unkindly labeled him "Sir Dinadan the humorist" and supplied him with hoary jokes of the chicken-crossing-the-road variety), but his presence is a reminder of the broad variety of incident in this book, from low comic horseplay through the high and solemn mysteries of the Grail. Few romances contain much in the way of humor, and we seldom see romance heroes carrying on like high-spirited boys to the approving delight of the other characters. Guenevere, the distant *domina* of *Sir Lancelot* and most other previous romances, is here shown as much more a woman, a hearty character who relishes a good laugh. When, at the tournament of Surluse, Lancelot playfully knocks Dinadan senseless, dresses him in a woman's garment, and brings him into the hall, Guenevere laughs so hard that she falls to the ground (x.49). We may deplore her sense of humor, but we must also admire the sheer gusto of a character capable not just of ladylike smiles but of great belly laughs.

This is, much more than the previous tales, a work of strong and varied emotions, and Guenevere, like the other characters in this book, displays a whole range of emotional states—passion, anger, jealousy, and sorrow, as well as laughter and joy. Characters in *Sir Tristram* are capable of losing their tempers, as Lancelot does while jousting with Tristram (ix.36). And they can suffer from conflicting emotions, as shown best by Palomides, whose combination of genuine admiration for Tristram and uncontrollable jealousy of him is very convincingly set forth. Guenevere is possessed even of a fine cattiness. When Elaine comes to visit Camelot,

Than the quene sente for sir Launcelot and bade hym com to her chambir that nyght, "other ellys," seyde the queen, "I am sure that ye woll go to youre ladyes bedde, dame Elayne, by whome ye gate Galahad."

"A, madame!" seyde sir Launcelot, "never say ye so, for that I ded was ayenste my will."

"Than," seyde the quene, "loke that ye come to me when I sende for you." (xi.7)

There are few passages in Malory's earlier works that seem so clearly to catch the tone of living speech, and almost nothing like this in previous English romance—only Malory's own *Gareth* does so well. Yet this is not unusual in this tale, where the dialogue often carries a colloquial force and ease almost dramatic in quality. When Lancelot was tempted by the four queens in *Sir Lancelot*, he replied, "Yet had I lever dye in this preson with worshyp than to have one of you to my peramoure, magré myne hede" (vi.3). Alexander the Orphan, when confronted by a similar situation in *Sir Tristram* (he too a prisoner of Morgan and having learned of her intentions), is more direct: " 'A Jesu defende me,' seyde sir Alysaundir, 'frome suche pleasure! For I had levir kut away my hangers then I wolde do her ony suche pleasure' " (x.38). Malory usually handles dialogue well, and even in his early tales the characters speak with a directness and vigor unusual in earlier English romance. But, beginning in *Gareth* and much developed in *Sir Tristram*, the speeches seem much more lively and colloquial (a skill that Malory may have learned from *Tristan*, which handles dialogue in an easy and direct fashion—the quotation above is taken by Malory directly from the French).[7] For example, there is the matter of oaths and curses, which, as P. J. C. Field remarks, give a realistic dimension to dialogue, perhaps especially in the late Middle Ages, when the English aristocracy seemed particularly fond of such expressions.[8] There is hardly a curse in *King Arthur*, and in *Sir Lancelot* most of the characters do Chaucer's Prioress one better and use "by my faith" as their strongest oath. The somewhat more forceful language of *Arthur and Lucius* is almost always part of the alliterations carried over from the *Morte Arthure* (" 'By God,' seyde sir Gawayn"). But in *Gareth* and even more in *Sir Tristram* the characters swear vigorously and often. Oaths, exclamations, and proverbial phrases lend a colloquial flavor to the speech of these works: " 'What, nevewe?' seyde the kynge. 'Is the wynde in that dore?' " (vii.35); "I may well beare the blame, for my bak is brode inowghe" (x.78).

All this makes *Sir Tristram* one of Malory's liveliest works. It may also more interfere with than enhance its enjoyment by modern readers, for the frequent liveliness of the dialogue, the lifelike emotions often displayed by the characters, and the occasional veri-similitude of the narrative may only reinforce the reader's assumption that Malory was trying, and failing, to write a modern sort of narra-tive. This is unfortunate, for one of the main pleasures of the tale is its elegant thematic structure, which reveals Malory in the fullness of his narrative powers. In *Sir Lancelot* and *Gareth* Malory had shown that he could control a narrative by means of theme, but he was most suc-cessful (in *Gareth*) when he most freely invented his materials. In *Sir Tristram* Malory resolved the difficult problem of reducing a very complicated French narrative into a coherent work controlled by themes that seem, as in *Gareth*, inherent in the materials rather than, as in *Sir Lancelot*, imposed upon them.

More important to the works that followed, Malory now shows that he can maintain thematic control even over materials that have a historical structure. The French *Tristan* is a biography, and its basic narrative structure is supplied by the facts of Tristan's life. Malory does not remove this history. In his version the "horizontal" motiva-tion of historical narrative remains, both in the general movement of the narrative and in the cause-and-effect relations of some of the epi-sodes. Occasionally Malory even strengthens this motivation; he gives reasons for Mark's hatred and for Isode's love, and the actions of the characters often seem to grow quite naturally out of the situations. All this adds to the verisimilitude of the narrative and the characters, who are more lifelike in *Sir Tristram* than in any of the previous tales. Nevertheless, Malory is finally less interested in the history of Tris-tram than in the image of chivalry embodied in his career. That is why *Sir Tristram* ends with the hero at the summit of his career, happily in possession of the fair Isode and proved the equal of Lancelot. The his-tory remains incomplete, with "no rehearsall of the thirde boke" (though the essential facts have been given), but the themes are fully realized, and the image of the bright afternoon of Arthurian chivalry is complete.

Malory still compresses, reorganizes, and "anglicizes" his source in the manner we have examined in the preceding works (his tale is about one-sixth the length of the corresponding parts of the French *Tristan*). But now he is more comfortable with a longer form, and though he divides his narrative into units, they are stages in the thematic devel-opment rather than self-contained parts of a small cycle in the manner of *The Tale of King Arthur*. Also, he now writes a somewhat more complicated narrative, with more *entrelacement* than in his preceding tales, though this is more often an *entrelacement* of themes than of episodes, with the bracketing episodes and structural parallels serving to establish a series of significant analogies, so that the adventures of a single knight are extended to comprehend the adventures of many knights in one coherent work. [9] All this—the longer narrative form, the *entrelacement* of themes on a more extensive scale than in the preceding tales, and the "development by analogy"—is necessary to the creation of a comprehensive portrait of Arthurian chivalry, and it makes a more complicated narrative than any of the preceding. Yet *Sir Tristram* has the narrative virtues at which Malory aimed in his earlier tales, and, because the *Morte Darthur* is itself an education in the reading of romance, by the time the sympathetic reader reaches this tale he has been well prepared to understand and appreciate its more complicated structure.

The principal theme of *Sir Tristram* is clear: Tristram's attainment of full knighthood as one of the four best knights in the world. The main stages of his quest are to attain a seat at the Round Table, which he achieves at the end of the sixth chapter (taking Vinaver's divisions as "chapters"), to win full possession of his lady, which he achieves in the tenth chapter, and to bring the Saracen Palomides to baptism, which he does in the final paragraphs of the tale. This three-stage quest is contained within a two-part structure (parts 1-6, 7-15 in Vinaver's edition), roughly equivalent in length, except for the story of Lancelot and Elaine, which is bracketed within the conclusion to the second part. Much else is included within the parameters of the overall thematic structure. The adventures of Lancelot and La Cote Mal Tayle are included within the account of Tristram's quest for a seat at the Round Table. The stories of Lamerok and Alexander the Orphan are interwoven with the account of Tristram's final break with Mark and his union with Isode at the Joyous Garde. And within the story of Tristram's bringing Palomides to baptism are the tale of Palomides' own quest and the intercalated tale of "Lancelot and Elaine," with its accounts of Lancelot, Bors, and Perceval. Yet these other adventures are held firmly within the main theme, and by the use of analogy, contrasts, and parallels—such as the great tournaments that occur in each of the sections—the multiplicity of character and episode serves to illuminate rather than obscure the movement of the narrative within this sound, even elegant structure.

This thematic structure is Malory's own invention. In the French

Tristan, as in *Sir Tristram*, the first battle of the hero's career is with the Irish champion Marhalt, and the first stage of his career is his attainment of a place at the Round Table. The French narrative, as we have already remarked, is historical in structure. The fight with Marhalt is connected to Tristan's relations with Mark and Isode, but, aside from demonstrating his prowess, it has nothing to do with his achievement of a place at the Round Table. Malory creates a new role for Marhalt: he makes him a famous knight of the Round Table, a role already established in Marhalt's first appearance in the cycle, in the passage we examined at the end of *The Tale of King Arthur*. Tristram's killing Marhalt, now one of Arthur's knights, therefore defines his relation to the Round Table at the very beginning of the action: he begins as a foe of Arthur's knights and, like any worthy foe, he must end as a member of the Round Table. The duel with Marhalt thus initiates the theme of enmity and reconciliation that ends in the expected battle to a draw with Lancelot that finally qualifies Tristram for a place at Arthur's court. When he comes there he finds that Marhalt's seat now bears the legend "This is the syege of the noble knyght sir Trystramys" (x.6), and this stage of the narrative ends with a great feast and with Malory's careful recapitulation, lest we miss the thematic function, of Tristram's first battle. The theme initiated in that battle is now complete.

However, other themes have been begun and left incomplete, thus providing for the continuation of the narrative. Tristram is now a member of the Round Table, but he is still separated from Isode. He must prove his worthiness of her, break finally with Mark, and bring her to Joyous Garde—Lancelot's castle. Tristram continues to increase in renown, becoming ever more nearly equal to Lancelot, here living with Isode at Joyous Garde, as Lancelot and Guenevere do later. In the next stage of the action he will assume Lancelot's role as inductor of knights into a higher form of knighthood, when in the last episode of the tale he brings Palomides to baptism.

Palomides' baptism, the main unifying theme of the second part, is also Malory's invention.[10] In the French version Palomides is a Saracen and, as in Malory, his jealousy of Tristan is expressed in a recurring theme of enmity and reconciliation that must be resolved in a culminating duel. Malory's Palomides is not simply an enemy of Tristram but much more emphatically an unbeliever who must be brought to the Christian faith. He is labeled Palomides the Saracen when he first appears as Tristram's enemy, in the tournament in Ireland, where

Tristram earns the love of Isode. In his next appearance, when he kidnaps Isode and is then attacked by Tristram, Isode stops the fight: "And yett hit were grete pyté that I sholde se sir Palomydes slayne, for well I know that by the ende be done sir Palomydes is but a dede man, bycause that he is nat crystened, and I wolde be loth that he sholde dye a Sarazen" (viii.31). When Isode says that, we know that Tristram must never kill Palomides but must ultimately bring him to baptism as part of the general pattern of reconciliations (with Isode, with Arthur's knights) that has already been set in motion.

The battle to a draw between Tristram and Palomides, the required means of reconciliation, is twice scheduled and twice canceled, each time serving as a thematic bracket that binds together the major divisions. Tristram's quest for a place at the Round Table ends with his duel with Lancelot, but that fight was supposed to have been between Tristram and Palomides. The two had agreed to meet at the "perown" near Camelot, but Palomides, as we later learn, was imprisoned and could not keep the appointment, and Lancelot rode up instead. His duel with Tristram resolves the theme of enmity and reconciliation insofar as it concerns Tristram and Arthur's court, but it leaves Tristram and Palomides' enmity unresolved, thus serving to bind the first stage of Tristram's career to the second. Again, after Tristram is united with Isode at the Joyous Garde and the tournament of Lonezep has provided proof of Palomides' worthiness, the two schedule another duel. This time Tristram cannot keep the appointment, since he has been wounded, and the battle is again delayed, providing a thematic bracket for the "Lancelot and Elaine" section. When that is complete, the long-expected duel takes place, and it marks the end of the entire tale.

Within these larger thematic structures Malory reshapes the narrative to conform to thematic patterns that give both meaning and coherence to the parts. In the first stage of Tristram's career, his quest for a seat at the Round Table, the main thematic pattern is the proof-of-knighthood theme that we examined in *Gareth*, and in its broadest outline Tristram's early career is quite similar to Gareth's: each begins in an unpromising situation, Gareth a kitchen knave scorned by Arthur's knights and Tristram a Cornishman and therefore an object of scorn (as usual in the *Tristan* romances) to the knights of the Round Table (viii.16-17). Each begins his career with a duel with one of Arthur's best knights (Gareth briefly fights Lancelot, Tristram fights Marhalt) and then engages in a series of adventures in which he gains the love of a lady. Then, disguised, each triumphs in a tournament (Tristram at the Castle of Maidens). The identity of each is revealed at the end of the tournament, but then each rides off for another series of adventures that culminate in a duel to a draw; Gareth fights his brother, Gawain, and Tristram fights his best friend, Lancelot. In each case the duel to a draw is followed immediately by the hero's reception into the Round Table.

The sympathetic reader can hardly miss this, since he comes to *Sir Tristram* immediately after reading *Gareth* (and the intercalated story of "La Cote Mal Tayle" serves as a further reminder of this thematic pattern), nor can he easily miss the familiar romance motifs of which the major theme is composed: Tristram begins as a young unknown who comes to a foreign court seeking knighthood; he defends this court against a foreign enemy but is then exiled (by his wound) and goes to another foreign court where, disguised, he triumphs in a tournament and wins the hand of a princess (the "exile" motif we examined in *King Horn*). Then, as required in a "courtship" motif, he is separated from his love. He returns to Mark's court, where he engages in a fabliauxlike affair with Segwarides' wife and fights his first battle with Lancelot's kin, Bleoberis (viii.13-18): this episode is the beginning of the reconciliation, first with Lancelot's kinsman and then with Arthur's court, necessitated by the killing of Marhalt. Then, on Mark's orders, Tristram leaves Cornwall for a foreign land, where he fights another of Lancelot's kinsmen, Blamour, whom he magnanimously spares. He thus earns the friendship of all of Lancelot's kin ("reconciliation," which is almost always achieved by duels in romance), and by his victory in this duel, which he fought on behalf of Angwysh, Isode's father, he again earns possession of his lady (viii.24; as required in the "courtship" theme, where each separation requires a new battle to prove the hero's worthiness of his lady). On the way home he wins a victory at the Castle Plewre ("abolishment of ill custom") and earns the friendship, after the customary duel (viii.27), of Galahalt the Haute Prince (further reconciliation with Arthur's knights). Then he returns to Cornwall, where Palomides appears and abducts Isode. Tristram battles Palomides, but spares him at Isode's insistence (viii.29-30; the battles with Palomides thus serve as a convenient bracket to the courtship theme). Isode sends Palomides to Camelot with the message that there are but four true lovers in the world, "And that is sir Launcelot and dame Gwenyver and sir Trystrames and quene Isode" (viii.31).

This marks the end of the first stage of Tristram's quest for membership in the Round Table, roughly corresponding to the first stage of Gareth's quest, which also concluded with his winning the love of his lady. The narrative is composed of the motifs of exile, courtship, and reconciliation woven together to form a tightly structured unit. Even the fabliauxlike affair with Segwarides' wife has its place in the thematic structure—as an amusing ironic contrast to those other wives in *Sir Tristram* whose affections stray but who remain "true lovers," as a means of showing the beginning of Mark's hatred for Tristram, and as a way for Tristram to earn the friendship of Lancelot's kinsmen. Finally, and perhaps most important, the Segwarides episode has an educational function, necessary for the candidate for full knighthood, who must, like Gareth, learn courtly manners at the same time that he proves his military virtues. Later Tristram will show the same self-control in bearing insults as Gareth (when he must put up with the complaints of Persides and Palomides), but at this stage he is learning to be a true lover as well as a great knight, and his education appropriately contains a lesson in the character of women: after Segwarides' wife has scorned both him and Bleoberis, he concludes, "For her sake I shall beware what manner of lady I shall love or trust" (viii.18). Having learned this, he is ready to offer his love to a more worthy lady, La Beall Isode.

The second stage of Tristram's quest for a seat at the Round Table—and his ultimate rank as second only to Lancelot—is in its broad outlines a doubling of the first, perhaps necessarily so, since it is an extension of the usual proof-of-knighthood pattern (Gareth wins his lady and then goes disguised to the tournament; Tristram wins his lady, and then the second stage of his adventures intervenes before he goes to the Castle of Maidens). Again Tristram battles one of Arthur's knights, Lamerok (viii.33), and again this initiates an enmity-reconciliation pattern of action, especially significant since Lamerok is one of the four best knights among whom Tristram is to be numbered. Then, because of a wound, Tristram again travels to a foreign land to seek a cure at the hands of the king's daughter Isode, though this time Isode la Blaunche Mains, daughter of Howell of Britainy. Though his marriage to this Isode is never consummated (because, Malory says, the book "makyth mencion that the lady wente there had be no pleasure but kyssynge and clyppynge"; viii.36), it leads to a renewal of enmity with Lancelot, who swears that henceforth he will be Tristram's mortal foe. This must finally be resolved by the duel to a draw required as the conclusion of the proof-of-knighthood theme.

Again Tristram abolishes an ill custom (at Castle Plewre in his first set of adventures, now at the Isle of Nabon le Noir; viii.39). Then, just as the two battles with Palomides marked the limits of the first stage of his quest for a place at the Round Table, he now meets Lamerok again, battles him to a draw, and swears friendship (ix.10-11). Two of the four best knights are now reconciled, but Lancelot remains his mortal enemy. Therefore, when Kay, Tor, and Brandelys invite him to the Round Table, for "ye are the man called now moste of proues excepte sir Launcelot," he declines: "God thank them all . . . but as yet I fele well that I am nat able to be of their felyship, for I was never yet of such dedys of worthynes to be in the companye of such a felyship" (ix.15). Tristram not only must earn Lancelot's friendship, he must conform to the thematic pattern. Like Gareth, he must pass through stages, each qualifying him for the next. Though he is not yet of "such dedis," he is now worthy to undertake the final stage of his quest for membership in the Round Table—tournament (in disguise) and quest (for a duel to a draw).

The theme, as we have seen in *Gareth*, requires that Tristram prove himself in the physical presence of those whose regard he seeks, Arthur and Lancelot, and he must do so in disguise. Therefore, Tristram now begins concealing his name. He rescues Arthur but rides off without revealing his identity (ix.16). Then he returns temporarily to Cornwall, where he is again united with Isode. He becomes jealous of her kindness to Keheydyns (as Palomides is jealous of him), and this enmity again separates him from Isode. He runs mad for love (like Lancelot later), a necessary penance for his affair with Isode la Blaunche Mains (just as Lancelot's madness is penance for his affair with Elaine), and a necessary proof that, despite his lapse, he is indeed a true lover and therefore eligible for the level of knighthood to which he aspires.

When he is cured of his madness, he is formally banished from Cornwall (a necessity, since he must be released from his allegiance to Mark before he can become Arthur's knight), and leaving Isode behind, though having proved his worthiness of her, he sets out for Logres. After a series of adventures, which reassert the continuing themes of Tristram's relations to Palomides and Lancelot, he arrives at the great tournament at the Castle of Maidens, where he triumphs in disguise but is recognized and immediately leaves (ix.34-35). This is the pattern we saw in *Gareth* and, as in *Gareth*, Arthur's knights now set out in quest for him, and Lancelot swears he will not return to the court without Tristram.

Again a brief series of adventures serve as preliminaries to the
required duel to a draw. The enmity between Tristram and Arthur's
court is temporarily renewed when Tristram brings to the tournament
at Hard Roche the shield devised by Morgan to reveal Guenevere's
guilt, just as Lamerok had brought the magic horn to Mark's court.
Likewise, the enmity between Tristram and Palomides is renewed
when Tristram is imprisoned and must patiently bear Palomides'
insults (as Gareth and La Cote must bear the insults of the damsel
maldisaunt) and again when they agree to meet at the stone marker
that Merlin had placed near Camelot in *The Tale of King Arthur* when
he prophesied that at this "perowne" should fight "two of the beste
knyghtes that ever were in knyge Arthurs day and two of the best
lovers" (x.5). Palomides, as we later learn, is imprisoned, and the
knight who rides up to give battle at the appointed time is Lancelot.
He and Tristram fulfill the prophecy; both disguised, they fight for
four hours until they learn one another's identity and each surrenders
to the other. Tristram is thus finally reconciled with Lancelot (and
through him with Arthur and his court) and proved to be of such
deeds as show his worthiness of fellowship in the Round Table, where
he now takes Sir Marhalt's place, magically inscribed with his own
name.

The achievement of near equality with Lancelot completes another
thematic pattern. It was introduced immediately after the tournament
in Ireland, when a damsel tells Tristram that surely he must be the
great Lancelot. He replies, "Wete you well that I am nat sir Launcelot,
fayre damesell, for I was never of such proues. But in God is all: He
may make me as good a knyght as that good knyght sir Launcelot is"
(viii.10). God, and Malory, have done just this. This relation t
Lancelot informs the entire tale, and Malory emphasizes the analogy
throughout his entire *Book of Sir Tristram.* Yet in the first part of
Tristram's quest for knighthood, Lancelot hardly appears. His name is
constantly invoked, beginning with the damsel's mistaking Tristram
for Lancelot. Then come the battles with Lancelot's kin, Bleoberis and
Blamour, which end with the declaration that thereafter "all the bloode
of sir Launcelott loved sir Trystrames for ever" (viii.23). After the
encounter with Galahalt at the Castle Plewre, Lancelot appears briefly
in the narrative as the rescuer of Gawain. But, though Tristram says,
"Of all the knyghtes in the worlde I moste desire his felyship" (viii.27),
he and Lancelot do not meet. Indeed, he and Lancelot barely see one
another—except in tournament or when one or both are disguised—
until their battle at the "perowne," and though references to Lancelot

continue throughout the adventures following Castle Plewre, Lancelot himself plays no significant role in the tale until the intercalated story of "La Cote Mal Tayle."

The reader, who has not long before finished *The Tale of Sir Gareth*, finds much that is familiar in this tale, at least in the beginning, where we have the same "Fair Unknown" situation. But as the tale develops it becomes clear that Lancelot is the real hero. La Cote is often bested; Lancelot is the one who abolishes the evil customs and rescues prisoners, first from Brian de les Isles and then from Pleynorous, and the former enemy who surrenders to Arthur comes not from La Cote but from Lancelot. One has the impression that the story starts out as a tale of La Cote and then becomes a tale of Lancelot. In a sense, it is a tale of Lancelot from the beginning, for La Cote's career explicitly repeats Lancelot's own youthful adventures. When La Cote comes to the court and asks for knighthood, Lamerok and Gaheris urge Arthur to grant the boon, "For, sir, and ye be remembird, evyn suche one was sir Launcelot whan he cam fyrst into this courte, and full fewe of us knew from whens he cam" (ix.1). When La Cote is unhorsed time after time in his first few adventures, Mordred tells the lady to stop criticizing the youth, and he convincingly explains why young knights are often put to a disadvantage on horseback (as noted earlier). Then he adds: "For in lyke wyse, sir Launcelot du Lake, whan he was fyrste made knyght, he was oftyn put to the worse on horsebacke" (ix.4).

Lancelot even comes in for some of the abuse that La Cote must suffer, for when he joins the pair and attempts to mollify the lady's anger, she turns on him: "And ever that damesell rebuked sir La Cote Male Tayle, and than sir Launcelot answerde for him. Than she leffte of and rebuked sir Launcelot" (ix.5). This may be the natural outcome of intruding on private quarrels, but it is a most unusual touch in the theme of the "Fair Unknown," and it seems designed mainly to reinforce the parallel between La Cote and Lancelot. From this point on, Lancelot becomes the hero of the tale, rescuing La Cote from better knights and defeating the principal antagonists. Perhaps this is why Malory calls this story "La Cote Mal Tayle" at its beginning but refers to it differently at its conclusion: "Now leve we here sir Launcelot du Lake and La Cote Male Tayle, and turne we unto sir Trystram" (ix.10).

In the context of this whole section of *Sir Tristram*, the intercalated tale of La Cote thus serves as a reinforcement of the analogy between Lancelot and Tristram, a reminder that Lancelot, like Tristram, also began as an obscure knight and slowly worked his way to full knighthood. The "realism" of La Cote—the fact that young knights must learn how to ride and fight—contrasts with the great achievements of the youthful Tristram (who kills the more experienced Marhalt in his first battle), but it also reinforces Tristram's adventures, showing us not the unreality of his quest but other aspects of this theme, so that the quests of Tristram, La Cote, and Lancelot (perhaps also that of Gareth) unite to define more fully what the achievement of knighthood means.

After the story of La Cote is complete and Lancelot has thus been introduced into the action, he reappears throughout the rest of these first six "chapters." His adventures, mostly minor, are interwoven with the major adventures of Tristram, often in parallel forms, so that the suggested effect is of Lancelot following the same quest as Tristram, as indeed they are at the end, when each is explicitly seeking the other and thus moving toward the duel that Merlin prophesied. Immediately after Tristram settles his differences with Lamerok and rides away (ix.10-12), Lancelot appears, is momentarily Lamerok's enemy, and almost fights him but is then reconciled with him. Immediately before the tournament at the Castle of Maidens, and not long after Tristram has put to flight the thirty knights who intended to ambush Lancelot, Palomides rides up and unhorses Tristram; Lancelot appears, disguised, immediately avenges him, and then rides off (ix.28). At the tournament Lancelot shares the prize with Tristram on the third day, though he generously insists it be awarded to Tristram alone. When Tristram leaves, Lancelot sets out on a quest to find him (ix.36). And Tristram, after the tournament at Hard Roche, sets out to find Lancelot (x.1). When the two meet at the "perowne," Lancelot is also disguised, as if he were also proving his merits. Each has been engaged in a quest leading to this duel, Tristram directly and Lancelot by analogy, and when they meet we are well prepared to accept the equality this implies.

The next two stages of Tristram's career—his final winning of Isode and his reconciliation with Palomides—form a second half, which, like the first stage, has two divisions. This is linked to the first, as we have seen, by the incomplete themes of courtship (he is still separated from Isode) and reconciliation with Palomides. The two stages of Tristram's career in this half are not sharply distinguished, and it seems likely that Malory thought of the seventh through the thirteenth "chapters" (from "King Mark" to "Sir Palomides") as a single unit, roughly equivalent to the first even in length. As might be expected, the second part contains a number of parallels to the first. Again Tristram journeys to Mark's court, where again he fights a duel on Mark's behalf for the "trwage of Cornwall." Thus he again proves his right to La Beall Isode, and again he is exiled by Mark's treachery. In this part, as in the first, there is an intercalated tale of a young man who wears the pierced doublet of a father he is sworn to avenge (La Cote in the first part, Alexander the Orphan in the second). There are further parallels of theme and episode, and each part ends with a scheduled duel between Tristram and Palomides which does not take place. When they arrange for their second duel, Tristram reminds Palomides (and the reader) of the first: " 'But now I am remembred,' seyde sir Trystram to sir Palomydes . . . 'ye promysed to mete me at the perowne and the grave besydis Camelot' " (x.87). This is yet another speech of Malory's own invention, designed, like so much that he invents in this tale, to strengthen the parallel thematic structures.

However, this second part differs considerably in tone from the first. This stage of Tristram's career, his final winning of Isode, is the happiest part of his life, but his happiness exists within a context of treachery and impending tragedy. Many of the themes and motifs of the first part now reappear in an ironically reversed form. Immediately after Tristram is inducted into the Round Table, Mark, consumed by jealousy, sets out in disguise for Arthur's court. His journey (x.8-15) is a parody quest, a reversal of the usual journey of the virtuous young knight through a series of adventures to acceptance at Camelot. The old and evil Mark is mocked and humiliated (and, unlike Gareth and La Cote, learns nothing from it); his only victory is a treacherous murder of one of Tristram's knights, and his quest ends not with a duel to a draw with Lancelot but with Mark groveling before the great knight, who brings him as a disgraced prisoner to the court. Arthur generously forgives Mark, for Tristram's sake (x.16), and when Mark solemnly swears to be a good lord to Tristram, the two return to Cornwall together (x.22).[11]

Interwoven with this reconciliation, which the reader knows can only lead to a new betrayal, are the adventures of Lamerok, which contain the familiar motifs of the proof-of-knighthood theme. Lamerok abolishes an ill custom (x.17-18), fights to a draw with Palomides and exchanges vows of friendship with him (for all four of the best knights must finally be reconciled to one another), and then, appropriately disguised, he triumphs in a tournament. Having proven his worthiness of his lady, Morgause, he goes to her chamber. There, instead of a happy union, Gaheris enters and beheads Morgause, his own mother (x.24). When Lancelot hears of this, he warns Arthur that Gawain and his brethren will kill Lamerok, and we learn that in the quest of the Grail they kill Dinadan (x.25). Lamerok's quest had led to an outcome far different from what, on the basis of our previous experience of these motifs, we might have expected.

Lamerok provides an analogy to Tristram in the same way that Lancelot did earlier in the tale, though it is much less obvious. Few readers could miss the parallel between the two best knights even if Malory had not so often emphasized it (since the hero of *Tristan* was modeled on Lancelot).[12] Perhaps most readers would miss the more subtle analogy between Tristram and Lamerok did not Tristram himself draw the parallel: Lamerok, like Tristram, loves a lady who is (legally) in the control of his enemies. Isode is the wife of King Mark, who hated Tristram even before Isode came to Cornwall. Lamerok loves Queen Morgause, the mother of Gawain and his brothers, who believe, mistakenly, that Lamerok slew their father. (We might note that the discrepancy in ages between lover and lady is less important to the writer than the analogy this relation helps develop.) Because Lamerok fears the treachery of Gawain and his brothers, he will not even visit Camelot (x.49). His fears are well founded, for ultimately Gawain and his brothers do treacherously attack him, and Mordred kills him with a stab in the back. This detail of Lamerok's death is Malory's own invention. So too is Tristram's reaction:[13]

"And for suche thynges," seyde sir Trystrams, "I feare to drawe unto the courte of kynge Arthure . . . "
    "As for that, I blame you nat," seyde sir Gareth, "for well I undirstonde the vengeaunce of my brethirne." (x.58)

Yet, murderers as even Gareth admits his own brothers are, only Tristram fears to visit Camelot because of their vengeance. Apparently this is because he recognizes, as Malory intends us to recognize, in Lamerok's doleful career an analogy to his own. Much later in the *Morte Darthur* Malory reminds us of this parallel: "For there was never none so bewayled as was sir Trystram and sir Lamerok, for they were both with treson slayne: sir Trystram by kynge Marke, and sir Lameroke by sir Gawayne and hys brethirn" (xix.11).

Even before Tristram and Isode are united at the Joyous Garde, and well before Lamerok's death, the reader has been reminded that Tristram must eventually die at the hands of King Mark. At the end of "Alexander the Orphan," Malory—again in a passage of his own invention—tells us that Alexander and Tristram suffer the same fate:[14] "This false kynge Mark slew bothe sir Trystram and sir Alysaundir falsely and felonsly" (x.40). This is a sad conclusion to what is otherwise one of the happiest tales in the *Morte Darthur*. Alexander and his love, Alys la Beall Pelleron, are an attractive pair. Alexander is chaste and brave, Alys rich and beautiful, and there is great charm in the youthful enthusiasm apparent when they fall in love at first sight: "A swete Fadir Jesu! The I muste love and never othir!" "A Lord Jesu! Here have I founde my love and my lady!" (x.38-39). Moreover, Malory (again unlike his source) emphasizes that Alexander is of Tristram's family, Alys of Lancelot's. Their union in marriage seems a happy emblem of the friendship between the two greatest knights in the world, an assurance that though both Tristram's and Lancelot's loves must end sadly, the next generation at least will find happiness: "And so they wente into their contrey of Benoy and lyved there in grete joy" (x.39). The rhyme, which is probably unintentional, lends this an almost lyric note.

But the tale does not end here, and Malory adds the report—another in this series of ironic reversals—that Alexander, like Tristram, is treacherously murdered by his own uncle, King Mark.

The tales of Lamerok and Alexander thus lend a dark, ironic undertone to what is, from the standpoint of Tristram alone, the most happy period in his whole history. We need no "rehearsall of the third book" of the *Tristan* to tell us the sad outcome of Tristram's love for Isode, for we are told it, by direct statement and analogy, even as we are shown the lovers at their most joyful moments. Nevertheless, the movement of *The Book of Sir Tristram* is not toward the triumph of treachery (though we know that is Tristram's ultimate fate). Despite all the treacherous acts we hear about—the murders of Lamerok, Alexander, and Tristram—we only hear about them. We are not actually shown Lamerok's death, and we learn no details of the murder of Tristram until the Grail quest is concluded and we come to the beginning of the end of Arthur's knights. There is treachery and hate as well as loyalty and love in *Sir Tristram*, and, as a comprehensive survey of chivalry requires, there are evil characters as well as good—Mark, the bad king, Gawain and his brethren, the "four dangerous knyghtys" (x.63) in sharp contrast to the four best, and Breunys sanz Pité, the antitype of the good knight. But they fade into

the background in the final stage of Tristram's career, in which the
dominant theme is reconciliation.

In this stage Palomides comes to the foreground. As we have noted,
Palomides' religion has been stressed since the beginning of the tale,
and Isode has ordered Tristram to spare him, for she will not suffer
him to die unbaptized. In romance noble Saracens, like Priamus in
Arthur and Lucius, must earn baptism by their valor. At the tournament at Surluse, the Haute Prince is so impressed by Palomides' valor
that he urges him to become a Christian. This is analogous to the scene
in which Kay, Tor, and Brandelys invite Tristram to join the Round
Table and Tristram replies that he is not yet of "such dedis of worthynes." Palomides replies: "I woll that ye all knowe that into this londe I
cam to be crystyned, and in my harte I am crystynde, and crystynde
woll I be. But I have made suche a vowe that I may nat be crystynde
tyll I have done seven trewe bataylis for Jesu sake, and then woll I be
crystynde. And I trust that God woll take myne entente, for I meane
truly" (x.47).

He repeats the same sentiment before his battle at the Red City,
affirming again that he cannot be baptized until he had done his seven
battles ("within lystis," as he now specifies; x.63). Finally, before his
last duel with Tristram he tells him, " 'I have but one batayle to do,
and were that onys done I wolde be baptyzed.' 'Be my hede,' seyde sir
Trystram, 'As for one batayle, thou shalt not seke hyt longe' " (xii.13).
In short, for Palomides Christianity is a higher order of knighthood,
for which he must qualify himself by means of a quest. Thus, the
proof-of-knighthood, which ended tragically in the case of Lamerok,
appears again, giving shape to Palomides' quest to overcome the evil
within himself and to achieve both reconciliation with Tristram and
baptism. He engages in preliminary jousts (x.63-64), abolishes an ill
custom, wins the first day's prize at the tournament of Lonezep (x.65),
undertakes a new quest, and fights a duel to a draw with his own
brother (x.82-83), thus qualifying himself for the adventures that lead
to the final duel with Tristram (delayed to provide a bracket for the
Lancelot-Elaine story), which ends in Palomides' baptism, the sacramental symbol of reconciliation.

The story of Lancelot and Elaine, the last major section of *Sir Tristram*, functions in the larger economy of the *Morte Darthur* as a "first
chapter" of *The Tale of the Sancgreal*. It tells of the birth of Galahad,
introduces the Grail itself, and establishes the characters of Bors and
Perceval, who, with Lancelot and Galahad, are the four Grail knights

who replace the four best knights of the world as the narrative focus in the next tale. The story thus serves as the bracketing episode that binds *Sir Tristram* to *The Sancgreal:* first we are told the histories of Galahad, Bors, and Perceval; then we pause for the conclusion of the Tristram-Palomides adventure, and then *The Sancgreal* itself begins with the great feast of Pentecost, to which Tristram and Palomides come and at which Galahad makes his first appearance. Though it has been thought that the very existence of *Sir Tristram* disproves the idea that Malory intended his tales to form a coherent "hoole book of kyng Arthur," the presence of the Lancelot-Elaine story shows that *Sir Tristram* would be incomplete without *The Sancgreal* and *The Sancgreal* would lack a beginning without *Sir Tristram.*

The function of the Lancelot-Elaine story within *Sir Tristram* itself may not be so obvious. Its subject matter seems so unrelated to the rest of the tale that one is tempted to think that the whole story of Lancelot and Elaine could be removed without harming that story or *Sir Tristram* as a whole. Yet Malory brackets this story within the Palomides-Tristram adventure, as if to force us to consider it in that context and to recognize the significant analogies between this and the earlier adventures in *Sir Tristram.* The most obvious analogy is in the narrative organization. The general course of Lancelot's adventures in this last section—faithlessness, madness, proof of worthiness—is the same as in Tristram's adventures in the last part of the first section of *Sir Tristram.* Tristram journeyed to another kingdom where he succeeded in an adventure that won him the hand of the king's daughter, Isode la Blaunche Mains, whom he faithlessly married. He returned to his own country and was forgiven, but a new breach with Isode caused him to run mad for her love. Then he adopted a disguise and proved himself worthy of a place at the Round Table in a series of adventures that culminated in a battle to a draw with Lancelot, after which he came to Camelot. In "Lancelot and Elaine," Lancelot travels to another kingdom, the land of King Pelles, where he succeeds in an adventure (curing a maiden and killing a serpent; xi.1-2) that wins him the hand of the king's daughter, Elaine, on whom he faithlessly, though enchanted, begets Galahad. He returns to his own country, where he is forgiven, but a new breach with Guenevere causes him to run mad for her love (xi.8). Then he adopts a disguise (xii.6) and proves himself worthy of resuming his place at the Round Table in a series of jousts that culminate in a battle to a draw with Perceval, after which he returns to Camelot.

Besides the general parallel in narrative movement between Tristram's earlier adventures and Lancelot's, a number of motifs and themes from other parts of *Sir Tristram* reappear in this section. The treachery of Gawain and his brothers is recalled (in a passage of Malory's own invention)[15] when Perceval, Lamerok's brother, visits his mother. Jealousy again is important (in Guenevere and in Bromell la Pleche, who hopelessly loves Elaine and lies in wait for Lancelot; xi.3), but here, as in the Palomides story, the final outcome is reconciliation, for the dominant concern in the whole last part of *Sir Tristram* is sacramental (here the Grail, baptism in the story of Palomides).

Interwoven with the main theme of Lancelot's faithlessness, madness, and reassertion of worthiness are the stories of Bors and Perceval. Bors provides an obvious analogy to Lancelot. Immediately after Lancelot has seen the Grail and engendered Galahad, he disappears from the story (we learn that he is kept in Morgan's prison for six months, but nothing more), and Bors appears to defeat Bromell la Pleche, who is jealously waiting to waylay Lancelot. Then Bors sees the Grail, and we learn that he also has a bastard son, Helayne le Blank (xi.4). After further adventures with the Grail, Bors is sent to Lancelot to tell him to repent, for though he excels in earthly things he has many superiors in spiritual matters (xi.6). Bors then disappears from the tale until the end, where we learn that his bastard son is now fifteen years old and has gone to Camelot to be knighted, and that Galahad is now fifteen years old and will come to Camelot to be knighted at the next Pentecost (xii.10).

Perceval, the other Grail knight, is younger than Bors, and his set of adventures is suggestive of the usual proof-of-knighthood theme. He had appeared briefly earlier in *Sir Tristram* (x.23, 51, 54), but now he comes to the foreground in his first adventures. We learn that he began with a touch of the "Fair Unknown" about him, for he, like La Cote and Gareth, was mocked and scorned by Kay and Mordred (xi.12), and his quest concludes in a battle to the draw with Lancelot. First he frees Persides and fights a battle to a draw with Lancelot's brother, Ector. Both are cured of their wounds by the Grail. After this he disappears from the narrative, off on his quest for Lancelot, who has adopted the disguise of Le Chevalere Mafete and fights all comers at the Castle Corbin, where, after Lancelot has defeated five hundred knights, Perceval finally arrives. The two fight to a draw and then recognize one another (xii.8) and—when Lancelot learns that Guenevere has forgiven him—Perceval, Ector, and Lancelot set off for Camelot, where they are joyfully received.

The duel to a draw that culminates Perceval's quest to find Lancelot and proves him worthy of the Grail quest is also a culmination of Lancelot's own quest to prove his worth, the last stage of his penance (which began with his madness) for his disloyalty to Guenevere. The Grail quest can only be achieved by Lancelot's fathering of Galahad, which is a sin, albeit a *felix culpa*, both against the sternly virginal code of the Grail and Lancelot's own chivalric code. On both counts, he must redeem himself by reestablishing his worthiness; the brief imprisonment by Morgan adds further motivation for this. Hence, he must begin in a low position (his madness) and move through the initial humiliation to which knightly aspirants like La Cote and Perceval are subjected, to a series of knightly deeds culminating in a great feat of arms at a tournament (to which his Castle Corbin adventure is equivalent) followed by a battle to a draw (with Perceval, who is now assuming his role as the second-best of the Grail knights) and a triumphant reception at Camelot.

Lancelot's new proof of his merit also serves to bring him emphatically back to the reader's attention. Thus far in *Sir Tristram* we have followed the adventures of Tristram, Lamerok, and Palomides, each of whom appears in a proof-of-knighthood theme. The first of the four best worldly knights has played an important role throughout, but he had not yet followed a quest entirely his own. The story of Lancelot and Elaine provides the occasion for that quest and allows Malory to suggest a balance in subject as well as form between the beginning adventures of Tristram and the final adventures of Lancelot.

The story of Lancelot and Elaine is thus a necessary part of *Sir Tristram*, the structure of which would be greatly weakened if it were removed. And this story of seduction, illicit love, adultery, and jealousy fits easily into *Sir Tristram*, where these have been major concerns throughout; it would clearly not fit in *The Sancgreal*, with its arcane symbols and generally unlifelike characters.

The appearance of the Grail in *Sir Tristram* does cast a supernatural light on the action, lending new meaning to Palomides' quest for the sacrament of baptism and to Tristram's role as the inductor of his former foe not into the Round Table but into the new life of Christianity. Yet *Sir Tristram* also casts its more lifelike aura on the Grail. Elaine must seduce Lancelot because of the ancient prophecy, and their affair begins in an atmosphere heavy with Grail symbols and enchantment. But the next morning the atmosphere is one of lively realism. First

Lancelot is enraged with Elaine for her trickery, and he even draws his sword against her. She kneels naked before him, and he ends by gently kissing her, "for she was a fayre lady and therto lusty and yonge" (xi.3).

Lancelot does not callously desert Elaine, as the more chaste Bors apparently deserted Brandegoris's daughter; and Elaine, however much her initial action might have been governed by the Grail prophecies, really loves Lancelot. She visits Camelot, facing up to the imposing wrath of Guenevere, and she has Brusen again trick Lancelot into her bed—this time for pleasure rather than prophecy—where the two enthusiastically embrace, "as was a kyndely thynge" (xi.8). When she comes upon the mad Lancelot she is moved to tears. She arranges for his cure (by the Grail), and though he longs for Guenevere he stays with Elaine. She knows that she cannot have Lancelot's love, but he has hers: "I woll lyve and dye wyth you, only for your sake; and yf my lyff might nat avayle you and my dethe myght avayle you, wyte you well I wolde dye for youre sake" (xii.5). In this book of hopeless lovers, jealousies, and anger, this is an especially affecting expression of generous constancy. It helps make Elaine an attractive figure and perhaps thus helps the reader more easily forgive Lancelot his sins, both real and courtly.

More important, the realistic presentation of Elaine's passion for Lancelot keeps the story from being a merely mechanical and symbolic enactment of the Grail prophecies. The chief Grail knight, we know, must be descended from the blood of Pelles and Lancelot, a happy union in contrast to the unhappy outcome of the union of the families of Lancelot and Tristram in "Alexander the Orphan." The importance of families in *Sir Tristram*—the feuds and the alliances that are developed here—prepares us to accept this situation. The verisimilitude of the presentation lets us almost believe it. The appearance of the Grail and the beginning of the fulfillment of the Grail prophecies could have been the most symbolic and lifeless part of the whole book. Instead, this is its most emotional part: Elaine's passion, Lancelot's madness and penitence (told at much greater length than Tristram's), Bors's anger at Guenevere, Guenevere's jealousy—all provide the Grail with a context of turbulent and very human emotions. The adventures of the Grail will become more and more spiritualized and symbolic, even surrealistic, in the following *Sancgreal*, but we are here given the impression that the miracles begin in an almost real and very human world and develop by their own logic from that. This is by no means the least of Malory's achievements in this remarkable *Book of Sir Tristram.*

With the brief conclusion in which Palomides' jealous love is transformed into the same generosity of spirit shown by Elaine and in which he is then brought to baptism, the book ends, with "no rehearsall" of the third part of the French book. There can be none, for the work is complete as it stands. From the standpoint of "plot"—more properly, the "history"—a number of conflicts remain unresolved. The four "daungerous knyghtes," Gawain and his brethren, are still plotting against good knights and remain unpunished for their murder of Lamerok; Palomides, redeemed, is still pursuing his questing beast; and Breunys sanz Pité, unrepentant evil, is still at large. Most obvious, King Mark still plots against Tristram, whom we know he will finally kill.[16] These are all matters of the history of the Round Table, left unresolved to provide for the continuation of the cycle. The enmity of Gawain and his brethren for Lamerok and his kin, and by analogy for Lancelot, will be resolved only when Lancelot and Gawain meet for their final battle (xx.13), when the murder of Lamerok will be recalled to remind us of the analogy and thus add an extension of meaning to the final duel (Lancelot's last battle) and bind together the parts of the cycle. Likewise, the later history of Tristram and Mark is not properly a part of Tristram's rise to the highest form of knighthood, though our knowledge of Tristram's end provides an ironic counterpoint; it is rather an analogy to Lancelot's later career, and so we are not told the details of Tristram's death until they are needed to establish this analogy—at the moment of Lancelot's healing of Sir Urry (xix.11), his highest achievement, and at the moment of his break with Arthur (xx.6).

None of this would have fit in *The Book of Sir Tristram*, which is concerned not with the complete history of the knights—that belongs to the whole cycle—but with Tristram's rise to the highest form of earthly knighthood, symbolized by his attainment of the role of inductor of others into knighthood, usually restricted to Lancelot. Tristram's quest provides the thematic structure within which his is but one of many quests—those of La Cote, Alexander, Perceval, Lamerok, Palomides, and Lancelot. Each by parallel or contrast helps define the quest in which Tristram is engaged and, by the very multiplicity of perspectives, helps us to recognize that the real subject of this book is not Tristram's quest but knighthood itself, which is thus shown to be a more complicated matter than it appears to be in the story of any one individual. All the characters in this book—the evil as well as the "good knights"—supply varying perspectives on the code of chivalry, which had been abstractly stated in *The Tale of King Arthur* and exemplified in *A Noble Tale of Sir Lancelot* but is here shown to be not one but a copious variety of "worshipful ways."

The question that remains is one that may hardly have occurred to Malory or his readers but has become important in modern criticism: What was Malory's attitude toward the worshipful ways of chivalry? Did he regard chivalry as an abstract ideal, a part of a golden world in which the good and the perfect are the same? If he did, then the imperfect knights of *Sir Tristram* must indeed embody a "moral degeneration" that shows "not only the essential inadequacies of the chivalric society but the ways in which those inadequacies bring about the fall of Arthur's realm."[17] Malory, Vinaver wrote, would have "indignantly" denied such a proposition.[18] He might also have failed to understand it, for "the chivalric society" was for him not an abstraction but the society in which he lived, complete with the imperfections that always exist in this sinful world, and the worshipful way of chivalry was not a dream of the past but the standard by which good and evil knights are to be judged both in literature and in life.

III

Malory and Chivalry

7
Fifteenth-Century Chivalry

Why should Malory, or any other fifteenth-century writer, have chosen to compose a romance? Malory's time was almost three centuries removed from the first great age of romance, and it was a time in which realism was rapidly spreading through all forms of art. The genre of romance had grown old, and the fifteenth century would seem to offer barren ground for new growth. Yet this age of newly discovered realism witnessed a great outburst of creativity in romance, providing a new impetus and a new form for the prose romance, which now became the dominant mode of aristocratic fiction, as it was to remain for centuries to come. A taste for realism, which Malory's readers have so often admired, and an admiration for romance chivalry apparently complemented one another.

This is most obvious in *The Book of Sir Tristram*, Malory's fullest depiction of chivalry and one of his most realistic tales. The realism of *Sir Tristram* is not, of course, primarily a product of its structure, its narrative technique, or even of its occasional specific details and brief descriptive passages. It arises rather from the relative sense of probability in the adventures narrated, from the liveliness of the dialogues, and, most of all, from the attitude that Malory adopts toward his characters and expects his readers to share. At times he seems to regard Tristram as a real person, and he directly calls upon his readers to pray for Tristram's soul as earnestly as he begs them to pray for his own release from prison. This is perhaps understandable, for Malory and his contemporaries were convinced that Tristram had indeed once lived and that the story of his adventures was basically a "true history." However, at other times Malory explicitly asks his audience to judge the actions of Tristram and the other characters in the light of their own experience. He assumes that they share Tristram's (and Malory's) love of the hunt, admire his expertise at jousting, and know enough about jousting that, when Tristram is unhorsed, Malory can appeal to his readers, "men of worship," to remember that no one can always be victorious and that at times even the best may be overcome by a weaker man. The statement is a commonplace of fifteenth-century discussions of chivalry, though not of earlier romance,[1] and it has an obvious rhetorical function—a *captatio benevolentiae* that establishes a comfortable, semiconspiratorial relation between narrator and reader. Yet these appeals to the audience seem also to be based on the assumption that narrator, reader, and fictional character actually share a common experience of the chivalric life that is the main subject of both *The Book of Sir Tristram* and the *Morte Darthur* itself, as if Malory were dealing with an aspect of fifteenth-century life as well as Arthurian romance.

This was indeed the case. In the year 1469, when he finished the *Morte Darthur*, chivalry as Malory understood and described it was a fact of aristocratic life. It was, as we shall see, only a part of aristocratic life, for only in fiction were nobles always and everywhere engaged in peculiarly chivalric deeds. Nevertheless, Malory lived and wrote in the late Middle Ages, when, for the first time in Western civilization, noble gentlemen actually jousted to gain honor and please their ladies, tried to be true lovers, went on quests, and attempted to realize in their own lives the ideals of romance chivalry.

This is of great importance to our understanding both of Malory's realism and of his attitude toward chivalry. We often think of romance as the antithesis of reality, as a genre "that possesses the mystery and spell of everything remote and unobtainable."[2] Yet, as we have seen, fifteenth-century adaptations of older romance show little concern with mystery and spell; they concentrate instead, as Malory does, on action and "historical" fact. The new prose romances composed in this period characteristically emphasize realistic geographical settings, deal with the possible more often than the marvelous, and frequently employ realistic details of action, manners, and speech. The heroes of these romances are larger than life and engage in deeds greater than real men could have performed, and to that extent they do indeed share with the old romances a sense of the unobtainable. But that remains in the background, and to a surprising degree fifteenth-century romance is a realistic genre, elevated in style but often mimetically true to the aristocratic life of the time. Martín de Riquer's comparison of historical records to fifteenth-century Spanish and French romance led him to conclude that many of the prose romances of the time "are not pure fantasy but realistic reflections of the life of the time, based on social realities as firm as those that can be found in a fabliau, in a novella of Boccaccio, or, much later, in the Spanish picaresque."[3] Even Malory's Arthurian tales, more fantastic than many original fifteenth-century romances, reflect the real chivalry of the time, heightened and idealized but based firmly enough on reality that the gentlemen for whom Malory wrote could recognize the contours and many of the actual details of the chivalric life of their own day.

This is not the usual understanding of Malory's relation to fifteenth-century life, and to demonstrate this fact will require an extensive discussion and some repetition of historical facts that may already be well known to the reader. Yet they will bear repetition, for the problem of Malory's "realism" and the even more important interpretive question of Malory's relation to his subject depend on our understanding of his relation to the chivalry of his own time. For that we have been dependent on historians' interpretations of fifteenth-century life, and literary scholars have remained content with the interpretations provided by historians of some generations past. Whatever attitude critics in recent years have ascribed to Malory—nostalgic, revivalist, condemnatory—most have accepted without question R. W. Chambers' dictum: "The world to which the *Morte Darthur* belonged had passed away before the book was finished."[4] More recent studies, such as Arthur Ferguson's *Indian Summer of English Chivalry*, as well as Johan Huizinga's earlier *Waning of the Middle Ages*, should have taught us better, for they demonstrate how strong chivalric ideals remained in Malory's time and long after.[5] But, perhaps because Ferguson and Huizinga stress ideals rather than practices, students of Malory have continued to assume that by the fifteenth century the practices of chivalry had long since passed away, leaving only empty rituals and tarnished forms.[6] Malory must therefore have looked back on chivalry as with "a desire to oversimplify and turn away from the present,"[7] perhaps even with a sense of tragic despair, knowing that chivalry included within itself the causes of its own destruction.[8] Perhaps, as the most recent study has it, he even regarded chivalry with a critical realization of the "fallaciousness of reviving the moral demands of one age, the demands of a chivalric society, as a guide to another."[9] Each of these interpretations is possible, even inevitable, if we assume that the chivalry of Malory's day survived only as a historical and literary ideal, its actual practices long since abandoned.

Every reader of late medieval history is aware that this is not altogether the case, that there were knights in Malory's time who attempted to perform chivalric deeds, that there were great tournaments, and that jousting was an international sport eagerly cultivated by the leading nobles of the age. Yet these seem a poor thing, mere empty display, because most of us are convinced that these were the last vestiges of an earlier golden age in which large numbers of knights lived lives of pure and chaste devotion to the chivalric code. We owe this idea largely to Léon Gautier, who, unlike earlier historians who had placed the golden age of chivalry in the fifteenth and sixteenth centuries, was convinced that chivalry flourished and triumphed in the conquest of Jerusalem in 1099.[10] Gautier believed that chivalry was a stern and ascetic ideal, a true "eighth sacrament," as he called it, and it was based, he claimed, on ten commandments, which Gautier himself wrote on the basis of his reading of the chansons de geste.

The romances that succeeded the chansons de geste in the early twelfth century were also, Gautier believed, accurate reports of the daily life of the nobility, and they therefore showed that "the decline of chivalry set in sooner than one is apt to believe."[11] The decline, he explained, was probably due to the loose morals imported from the East (a touch of chivalry causing its own fall even this early), and the baneful influence of the Arthurian romances hastened the decay. There were, he observed, knights in the late Middle Ages, "But—what can one say?—the knights of the time no longer observed the commandments of ancient chivalry."[12]

Gautier's rigid exclusion of Arthurian romance from his exemplars of chivalry did not survive, but his conviction that there was an early golden age did, and as late as 1949 Gustave Cohen could still dismiss fourteenth- and fifteenth-century chivalry in the same way Gautier did almost a century before, by explaining that the knighthood of the later period was no longer "a wandering life, consecrated to the redressing of wrongs and the protection of the weak by individual intervention to correct social injustices."[13] Certainly there is none of this sort of naiveté in Sidney Painter's or Richard Barber's histories of chivalry[14] or in the works of Huizinga and Ferguson, but even in reading these scholars one feels the faint presence of Gautier's idea that chivalry began in a burst of glory and then declined into its waning or Indian summer rather than, as earlier historians believed, "progressed" to its flowering in the late Middle Ages and early Renaissance.

There was, of course, no golden age, no period of history in which noble warriors universally followed the improbably pure standard of conduct that Gautier attributed to the early crusaders. As Painter writes, if the ideals of chivalry had ever had any widespread effect on society, "One would expect to find a time when knights refrained from rapine and casual manslaughter, protected the church and the clergy, and respected the rights of helpless non-combatants in war. I find no evidence this was ever the case."[15] Certainly the late Middle Ages generally offer as dismal and unromantic a prospect as any other period, perhaps more, since they are better documented. Kenneth B. McFarlane has wisely observed: "It is obvious that those who wish to believe in a golden age when men's appetites were subdued by simple faith are well advised to seek it . . . in the period before 1066, for which there are practically no records. It is odd that it is the very richness of their sources which have given the later Middle Ages a bad name."[16]

Yet if there was a golden age of chivalry, a time when men at least tried to be chivalric knights, it was from the fourteenth to the sixteenth centuries. The ideals of chivalry seem to have been largely a literary invention, and it was not until the late Middle Ages that even the nobility was much influenced by literature. There were few knights in the twelfth or even the thirteenth century who had either the leisure or the literacy to hold the mirror of life up to art. Consequently the ideals of chivalric literature spread slowly, and not until the late fourteenth century was chivalry widely accepted by the nobility.[17] Thereafter the chivalric movement spread rapidly. This was, as Huizinga has described it, an age of "applied" literature.[18] Throughout Europe nobles strived to emulate in life the deeds they read about in literature, so that by the end of the fifteenth century chivalric idealism, far from being obsolete, affected "the entire politically active element of the commonwealth."[19]

The importance of literature in shaping the style of the aristocratic life was explained in this way by Baron de Lettenhove, the editor of Froissart:

The history of chivalry is naught else but the picture of the admirable

influence exercised by literature, in the name of religion and civilization, on the violent and brutal passions encouraged and propagated
by war. If Froissart and the other chroniclers of the time admire and
exalt chivalry, it is because they perceive that in subjecting kings
themselves to the duties of chivalry, and in placing the whole career of
a knight between the two extreme limits of a romance which was read
to him in his youth, and the chronicle by which his life was judged at
the end, they succeeded in giving to letters in the feudal world a more
exalted place than that which they had ever attained in Greece or
Rome.[20]

The good baron may exaggerate. Certainly it would be an exaggeration to say that the brutality of the Hundred Years' War was much
mitigated by chivalric ideals, which clearly affected the surface much
more than the substance of late medieval life.

Nevertheless, the romances provided an image of a secular golden
age that defined worldly virtue for the late medieval aristocracy.
Many aristocrats, if not most, were of course interested only in the
appearance of virtue, but whether one aimed to achieve the appearance or the reality, the means were clear: one must imitate in life the
manners and deeds of the heroes of antiquity. Richard II in England
and Charles VI in France were among the leaders of this movement,
sponsoring extravagant tournaments and chivalric ceremonials of the
sort that had heretofore existed mainly in the literary imagination. As
the chronicler of Saint Denis remarks when describing the knighting of
Louis of Sicily and Charles of Anjou at the court of Charles VI, this
was done according to the "ancient customs," and thus "these may
appear strange and extraordinary to those who know nothing of the
antique customs of chivalry."[21] They would have appeared less
strange to the next generation, Malory's, when the imitation in life of
the customs of the old romances had become widespread.

The idea that one could imitate in life the manners of the heroes of
romance seems absurd if we assume, as many older historians did,
that feudalism and chivalry were indissolubly mixed and that the disappearance of feudalism (which had, if not disappeared, greatly
changed in form by the fifteenth century) necessarily removed the
social basis of chivalry.[22] Certainly the chivalry of the eleventh and
twelfth centuries was a part of feudalism, and loyalty remained the
essential knightly virtue throughout the entire period. However, the
objects of knightly loyalty changed, and the romances that shaped
later ideals of chivalry had little to do with feudalism. The hero of a
romance is typically a landless knight, one who makes his way with

his sword and is too busy jousting and questing—engaged in the ceremonialized forms of combat typical of romance—to worry much about feudal obligations. The romance knight fights for honor and renown rather than for religion or his lord, and, insofar as feudal holdings are concerned, he fights *for* land, not because of it. Even if he should be heir to a kingdom, he is typically deprived of it (by a wicked steward, the upstart middle class) and must prove his worthiness in order to regain it.

Indeed, there seems to be an inverse relation between the weakening of feudal ties and the rise of romance chivalry. One might speculate that as power shifted away from the old agrarian aristocracy, from those who held land to those with skills and money, the almost inevitable response of the nobility was an insistence upon those qualities that set them apart as a class and an emphasis on an ideal of noble conduct that defined that class. If power and money were moving into the control of men of low blood with no sense of chivalry, how much more precious honor and high birth, to which the lowborn could not aspire! The middle class seems to have been rising since the Flood receded, and in every period since the Conquest one can find nobles complaining about upstart commoners, but in the fourteenth and fifteenth centuries the knightly class seems to have felt more threatened—perhaps with better reason—than in former times. In fifteenth-century books of protocol, such as John Russell's *Boke of Nurture*, we learn that a marshal at a feast had to worry about such ticklish questions as who rated higher, a poor noble or a wealthy commoner. And where did one seat the parents of a lowborn person who held a high office? And what did one do with a woman of low blood who was married to a knight?[23] The reaction of the nobility of the period was an increased insistence on the importance of noble blood, the beginnings of a definite and conscious class structure, and an enthusiastic cultivation of the ceremonial forms of chivalry.[24]

The feudalism that survived in Malory's England was what has sometimes been known as "bastard feudalism," a contractual, monetary rather than strictly feudal (land-based) relation between a great lord and a lesser nobleman; the great lord would pay a fixed fee or offer political protection in return for feudal services.[25] Loyalties shifted easily, and the lesser gentry tended to seek a "good lord" rather than serve a "natural" feudal overlord. Powerful men and their families thus gathered great retinues in order to grow more powerful, and the whole fluid scene was a long way from the ideally ordered and unchanging state to which earlier feudalism had at least aspired. Yet men of the time did not much notice how greatly feudal practices had changed, and those that they saw in their most accessible sources of earlier social history, the romances, were much like their own.

Indeed, the political organization of Arthur's England in Malory's book is surprisingly similar to fifteenth-century actuality.[26] The king presides over great family groups—Lancelot and his brethren, Gawain and his—who owe their first loyalty to their family leader (Lancelot's brethren once plot even to kill Tristram) and who look remarkably like the great families that controlled the destiny of Malory's England. A strong man can become more powerful, as Gareth does; his opponents seem to live in a feudal vacuum, as some did in the Wars of the Roses, when no man could be sure to whom he owed allegiance and lesser men necessarily shifted from one lord to another, seeking the security a great lord could afford. Each of Gareth's opponents shifts his loyalty from his former overlord to his new conqueror and swears homage in terms reminiscent of fifteenth-century feudal contracts.[27] Gareth thus builds the elaborate retinue that defined "great estate" in the fifteenth century, complete with the ceremonial officers so essential to the household of a great fifteenth-century lord.

Likewise, Tristram's obligation to Mark seems to depend more on Mark's good conduct than on any inviolable feudal bond, and, like many in the fifteenth century, Tristram easily serves two lords at once, Mark and Arthur. He leaves Mark's service when he thinks Mark has behaved badly, thereby in effect negating the feudal contract, and he returns only when his friends make Mark swear to be a "good lord" to Tristram, a phrase and practice reminiscent of the Pastons' maneuverings to gain "good lordship."[28] The "good lords" who gather great retinues confront the king constantly with the problem of the "overmighty subject," such as Gawain, who forces Arthur into the war with Lancelot, another subject grown so powerful that he can flaunt the royal authority. Arthur's problem in fiction is not far from the problems Edward IV and Henry VI faced in Malory's own time.

The people in such a period shift their loyalties all too easily from one king to another, as they alternated in actuality between Henry and Edward. In the *Morte Darthur*, when Mordred seizes the throne, "Than was the common voyce amonge them that with kynge Arthur was never othir lyff but warre and stryff and with sir Mordrede was grete joye and blisse" (xxi.1). Malory's contemporary, John Wark-

worth, made almost exactly the same point in his analysis of the political situation in England at this time: "The common people said if
they could have another king he would regain all his lost possessions,
and amend every corruption in the state, and bring the realm of
England into prosperity and peace; nevertheless, when King Edward
reigned, the people expected all the aforesaid prosperity and peace;
but one battle after another, and much trouble and loss among the
common people."[29] Malory himself was struck by the resemblances
between Arthur's problems and those of his own troubled times, and
he could not forbear directly addressing his readers:

Lo ye all Englysshemen, se ye nat what a myschyff here was? For he
that was the moste kynge and nobelyst knyght of the worlde, and
moste loved the felyship of noble knyghtes, and by hym they all were
upholdyn, and yet myght nat thes Englysshemen holde them contente
wyth hym. Lo thus was the olde custom and usayges of thys londe, and
men say that we of thys londe have nat yet loste that custom. Alas!
thys ys a great defaughte of us Englysshemen, for there may no
thynge please no terme. (xxi.1)

Men did indeed say this. Not twenty years before, Charles d'Orléans,
noting the problems of Henry VI, had written:

> Have not the English frequently betrayed their kings?
> Indeed yes; everyone knows of this.
> And again the king of their country
> Is now in perilous balance.
> Every Englishman strives to speak ill of him.[30]

This fact did nothing to shake Charles's faith in chivalry; he saw the
situation rather as a convenient opportunity for the king of France to
be "vaillant" and renew the war.

Malory's complaint about the fickleness of his time, like Caxton's
lament that the knights of his day were not as they had been of old,
has been used to reinforce the idea that fifteenth-century chivalry was
only a thin imitation of an earlier, better time, when noble self-sacri-
ficing knights actually lived lives of disinterested goodness. Students
such as Raymond Kilgour, in his *Decline of Chivalry*, rely on contemporary complaints as their main proof that chivalry in this century
was in a sorry state.[31] This misses the point. Chivalry is, among other
things, a moral code, and those who admire chivalry are by definition
moralists. Morality, of whatever sort, was always better in the past, is
always sadly declined in the present, and is therefore always in need of
revival. That is why the history of chivalry is a history of "revivals,"

characterized always by the conviction that the chivalry of the present day is but a sad shadow of some former time. In the twelfth century John of Salisbury complained at length in his *Policraticus* that the knights of his time had deserted the old ideals and had become vain, gluttonous, cowardly, and interested only in empty display.[32] About the same time Chrétien de Troyes began his *Ywain* with a lament that courtesy no longer existed. "But let us leave those that are living," he writes, "for I take it that a courteous man, though dead, is better than a living knave."[33]

Chrétien thought that courteous men had lived in distant antiquity, and John of Salisbury was convinced that there had been good knights in the previous age, before the Norman Conquest, when Harold, John's ideal, dealt with the Welsh in a satisfactorily bloodthirsty way. John could not know that later chivalric moralists would take his own time as the ideal age, for the age of perfect chivalry tended to move forward in later times. The latest chivalric moralist, Marc Vulson de la Columbière, was convinced that the chivalric life was still possible when he wrote his *Vray théâtre d'honnevr et de chevalerie* in 1648. The nobles of his own time, he sadly reported, had deserted the old ideals, and he published his narratives of great chivalric deeds—drawn mainly from the late fifteenth and sixteenth centuries— in the hope that they would inspire his contemporaries "du bien desir de les imiter et de les suivre."[34] His preface, Vinaver writes, bears a striking resemblance to Caxton's, "and his object is not much different from Malory's noble end."[35] Vulson was convinced that chivalry still flourished in the late sixteenth century. But that was when Sir Philip Sidney and Sir Henry Lee were participating in the Accession Day Tilts, which were a serious attempt to encourage a renewed "Protestant chivalry" by reviving the practices of the courts of Henry VIII and Edward IV, following the "ancient" rules drawn up by John Tiptoft in 1466.[36] Caxton, who lived during Edward's reign, was sure that the chivalry of his own time was a poor thing compared to the greater days of Henry V. But a sermon writer of that reign tells us that "the days are evil," whereas in the past "there were many strenuous knights in this land, alike of the Round Table as of the garter."[37] But at the time that Edward III founded the Order of the Garter to revive the ancient virtues of his grandfather's reign, chivalry, so Bishop Thomas Brinton stated, was in a very sad state.[38] Times were equally bad during the reign of Edward II, when, according to a contemporary poet, the nobles of the day were mere "carpet knights";[39] before that, when Edward I attempted to revive the ancient virtues, they must have been sadly needed, for even in the early thirteenth century the English preacher Odo of Cheriton was deploring the decline of knighthood and the French poet Guérin complained that knights everywhere were marrying commoners for the sake of money and thus chivalrous deeds were put aside and "nobility perishes."[40] In fact, as Gerald Owst has shown, the attack on the degeneracy of contemporary knighthood was almost a pulpit tradition, and the words of the twelfth-century churchman Peter of Blois were repeated, often little changed, throughout the centuries that followed; as Owst says of medieval preachers from the twelfth to the fifteenth centuries, "All, with one accord, look back from their own day to some golden age of chivalry in the past."[41] The same can be said of admirers of chivalry such as Caxton and Vulson de la Columbière.

Modern historians have nevertheless tended to agree with Caxton that chivalry was sadly declined in the fifteenth century. Of course, some historians have looked eagerly for signs of its decay, as did Charles Plummer, who scorned a code that "failed to conceal its ingrained lust and cruelty, and its reckless contempt for the rights and feelings of all who were not admitted within its charmed circle," or E. A. Freeman, who regarded chivalry as an outmoded aristocratic ideal as opposed to "the more homely virtues of an honest man and good citizen."[42] Even a sympathetic historian cannot miss the fact that there was a considerable discrepancy between ideals and actualities in the late Middle Ages, and the more we know about this period, like any other, the less ideal it seems. Caxton could see the faults of his own time but not those of the reign of Henry V, on whom he could look back as a mirror of chivalry, a worthy successor to Arthur.[43] The modern historian, who knows more about Henry's reign than Caxton did, must probably conclude with Painter that "Henry V and Bedford were cold-blooded conquerors, not chivalrous adventurers."[44] However, this could be said of rulers in any period, perhaps including our own. It is not remarkable that Henry V had a streak of the scoundrel in him; what is remarkable is that he strove at least to appear to be a chivalric conqueror on the pattern of the kings of old romance, challenging the dauphin to single combat in the style of Arthur. For him, chivalry defined a mode of conduct to which even kings must conform.

Of course, chivalry is an especially slippery abstraction, and where, when, even whether it existed depends on how one defines it. In its most abstract sense, Sir Walter Scott's idea that chivalry is a generosity of spirit, chivalry can and does exist in every time and place, for there are always some whose lives are occasionally sparked by a generous sense of personal integrity and consideration for others.[45] Likewise, if we think of chivalry simply as "the ideals and practices considered suitable for a noble,"[46] then we will find as many chivalries as there are times and places, since every society has a noble ideal, even though each may define "noble" in its own way. Only when we insist that chivalry be defined by some rigid code, such as Gautier's "ten commandments," can we decide that any one period had "true chivalry" and some other only a pale imitation.

Malory and his contemporaries were convinced that there was indeed such a code, a definite set of ideals and practices that defined what they called the High Order of Knighthood. A man who offended against that code was not worthy of knighthood in either fiction or life. When Lancelot hears of the conduct of Perys de Foreste Savage, he angrily asserts, "He doth shame unto the Order of Knyghthode and contrary unto his oth. Hit is pyté that he lyvyth!" (vi.10). Apparently Malory's contemporaries agreed. The chronicler Richard Grafton tells us that in 1463 one Rauf Grey, who was guilty of treason, "was disgraded of the high order of knighthood by cutting off his gilt spurs, rending his coat of arms, and breaking his sword over his head; and finally, his body was shortened by the length of his head."[47]

In its simplest aspect, the fifteenth-century code of chivalry was that to which Malory's knights must swear when the Round Table is first founded:

Never to do outerage nothir morthir, and allwayes to fle treson, and to gyff mercy unto hym that askith mercy, uppon payne of forfiture of their worship and lordship of kynge Arthure for evirmore; and allwayes to do ladyes, damesels, and jantilwomen and wydowes sucour, strengthe hem in hir ryghtes, and never to enforce them, upon payne of dethe. Also, that no man take no batayles in no wrongfull quarrell for no love ne for no worldis goode. (iii.15)

These are the basic virtues of knighthood, not very much different from those proclaimed at the council of Clermont as a guide for the first crusaders, though now there is less emphasis on service to the church and more on the social virtues necessary to the maintenance of the "common good."[48] As Charles Moorman writes, the knighthood of Malory's Round Table is "an attempt to create a new kind of chivalry, only hinted in the sources, a chivalry based on corporate values, in which the virtues of the romance tradition—the sense of honor and integrity, courage and prowess—would remain but would be diverted into socially useful standards."[49]

This is true, but the attempt was not Malory's alone. The late medieval belief that knighthood served the common good—"socially useful standards"—was almost universal by Malory's time. The Chandos Herald praised Edward III for maintaining the "bien publique," Christine de Pisan explained the obligations of chivalry to "la bien commune" and "la chose publique," and Malory's contemporary, John Hardyng, whom we know Malory read carefully, stated that Arthur's knights were sworn to defend

> The faith, the church, maidens, & widowes clene,
> Children also, that were in tender age,
> The commun profit ever more to sustene.[50]

The theme is found in Lydgate's account of the Round Table in *The Fall of Princes*, in the fifteenth-century poem *Knyghthode and Bataile* ("Res publica right commendabil is / If chevalers and armys there abounde"), in Caxton's *Book of the Ordre of Chyvalry*, and in many another work.[51] Moreover, it clearly underlies the oath taken by actual fifteenth-century knights of the Bath, who were charged to defend the faith, to be true of their word, to "sustain widows in their right at every time they will require you, and maidens in their virginity, and help them and succor them," to sit in no wrongful judgment, and to punish murderers and extortioners. When Rauf Grey was degraded of the order of knighthood, the heralds specifically reminded him of his violation of this oath.[52] Malory's formulation of the basic knightly code thus reflects the common understanding of his contemporaries. Even the injunction about ladies—"never enforce them"— which Vinaver thought inappropriate to a knightly vow, was not out of place. A contemporary French version of the oath administered to knights of the Round Table specifies that the knights were sworn not to take or touch any lady or damsel whom they had won by force of arms "unless she consents to it."[53] The oath of the knights of the Bath, "to sustain . . . maidens in their virginity," seems to imply the same, and being "forced" appears among the sufferings of fifteenth-century ladies that heralds were sworn to alleviate.[54]

Important as the code was, one could not become a knight simply by acting like one, for knighthood was restricted, at least in theory, to those of noble birth. The Wife of Bath's views on gentility show that there was a more democratic point of view, and John Tiptoft, in his *Book of Noblesse,* argued that true nobility rests in "a man's own virtue and manhood" and not in "the nobleness of birth" (pp. 226-227). This, however, is definitely a minority view. Malory and most of his contemporaries remained convinced that only those of noble birth could become knights. The author of *The Boke of St. Albans* (1468) disposed easily of the old revolutionary slogan "When Adam dalf and Eve span / Who was then the gentleman?" He wrote, "A bondsman or churl will say we all come of Adam. So Lucifer with his company might say we all come of heaven." He explains that Adam and Eve had no lineage and that therefore it is absurd to ask "Who was then the gentleman?" Lineage began with Adam and Eve's children, with some doomed to churldom and some destined for nobility.[55] Other writers are equally explicit. The author of *Knyghthode and Bataile* inserts an elaborate explanation of why knighthood is restricted to noblemen (vv. 271-279), a passage that Vegetius (the author of the *De re militari,* the source of this work) would have found puzzling indeed. Caxton, whom editors of Malory so often characterize as a shrewd businessman, supported the theory even at the expense of possible sales, explaining in the colophon to his *Book of the Ordre of Chyvalry* that his book "is not requisite for every common man to have but to noble gentlemen that by their virtue intend to come and enter into the noble order of knighthood."

The distinction was apparent in life as well as theory, and it was generally assumed that gentle blood was a prerequisite and that knighthood was reserved, in the words of a summons to Parliament in 1422, to those "gentlemen of birth . . . able to be knights."[56] Jousting, which in the late Middle Ages was an essential part of chivalry, was restricted specifically to the nobility, and challenges usually specified that only a gentleman might accept. Malory's famous contemporary, Jacques de Lalaing, announces in one of his *chapitres d'armes* that he will fight with anyone, "pourvu qu'il soit gentilhomme de toutes lignees."[57]

Malory is equally firm on the restriction of knighthood to the nobly born. Lancelot, despite Gareth's proven prowess, will not knight him until he knows "of what kyn ye be borne" (vii.5). Later he assures Arthur that he knows Gareth's name and lineage, "Or ellys I wolde nat have yeffyn hym the Hyghe Order of Knyghthode" (vii.18). The consequences that might have come from granting a churl this honor are shown in the experience of King Harmaunce of the Red City, who raised two children, apparently without knowing their low birth, only to have them betray and kill him. Malory is moved to intrude on his narrative, and as usual when he does so, it is because a point of the noble life is concerned: "And as ever hit is an olde sawe, 'Gyeff a churle rule and thereby he woll nat be suffysed,' for whatsomever he be that is rewled by a vylane borne, and the lorde of the soyle be a jantylman born, that same vylayne shall destroy all the jeauntyllmen about hym. Therefore all the astatys and lordes, of what astate ye be, loke ye beware whom ye take aboute you" (x.61). This attitude is far from Chaucer's more humane view, but it seems to reflect the beliefs of the fifteenth-century gentry to which Malory belonged and for which he wrote.

The one apparent exception to this rule is Tor, the reputed son of Aryes the Cowherd (whom Arthur does dub despite the fact that he does not yet know that he is King Pellinor's son), who shows his noble birth by his actions. As Aryes explains, "Thys chylde wol not laboure for nothynge that my wyff and I may do, but allwey he woll be shotynge, or castynge dartes, and glad for to se batayles and to beholde knyghtes. And allweyes day and knyght he desireth of me to be made knyght" (iii.3). Noble blood compels one to noble action, to deeds of prowess. The six knights who jousted to celebrate the marriage of Richard, Edward IV's son, in 1477 declared in their challenge that deeds of prowess were laudable and "This considered must move and stir all noble courages to employ their persons in these causes."[58] When Perceval's mother begs him and Agglovale to remain with her, he replies: "A, my swete modir . . . we may nat, for we be comyn of knynge bloode of both partis. And therefore, modir, hit ys oure kynde to haunte noble armys and noble dedys" (xi.10). Indeed, the gentleman who does not haunt noble deeds is guilty of sloth. As Hardyng and many another put it, "Honour and ease abideth nat together," and as late as the time of Vulson de la Columbière chivalric deeds would be recommended as a way of avoiding base "idleness."[59]

"Honour"—or, to use Malory's favorite word, "worship"—is the central concern of fifteenth-century knights in both fiction and life. It is a precise concept, and when Malory refers to his readers as "men of worship" he is not being merely polite. "Worship" is the proper quality of a good knight. The basic ethical code of knighthood to which Arthur's knights swear is of primary importance, since, like the evil knights in Malory or Rauf Grey in life, one can lose worship by committing the crimes it specifies. But one gains worship (emblemized in

Malory by membership in the Round Table) only by means of knightly acts. When Arthur knights Tor, he tells him "Be ye a good knyght"— the exact words used by English kings when creating knights of the Bath in the fifteenth century.[60] Then Arthur adds "and if ye be of proues and worthynes ye shall be of the Table Rounde" (iii.3). Real knights of the Bath were likewise admonished to gain worship by prowess and worthiness. The new knight had to wear a white lace on his shoulder

Unto that time that he get some manner of worship by deserving by witness of worthy knights and squires of arms and heralds duly afterward reported; which report must enter into the ears of the worthy prince that hath made him knight, or of some other, or else of some noble lady, for to take away the lace from the shoulder, saying thus: "Right dear lord, I have heard so much of your worship and renown that ye have done in diverse parts unto the great worship of knighthood to yourself and to him that made you knight, that [ye] deserve and right well that this lace be put and take away."[61]

A desire for this sort of good reputation, "worship and renown," had been a concern of noble warriors since at least the days of the *lofgeornost* ("most eager for praise") Beowulf, but the qualities of a worshipful warrior are now far more elaborate than those that one can earn by simple prowess (and Arthur specifies "worthynes" as well as "proues" to Tor). The noble warrior must aspire to the model knighthood defined by Ector in his threnody for Lancelot.

Thou were hede of al Crysten knyghtes . . . thou were never matched of erthely knyghtes hande. And thou were the curtest knyght that ever bare shelde! And thou were the truest frend to thy lovar that ever bestrade hors, and thou were the trewest lover, of a synful man, that ever loved woman, . . . and thou were the godelyest persone that ever cam emonge prees of knyghtes, and thou were the mekest man and the jentyllest that ever ete in halle among ladyes, and thou were the sternest knyght to thy mortal foo that ever put speere in the reeste. (xxi.13)

This is clearly an ideal of conduct much different from that of the early crusaders. The knight remains a Christian warrior, and Malory, by his emphasis on "erthely" and "synful," shows his awareness of the superiority of the perfect but impractical "celestial chivalry" of the Grail. Nevertheless, in this model of human knighthood earthly qualities are of great importance. Courtesy is as important as prowess, and so are manners ("jentyllest that ever ete in halle") and even good looks ("godelyest persone"). We see some of the same concern with good manners in the biographies of contemporary knights. The biographer of the earl of Warwick, regarded as the "fader of curtesy" in Malory's lifetime, gives as careful attention to the excellence of his hero's table manners as to his martial exploits. When Warwick visited the king of France, he sat at the high table and "so mannerly behaved himself in language and nurture that the Kyng and his lords with all the other people gave him great laud."[62] The mention of Lancelot's good looks in the catalog of his virtues is a reminder that fictional heroes are now handsome as well as brave and true. Malory's Scottish contemporary, Sir Gilbert Haye, specifies in his *Buke of Knychthede* that "beauty" is among the characteristics essential to a knight and that a man deformed in any manner in either body or visage must be denied knighthood, "the which excludes utterly all ignobility and vileness."[63] Even as late as the time of Sir William Segar, Queen Elizabeth's garter king of arms, it was assumed that a knight must be not only noble, skilled, and strong but also "well favored of face and comely."[64]

The ideal knight was, in short, a courtier as well as a warrior and, more important, he was a lover. In life as well as literature, "courtly love," or better, "chivalric love," became a serious concern of those who aspired to knightly virtue. The term "courtly love" is not in very good repute nowadays. It has become customary to deny that it even existed, and influential critics have warned us that to speak of courtly love in relation to late medieval authors such as Chaucer is "to foster a kind of historical desecration."[65] However, recent discussions of chivalric love have focused almost exclusively on the time when it was thought to have begun, the twelfth century. Older scholars, such as Gaston Paris, read the romances of Chrétien and the rules of Andreas Capellanus as social documents, and they were convinced that the noble lords and ladies of the court of Champagne actually lived and loved according to the precepts of courtly literature, with knights worshipping their ladies, usually from afar, and the countess presiding over solemn courts of love. More recently scholars such as John Benton, who studied the historical documents as well as the literary remains of the time, have demonstrated what should have been suspected all along: chivalric love was a matter of literature rather than life, and aside from the lyrics and romances of the time there is no evidence for the existence of courts of love, of the service of ladies, or of any of the manners and attitudes that we associate with this concept.[66]

I suspect that there must have been some traces of chivalric love in the life of the time. Surely there must have been some clever squires

who recognized the tactical advantages of "luf-talkynge" to young
ladies with a taste for literature. Certainly in later times unscrupulous
suitors were not above such stratagems. Henry, duke of Lancaster,
admits in his *Livre de seyntz medicines* that he was guilty of this in his
youth, and the Knight of La Tour-Landry warned his daughters
against such deceivers.[67] Likewise, there must have been a few salons
even in twelfth-century France in which *questions d'amour* were
debated, however lightheartedly, and in which sophisticated nobles at
least pretended to play the elaborate game of chivalric courtship as
described in the romances. That chancery records, chroniclers, and
sober ecclesiasts do not mention such frivolities is hardly surprising;
they are silent about many other aspects of the social life of the time. It
does not therefore follow that chivalric love had no basis whatsoever
in early medieval life and that any work which uses its conventions is
necessarily ironic, as D. W. Robertson would have it. It does follow,
however, that such courtly love as did exist was at most a marginal,
mainly literary phenomenon rather than a serious aspect of aristocratic life. One can hardly imagine a twelfth-century chronicler
praising a contemporary noble because he carried on in the manner of
Lancelot or Tristan.

That is exactly what fifteenth-century chroniclers and biographers
did, for in the late Middle Ages the situation was much different.
Sober historians believed that the Arthurian romances were true histories, accurate portrayals of ancient virtue. If the heroes of that
golden age were great lovers, then the heroes of the present must emulate them; the author of *Le livre des faicts du mareschal de Boucicaut*
explains the moral basis of love:

Who can be brave without love? Indeed, no one. Love banishes fear
and instills bravery, making one forget all pain and willingly perform
the labors that he undertakes for the one he loves . . . Thus one reads
of Lancelot, of Tristan, and of many others whom love brought to the
attainment of goodness and renown. Likewise, living in our own times
there are many such nobles in France and elsewhere whom we have
seen and yet see; thus one speaks of Othe de Granson, of the good
Constable of Sancerre, and of many others whom it would be long to
name and whom the service of love made valiant and virtuous.
(P.393)

Othe de Granson, the friend of Geoffrey Chaucer, and Boucicaut
himself, who was marshal of France, were important men of the time,
who virtuously strove to be good lovers as well as great warriors.

Fifteenth-century readers thus had no reason to doubt that courtly love existed. They had the historical evidence of the old romances that chivalric love, service to one's lady, was the source of chivalric virtue. And in the biographies of late medieval knights such as Boucicaut or Jacques de Lalaing they were shown that instruction in love was a necessary part of the education of a young knight who aspired to virtue.[68] The good Constable of Sancerre, Othe de Granson, and many others were living proof that the old love of the romances did exist in the real life of the times.

Of course, one may doubt that pure chivalric love was always and universally practiced even by exemplars like Boucicaut; the chivalric biographers and chroniclers of the fifteenth century probably selected and distorted in their way as much as the monastic chroniclers of the twelfth century did in theirs.[69] Nevertheless, throughout the fifteenth century knights at least publicly accepted the idea that love was the source of chivalric virtue, and they strove to do honor to their ladies. As late as the sixteenth century, Brantôme gives many examples of his own contemporaries, such as the chevalier de Bussi, who told Brantôme that he fought his celebrated duels and battles "not for the service of his prince, not for ambition, but for the sole glory of pleasing his lady." Brantôme proves that this is virtuous by using much the same argument as the author of Boucicaut's biography had used two centuries before: "And why have so many brave knights errant of the Round Table and so many valorous paladins of France in times past undertaken so many wars, so many long voyages, done such great expeditions, if not for the love of beautiful ladies whom they served or intended to serve?" (Oeuvres, IX, 390).

Though chivalric love is as difficult to define in the late Middle Ages as such abstractions are in any period, there was considerable agreement about its main characteristics. Of the many works devoted to defining love, Les cent ballades, composed in the late fourteenth century by four knights, including Boucicaut, to pass the time on their way to the Holy Land, is an especially clear statement of the commands of the God of Love and an especially interesting one, since we know that Boucicaut attempted to follow these commandments in his own life.

The basic commandment of the God of Love is that the lover be a loyal servant of his lady and seek renown by chivalric deeds in order to be worthy of her love. He must have the usual courtly virtues—good looks and good manners—as well as the military virtues, and the model lover-knight of the *Cent ballades* is well summarized in Ector's characterization of Lancelot at the end of the *Morte Darthur*. The lover, so we learn from the *Cent ballades*, must also maintain secrecy. This is common in late medieval discussions of love, not because adultery is condoned (neither it nor marrige is even mentioned) but because the great lovers of old maintained secrecy. Boucicaut in his own life kept his love secret even from the object of his desires, not daring to mention it until by martial deeds he had proven himself worthy of his lady's regard.

However vague the details of chivalric love might have been, they were well enough understood to be regarded as a set of laws, worthy of serious discussion. Though modern scholars have proved that there probably was no actual court of love in twelfth-century Champagne, late medieval readers had the authority of writers such as Andreas to prove to their satisfaction that such was indeed the ancient practice. And thus we find that in the year 1400 Charles VI of France founded a real Court of Love.[70] It had an elaborate set of rules and ceremonials and a long list of officers, among whom were the most important poets and nobles of the time, including the bishop of Paris. Like the various *puys* (some of which were also devoted to chivalric love), its concern was mainly literary. Its feast was Saint Valentine's Day, when amorous poems were read by the members. The rules specified that these works were not to be mere literary exercises, for each poet was obligated to write "about his own *amoreuse* and none other."[71] Moreover, the poems had to redound to the honor of ladies; there was an elaborate ceremony of degradation for any member who violated these rules, and the court issued a formal writ of banishment against Alain Chartier for writing *La belle dame sanz merci*.[72]

It all sounds like a solemn game, and doubtless for many of the participants it was, but the line between earnest and game is not easy to draw in an age so devoted to ceremony as this, and clearly some members of the court were sincerely devoted to *Amour*. Pierre de Hauteville, who held the office of *Prince d'Amours*, directed that on his tomb in the Church of Saint-Jacques de Tournai should be inscribed: "Here lies the noble Pierre de Hauteville . . . This . . . Pierre was known in his days as the Prince d'Amours . . . May all loyal lovers pray for his soul. Amen."[73] Boucicaut, who was also a member of this court, likewise took his duties seriously. He founded a special chivalric order, L'escu vert à la dame blanche, to honor ladies and "defend them in their rights."

There was a basic confusion about chivalric love, because the great lovers of old, such as Lancelot and Tristan, had been adulterers, and probably also because the service of ladies sometimes had that outcome even in the fifteenth century. Responsible public figures such as Boucicaut obviously could not condone adultery, and we therefore find a good deal of discussion about the differences between "true love" and lechery, or "false love." A devotion to true love would allow even a strict moralist such as Christine de Pisan, who was shocked by the immorality of the *Roman de la rose*, to celebrate the true servants of the God of Love.[74] The *Lois d'Amor* promulgated in 1356 by the Académie de jeux floraux, a forerunner of the Court of Love at Paris, defines love mainly as religious devotion, though chaste earthly love was also allowed.[75] This organization was a *puys* devoted to the encouragement of love poetry. It held its fête (as it still does) on the first of May, when the consistory of the Docteurs de la gaie science awarded the title of *Fin amant* to the winner of a poetic competition. The rules specified that the poems must be of sound virtue: "It goes without saying that anyone who seeks to compromise the feminine sex or whose writings tend to a culpable end, will be unworthy to receive a prize. Likewise, the author who writes of love, if he does not address himself to God or the Holy Mother, will be subjected to a careful examination by the *Mainteneurs* [the seven principal officers] and made to affirm, on oath, the purity of his intentions." The fourteenth-century Mainteneurs of the Jeux floraux were aware that there is good love and bad: "We must take the word love in a good sense, and indeed it is only spiritual love (*amor psychique*), honest love (*amor honnete*), and pure love (*amor pur*) which we shall always maintain here, and not the other sort, which will always be banished."[76]

As might be expected, it was generally held that true love flourished in the past but was nowadays fallen on evil times, when "the other sort" generally prevailed. Thus, as we have seen, the author of *Le livre des faicts du mareschal boucicaut* specifies that his hero follows the dictates of true love, pursuing love for honor and virtue rather than the delectation of the body, bestowing his devotion upon a worthy object, and keeping his passion secret, not even daring to speak to his lady, but rather singing, writing poems, dancing, jousting, tourneying: "But he was not so bold as to speak plainly his thoughts, as do those deceivers nowadays [*temps present*] who without desert go boldly to ladies and demand that they be loved" (p. 397). Malory is of the same opinion: "But nowadayes men can nat love sevennyght but they muste have all their desyres . . . But the old love was nat so. For men and women coude love togydirs seven yerys, and no licouris lustis was betwyxte them, and than was love trouthe and faythefulnes. And so in lyke wyse was love in kynge Arthurs days" (xviii.25).

Malory's idea of love was that of his time. His fictional knights, like contemporary real knights, strive to win honor for the sake of their ladies, thus becoming virtuous through love, and his ideal lover is a "trew lover," the *Loyal amant* of Boucicaut and many another writer of his day. The deeds that Malory's knights perform on behalf of ladies are extravagant, but hardly more extravagant than those of real knights of this period. Most readers of Froissart will recall the famous episode in which some of Edward III's knights, setting out for France, vowed to wear patches over their right eyes until they had struck a blow for their ladies' sake (and did so).[77] In the early fifteenth century Galeot of Mantua was so enamored of Joan of Padua that in return for a single dance he set out on a quest and sent back two knights prisoners, as Lancelot sent his noble captives to Guenevere.[78] The sixteenth-century ladies whom Brantôme knew received even more extravagant service from knights such as the chevalier de Lorge, who at the court of Francis I unhesitatingly leaped unarmed into an arena, where two lions were fighting, to fetch a glove that his lady had thrown there in order to test his courage.[79]

That was going a bit far, and de Lorge angrily left his lady for another. Malory's Tristram has a similar experience, when Segwarides' wife insists that he fight on her behalf, even though her husband is present, and then goes off with another when he fails to do so. Tristram learns the first rule of love, which is, as the author of the *Cent ballades* specified, that one must love a worthy object: "I shall beware what maner of lady I shall love or truste" (viii.18). Isode is a worthy object, and she and Tristram exemplify Malory's principle that "there was never worshypfull man nor worshypfull woman but they loved one bettir than another" (xviii.25). Isode proves this when she generously refuses to keep Tristram with her at the Joyous Garde, basely enjoying himself when he should be engaged in acts of chivalry. She tells him,

"What shall quenys and ladyes say of me? 'Hyt ys pyté that I have my lyff, that I wolde holde so noble a knyght as ye from his worshyp.' "

"So God me help," seyde sir Trystram unto La Beall Isode, "hyt ys passyngly well seyde of you and nobely counceyled. And now I well understonde that ye love me." (xii.11)

Ladies in real life seem at least sometimes to have done the same. When Bertrand du Guesclin married his lady Tiphaine, he stayed at home with his new wife, neglecting his knightly duties. "But she upbraided him with this remonstrance, how that before their marriage folk did talk of naught but him and his gallant deeds, and henceforth she might well be reproached for the discontinuance of her husband's fair deeds and good renown. This she said was a very great disgrace to her and him, that he had now grown such a stay-at-home, and she did not cease her chiding until she had roused in him his former spirit and sent him back to the wars, where he did even doughtier deeds than before" (Brantôme, *Oeuvres*, IX, 394).

Du Guesclin's lady was his wife, and, as we have noted, the one rule of courtly love that was not promulgated in the late Middle Ages was Andreas's dictum that love is impossible between a man and wife. That was a harmlessly amusing idea so long as chivalric love was mainly a matter of literature rather than life. When chivalric romances became a guide to conduct, the condonation of adultery was no longer acceptable. This may be why English romances, which are all from this later period, seem so moral when compared to their French antecedents.[80] Though fifteenth-century nobles were eager to be known as model lovers equal to Tristram or Lancelot, they obviously did not want to be known as adulterers. Consequently much of the chivalric love of the time is a matter of abstract service to ladies. Malory's older contemporary, the earl of Warwick (Richard Beauchamp), won such favor in the eyes of Sigismund's empress that she showed him "great love and favor" and wore his insignia. But that is as far as their relation went, and, so far as his biographer is concerned, it is as close as he ever came to having a relation of any sort with an actual lady. The reader of the biography is surprised at the end of the work when Warwick's wife and children appear; they had not been mentioned before.[81] Only the sixteenth-century Squire Meldrum, among the subjects of late medieval chivalric biographies, had a lady whom he loved *paramours*, and Sir David Lindsay is moved to assure his readers that though Meldrum never did get around to marrying the lady he was at least superior to Lancelot, since he was not guilty of seducing his king's wife. Yet Lindsay also uses Lancelot as the standard of knighthood, for though he was an adulterer he was a true lover and remained the standard of knightly chivalry.

The fiction of the time is usually as chaste as, according to chivalric biographers, ideal knights in real life were. The author of *Ponthus et la belle Sidoine* is at great pains to remove any suggestion of unchastity from the Horn story that he adapted for his romance, and when Ponthus and Sidoine are finally about to be married, Ponthus explains away any suspicions the reader may entertain: "I make myn avow to God that I never kissed her requiring villainy when I went out of this country, ne I never thought to do otherwise to her than I might to mine own mother" (p. 108). This delights Sidoine—"When Sidoine herd these words, she had great joy in her heart and loved him much better." The neighbors have their doubts: "Some said he was a trewe knight, and some said he would not abide so long unmarried but that he hoped to have some solace of her and she in like wise of him" (p. 109).

The author of *Ponthus* was free to change his tale in a manner denied to Arthurian romancers, whose materials were historical, at least in theory, and who therefore had somehow to reconcile the facts that Tristram and Lancelot were the greatest of earthly knights and yet adulterers. John Hardyng solved the problem by simply asserting that love in those days made "knightes worthy and coragious and gentilwomen to lyve in great clennes":

> Ther was no knight accompted of honoure
> But if he wer in warre approued thrise,
> Nor with ladies beloued as paramoure:
> Which caused knyghtes armes to exercyse,
> To be vertuous, and clene of life and wise:
> It comforte also ladies and theyr femynitee
> To lyve and more in perfite chastitee.   (P. 130)

Hardyng's account of Arthurian history is so brief that he could ignore the problem of reconciling "paramoure" with perfect chastity. Malory could not, and he therefore had to find a means of mediating between his convictions and his inherited plot. The most obvious attempt is just before "The Knight of the Cart" in *The Book of Sir Lancelot and Guenevere*. Malory insists that Lancelot and Guenevere engage in "vertuous love" which, far from causing the fall of the Round Table and thus leading to blame and punishment for Guenevere, "Whyle she lyved she was a trew lover, and therefore she had a good end" (xviii.25). This, as we have seen, is because love in Arthur's time was not as it is nowadays, when "Men can nat love sevennyght but they muste have all their desyres."

There are contradictions and ambiguities in Malory's handling of this problem. When he is free to invent, as in *Gareth*, marriage is clearly preferred to love *paramours*; this was usually the case in fifteenth-century fiction. Elsewhere, constrained by history, he must present the adulterous loves of Tristram and Isode and Lancelot and Guenevere, and sometimes he seems positively to admire these affairs. His contemporary, Johonet Martorell, the author of *Tirant lo blanc* (another knight-romancer), had a similar problem, for one of his main characters is the lover of the empress of Constantinople; he solves his problem simply by ignoring it and assuring his readers that the character (like Malory's Lancelot) is rewarded for his knightly deeds and raised to Heaven by innumerable angels. Malory is a bit more attentive to moral matters than that, and, as the end draws near, he does his best to redefine love in a manner that will deflect at least part of the blame from his hero and make the "old love" of Lancelot and Guenevere acceptable to his readers. Even God is invoked for this purpose, when Lancelot points out that he could not have defeated those who accused him of adultery (and surprised him *in flagrante delicto*) "had nat the myght of God bene with me" (xx.15). Malory's concern to excuse Lancelot's adultery, though it has something of the arbitrary method of *Tirant* about it, shows that he is indeed the contemporary of the authors of works such as *Paris et Vienne* or *Ponthus et la belle Sidoine* rather than of earlier romancers, such as Thomas of Britainy or even Chrétien de Troyes.

However, the most important fact about Malory's treatment of courtly love is that it would have seemed to his readers not an improbable fiction, an irony, or even necessarily a sin, for it was an aspect of the noble life as they knew it. Great nobles of the time aspired, at least in public, to be servants of the God of Love; serious poets and men of affairs, like the members of the Court of Love at Paris, pondered questions of love; it was generally agreed that chivalric love was the source of chivalric virtue, and the conventional words and gestures of the courtly lover had become part of the language of the upper classes. By Malory's time we find evidence of this even in the *Paston Letters*. When John Paston III sought Margery Brewys as a wife he labored long (first drawing up a much-corrected draft) to write his intended in the character of a courtly lover:

Mistress, though it be that I, unacquainted with you as yet, take upon me to be thus bold to write unto you without your knowledge and leave, yet mistress, for such poor service as I now in my mind owe you, purposing, ye be not displeased, during my life to continue the same, I beseech you to pardon my boldness and not to disdain but to accept this simple bill to recommend me to you in such wise as I best can or may imagaine to your most pleasure . . . And, mistress, I beseech you in easing of my poor heart, that was sometime at my rule, which now is at yours that I may have knowledge of your intent and how ye will have me demeaned in this matter. And I will be at all seasons ready to perform in this matter and in all others your pleasure as far forth as it lieth in my poor power to do so. (Letter 373)

Gawain with his "olde curteisye" could hardly have done better, and John Paston doubtless at least liked to think that he could have understood some of Lancelot's problems, since he, like the great Lancelot, had lost control of his heart.

Margery Brewys replied in kind. She was moved even to verse when she replied to her own "well beloved Valentine" and described the pains of love and its necessary secrecy:

> For there wottes no creature what pain that I endure,
> And for to be dear, I dare it not discure.   (Letter 415)

Like the Maid of Astolat, she would not be moved by better advice:

> And if my friends say that I do amiss they shall not me let for to do,
> Mine heart me biddes ever more to love you.

And she begged John to keep their love secret: "And I beseech you that this bill be not seen of none earthly creature save only yourself."

While John and Margery wrote one another in the characters of courtly lovers, many of the greater nobility were not only talking but acting the parts. Great ladies presided over tournaments in which knights fought for their honor. Knights toured Europe challenging others to fight for their ladies. Others swore to perform great deeds for their ladies' sakes, and sometimes they even fulfilled their vows. All this was, of course, theatrical, literary, and usually chaste, and it seldom interfered with other business. While John Paston and Margery Brewys wrote their courtly love letters, hard negotiations went forward about the amount of the dowry. Moreover, the same knights who enjoyed acting like courtly lovers were capable of a coarseness only slightly less brutal than that of our own time.[82] Yet occasionally even in the lives of the practical Pastons the conventions of courtly love became real and provided for tales of chivalric love real-life analogues that placed even the old extravagances within the realm of the possible.

8

Knighthood in Life
and Literature

The case of chivalry in its more general sense is much the same as that of courtly love. Romance chivalry—the idea that a knight must perform deeds for the honor of his lady and to acquire "worship"—was in the twelfth century a literary ideal, with only an indirect relation to the life of the times. The early romances present a heightened and purified image of the life that some of the more sophisticated twelfth-century nobles might have wanted to live if they had been blessed with the wealth and leisure to do so. But we know of none who, gorgeously equipped, jousted for the sake of honor, went on knightly quests for the sake of their ladies, and lived by the code of Lancelot or Tristan. In England William the Marshal (1144-1219) came closest to leading a life of chivalric adventure, for in his youth he traveled about Europe as a knight-errant taking part in tournaments, and he became one of the most famous and successful jousters of his time. His life, *L'histoire de Guillaume le Maréchal*, provides our fullest surviving portrait of an actual knight of the late twelfth century. This work was written between 1226 and 1231 at the command of William's son and of his old friend Jean d'Erlee.[1] We may therefore assume that it places William in the most favorable possible light, and the author does indeed represent his hero as the ideal knight. But William fulfills the ideal of his own times. He is loyal, generous, wise, brave, and admired by the ladies. But he is no servant of the ladies. As Sidney Painter writes, "William's code is not the chivalry of a Lancelot or a Galahad but one that is purely military and feudal."[2]

163

Though William's greatest virtue is *largesce,* as one might expect in a romance written by a professional minstrel, his main interest in knightly jousting is the profit that he gains from it. This is typical of his time, when tourneys were not so much a way of gaining worship as commercial undertakings, a means by which a landless knight, as William was, could become rich. There was thus little bother with knightly courtesy. At a tournament at Saint-Pierre-sur-Dive, when William and his companions were at dinner, a wounded knight rode by and then, fainting, fell from his horse, broke his arm, and lay helpless. William leaped from the table, rushed out, seized the fully armored knight, tucked him under his arm, and returned to his companions, throwing him at their feet and saying, "Here, this will pay your debts."[3]

From 1177 to 1179 William and his partner, Roger de Gaugi, lived as knights-errant, touring the Continent to participate in tournaments; in less than a year they defeated 103 knights.[4] But before they set out, he and Roger carefully drew up an agreement of partnership in order to split the profits they expected to make. Such agreements were not unusual: Richard I and Philip of France drew up a similar agreement before they set out on the Third Crusade. What is unusual, from the standpoint of later chivalric biographies, is the biographer's matter-of-course acceptance of the idea that profit is important in knightly enterprises. Later knights at least pretend to fight for honor alone. William fights for honor and plunder. Even on his deathbed he proudly recalls the wealth he has gained by his victories over five hundred knights, from each of whom he took horse, armor, and ransom.[5] This is closer to the dying Beowulf looking with satisfaction on the booty he has won than it is to the exploits of the Chevalier Bayard. Bayard, who lived in the sixteenth century, at the other end of the chivalric age, once captured the treasurer of the Spanish army, who was carrying 15,000 ducats. When his companion insisted on a half share (though he had not been present at the capture), Bayard refused, and he was upheld by the Court of Chivalry. Then, having satisfied his honor, he gave half of the money to his companion, gave the other half to the soldiers of the garrison, and released the Spaniard without ransom, allowing him to keep all his personal possessions.[6] This is an act of bravado and *largesce* comparable to William's in the tournament at Saint-Pierre-sur-Dive, but Bayard's *largesce* extends even to the captive Spaniard, and he would have been as horrified by William's unchivalric concern with profit as William would have been amused by Bayard's innocence. William learned early in life that ran-. som is the main business of a knight.[7] How else, he would have asked, could one maintain the *largesce* essential to knighthood?

In the later chivalric biographies one hears somewhat less about *largesce* and almost nothing about the booty necessary to maintain it. Plunder and ransom, of course, remained the main business of war; Bayard's companion was clearly aware of this, and many knights setting off for campaigns during the Hundred Years' War made business agreements similar to that between William and Roger de Gaugi. But honor rather than profit was now becoming the more acceptable public motive. Jousting and tournaments became entirely matters of honor. Ulrich von Lichtenstein, who jousted his way through Europe a generation later than William, consciously patterned his actions on the heroes of romance (and was fond of jousting disguised as King Arthur or even Frau Venus), and though we hear much of the honor he gained in the tourneys, we hear nothing of the profit.[8] How greatly matters had changed between William's day and Malory's is shown by the fact that in *The Book of Sir Tristram* the "evil custom" abolished by Lamerok at one castle is simply the ordinary rule of tournaments in the earlier period: each passing knight must joust, and if he loses, "He shall lose his horse and harnes and all that he hath, and harde if he ascape but that he shall be presonere." That was the whole point of jousting in William's time, but when Palomides hears of it he is deeply shocked: "So God me help . . . this is a shameful and vylaunce usage" (x.17).

By the time Malory wrote this, the most one could earn by jousting was honor and perhaps a jewel if he won one of the prizes.[9] The old custom of the victor's claiming the horse and armor of his opponent survived only in his claim to, in the words of a challenge issued in 1438, "his helm or other a blymaunt the which he wears upon his head for to bear unto his lady."[10] A landless knight could hardly make his fortune in the lists, for expensive special armor was now required, and as often as not the victor of a passage of arms—the best way to gain worship at this time—was expected to give handsome presents to those whom he defeated and then, as sponsor of the jousts, provide a great feast for all who attended. A young squire like John Astley could earn a handsome reward from his king for fighting in the lists, but unless one had this sort of patronage he could hardly afford to enter and pay the many fees required, including even "nail money" to the heralds (a fee for nailing up the shields around the lists).[11] It cost the

Bastard of Burgundy 3,000 écus to accept the challenge of Lord Scales in 1467,[12] and though few knights who jousted bore expenses that great, it is clear that the profit motive was completely gone from fifteenth-century tournaments and that honor and worship themselves were proving quite expensive.

Even warfare was now ostensibly conducted to gain honor rather than profit. This was, of course, more pretense than fact, but perhaps pretense is the best index to the moral ideals of any age. William the Marshal's contemporary (and probably his friend), the troubadour Bernart de Born, frankly delighted in the prospect of loot, and he apparently saw nothing unchivalric in the *sirventes* he wrote to Richard I and Philip August urging war for the sake of the plunder it would bring.[13] Fourteenth- and fifteenth-century nobles were clearly just as eager for the wealth a successful campaign could bring, and they doubtless agreed with Joan of Arc's captain, La Hire, who said, "If God were a soldier He would be a pillager."[14] Yet they preferred their poets to sing about honor and renown. *The Life of the Black Prince*, written by the Chandos Herald, shows how much attitudes had changed. Like the minstrel-author of William's biography, the Chandos Herald presents his hero as an ideal knight, but now—in the fourteenth century—the ideal knight is motivated entirely by honor, and we hear little of the plunder Edward and his army actually gained.

It is significant that Edward's biographer was a herald rather than a minstrel and that the records of his knightly victories were kept by heraldic historians rather than clerks like the one who kept track of William's jousting, more in the manner of an accountant than a recorder of noble deeds. In the late Middle Ages the heralds became the official historians of the nobility, and they had the duty of recording the great chivalric deeds of the present and scaling them, as does the Chandos Herald, against the deeds of Caesar and Arthur, so that we are given the impression that the present may at least aspire to equal the past. The heralds, of course, presented their subject in the most favorable light; a fifteenth-century herald's oath specified that if he should hear something unfavorable to lords and ladies, "Ye keep your mouth close and report it not forth but to their worship and the best."[15] Nevertheless, heraldic records were meant to be official and accurate histories. The Chandos Herald was thus careful to record each deed in precise detail, with long lists of the participants that remind one not only of early romances, such as the *Estoire de Merlin*, but also of Malory's catalogs of names and his careful specification of the participants in tournaments. Such details seem tedious to the

modern reader, but for fifteenth-century noblemen they may have
added a touch of verisimilitude, lending Malory's fiction some of the
tone of the works of contemporary heralds and chivalric chroniclers,
such as the Chester Herald in England and Olivier de la Marche in
Burgundy, who aspired to record in exact detail the noble deeds of
their age.

The Chandos Herald, who wrote a century before Malory, still
regarded chivalry as largely a matter of warfare rather than jousts and
service to ladies. In his work "We have little talk of 'ladye loves,' nor
any dwelling on the gaieties of times of peace or the feats of tournaments or the revelries of the hall."[16] A generation later, when Froissart
lived and wrote, the ideals of chivalry were becoming a generally
accepted part of the noble ethic. War was becoming—at least in aspi-
ration—an extension of the tournament (rather than the reverse), and
even powerful princes were beginning to attempt to imitate in life the
deeds they read about in romances. Tournaments, "lady loves," and
the gaieties of chivalric courtesy were becoming an important means of
acquiring "worship," and Froissart in his *Chroniques* paid as careful
attention to those forms of chivalry as to the battles he narrated. The
imitation of romance in life had become an essential part of chivalry.

In earlier times, jousts, tournaments, and knightly duels were
generally regarded as at best frivolous and at worse damnable. They
were forbidden by the decree of the council of Clermont, and Innocent
III specified that those killed in tournaments should be denied Christian burial—"extra ecclesiam tamen careat sepultura."[17] This attitude
persisted until well into the fourteenth century, when Bromyard
reminded his hearers that jousting was forbidden by the Church and
added that "the tournaments of the rich are the torments of the
poor."[18]

In England tournaments were rare until late in the thirteenth century. William the Conqueror had forbidden their importation from
France, and they did not appear until the troubled reign of King
Stephen (1135-1154).[19] Henry II disapproved of them, though his son,
Young King Henry, went to France to joust. Even a great warrior like
Richard I never pretended to be a romance knight, battling in the lists
for the honor of his lady (women were banned from his coronation
feast), or a king of romance, presiding over jousts. As Richard Barber
writes, "He left such frivolous matters to lesser princes, such as the
counts of Hainault, and no chronicler ever saw their fondness for
tournaments as anything other than youthful folly."[20] Indeed, when
Richard saw that the youth of his own realm were determined to joust,

he characteristically turned their folly to his own financial advantage: he licensed tournaments and extracted a fee from all who wished to participate. The chronicler William of Newburgh explained that Richard established these tournaments to encourage military discipline, but the size of the fees seems to show that profit rather than skill was uppermost in Richard's mind: they ranged from twenty marks for an earl down to two marks for a landless knight.[21]

What the Church regarded as sinful and Richard saw as a source of revenue had become by Malory's time a noble and virtuous pursuit. Jousts, wrote Malory's older contemporary, Nicholas Upton, were necessary "to prove one his strength and manhood; which manhood and fortitude is a moral virtue; yea, and also one of the cardinal virtues."[22] Much more so the tournament with its "feats of the necessary discipline of arms," as a fifteenth-century challenge put it, "to the experience and enabling of nobles to the deserving of chivalry, by the which our mother church is defended, kings and princes served, realms and countries maintained in justice and peace."[23] The idea that tournaments had a direct military and moral value survived even in the Elizabethan Accession Day Tilts and in Vulson's seventeenth-century *Vray théâtre*.[24]

An even more important justification for tournaments in the fourteenth and fifteenth centuries was the authority of ancient tradition. This, of course, was based not on a knowledge of actual conditions in ancient Greece and Rome (where chivalry was thought to have originated) or in the days of King Arthur but on the romances themselves. As early as the thirteenth century, tournaments begin to be imitations of romance chivalry, with knights appearing in the characters of Lancelot and Tristan (as they did in Cyprus in 1223), and the tournaments tending to be pageantlike recreations of the Round Table.[25] Edward I, a great reader of romance—Rusticiano da Pisa dedicated his compilation of Arthurian romances to him—seems consciously to have used his "Round Table" in an attempt to recreate Arthurian chivalry, just as Edward III decided to found the Order of the Garter in imitation of the Order of the Round Table.[26] In the fifteenth century, tournaments became even more elaborate recreations of romance, leaning often toward pedantry in their attempts at historical accuracy. The late fifteenth-century *La forme des tournoys et asemblees au temps du roy Uterpendragon et du roy Artus* is a set of tournament rules carefully culled from early romances.[27]

There is more than a touch of the theatrical in all this, as there is in the use of the word "triumph" as a synonym for "tourney" and in

Malory's use of the phrase "play his pageant" to describe a knight's participation in a tournament.[28] But, theatrical as such tournaments were, they seemed to participants and spectators more noble emulation than playacting. It is difficult to think of a more elaborately contrived and stage-managed tournament than that held to celebrate the wedding of Edward's sister Margaret to Charles of Burgundy in 1468, characterized by a twentieth-century historian of tournaments as mere "buffoonery."[29] But the heralds and chroniclers who recorded the event regarded the whole affair as an admirable enterprise, worthy of more elaborate records than we have for any contemporary battle.[30]

The more romantic life became, the more realistic romances seemed, so that sometimes, as Martín de Riquer has shown, it is difficult to separate fiction from reality both in fifteenth-century romances and in contemporary chronicles; the fiction seems real, the chronicle fiction. Riquer's study is restricted to Spain and Burgundy in the first half of the fifteenth century, but it can easily be extended to England, where chivalric deeds were also eagerly cultivated. Johonet Martorell, the author of *Tirant lo Blanc*, set part of the action of his romance in England, which he himself had visited as a knight-errant, and another of Malory's contemporary knight-romancers, Antoine de la Sale, regarded the English as admirably proficient in chivalric ceremonial— "The most ceremonious people in matters of honor that I have ever seen."[31] Riquer's best example of the interrelation of literature and chivalric life—his study of the "impresa del braccioletta"[32]—applies to England as easily as to the Continent, and indeed is a necessary part of the history of the great chivalric duel held at Smithfield in 1467 between Lord Scales, one of the most celebrated English knights of his time, and Anthony, the Bastard of Burgundy, one of the most accomplished jousters on the Continent.

The "impresa del braccioletta" (*emprise de bracelet*) was based on the custom of a knight-errant's wearing a special device, an *emprise* (in this case a bracelet or leglet), which he has vowed not to remove until he has jousted with some suitable opponent. Knights in romance had sometimes carried a special heraldic symbol on their quests, as La Cote Mal Tayle carries the shield that the maiden brought to Arthur's court and that he must carry until he has completed the quest he has undertaken. In the late fourteenth century it became fashionable for real knights to adopt some heraldic emblem as a form of announcing their readiness to joust. Boucicaut, for example, had shields hung up at St. Engelbert, which, as in the romances, a prospective opponent

would touch as a challenge to joust. Other knights of the time took to
carrying about such emblems. For example, Sir Piers Courtenay, a
famous English jouster of the last decade of the fourteenth century,
had a new surcoat made with the emblem of a falcon on it and this
legend:

> I beer a falcon, fayrest of flith,
> Qwha so pinchez at hir, his deth is dith,
> In graith.[33]

A Scotish knight, Sir William Dalzell, saw the device and rushed to
buy a new surcoat, in which he soon appeared before Sir Piers. It had
a magpie upon it and this legend:

> I beer a pye pykkand ay a pes,
> Qwha so pillis at hir I pik at his nese,
> In faith.

Sir William was as good as his word, and in the fight that followed Sir
Piers lost his two front teeth.

This custom of wearing a special device, an *emprise*, as an invitation
to joust had apparently become well established by the early decades
of the fifteenth century, for Riquer tells us that on St. Sebastian's Day
in 1431 a Spanish knight, Bernat de Coscon, was walking in the streets
of Sarragoza, wearing the device of an arm pierced with an arrow, as
he was accustomed to do on this day in honor of the saint.[34] Another
knight, Antonio de Monte Aperto, seeing this emblem and mistaking
it for a chivalric *emprise*, immediately challenged Bernat to joust.
Bernat refused, because of the day, but agreed to satisfy Antonio on
another occasion. Antonio thereupon drew up his "chapters of arms,"
the formal challenge with the rules for the combat, calling them the
"Capitoles de la empressa del Bracelot." Probably as an allusion to
Bernat's votive device, he announced that his *emprise* would be an
armlet, and then to add dignity to the occasion he drew upon the "Joie
de la court" theme of works like Chrétien's *Erec*, and explained that he
was the prisoner of his lady, who had commanded him to wear the
armlet until someone (that is, Bernat) agreed to joust with him in the
manner outlined in his chapters and in "the honor of the lady whom I
love." Bernat accepted the challenge, and the desired duel took place.

A few years later, in 1445, a Sicilian knight, Giovanni di Bonifacio,
who was in the service of the king of Aragon (and therefore probably
knew of Antonio's adventure) added the theme of the quest to the
"emprise del Bracelet." He traveled to the court of Burgundy,

"wearing on his left leg an iron in the manner and fashion of the irons worn by slaves, hanging from a little chain of gold."[35] His chapters proclaimed that he would fight for his lady's honor with any knight in the court. The young Jacques de Lalaing accepted his challenge, to the great satisfaction of all concerned.

The next year Jacques himself, inspired by Giovanni's visit, undertook a similar adventure, vowing that he would wear on his arm "a bracelet of gold to which he had attached a lady's kerchief as a favor (*un couvrechef du plaisance*)."[36] In July 1446 he sent out heralds with his challenge, his *chapitres d'armes*, specifying that whoever should touch his *emprise* (restoring the older practice, overlooked by Antonio and Giovanni) would be, providing he was of suitable birth, bound to deliver Jacques from his vow by battle. He journeyed through Spain and Portugal seeking an opponent until Diego de Guzmán solemnly touched his *emprise*, and the two met in a magnificent duel in 1448 in Valladolid.

The following year Jacques delivered his challenge to James Douglas and journeyed to Scotland, where he and his companions fought with Douglas and other Scottish nobles. Then he went to London, carrying the same "braclet d'or" that he had worn to Spain. However, King Henry VI refused to allow any of his knights to accept the challenge, probably for political reasons rather than any objections the saintly Henry may have had to jousting. His son was an enthusiastic jouster, and when Henry granted a judicial duel in 1453 the order specified that the scaffolds should provide a place for the king to have a good view of the proceedings.[37] Nevertheless, Henry's knights were not to be deprived of their pleasure, and as soon as Jacques returned to Burgundy, an English squire, one Thomas (probably Thomas Kay), arrived with his own challenge. The duel took place in Bruges in the presence of the duke of Burgundy and many English and Burgundian nobles. The fight was furious—axes were the weapons—and Jacques was badly wounded.

From the real lives of knights like Giovanni di Bonifacio and Jacques de Lalaing, the "impresa del braccioletta" passed into literature. It appears next in Antoine de la Sale's romance, *Petit Jehan de Saintré*.[38] The romance is set in the fourteenth century, when a Jehan de Saintré actually lived, but it is based on fifteenth-century life, and it is a didactic work, a handbook of chivalry for fifteenth-century gentlemen. Little Jehan's adventure with the "impresa del braccioletta" is, as Riquer demonstrates, based directly on the real-life adventure of

Jacques de Lalaing. In this romance version, the idea that the knight carries his *emprise* on behalf of a lady is given substance by making the adventure result not from the hero's vow but from his lady's command. Jehan's chivalric career begins when his lady, the Lady of Belles Cosines, tells him he must wear a golden armlet, adorned with precious stones. She explains (adding—a touch Malory would have appreciated—that she will finance the enterprise) that he must wear the armlet for a year, seeking a gentleman "de nom et d'armes sans repreuche," who will battle him on horse and foot, and she tells him to send out his heralds to announce this fact and find a knight who will deliver him from his charge. Jehan does so, and he finds a suitable adversary, as Jacques did, in Spain.

Had Riquer extended his researches to England, he would have found the next development of the "impresa del braccioletta" in one of the most famous duels to occur in Malory's lifetime, the battle between Anthony Woodville, Lord Scales, and the Bastard of Burgundy.[39] The episode in *Petit Jehan de Saintré* had been based on life, and now this episode in life seems almost to have been based on *Petit Jehan*. When Lord Scales, who was Edward IV's brother-in-law, was at court one day, he was surprised by a group of ladies, who atttached a golden ring adorned with pearls to his leg. On it was a richly enameled *fleur de souvenance* (a forget-me-not), and with it came the ladies' command that Scales wear the ring until he had done battle with a great knight "of four lineages and without any reproach." The situation is the same as in *Petit Jehan*, and even the words of the command are similar ("de nom et d'armes sans repreuche"), though this is a common formula. The ring is worn on the leg (as in the case of Giovanni di Bonifacio) rather than the arm, but this is perhaps an allusion to the insignia of the Garter. It is a scene from romance realized in life.

Scales, nevertheless, did exactly as he was commanded, for he probably did not consider the event romantic playacting so much as a necessary part of the chivalric life. He had perhaps heard of Jacques's adventure, and he surely knew that the knights of the Bath wore a white lace on their shoulder until they achieved some worshipful adventure. He therefore sent his herald to one of the most famous knights in Europe, the Bastard of Burgundy, who solemnly touched the *fleur de souvenance*, and in 1467 the battle was fought on horse and on foot at Smithfield, near London. The lists were constructed at great expense, and the ceremonies were of such magnificence that even the Burgundian chronicler Olivier de la Marche was deeply impressed. Much of the panoply may have been due to the fact that the Bastard came partly as an ambassador to arrange the marriage of Margaret of York to Charles of Burgundy. Nevertheless, the fight was furious. The weapons were not rebated (dull) but sharpened weapons of war, and the duel was therefore regarded by at least one London chronicler as for "life and death."[40] The first day the fight was with lances and sword on horse, and the Bastard, according to the same chronicler, was cast down "horse and man." This may have been the fault of the Bastard's horse. At least he thought so, and he told Olivier de la Marche, "Doubt not, he has fought a beast today, and tomorrow he shall fight a man."[41] Malory's knights often react in the same manner to being unhorsed: "For thoughe a marys sonne hath fayled me now, yette a quenys sonne shall nat fayle the!" (viii.33; cf. viii.22, xx.22). Tempers may have been short the next day, when the fight was on foot and with battle-axes. Scales fought with his visor raised, a daring act given the use of sharpened weapons, and the battle became so furious that King Edward had to stop the fight: "Then the king, perceiving the cruel assail, cast his staff and with a loud voice cried, 'Whoo!' Notwithstanding, at the departing there was given two or three great strokes, and one of the ascot's staffs broke between them."[42] As Lancelot tells Arthur, knights sometimes lose their tempers in tourneys. This happened to Lord Scales in a tournament in 1477,[43] and it is likely that if Edward had not stopped this battle there would have been an unfortunate international incident.

The fight was therefore stopped in the same way and in the same words as we read in Malory's account of a duel between Palomides and a strange knight (Lamerok) with the Haute Prince and Lancelot sitting as judges: "Then the Haute Prynce and sir Launcelot seyde they saw never two knyghtes fyght bettir; but ever the straunge knyght doubled his strokys and put sir Palomydes abak. And therewithall the Haute Prynce cryed 'Whoo!' " (x.44). Then, when King Edward had stopped the fight, there followed the usual outcome of a draw in romance: the reconciliation of the two knights, who swore henceforth to be friends and brothers in arms. Moreover, they kept their oath. The next year, 1468, at the great tournament at Bruges, Scales would not fight against the Bastard of Burgundy. He jousted with Burgundian knights, "but not with the Bastard, for they made promise at London that non of them shold never dele with othyr in armes."[44] It was just as well, for in the jousting the Bastard was badly injured.

Lord Scales died (by execution) before Caxton printed Malory's work, but if he could have read the *Morte Darthur* in manuscript he would have relished the great duels, which not only have the same general shape as the great jousts in which he took part but echo the very sounds that he knew so well—the trumpets and minstrelsy, the heralds crying "Leches les alere!" and the king shouting "Whoo!" (xix.9). Had Scales lived he would doubtless have been a reader of Caxton's edition, for he was a patron of Caxton and a man of letters as well as the most celebrated jouster of his time. He translated the *Dictys and Sayings of the Philosophers* and the *Moral Proverbs* of Christine de Pisan, both of which Caxton printed.

Scales's combination of chivalric and literary abilities was not unusual in the fifteenth century, for chivalry and learning were thought to be closely related. As the biographer of the marshal Boucicaut put it: "Two things have by the will of God, been established in the world, like two pillars to sustain the order of divine and human laws . . . These two flawless pillars are chivalry and learning, which go very well together."[45] They do indeed, and the great patrons of learning in Malory's time, such as the dukes of Burgundy or King René of Anjou, were also the great patrons of chivalry. Antoine de la Sale's account of the education of his ideal knight, Jehan de Saintré, contains a massive reading list, mainly in classical and religious texts, and though probably few actual knights read so ambitiously as Jehan, the illiterate of the twelfth century had long since passed from the scene, and a good number of knights—like la Sale himself and of course Malory—were men of letters. As Sir William Segar observed as late as 1602, "Indeed, very rarely doth any man succeed in arms that is utterly ignorant of letters."[46]

In England the union of arms and letters was perhaps best exemplified in John Tiptoft, the earl of Worcester. He is known best to students of literature as one of the earliest English humanists, famed even in Italy for his command of Latin oratory. It was said that his eloquence brought tears to the eyes of the great humanist Aeneas Sylvius, Pius II. Like Scales, Tiptoft was also a translator whose works—English versions of Cicero's *De amicitia* and Buonaccorso's *De vera nobilitate*—were published by Caxton. When Tiptoft was executed (deservedly; he also found time to earn the sobriquet Butcher of England), "the axe destroyed in that one head more learning than remained in all the surviving nobility of England."[47]

Yet Tiptoft was also an expert on matters of chivalry. He was Constable of England, chief authority in matters of chivalry. In 1466, at the command of Edward IV, he drew up the rules for jousting, *Ordinances for Justes and Tournaments*, which were used for the next hundred fifty years in England.[48] As Constable he presided over the joust between Lord Scales and the Bastard of Burgundy as well as the other jousts that occurred on the following days, and he performed his duties so skillfully that he earned the praise of Olivier de la Marche, who as maître d'hôtel of the court of Burgundy was a strict judge of such matters.[49]

As Constable it was also Tiptoft's duty to write a report of the joust. He prefaced his report with a statement that shows how deeply life and literature had become intertwined by this time, since his justification for writing his report of a real event is strikingly similar to the justification that Caxton used twenty years later for printing Malory's account of fictional events: he explains that "by virtue of the said office to us commit, it appertaineth not only to do put in writing all the noble deeds of arms which in our time have been accomplished" so that they will be remembered, but also to make them known in other lands, "That other worthy men to their ensaumple should encline them to apply to such and semblable deeds and that by such noble exercises of armes the augmentacioun of worthy knighthood should be the more and longer continued."[50]

Another official at the duel between Scales and the Bastard of Burgundy was Sir John Astley, who if not a patron of literature was at least the owner of an important manuscript of chivalric ordinances (including Tiptoft's), accounts of contemporary deeds of chivalry, and literary works (such as Scrope's translation of the *Epistle of Othea*).[51] He was also a skilled knight. In 1438 he fought Pierre de Massé in answer to a challenge—"half at my request and half at his"—before the king of France; Astley killed his opponent. Again, in 1442, when Philip Boyle of Aragon came to London carrying his challenge, Astley accepted the challenge and fought at Smithfield, using sharpened weapons, and he did so well that King Henry VI knighted him and granted him a pension of 100 marks a year. Boyle survived and later visited England as Spanish ambassador.[52] Astley fought at least one more important duel, against Francis de Surienne;[53] he became a knight of the Garter in 1461 and lived until 1486, a year after Caxton published the *Morte Darthur*. Given Astley's interest in chivalric matters (as shown by his manuscript), he could well have been one of the "noble gentlemen" who urged Caxton to publish Malory's work.

If Astley did read Malory, he probably read the accounts of duels with special care, both the duels of chivalry such as those in which he himself had fought, and the judicial duels, such as Palomides fights at the tournament at Surluse and Lancelot fights on Guenevere's behalf against Mellyagaunce and Mador de la Porte. Astley seems to have been something of an expert on judicial duels; he was appointed to serve as an official at the duel between John Lyalton and Robert Norreys in 1453, and he served again in 1456 at the duel between John David and his master (who was drunk and easily killed by David).[54] The most elaborate judicial duel in Malory, that between Lancelot and Mador de la Porte, follows the general outline of procedure set forth in Gloucester's rules for judicial combat, which governed the duels at which Astley helped officiate (he also owned a copy).[55] Mador formally "appeled" the queen of treason, "For the custom was such at that time," Malory explains, "that all maner of shamefull deth was called treson" (xviii.4).[56] The king assigns a day for the trial of arms, and on the morning assigned the queen is put in the Constable's custody, and the fire is prepared. There are lists for the battle, spectators, and a tent for each of the combatants. The appellant, Mador, and defendant, Bors, formally swear. Mador takes the field first. And, when Lancelot has appeared, taken Bors's place in the fight, and defeated Mador, there are "knights parters"—the knights whom Gloucester specified were to assist the Constable in "departing" the combatants—to conduct the wounded Mador to his pavilion. Malory's mention of the Constable and his assistants (neither appeared in his source) seems to indicate that in writing about this fictional duel he was reminded of actual judicial duels, and, perhaps without thinking too much about it, supplied the expected details.

Lancelot's duel with Mador is thus a good example of the blending of fiction and actuality that readers such as Astley would have found in the *Morte Darthur*. Certainly Astley had never seen a judicial duel in which one of the combatants suddenly appeared and fought incognito, as Lancelot does, for the rules of combat were very clear about the proper identification of the participants. But this bit of romance fiction exists within a context of recognizable reality. The same is true of the other judicial duels in the *Morte Darthur*; the casting of the glove, the appointment of judges, the erection of lists all provide verisimilitude for the fiction. Even Palomides' beheading of his opponents, Generydes and Archades, was not entirely out of the range of actuality. Exactly the same thing happened—the victor beheading his defeated opponent—in a judicial duel fought before an

English judge in Ireland in 1586, over a hundred years after Malory's book appeared in print.[57]

Indeed, the even later career of Captain John Smith, of Virginia fame, provides a striking real-life analogue to Palomides' duel with the Saracen champions.[58] Smith tells us that he jousted in full armor before the noble lords and ladies of the duke of Transylvania's court against the Saracen champion of the Turkish army. Smith killed his opponent with his lance and then, like Palomides, beheaded him. The next day, again like Palomides, he was challenged by a second Saracen champion, whom he also killed and beheaded. Smith went Palomides one better, for he faced a third Saracen, though this time he killed his opponent not with a lance but with a pistol. We may doubt the whole truth of Smith's account, just as we may doubt that Smith's contemporary, Lord Herbert of Cherbury (1583-1648), was really the chivalric knight-errant he claimed to be in his autobiography.[59] But Smith's contemporaries believed him and found nothing incredible in the idea that a seventeenth-century gentleman would wear full armor and engage in chivalric jousts *à outrance* (to the death).[60] And probably Lord Herbert actually did challenge a Frenchman to a duel "because I thought myself obligated thereunto by the oath taken when I was made a knight of the Bath."[61] Ideas of chivalry survived even in the seventeenth century. The difficulty, as a contemporary observed, was that by this time the country was so well governed there was "no employment for heroickal spirits."[62]

The survival of the knightly duel for so long after Malory's time may come as a surprise to those readers who believe that chivalric practices were dying in Malory's day. The judicial duel was indeed regarded with suspicion by many in the fifteenth century, and few were fought, but the closely related chivalric duel was gaining in popularity, and men were "appealed" for "treason," which, as in Malory, meant not *lese majesté* but betrayal of one's knightly oath; hence it is possible for a king, like Mark, to be guilty of "treason" toward his subject, Tristram.[63] The judicial duel itself long remained at least theoretically possible; as late as the eighteenth century Parliament defeated an attempt to abolish it, and it was defended as one of the pillars of the English constitution. The last judicial duel arranged, though not fought, in England was in the year 1817, and the custom was not abolished until 1819.[64]

Sir John Astley and others of Edward IV's court would have known in life another of the conventions of romance, the knight-errant, who travels about Europe, as did Jacques de Lalaing, seeking battle in whatever courts he visited. Philip Boyle, whom Astley fought *à outrance*, was such a knight, who journeyed from Spain to England, seeking opponents.[65] He was one of a number of Spanish knights-errant who visited England, including Pedro Vasquez, who died in 1477, and whom Riquer suggests as the model for the hero of *Tirant lo Blanc*.[66]

The author of *Tirant lo Blanc*, the Spanish knight Johonet Martorell, was in England in 1438 and 1439, just a few years before Astley's duel with Boyle. Martorell came to ask Henry VI to preside at a duel to the death between himself and Joan de Monpalau, who had broken his word to marry Martorell's sister. Henry agreed, and the duke of Huntington's herald carried Martorell's challenge, but the fight did not take place.[67] Nevertheless, Martorell was so impressed by the English chivalry that he used England as the setting for his romance, and made Tirant an English knight of the Garter. He drew on English traditions (his is the earliest record of the story of Edward's founding the order to honor the garter dropped by the countess of Salisbury), on English literature (*Guy of Warwick* is one of the principal sources of the first part), and perhaps even on English life, for it has been suggested that some of the details of Tirant's career are based on the life of Richard Beauchamp, the most celebrated English knight of the early fifteenth century.[68] Martorell, who began writing his romance in 1460, must have been almost an exact contemporary of Malory, as well as of Antoine de la Sale, another knight who wrote romances during Malory's lifetime.[69] We know that Martorell and la Sale drew on their own chivalric experiences for their works, and its seems likely that Malory did the same.

Knights from Hungary, Germany, Burgundy, and France also came to England seeking duels and jousts, and English knights traveled to the Continent for the same purpose.[70] The English squire Thomas, who wounded Jacques de Lalaing, was such a knight-errant, as was John Chalons, who killed a French knight, Louis de Beul, in Paris in 1449. Richard Beauchamp, the earl of Warwick, traveled throughout Europe seeking duels and tournaments. Knight-errantry was, in short, a widespread activity in the fifteenth century. I have already mentioned Galeot of Mantua, who journeyed about Europe for an entire year and sent back at least two captives to Joan of Padua, in the manner of Lancelot sending his prisoners to Guenevere, but perhaps Galeot's conduct is less remarkable than that of his prisoners, who actually came to surrender to Joan. She could have done with them as she wished; the canons of St. Peter's Church in Rome held—and badly mistreated—a knight who had been sent to surrender to them. But Joan was as magnanimous as Guenevere, and she set her prisoners free.[71] Few carried knight-errantry that far, but clearly when fifteenth-century readers such as Sir John Astley read of Malory's knights traveling about seeking adventures or going to a foreign court to joust, as Lamerok comes to Mark's (vii.33), they would have recognized not just a romance convention but a fact of the noble life of the times.

Another fact of experience in Malory's time was the *pas d'armes*, in which a knight sets himself up at a given spot, often on or near a main highway (hence *pas*) and offers to joust all comers. This is a familiar motif in romance, perhaps originating in something like the "Joie de la court" episode in Chrétien's *Erec*, in which the hero is commanded by his lady to battle all comers until he is himself overcome and relieved of the obligation (the situation of the Red Knight of the Red Lands in *Gareth*). Or a knight may set up in the manner of Alexander the Orphan, defending his lady, la Beall Pylgryme, and fighting all comers on her behalf for the space of an entire year. This literary motif was imitated in life by the famous Marshal Boucicaut, who in 1390 held a *pas d'armes* at St. Englebert near Calais. Two shields were suspended from a tree, and a challenger could choose to fight with either rebated weapons or sharpened, depending on which shield he touched. The *pas* was maintained for thirty days, with great ceremony and feasting.[72]

In 1434 the great Spanish knight Suero de Quiñones held a *pas d'armes* even more directly patterned on romance, the famous Paso honoroso. He announced that he was the "prisoner" of a great lady (apparently on parole) and that he could be released only if he and his companions defended against all comers the road leading to St. James of Compostella, theoretically denying passage to all.[73] The resemblance to Mabinograins in the "Joie de la court" episode in *Erec* (as well as to Malory's *Gareth*) is obvious, and the whole affair was conducted with literary overtones (it has been suggested that Suero patterned his life on that of *Amadís de Gaul*)[74] and with great magnificence. Suero and his companions held the passage at a bridge near Leon for an entire month, fighting 705 duels with sixty-eight knights, with one killed and several wounded.

Whether or not El paso honoroso set the fashion, the *pas d'armes* became widely popular in the decades that followed, often in

increasingly elaborate forms. In 1443 at the pas de l'arbre de Charlemagne, near Dijon, thirteen Burgundian knights jousted for six weeks
against all comers, who arrived from all over Europe to participate.[75]
(Each of these was an international event that was, like the great
tournaments of the time, announced by heralds to courts throughout
Europe.) In 1446 King René of Anjou, one of the most cultured men of
his time and an enthusiastic jouster (he wrote a book on the subject),
celebrated the departure of his daughter, Marguerite of Anjou, to
marry Henry VI of England by staging the magnificant Pas de la
joyeuse garde.[76] A castle (the Joyeuse garde) was erected, complete
with unicorns, lions, and tigers from the royal zoo, and René, disguised as Lancelot, defended the castle, with his lady (his wife) taking
the part of Guenevere, and with many English knights participating,
including the duke of Suffolk (who is remembered now more for his
poetry than his chivalry). In 1449 the adventure of Alexander the
Orphan was realized in life in the Pas de la belle pèlerin, in which the
Bastard of St. Pol, disguised as Lancelot, defended "la belle pèlerin"
for a month at the place on the road between Calais and St. Omer,
known as "Beau jardin et a present le Crois de la Pèlerin."[77] As it
happened, this was a time of war, and only one challenger, an aged
German, turned up to joust. Nevertheless, the *Crois de la pèlerin* was
solemnly erected to memorialize the joust—as Merlin raised the
"perowne" near Camelot to mark the site of the duel between Balin
and Balan—and fifty years later the great sixteenth-century knight-
errant, the chevalier Bayard, "piously went to visit this cross as if on a
pilgrimage."[78]

That same year Jacques de Lalaing undertook to defend the
Fontaine des pleurs on behalf of his "Dame des pleurs" for an entire
year, from November 1449 to October 1450.[79] It was an elaborate setting, with shields in various colors for the challengers to touch, the
lady herself in attendance, and a script, in verse, for a pageant to mark
the end of the adventure. Lalaing, like a true romance knight, was disguised as the "knight of the Dame des pleurs," and his *chapitres* provided that if a knight was unhorsed he had to wear a golden bracelet
for a year or until he found a lady who would free him on condition
that he serve her. The shields from this event were later hung in the
Church of Notre Dame in Boulogne, solemnly dedicated to the Virgin.
Such passages of arms continued to be held throughout the century,
culminating in the famous event at Sandricourt in 1493, where, at the
conclusion of the formal jousting, the participants rode out with their

ladies, jousting with all whom they encountered, "as once did the knights of the Round Table."[80]

The popularity of this form of jousting was such that tournaments tended to follow its pattern, with either individual jousts, cast in the form of a *pas d'armes* and followed by a general melee, or with the knights divided into two parties, the *tenans* (those who hold the *pas*) against the *venans* (those who come to it), though in this case the *pas* might be a barrier or a castle. In 1467 Sir John Paston took part in a tourney at Eltham, with King Edward, Lord Scales, Sellenger, and Paston "within" (that is, as *tenans*), and the Lord Chamberlain, Sir John Woodville, Sir Thomas Montgomery, and John Appere "without" (as *venans*).[81] This was a minor tourney, but apparently it was the sort of tournament that Malory describes in *Gareth*, in which there is a Castle Perilous and knights "within" to battle those "without" (vii.28), a convention a trifle puzzling to the modern reader (since Malory does not bother to explain why some are within the castle and some without) but easily comprehended by his contemporaries, who could have seen or heard of such affairs.

Such combinations of tournaments and passages of arms remained popular for the rest of the century. One was held in Paris in 1468, another in Ghent in 1469, one in London in 1474, and in 1477 six gentlemen challenged all comers to honor the marriage of Richard, King Edward's son, to Anne Mowbray; Lord Scales fought disguised as a "white hermit" and very nearly killed Thomas Hansard.[82] Later in the century, by the reign of Henry VII, the challenge to all comers was the usual form of a tournament, and at Richmond a *pas d'armes* was held for an entire month, during the course of which Sir James Parker was killed.[83] But perhaps the most famous tournament in which English gentlemen participated in the fifteenth century was the Pas de l'arbre d'or, held at Bruges in 1468 to celebrate the marriage of King Edward's sister, Margaret of York, to Charles of Burgundy.[84] Caxton was probably present at this elaborate affair (Margaret became his patron), and it was once speculated—without foundation—that Malory himself was in Bruges at the time.[85] It was an elaborately staged affair, with a golden tree, a distressed damsel, a dwarf, a giant, and courtly ceremonies that left English spectators almost speechless. And it was a grand tournament: the Bastard of Burgundy was injured, Philip of Poitiers was badly wounded, and the melee so got out of hand that the duke himself had to ride into the lists waving his baton and shouting to the knights to stop on pain of death.

Such affairs were so elaborate, almost as much masque as tournament, that one must remind himself that they remained dangerous. The object of jousting was never to kill or to maim. Even in William the Marshal's rougher age the combatants knew that a dead opponent paid no ransom. In the fifteenth century the *chapitres* of challenges normally contained a phrase such as "God forbid" when specifying the rules that applied if one of the fighters was injured. Special armor was used to lessen the risk of injury; the barrier was introduced to separate the charging horses and prevent head-on collisions; and, since the object was purely to win "worship," Jehan de Saintré's lady specified that a jouster must not even be angry with his opponent (p. 190).

All this, along with the extravagant pageantry, appears to be pretty poor stuff to most historians of the tournament, who sometimes seem a rather bloodthirsty lot, delighted to find that some sixty knights were killed at a tournament near Cologne in 1240 and a bit contemptuous at later, less bloody affairs. Most fifteenth-century tournaments were bloodless, and evidently even the spectators approved. In Chaucer's *Knight's Tale*, when Theseus orders that the tournament between Palamon and Arcite be *à plaisance*, the voice of the people "touchede the hevene: 'God save swich a lord, that is so good, / He wilneth no destruccion of blood!' " (vv. 2561-64). Nevertheless, jousting remained a dangerous sport. Frequently, sharpened weapons were used, and sometimes special protective armor was forbidden, as in one of Henry VII's tourneys in which it was specified that only plain "hosting armor" is to be worn, "such as they will use in time of war."[86] Jousting remained dangerous even when special armor was worn and rebated weapons were used. As late as 1515 several knights were killed at a tournament in Paris.[87] In 1518 Charles V rode in a tournament in which seven knights lost their lives. Henry VIII was nearly killed while jousting, and in 1559 Henri II, king of France, did indeed lose his life while jousting before his assembled court. The next year the duc de Montpensier, a prince of the blood, was killed in the same way.

Real fifteenth-century passages of arms are reflected in fifteenth-century literature. One example known to English readers of Malory's time is in *King Ponthus*, which, as we have noted, is an adaptation of *Horn et Rigmel*. At the point where in the older work the hero leaves for exile in Ireland, the fifteenth-century author substitutes a *pas d'armes* (pp. 40-44). Ponthus disguises himself as "the Black Knight with the White Arms" and sets up his *pas* in a nearby forest. He sends a dwarf to announce that he will be there at prime each Tuesday for an entire year. On a tree he will hang a shield, which each challenger must touch. When he touches the shield, a dwarf will blow a horn, and from the pavilion will emerge an old damsel, accompanied by a hermit, who will announce to the challenger that the Black Knight will soon be ready to fight. There are many other provisions described, including prizes, a feast for the combatants at the conclusion of the adventure, and a marvelous well, like that in *Yvain*. In all, this seems the most fantastic episode in the whole romance. Yet it is in some ways the most realistic. The author even specifies that Ponthus hires the dwarf to act as his herald, goes to town to hire a suitably aged lady to play the part of the damsel, and himself assumes the role of the hermit (followed by a quick change into the role of the "black knight sorrowing bearing arms of white"). The whole elaborate adventure is based on the actual practices of real knights of the time, and apparently the author felt that the effect of the narrative was enhanced rather than diminished by the realistic details that underscore the dramatic, playacting element that surrounds the jousts.

Likewise, the most realistic of the *pas d'armes* in the *Morte Darthur* is the most fantastic, that held by Lancelot when he is in exile from Guenevere, staying with Elaine at the Castle of Blyaunte (xii.6). First Lancelot, like his real-life counterparts, changes the name of the place: "Lancelot lat calle hit the Joyus Ile." Then he adopts a fanciful *nom de guerre*, "and there was he called none otherwyse but Le Shyvalere Mafete, 'the knyght that hath trespast.' " He adopts a symbolic heraldic device, "late make him a shylde all of sable and a quene crowned in the midst of silver and a knight clene armored knelynge afore her." Like Ponthus, he sends out a dwarf to make a "cry, in hyring of all the knyghtes, that there ys one knyght in Joyus Ile, which is the castle of Blyaunte, and sey that his name is Le Schyvalere Mafete and woll joust ayenste knyghtes all that woll come." Again like Ponthus, he specifies prizes ("a fayre maydyn and a jarfawcon"). In three days he jousts far more—five hundred—than any living knight in the fifteenth century, but, like most of the *pas d'armes*, the affair is bloodless and capped with grand festivities: "And there was nat one slayne of them. And aftir that sir Launcelot made them all a grete feste."

Likewise, the grand tournaments in the *Morte Darthur* reflect the customs of Malory's own time, and the more elaborate they are the more closely they resemble real tournaments. Most of the jousting in the book is relatively informal, as was probably also the case in Malory's time, when only the great chivalric festivals were fully recorded, and lesser affairs passed unnoticed, probably because they were so common. We know of the tourney at Eltham, in which Edward IV himself took part, only because Sir John Paston was one of the participants and happened to write home about it. And we know that Henry VI's son and his companions frequently engaged in jousting only because Fortescue happened to mention it in the preface to his *De laudibus legum Angliae*.[88] Probably most of Malory's readers knew best about informal jousts of this sort.

Nevertheless, Malory's contemporaries would have found many familiar details in his tournaments. The "customs" of the various castles and bridges are obviously similar to those of contemporary passages of arms, even to the specification of what forms of combat may be used (thus one of Dinadan's opponents will fight only on horseback, for that is "the custom of this place"; x.10). Malory's knights, like knights in the fifteenth century (but not before), have special armor for jousting ("the harneyse that longed unto josten-ynge"; xiii.6), and his tournaments are great displays, with minstrelsy and special scaffolds for the spectators. The usual order of events is first individual jousts and then the grand melee, and, as was the custom, first lances are broken, "Than whan this done was drawynge of swerdys" (vii.30). There are prizes for the best jousters, and feasts and dancing to conclude the festivities.

When Malory invents a tournament, as he does in the cases of the tourney in *Gareth* and "The Great Tournament" in *The Book of Sir Lancelot and Guenevere*, the tournaments are even closer to life, for Malory—probably without thinking about it and simply drawing upon his own experience—makes these tourneys affairs that are regulated by heralds who keep score and award the prizes on the basis of their record. In *Gareth* we read, "All this was marked wyth noble herrodis, who bare him best, and their namys" (vii.28). In "The Great Tournament" we are even given the actual score: "The pryce was yevyn unto sir Launcelot, for by herowdys they named him that he had smytten down fifty knyghtes, and sir Gareth fyve-and-thirty knyghtes, and sir Lavyne four-and-twenty" (xviii.24). Score keeping by heralds is unknown to either life or romance in earlier times, and this is the earliest example in English romance of the practice. (David Aubert's *Three Kings' Sons*, written in Burgundy in 1463, is an early Continental example.) It is typical of real tournaments in the later fifteenth century, however; John Tiptoft's *Ordinances* consisted of rules for score keeping and were used for the score cards ("jousting cheques") that have survived from the sixteenth century. Likewise, in another tournament of Malory's invention, that which concludes *Lancelot and Guenevere*, the prize is specified as not simply the "prys" or the "gre" but a diamond such as was offered in real life as the prize for the tournament held to celebrate Prince Richard's marriage in 1477.

By the time Malory was writing about such tournaments, the process of life's imitating art, described by Baron de Lettenhove, was complete, and one hardly knows which came first: Did Malory specify a diamond as a prize because that was the custom of tournaments such as the one at Richmond in 1477? Or was the prize at Richmond a diamond because of the tournament in Malory? The process, as Riquer describes it, is like that of the modern cinema. The cinema imitates life; life in turn imitates the cinema; and then the cinema imitates life, with the expected distortions at each stage.[89] Noblemen of the early fifteenth century patterned their tournaments on romance, with a few practical changes, such as the office of heralds. Romancers like Malory or David Aubert then patterned their tournaments on life, incorporating contemporary practices into their heightened accounts. Then the nobles of the late fifteenth and early sixteenth century patterned their tournaments on these romances. A jouster of the thirteenth century, transported to the sixteenth, would have been baffled by the heralds, barriers, and score keeping. The participants would have been sure that their practices were ancient, authorized by "old romances" that writers such as Malory claimed to have transmitted unchanged from their ancient sources.

9

The Realism of
Fifteenth-Century Romance

How deeply literature influenced the lives as well as the sports of later medieval knights is shown by the chivalric biographies of men such as Marshal Boucicaut, Jacques de Lalaing, the earl of Warwick, or Chevalier Bayard. Even when one makes allowances for exaggeration by the biographers and for the selective nature of the events they chose to relate (and others that they must have ignored), we are left with the fact that noblemen such as these consciously patterned their lives on the conventions of romance. The last English chivalric biography—Sir David Lindsay's *Squyer Meldrum*—tells the life of an actual Scottish gentleman who, Lindsay says, performed deeds for his lady's honor greater than Lancelot or Tristram ever did. In 1518 Meldrum (who died in 1560) fought a single combat against the English knight Talbert during the siege of Montreuil. As C. S. Lewis wrote, "The circumstances of Meldrum's battle with the English champion in France might have come straight out of the pages of Malory."[1] So too could his exploits when he and his paramour, the Lady Gleneagles, were ambushed by his enemies and Meldrum fought them off single-handedly. In a sense, the adventures did come from the pages of Malory, for Meldrum, like his contemporary, the great Chevalier Bayard, still lived in a time when men were attempting to emulate in real life the heroes of romance. The depth of the interplay between life and romance in the late Middle Ages is shown by the fact that *Squyer Meldrum*, which is the last as well as one of the best of the verse romances, is a work not of fiction but of fact.

Given this sort of historical context, it is not surprising that scholars have found a number of real-life analogs to characters in the *Morte Darthur*. C. O. Parsons noted that a much earlier David Lindsay (who died in 1407), fighting the English Baron de Welles in London in 1390 in a duel *à outrance*, threw his opponent to the ground, slipped his dagger through the greaves of his armor, and then chivalrously arose and granted de Welles's life to the queen.[2] Parsons notes the similarities to Lancelot's duel with Mador de la Porte (xviii.7), and he shows too that Mordred's death is very similar to that of one of Lindsay's opponents, as narrated by the chronicler Wintown. In an article called "Sir Thomas Malory—Historian?" Nellie S. Aurner found historical analogs for a great many of the characters in the *Morte Darthur* and, though few would agree with all her identifications, many critics have thought that the *Morte Darthur* is at least partly historical and have found in Arthur's Continental campaigns traces of the career of Henry V, king of England in Malory's youth.[3]

Perhaps the most striking similarities between fifteenth-century history and Malory's fiction are to be found in the life of Richard Beauchamp, earl of Warwick, whom I have already mentioned a number of times. Warwick, who died in 1435, was once thought to have been Malory's captain at the siege of Calais, and it has been argued that Malory based the figure of Gareth on his old commander. However, William Matthews has shown the improbability that the Thomas Malory who served at Calais and was so frequently in trouble with the law is the same Thomas Malory who wrote the *Morte Darthur*, and it is therefore at least doubtful that our author knew Warwick in person.[4] Nevertheless, it is very probable that Malory knew something of Warwick and his celebrated deeds, either by hearsay or by written accounts such as that contained in the Lansdowne Manuscript. The fullest account of Warwick's career is the pictorial biography, *The Pageant of the Birth, Life, and Death of Richard Beauchamp, Earl of Warwick*, which was written sometime in the late 1480s.[5] This reads more like a romance than a true biography, and we might suspect it to be purely fiction if it were not substantiated by other records. Warwick's early life followed the pattern that we know from Malory's romances: he was knighted, and then he triumphed in the great tournament given to celebrate the marriage of Henry IV to Joan of Navarre, where he did such deeds "as redounded to his notable fame and perpetual worship" (5). He then went off to fight his king's enemies and thus earned a higher form of knighthood, reception into the Order of the Garter. The pattern of tournament-quest-higher form of knighthood is characteristic both of Malory's heroes and of knights in real life, such as Jacques de Lalaing, who in the 1440s jousted before his king, went on a quest (the "emprise del braclet"), defended a *pas* (the Fountaine des pleurs), and earned a higher form of knighthood. Malory's knights earn a place at the Round Table, Warwick the Order of the Garter, Jacques the Toison d'or (the Burgundian Order of the Golden Fleece).

Warwick then set out for the Holy Land, pausing in Paris to visit the king of France (whom he impressed with his good manners) and in Mantua to visit the famous Galeot (whose quest in honor of Joan of Mantua is mentioned above) and to battle Sir Pandolf Malatete, whom he nearly killed: "If the lord Galeot had not the sooner cried 'peace!' Sir Pandolf sore wounded on the left shoulder had been utterly slain in the field" (13-14). In the Holy Land he met a Saracen lord reminiscent of Palomides: at dinner Sir Baltirdam secretly told Warwick "that in his heart he durst not utter his concept yet he faithfully believed as we do" (19). Then he returned by way of Russia, Lithuania, Poland, Prussia, Westphalia, and Germany, and "In this journey Earl Richard got him great worship at many tournaments and other faites of war" (22). Later, after his adventure at Calais, to which we shall return, he went with an English embassy to the council of Constance, where he was challenged to joust by a "Great Duke." He killed his challenger in the lists, thereby winning the favor of the empress, who witnessed the battle and was so taken with the conqueror that she insisted on wearing his emblem. More important, he won the praise of the emperor: "And the Emperour said to the king that no prince christian for wisdom, nurture and manhood had such another knight as he had of the Earl of Warwick, adding thereto that if all courtesy were lost yet might it be found again in him. And so for ever after by the Emperours authority [he] was called the Father of Courtesy" (35).

Warwick's most flamboyant knightly adventure was the *pas d'armes* that he held on his way to take command of the English troops at the siege of Calais in 1419. He wanted to perform a "new point of chivalry" (24), and he decided to hold a three-day tournament on the pattern of romances such as *Richard the Lion-Hearted* or *Ipomedon*. He had three shields painted, one depicting a lady and a green and black knight, another a lady and a green knight, and the third a knight called the "chevalier attendant." He then sent his challenge to the French camp, where three French knights, two of whom used *noms de jouste*, "le chevalere rouge" and "le chevalere blanke," accepted his offer. The first was a famous jouster who with fifteen companions was waiting for a scheduled joust *à outrance* with fifteen English knights. Warwick, fighting as the Green and Black Knight, at the third course, bore him down "horse and man," says the author of a contemporary account in the Lansdowne Manuscript.[6] Then he "returned unknown to his Pavilion" (29). The next day, fighting as the Green Knight, he struck down the Chevalere Blanc, and again, according to the Lansdowne account, "He kept ever his umbrere down, for he would not be known in the field." The third day, this time wearing the arms of his "ancestor," Guy of Warwick, he defeated his third opponent, and, when the onlookers claimed that Warwick must have tied himself to his horse, he jumped from the saddle and, fully armed, leaped back on his horse again. Then, his *emprise* successfully concluded, he presented each of his opponents with the gift of a handsome horse and entertained them with a great feast. The Frenchmen then returned to their army, Warwick to his, and the war resumed.

A number of scholars have suggested that Malory may have based Gareth's somewhat similar exploit on the real-life adventures of the earl of Warwick, and Vinaver some years ago speculated that even the name Beaumains may have been based on Warwick's family name, Beauchamp.[7] All this seems doubtful (and Vinaver no longer holds this opinion), but clearly fifteenth-century gentlemen who knew of Warwick's exploits would have read the account of Gareth's triple disguise not as an improbable fiction but as an only slightly heightened account of events that occurred in life.

The style of fifteenth-century life was often so flamboyant that it may be that some of the deeds of Arthur that seem most romantic to the modern reader seemed most lifelike to Malory's contemporaries. For example, we have already noted the similarity of Arthur's invasion of France (in *Arthur and Lucius*) to Henry V's French campaign. This is the one historical parallel that some critics of Malory still accept. Yet the parallel of Arthur's campaign to Henry's depends on the readers' fairly close knowledge of Henry's movements, and perhaps some, who lacked this knowledge, may have found the most realistic part of Arthur's campaign not in the route his army takes but in the romantic manner in which the campaign begins (with a set of chivalric vows) and ends (with Arthur killing Lucius with his own hands). The vows that Arthur's knights make in the council that precedes the invasion of France came to Malory from the alliterative

Morte Arthure, whose author in turn drew on the French romance about the vows made on the carcass of a peacock by Alexander's knights, the *Voeux du paon*. This romance seems to have been the inspiration for a vogue of sets of chivalric vows made on the carcasses of various birds. Edward I is said to have begun his war with Scotland because of a vow made on a roast swan.[8] The *Voeux du heron*, a late fourteenth-century poem, tells us that the Hundred Years' War began with a series of vows made by Edward's knights on the carcass of a heron. There is no historical basis for this, and the poem may have been intended to criticize rather than praise King Edward. If so, Philip the Good missed the point, for in 1454, in response to the pope's plea to mount a crusade against the Turks, Philip held his celebrated Voeux du faisan (the Vows of the Pheasant), in which he and his knights vowed to set out on a crusade and Philip himself swore that he would face the Grand Turk in single combat.[9] These vows, like so much in Philip's life, are a strange combination of artificiality and sincerity, and though Philip was acting in response to the pope's plea and did indeed in 1456 send his son and 4,000 men to serve under the pope's banner, it is unclear how serious he was about the whole business. Nevertheless, Philip's real-life vows—more fantastic in form and setting than the sober avowals of Arthur's knights—provide a realistic basis for the vows of Arthur and his knights to fight Lucius and his Saracen allies. Such scenes, Malory's readers knew, not only could but did happen in life.

Philip had sworn to meet the Grand Turk in single combat, just as Arthur does meet and slay with his own hands the Roman emperor. The idea of one ruler's meeting another in battle may seem to us pure fiction, but it was not so in the fifteenth century, when kings were still expected to be warriors and lead their troops in battle, as Henry VI and Edward IV did. Moreover, they were expected to be skilled knights, able to defend their nation's honor in chivalric duels, and challenges between national leaders were the order of the day. Just a few years before the Vows of the Pheasant, Philip the Good had issued a challenge to Humphrey, duke of Gloucester, and whatever Philip's intentions regarding the Grand Turk may have been, he seems to have been very serious about his intended duel with Humphrey: he ordered special armor, went into training, and even gave up drinking, and he seemed to be sincerely disappointed when a papal bull forbad the scheduled fight.[10] Previously Richard II of England had challenged Charles VI of France, Louis of Orléans had challenged Henry IV, and Henry V had challenged both the Dauphin and Philip the Good.[11]

None of these projected duels ever took place, and we may well suspect that most of them were delivered for their propaganda value. But that itself indicates the importance and credibility of the idea in Malory's time. Moreover, the challenge was a convenient means of declaring war—which was done by sending one's herald, in the same way the knights-errant delivered their challenges—and such challenges were used in private battles in England during Malory's lifetime. The most notable of these, the battle of Nibley Green in 1470, began with a challenge to a duel, "according to the honour and order of knighthood," and, this being refused, a battle followed, with the loss of one hundred fifty lives.[12]

The idea that national leaders might settle questions of policy by single combat—without further loss of Christian blood, as the form went—survived until well into the sixteenth century, and as late as 1590 Henri IV challenged the duc de Mayenne to settle the fate of France in single combat. Arthur's challenge to Lancelot (xx.11)—another fifteenth-century royal challenge to a duel that does not take place—like his defiance of Lucius, is thus not only a gesture of romance chivalry but a reflection of the realities of the time.

As these historical challenges show, chivalry was not only an ideal to which fifteenth-century monarchs paid lip service, it was also an important instrument of national policy. The great tournaments, such as the duel between Lord Scales and the Bastard of Burgundy, were diplomatic as well as chivalric occasions,[13] and even half a century later, when Henry VIII and Francis I met on the Field of the Cloth of Gold, the purpose was not merely to dazzle their subjects with a chivalric display; it was also to establish a *rapprochement* between the European powers on the basis of chivalry.[14] The idea that this was possible, that real kings might base their actions on chivalry rather than self- or national interest, seems absurd today. Yet there were rulers in the late Middle Ages who did sometimes place honor before national advantage, usually, it must be said, with disastrous results. King John of France, that "knightly muddlehead," as Johan Huizinga calls him, lost the battle of Poitiers at least partly because chivalry was more important to him than elementary tactics.[15] Then, having lost the battle, his sense of honor dictated that he grant the duchy of Burgundy to the bravest of his sons—a grand gesture that gravely imperiled the French nation. Yet he was remembered even in Malory's lifetime as a model of chivalry and kingly morality.[16] John may therefore have lost the war, but he won what seemed to many in his time more precious—knightly renown.

John's example was followed by other kings and rulers. Charles the Fearless, last duke of Burgundy and husband of Caxton's patroness, Margaret of York, was also more interested in chivalry than was good for him, and he lost both his life and his dukedom as a result.[17] So too did James IV of Scotland, who, half a century after the *Morte Darthur* was written, died at Flodden Field (1513) and left his kingdom crippled because of his devotion to chivalric honor. James was a great reader of romance and an enthusiastic jouster (he liked to disguise himself as Arthur or the "Chevalier Salvage"). He got into the war with England partly because he fancied himself the chivalric servitor of the queen of France—who wrote him in the character of a damsel in distress, begging his help—and partly because Louis XII of France promised him that once the English were disposed of, James could lead a crusade of Christian princes to reconquer the Holy Sepulcher.[18]

With this assurance, James invaded England, but then he dallied at the Castle Ford, which he failed to destroy, so it was said, because he had fallen in love with Lady Heron, the fair chastellaine. When Surrey led the English army North, James could have attacked and destroyed his enemies while they were still assembling. But Surrey, realizing his own danger and knowing James's chivalric temperament, sent his herald to the Scottish camp with a formal challenge to a battle on a given day, just as the armies of Mordred and Arthur meet on a set day of battle (xxi.3). James chivalrously accepted and sat with his army, waiting for the English to bring up the necessary reinforcements. Then, as the newly orphaned James V complained:

The King our father remained in the enemy's country with the peers of the realm, expecting battle at a pre-arranged time and place. But the English, intent on deceit, took care not to fight at the pre-arranged time and place nor on the day appointed . . . Our dearest father, made impatient by the very sight of the enemy, rushed too boldly upon them . . . our nobles fell at the head of their men or fighting beside them. It was different with the enemy; every one of their leaders remained with the supports or in the rear.[19]

Young James was not complaining about his father's conduct; he was commending it in this letter to the Danish court, hoping that the Danes would be so moved by James IV's chivalry and so disgusted by the unchivalric conduct of the English that they would come to the aid of Scotland. The nation sorely needed it; James's fatal error of leading his troops in a brave charge against the strongest part of the English line resulted in his death, the loss of many Scottish nobles, the massacre of much of his army—the poet William Dunbar may have been among the slain—and a defeat that crippled Scotland. Yet James received the ultimate tribute from his people: the rumor that he, like Arthur, was not dead but would return.[20]

James, it was believed, had gone not to Avalon but to the Holy Land. This, inspired by James's own enthusiasm for a crusade, is a reminder of the importance of the idea of a new crusade throughout the late fifteenth and early sixteenth centuries. This idea is invoked in the final lines of the *Morte Darthur*, in which Lancelot's comrades, following his last wish, go to the Holy Land and do "many battles upon the myscreauntes, or Turkes." The fall of Constantinople to the Turks in 1453 had sent a shock through Christendom that continued to reverberate for many years, and even decades after the event chroniclers like Fabyan expiated at length on the atrocities committed by the Turks against the Eastern Christians.[21] The popes urged the kings of Europe to join in a new crusade; one such appeal was the occasion of Philip of Burgundy's Vows of the Pheasant, and though Philip did not go crusading, he did, as we have noted, send 4,000 men to serve under the pope's banner. Pius II urged Edward IV to join the Venetians in their war with the Turks. Edward pleaded the war with Scotland as an excuse, but even he may have taken account of popular interest in such a project, for the proclamation for one of his tournaments specified that military exercises of this sort were necessary not only for the defense of the nation but to prepare for fights against "myscreauntes."[22] In the year that Malory was writing the lines about fighting against the "myscreauntes, or Turkes," two Greek churchmen were keeping the idea alive, for they were traveling about England collecting funds to ransom their countrymen from "the cruel Turk, enemy of the church and christian faith."[23]

It is not surprising that crusading plays an important role in so many fifteenth-century romances. As William Matthews has noted, crusading is a recurrent theme in the Thornton Romances.[24] In David Aubert's *The Three Kings' Sons* the warfare is entirely directed at the Turks. In Antoine de la Sale's *Petit Jehan* the hero realizes the dream of Philip the Good and does indeed kill the Grand Turk. In Martorell's *Tirant lo Blanc*, Tirant recaptures Constantinople from the Turks and himself assumes the imperial throne of the restored Christian Eastern empire. The hero of *Sir Degravant*, like the surviving knights of the Round Table, ends his life fighting for his faith in the Holy Land: "At Port Gaff he was slon / For-iusted with a soudon" (vv. 1913-14). All these romance knights, and others, fulfilled in fiction the dream of many a knight in life, and, as shown by the elaborate plan drawn up by Monstrelet and by the policies of the popes themselves, such a dream seemed to many well within the realm of possibility.[25]

Lancelot dies not in battle against the Turks but in a hermitage, withdrawn from the world and doing all manner of bodily penance. This seems to many readers an almost explicit rejection of chivalry, an acknowledgment that the life of earthly knighthood has failed and that the only hope is in the rejection of the world implied by Lancelot's retreat. However, the retirement of a knight to a hermitage is almost a convention of romance, and both the Vulgate *Lancelot* and the *Morte Darthur* are well populated with knights—such as Malory's Sir Bawdwyne, Sir Ulphin, and Sir Brastias—who end their days in hermitages, where they serve as friends and helpers to the good knights who remain in the world. Indeed, at one point Malory says that in Arthur's days only "men of worship and proues" could become hermits.

To become a hermit in romance is not necessarily to reject worship and prowess. The hermit-knight in *The Tale of the Sancgreal* who breaks the rule of his order and takes up the sword to maintain the rights of his family against the mighty earl of Vale (xv.1) is not punished but miraculously rewarded by God for his knightly deed. Likewise, Lancelot's companions, Bors, Bleoberis, and Blamour, who have become hermits along with Lancelot (xxi.10), are commanded by Lancelot to leave the hermitage and carry on the chivalric life, fighting the "miscreauntes" in the Holy Land (xxi.13). In this role as adviser to his companions, Lancelot has something about him of the most famous hermit-knight in chivalric literature, the narrator of Ramon Lull's *Order of Chivalry*, an old knight, now retired to a hermitage, who gives advice to a young man about to begin a chivalric career. In Olivier de la Marche's allegorical *Le chevalier délibéré*, the hero is likewise advised by a hermit, who had been a "Cheualier errant par le monde" and is now retired to a hermitage (p. 12), and la Marche's poem ends with the knightly narrator himself, advanced in age, donning the armor of Repentance.

The close relation between the eremitical and chivalric lives in romance was apparent in life as well as literature. Hermits frequently appeared as characters in the dramatic displays surrounding tournaments and *pas d'armes*, and sometimes knights even fought in this guise, as Lord Scales once jousted as the White Hermit. Much later, Sir Henry Lee enacted the retirement of a knight to a hermitage when, too old to continue jousting in the Accession Day Tilts, he formally retired and assumed the role of an aged hermit.[26] He followed the advice of Stephen Scrope, Malory's contemporary, who urged knights too old for chivalric feats to turn to spiritual ones.[27] Knights did so, symbolically in the cases of those nobles who sought burial in the garb of religious orders, or intermittently, like Philip the Good of Burgundy, who was accustomed to retire from the world for days at a time, living only on bread and water, or even actually, like the duc de Clèves, who retired to a "hermitage" with his entire court. His arrangements were somewhat less than rigidly ascetic, for the duke took twenty personal servants with him to the hermitage, along with all his courtiers, and, as Monstrelet reported, the duke and his fellow hermits lived not on herbs and water but on the finest meats and wines.[28] Much later Emperor Charles V, who had translated *Le chevalier délibéré* into Spanish, also retired to a contemplative retreat.

Monstrelet was amused by the hypocrisy of the duke's withdrawal from the world. Malory might almost have approved of it, for his hermit, Sir Bawdwyne of Britain, maintains a household as grand as that of the duc de Clèves, well stocked with wines and noble foods: "For in thos dayes hit was nat the gyse as ys nowadays; for there were none ermytis in tho dayes but that they had bene men of worship and proues, and tho ermytes hylde grete housholdis and refreysshed people that were in distresse" (xviii.13). Malory's apparent confusion of the ascetic and noble styles of life is not surprising in an age that cultivated extremes in the manner of Philip the Good, who could move from luxurious feasting to penitential fasting without worrying much about inconsistency. What seems shocking in life (the duc de Clèves's "hermitage") seems admirable in romance (Bawdwyne's "grete houshold"). Likewise, we are apt to be shocked when Gawain in the Grail quest refuses to do penance ("I may do no penaunce for we knyghtes adventures many times suffir grete woo and payne"; xiii.16) and is too rushed to stop for counsel from a hermit. But our sense of shock should perhaps be tempered by the similar real-life experience of the Gascon knight, Etienne Vignoles, called La Hire. In the year 1427, rushing to take part in an attack on the English, La Hire stopped to demand absolution from a priest. He had no time, he said, to confess in detail, for he had done the sort of things men of war are accustomed to do. But he did take time for a brief prayer: "God I pray that you do today for Lahire what you would want Lahire to do for you if he were God and you were Lahire."[29] La Hire, the chronicler adds, thought this was a very good prayer, and perhaps it was, for he later became one of the most celebrated captains of Joan of Arc. Gawain too, we might note, dies like a good knight despite his sins during the Grail quest, and, for his knightly deeds, God allows him to return from death to warn Arthur against the coming battle with Mordred.

In contrast with the rather doubtful piety of the duc de Clèves and La Hire are the many examples of extreme penance and asceticism, for this was a time when religion as well as literature affected life in dramatic and exaggerated forms. Lord Scales, who had most enthusiastically imitated romance in his joust with the Bastard of Burgundy, seems to have carried his imitation of romance to the end, and he died in a manner reminiscent of Lancelot's penance at the hermitage. He spent the night before his execution writing a poem on the vagaries of Fortune, the burden of Lancelot's lament, and after his death he was found to have been wearing a hair shirt.[30] Scales's sincerity cannot be doubted, yet this final act seems no less an imitation of romance than his earlier adventures. Likewise, when John Tiptoft went to the block, he begged his executioner not to strike cleanly but to cut off his head with three strokes in "honour of the Trinity."[31] It is difficult to avoid thinking not only of Christ's Passion but of *Sir Gawain and the Green Knight*.

There is no doubt that Tiptoft was thinking only of his faith, but he chose to symbolize this in a manner that would fit easily into a fictional romance or a fictionalized saint's life, as if he saw the contours of his own life in terms of literature. Perhaps he did, for the deeds of romance heroes had moved from the realm of fiction to the real world. Knights such as Suero de Quiñones, Jacques de Lalaing, Richard Beauchamp, and many lesser nobles enacted in real life the quests, vows, and disguises of chivalric romance. To the chroniclers and heralds of the time these real-life deeds became new "examples" equal to those of old "auctoritee" in their power to inspire others so that, as Tiptoft wrote of Scales's deeds, "worthy knighthood should be the longer continued." As I have remarked, Tiptoft's justification for recording contemporary deeds of chivalry is nearly the same as Caxton's reasons for printing the *Morte Darthur*; Tiptoft's facts and Malory's fictions are equally representative of fifteenth-century life, and when Caxton, in his well-known address to the knights of England (in *The Ordre of Chyvalry*), urges his readers to emulate the great deeds of chivalry, he urges them to read both romance ("Of the

Holy Grail, of Lancelot, of Galahad, of Tristram, of Perceforest, of Perceval, of Gawain and many more") and recent history: "Read Froissart. And also behold that victorious and noble king Harry the fifth, and the captains under him." The jumbling together of history and romance made some sense in a time when chivalric romance and life itself were more closely related than at any other time in history.

Malory is thus a "realistic" writer not because he is realistic in method but because his subject, chivalry, was itself real. Malory's much-admired (though relatively rare) lifelike details should be considered in this context. Mordred's use of siege guns is not an "anachronism" but a reflection of the sieges of the time. Likewise, Guenevere's expenditure of 20,000 pounds in her search for Lancelot, or Lancelot's offer of a handsome dowry, 1,000 pounds per year, to the Fair Maid of Astolat are not, as some readers seem to think, "middle-class" touches that reveal Malory's essentially unchivalric common sense. They certainly reveal his practicality, but in Malory's time chivalry itself had practical as well as ideal aspects, and similar practical details are found in almost all aristocratic fifteenth-century romances, even the more fantastic ones, such as *Arthur of Little Britain*, in which the exact amount and disposition of a dowry is specified as precisely as Lancelot's offer to the Maid.[32]

Indeed, because he writes in the compressed style of English verse romance, Malory seldom achieves (or aspires to) the elaborate realism of his Continental contemporaries. C. S. Lewis, discussing Malory's use of detail, remarks on the "laundry list" sort of realism in Malory's cataloging exactly how Lancelot's blood soiled Guenevere's bed in the Mellyagaunce section of *Lancelot and Guenevere*.[33] But there is nothing in Malory to equal the ledger-book realism of Antoine de la Sale's *Petit Jehan*:

And when evening had come, he opened the gate of the garden and there awaited Madame, who did not long delay. Then was there such cheer between them that no man or woman can think of it unless Love has taught them. Then she said to him, "My only lover and my sweetest thought, you can not be here long: kiss me for true love's sake. And take here in this little purse one hundred and sixty *écus*, which I give you to buy a noble, energetic, and handsome riding horse, which should be lively and spirited, whatever he may cost you, up to eighty *écus*. And buy another of sound body for everyday riding, costing up to twenty *écus*. And buy a pair of horses to carry your baggage and your servant for thirty *écus*. That is one hundred and thirty *écus*.

With the thirty *écus* that remain, have suitable harness made of
beautiful cloth, and dress yourself and your servants in your livery
when you go out riding. And spend what remains on yourself as long
as it will last. When it is gone, you need only make our signal, nothing
more." And with these words she said, "Farewell, my love, all my
hope and all my welfare!"

"And farewell, Madame! Farewell, my treasure! Farewell, she who
can command me most and whom I must and will most obey!"

And with these words they parted. (Pp. 104-105)

One can hardly imagine a better illustration of the combination of
extravagant romantic gesture and solid practicality that characterized
the noble life of the fifteenth century.

This mixture of chivalric rhetoric and financial common sense
seems incongruous only if we assume that chivalry had no direct relation to life. Malory's Scottish contemporary, Sir Gilbert Haye, would
probably have approved of the prudent attention to financial matters
in Antoine de la Sale's *Petit Jehan.* In his translation of Lull's *Order of
Chivalry,* Haye does not hesitate to add to his source explicit comments on the state essential to knighthood—not only good horses
and armor but handsome clothing and servants—and he maintains
that a knight should possess lands as well as honors.[34] This concern
with practicalities is not a sign of a weakening of the older idealism
but evidence that the old ideal is now accepted as part of life.

Chivalry in the *Morte Darthur* is thus neither nostalgia nor escape.
A fifteenth-century knight like Sir Thomas Malory could hardly
escape chivalry, which was not one of a series of possible life-styles
but a definition of the noble life itself. The only alternative to a life of
chivalry is that which appears, though only intermittently even there,
in *The Tale of the Sancgreal:* withdrawal from the world. Even that,
as we have seen, is a part of the chivalric life, and it is a solution to an
individual's problems, not to the problems of the world. To write
about chivalry is not to avoid these problems but to illuminate them.
Just as there are good and evil knights in romance, all to be judged by
the code of chivalry, so there are good and evil knights in life, whose
morality can be judged by the same standard. Certainly Malory was
aware of the evils of his time, and perhaps—since the admirer of chivalry is by definition a moralist—he was more keenly aware of these
evils than many of his contemporaries. We can feel his enthusiasm for
the great deeds of a Tristram or a Lancelot; we can also feel some of
the agony Malory felt for his own times when he directly calls upon
his readers to recognize the analogy between Arthur's problems and

those of England in 1469, when the North was already in open rebellion and one king, Edward, ruled in England, while another king,
Henry, was exiled in France preparing for the invasion and civil war
that came once more in 1470, just a few months after Malory finished
his book. Probably Vinaver was right when he maintained some
decades ago that Malory's work might never have been written had it
not been for the troubles of England during the Wars of the Roses,
"faced with the horrors of internecine strife and the uncertainty of the
future."[35] Malory's book reflects some of the evil of the chivalry of his
own time as well as some of its good. That the *Morte Darthur* has
seemed to some modern readers an exposure of the weaknesses of the
knightly code is due to their idealism rather than to Malory's, for he
saw chivalry not as a dream of perfection but as a mode of life, and his
book serves both as a measure and as a mirror of his own times.

To some extent, then, Malory's book is in the tradition of other fifteenth-century romances, such as *Ponthus et Sidoine* or *Petit Jehan*,
which are handbooks of noble conduct designed to instruct their
readers in the ways of chivalry by means of examples of proper and
improper conduct. Indeed, almost all fifteenth-century romances have
something of the "courtesy book" about them, for, as we have seen,
both history and romance were thought to have a direct didactic value
by providing exemplars of noble conduct. Thus Caxton advised the
readers of the *Morte Darthur* to "take the honest acts in their remem-
brance, and to follow the same . . . Do after the good and leave the
evil, and it shall bring you to good fame and renomee." Most likely
Caxton's readers followed this advice. As William Schofield wrote,
"All the fifteenth century would have recognized in it much more
clearly than we a true guide for gentlemen's careers; they could have
understood better the mode of battle and tourney, whereby heroes
still won renown; they could hardly fail to be aroused by seeming
parallels in the Arthurian past to the events of their own present,
which have little concerned men since."[36]

Even in Malory's day such events concerned only the aristocracy,
and Malory's "realism" must finally be seen in that context. His
realism is narrow, as narrow in its way as that of *Maître Pathelin* or
Les cent nouvelles nouvelles. Consequently, the book has seemed to
critics such as E. K. Chambers to have no relation to life: "Of the
England of the fifteenth century, exhausted by generations of dynastic
quarrels, of England as we find it depicted in the Paston Letters , of the
complete breakdown of law and order, of the abuses of maintenance

and livery and private warfare, of the corruption of officials, of the
excessive taxation, of the ruin of the countrysides by the enclosure of
agricultural land for pasture—of all this we find no consciousness
whatsoever in Malory's pages."[37] Almost exactly the same criticism
has been made of *Petit Jehan de Saintré:* "The world outside, the
middle class life of the towns, the sordid misery of the peasants, the
devastated country, are not so much as hinted at. They might never
have existed."[38] For the narrowly aristocratic circle of Antoine de la
Sale's readers they did not exist, just as the common soldiery did not
exist for the chroniclers, who would carefully enumerate the deaths or
captures of noble men but would dismiss the lesser casualties as "others
of no name." The same chroniclers who would narrate in careful detail
a famous joust would pass over in a phrase or two the pillaging of
the countryside or the ravaging of a town. From the viewpoint of
the chivalric writers and their audiences, such matters were of little
concern, of as little concern as chivalric jousting and noble deeds were
to most of the Pastons.

It is therefore as vain to look in the pages of Malory for the Pastons'
England as it is to search the Pastons' letters for Malory's world—and
it is, of course, a mistake to think that either gives us a full report of
fifteenth-century life. Malory, as Schofield so well demonstrates,
writes not for the whole range of fifteenth-century society but for a
small audience—gentlemen like himself, who shared his love of
hunting, jousting, and literature.[39]

Most of the Pastons were not of that sort. Old John Paston was
apparently no great reader, and he once paid a fine rather than accept
knighthood and the duties that went with it. He did allow his son to be
knighted, but he did so in the hope that some business advantage
would come of it, and when none did, he branded young Sir John a
mere "drone."[40] So perhaps did Sir John's brothers. In 1467 Sir John
wrote home in great excitement about his jousting at Eltham: "My
hand was hurt at the Tourney at Eltham upon Wednesday last. I
would you had been there, for it was the goodliest sight that was seen
in England this forty year of so few men." His brother, back home at
this time and more concerned about the family's business than aristocratic frivolities, dourly replied: "And whereas it pleaseth you to wish
me at Eltham at the Tourney for the good sight that was there, by
troth I had lever see you once at Caister Hall than to see as many
king's tourneys as might be betwix Eltham and London."[41]

One may doubt that Sir John's father would have found much to interest him in Malory. Sir John, on the other hand, was a devoted reader of romances, tracts of chivalry, and other forms of literature, and his reading affected his view of life.[42] When he witnessed the great chivalric gathering at the Pas de l'arbre d'or at Bruges in 1468, he saw it in the light of his reading: "And as for the Duke's court and as of lords, ladies, and gentlewomen, knights, squires, and gentlemen, I never heard of none like to it, save King Arthur's court."[43] His letter communicates some of the same awed excitement we feel in Shakespeare's account of the Field of the Cloth of Gold:

> When these suns
> (For so they phrase 'em) by their heralds challenged
> The noble spirits to arms, they did perform
> Beyond thought's compass, that former fabulous story
> Being now seen possible enough, got credit,
> That Bevis was believed.   (*Henry VIII*, act 1, sc. 1)

When Sir John turned back from life to his books of romance, no doubt the deeds of Arthur and his knights got credit, for their adventures were little more fantastic than those he had witnessed with his own eyes at Bruges.[44] For such readers the *Morte Darthur* was not a work of nostalgic fiction; it was a mirror in which they could see and judge the noble life as they knew it. This is the final answer to the question posed at the beginning of this section: Why should Malory, or any fifteenth-century writer, have chosen to compose a romance? He did so because in his age romance dealt not with the remote and dreamlike but with the contemporary and real concerns of the class to which he belonged, presenting at once an exemplification and a vindication of the chivalric life to which virtuous men aspired. Yet Malory's task was more difficult than those of many contemporary romancers, for to write the history of the Round Table in the fifteenth century was to write about what the late Middle Ages had come to regard as the finest realization of the chivalric ideal; yet that history was inherited from an earlier time and from earlier writers, such as the Cistercian prose romancers, for whom the wordly ideals of chivalry were anything but admirable.

IV

The Fall of Camelot

10

The Tale of the Sancgreal

When Malory turned to the *Quest del Saint Graal*, the *Mort Artu*, and the stanzaic *Morte Arthur* for an account of the final movement of Arthurian history—the decline and fall of the Round Table—he faced a difficult problem. It is not simply that his heroes have to die. All must die, even in romantic biography, and Arthur and his knights die heroically; in the chronicle versions Arthur's death even enhances his heroism, since he dies at the hand of the traitor Mordred, as if only treachery could avail against so great a figure. The difficulty lay rather in the "historical" causes that the thirteenth-century prose romancers had adduced to account for Arthur's death. By the time the Vulgate Cycle was assembled, the simple chronicle account of Arthur's career had been elaborated to contain a great collection of other stories—the Grail quest, the love of Lancelot and Guenevere, the feud between the houses of Lot and Pellinor, and the assorted marvels, loves, and adventures of the knights of the Round Table. The architects of the prose cycles created a coherent structure for these diverse materials by the techniques of historiography, establishing not only a chronological but also a causal framework for the whole. They were in this sense historians, interested in the causes of events, rather than romancers, and, as Jean Frappier has shown, the early parts of the Vulgate Cycle are "retrospective sequels," written after the concluding parts in order to establish a full history to account for the later events.[1] Indeed, the whole Vulgate Cycle as it now exists (*Estoire del Saint Graal, Estoire de Merlin, Lancelot, Queste, Mort*

Artu) has been recast along the lines of a "retrospective sequel" designed to show the historic causes of Arthur's fall.

None worked more diligently to this end than the Cistercian author of the *Queste del Saint Graal*, which is the most important branch of the Vulgate from this historical point of view and which deeply influenced the whole cycle. The *Queste* necessitated the new introduction provided by the *Estoire del Saint Graal*, and it greatly affected the tone of parts of the *Estoire de Merlin*. Likewise, it exerted a powerful influence upon the composition of the *Mort Artu*. Only the *Lancelot*, which was composed before the *Queste*, remained untouched by its spirit.

The authors of the *Queste* found the explanation for Arthur's fall in that cause which monastic historians customarily assigned to any social disaster: sin. Arthur and his knights fall because of the sin of lust that affects all earthly knighthood. The Grail quest, the greatest adventure of the Round Table, is the story of the Round Table's utter failure, its incapability of achieving the Grail because of its sin, for which its destruction is the just and inevitable punishment.[2] Likewise, the authors of the *Estoire de Merlin* scatter dire prophecies throughout their narrative, and, expanding on the theme of lust, they provide a historical explanation for Mordred's betrayal of Arthur: Mordred is the emblem of Arthur's lust, the product of his incestuous union with his own sister. Mordred's treachery—an act of simple political ambition in the chronicles—thus becomes in the Vulgate Cycle a just retribution for Arthur's own sin.

The authors of the prose *Lancelot* were somewhat less concerned about sin than the Cistercians, yet they too developed an explanation for the fall. Lancelot's love for Guenevere and Morgan's continuing evil plots to reveal it to the king are a constant reminder that the unity of the Round Table is only temporary and that one day this love will be revealed and the Round Table inevitably split. Likewise, the enmity between the houses of Pellinor and Lot, which is developed in the *Lancelot*, provides a cause for Agravain's ultimate betrayal, which leads to the war between Arthur and Lancelot, breaks the fellowship of the Round Table, and thus enables Mordred's treachery to come so close to success. These themes are all incorporated in the prose *Tristan*, where the tragic history of Tristan and Iseult, parallel in so many ways to that of Lancelot and Guenevere, provides a dark foreshadowing of the future.

Finally, the author of the *Mort Artu* draws all these strands together to weave a web of fate in which Arthur, Lancelot, Gawain, and the entire Round Table are hopelessly entangled. His tone is more compassionate, less condemnatory than that of the author of the *Queste*, and his protagonists suffer from Fortune as well as their own crimes.[3] But the final cause of the disaster is much the same as the cause of the failure of the Round Table in the Grail quest: Arthur and his knights trust too much in this fickle world. Salvation lies only in a penitential rejection of this realm of sin, ruled by Fortune. One must scorn it, as Galahad did, or as Lancelot and Guenevere finally do when they withdraw to religious retreats to atone for their worldly sins.

This gloomy view of Arthurian history did not completely prevail, for medieval readers of the Vulgate Cycle could evidently relish both the story of Lancelot's earthly deeds and the tale of his humiliations in the Grail quest, and apparently they were not worried about trying to reconcile the two. Moreover, through most of the Vulgate Cycle— almost all of it until the *Queste del Saint Graal*—the historical framework is little more than a framework, apparent only in occasional reminders of what is to happen far in the future and of relatively little importance to the adventures at hand. Only in the *Queste* and *Mort Artu* do the historical patterns converge in their tragic consequences. Nevertheless, in late medieval literature this image of Arthur as a victim of sin or of Fortune does have an effect, and he becomes a somewhat ambivalent figure, frequently an object of condemnation rather than an exemplar of noble conduct.[4] Furthermore, though the chronicles maintain the image of Arthur as a perfect king (heaping abuse on Mordred and Guenevere as a means of fixing the blame for the fall), the Grail quest, in which the Round Table appears in its least attractive light, had become an essential part of the history, an episode that had to be included even in so brief an account of Arthur's career as appears in Hardyng's *Chronicle*. As Valerie Lagorio has shown, the tale of the Grail became more popular in England in the fifteenth century than it had ever been, and there was a growing cult of Joseph of Arimathea, who became, at least as far as the populace was concerned, St. Joseph of Glastonbury.[5]

Malory had little choice; he had to include the story of the Grail quest, and he therefore had to deal with a work much different in tone and effect from the celebration of secular chivalry in the *Tristan*. The *Queste del Saint Graal* flatly condemns the Round Table and its values, and the *Mort Artu*, on which Malory drew for the tale of Arthur's death, is a demonstration of the weakness of the chivalric code, an account of the catastrophe to which it, like any earthly value, must inevitably lead. Moreover, to be true to his history, Malory had to include all the other historical explanations of Arthur's fall that the thirteenth-century romancers had so skillfully interwoven with the original chronicle account. The last three tales of the *Morte Darthur* are therefore rich in historical causes for the final disaster, and so long as we read them with an eye to historical cause and effect we find good evidence for considering the *Morte Darthur* a tragedy, with Arthur and his knights suffering the just consequences of their own sins. This interpretation is, of course, very congenial to those who would read the *Morte Darthur* as a realistic novel built upon a cause-and-effect plot. Furthermore, this reading has validity, for the "historical" plot is indeed part of the *Morte Darthur*, as it is of every prose cycle. The tragic interpretation of the *Morte Darthur*, which has prevailed for the past hundred years, has a solid basis in the text.[6]

Chaucer's Monk, in his more solemn moments, would probably have delighted in the tragic aspects of the book. The Knight would have felt otherwise:

> I seye for me, it is a greet disese,
> Whereas men han been in greet welthe and ese,
> To heeren of hire sodeyn fal, allas!
> (*Nun's Priest Prologue*, vv. 2771-73)

He preferred comedy:

> And the contrarie is joye and greet solace,
> As when a man hath been in povre estaat,
> And climbeth up and wexeth fortunat,
> And there abideth in prosperitee.
>
> (vv. 2774-77)

Malory too was a knight rather than a monk, more precisely a fifteenth-century English knight rather than a thirteenth-century Cistercian monk. In the early thirteenth century, romance chivalry remained largely an ideal of secular literature, and secular ideals of any sort were not likely to find much favor with monastic writers of the time. The Church itself remained opposed to chivalric activities such as tournaments, and it had little sympathy with any form of knighthood that was not clearly in its own service. By the fifteenth century, chivalry had become respectable in the eyes of both Church and state, and the chivalric code of Arthur's knights had become the ideal of an important segment of society, that to which Malory and his noble readers belonged.

Malory obviously could not, and would not, reject the religious values of the *Queste*, which had shaped its narrative, and he had to remain true to the history of Arthur's fall as it had been told in the *Mort Artu*, complete with the war between Lancelot and Arthur, which is caused in large part by Lancelot's adulterous love of Guenevere. He therefore could not avoid writing a tragedy that must have been a "greet disese" to a late medieval admirer of Arthurian history. But Malory also had to hold true to his own conception of his heroes and to his own conviction of the value of the secular chivalry they exemplify.

Malory solved this problem by his most skillful use of thematic structure. In *Sir Tristram* Malory had learned how to impose a thematic structure upon a historically ordered narrative, but in that tale the historical structure could remain well in the background. In the last three tales, the historical structure comes to the foreground as the heroes move to their inevitable tragic fall. Yet, interwoven with the historical tragic narrative is a thematic "comic" narrative, one of "joye and greet solace," that leads to the vindication of Arthurian chivalry. We can see evidence of this complex double view of Arthur's fall as early as *The Tale of King Arthur*, in which the final catastrophe is first foretold. When Arthur incestuously fathers Mordred, Merlin prophesies the fall of Arthur and the Round Table because of the king's "fowle deedis": "Ye have done a thynge late that God ys displesid with you, for ye have lyene by youre syster and on hir ye have gotyn a childe that shall destroy you and all the knyghtes of youre realme" (i.20). This is essentially what Merlin says in the French source, and it is part of the historical narrative structure that leads to the final tragedy. But then Malory adds a prophecy of his own: " 'But I ought ever to be hevy,' seyde Merlion, 'for I shall dye a shamefull dethe, to be putte in the erthe quycke: and ye shall dye a worshipful dethe.' " This is part of Malory's thematic structure, which casts the events of the final tales into a new perspective that complicates and complements without contradicting the historical: Arthur's fall is at once a punishment for his sins, true to the history, and a "worshipful" end, true to the chivalric ideal.

Consequently, the final tales of the *Morte Darthur* can be read both as the tragedy of Arthur and his knights, with the condemnation of their "fowle deedis" implicit in the Vulgate history, and as a "comic" affirmation of their "worshipful" lives and values. In recent years critics have so concentrated on the tragic aspects of the book that it has become almost a commonplace that the final tales are a melancholy demonstration of the failures of Arthur and the Round Table, which was doomed to tragedy because of its internal flaws. Caxton, who seems to have had a clear idea of the complexity of Malory's work, knew as well as we that the book ends with the "most piteous" death of King Arthur "saunz gwerdon." Yet he recommended it to his noble patrons as a work whose chief interest lay in the joyous and pleasant histories of that "most renommed, fyrst and chyef of the Thre best Crysten, and woorthy, Kyng Arthur."

Certainly modern criticism of the *Morte Darthur* has greatly enriched our understanding of Malory's book and shown conclusively that it is much more than the simple collection of joyful tales that Caxton urged upon the nobility of his time. Yet, with the disappearance of Caxton's joyous interpretation, the *Morte Darthur* has lost a whole dimension of pleasure and meaning. To emphasize the joy and ignore the tragedy would obviously oversimplify Malory's book. But to concentrate entirely on the tragedy and thereby miss the joy, as some critics now do, is also an oversimplification. In *The Tale of the Sancgreal, Lancelot and Guenevere*, and *The Death of Arthur* Malory presents a continuing historical and thematic narrative that is anything but simple. These last three tales are more subtle and artful than even their more obviously sophisticated sources, and they reveal a mind that is a good deal more complex than we usually encounter in fifteenth-century romance.

The Tale of the Sancgreal may seem of itself sufficient refutation of my characterization of Malory's method, for it is generally regarded as the least original of all Malory's tales. So far as the *matière* is concerned, this is quite true. Malory considered the *Queste del Saint Graal* "one of the trewest and of the holyest that ys in thys world," and he treated it with unusual respect. He greatly compressed the French narrative, mainly by drastic reductions in the elaborate explanations provided by assorted holy men and recluses for every adventure and dream, but he made few changes in narrative and structure. He added little of his own invention, and that mainly in comment and dialogue; only one scene in the entire tale, the final one, has no counterpart in the French work. He omitted very few episodes from the French, and he followed without deviation the order of narrative that he found in the *Queste*. The result is a more nearly straightforward job of translation and reduction than any of his other works. Yet Malory's *Sancgreal* is nevertheless an "original" work, a tale much different in tone and meaning from the French *Queste del Saint Graal*, because although Malory does not greatly alter the *matière* of his source he drastically alters its thematic meaning.

Malory's decision not to tamper much with the *matière* of the *Queste* was probably due not only to his respect for the story but to the fact that the French tale already had the sort of narrative structure that he admired. Stripped of most of its allegorical explication, the *Queste* has a simple and relatively straightforward narrative line, complete with parallels and brackets of the sort that Malory worked to achieve in his other tales. What interlacing there is in the *Queste* is of much the same sort as in Malory's *Sir Tristram*, with the stories of Bors and Perceval bracketed within the adventure of Galahad, just as the tales of Alexander the Orphan and La Cote Mal Tayle are bracketed within the adventures of Tristram. And in each tale the success of Tristram and Galahad is measured against the figure of Lancelot, whose adventures are interspersed throughout both narratives and thus provide a main source of coherence in each.

Moreover, the *Queste del Saint Graal* has the same thematic organization as Malory's other tales, and it is built upon some of the same themes and motifs. It is yet another in the series of quests for perfect knighthood that are the main concern of all the tales in this central part of the *Morte Darthur*, though now the perfection is celestial rather than earthly. Through the first two-thirds of the tale, the adventures of Galahad follow much the same proof-of-knighthood pattern as we examined in *Gareth* or *Sir Tristram*, and, as in *Sir Tristram*, the achievement of full knighthood is related to fellowship in a select group of "four best knights." Galahad, like so many aspiring young men in the previous tales, comes to Arthur's court seeking knighthood. He is granted this (by Lancelot, as usual), and at once he takes his place at the Round Table. Immediate reception into the Round Table is indeed unusual, but now the movement of the theme is not toward Arthur's court but beyond it, and membership in the 150 knights of the Round Table is prerequisite to membership in the group of 150 knights who seek the Grail.

Nevertheless, Galahad's actions follow the familiar pattern: he receives knighthood, triumphs in a tournament (xiii.6), and leaves on a quest in which he abolishes an ill custom and frees captives (xiii.14-15). Then, disguised, he outjousts Arthur's knights, Lancelot and Perceval, and, still disguised, rescues Perceval (xiv.4) and triumphs in a final tournament (xvi.1). This victory completes the proof of Galahad's worthiness of the Grail quest, and it is the last earthly adventure in the tale (Gawain and the other unsuccessful knights return to Camelot at this point). Immediately after the tournament Galahad is united with Perceval and Bors, and the achievement of the Grail begins. All that is lacking from the pattern is the required fight to the draw between each of the "four best." Perceval seems to be aware of this, for when he is unhorsed by the disguised Galahad he is determined to fight for revenge. But his aunt, now a recluse, warns Perceval against this, since Galahad can never be overcome by earthly knights' hands (xiv.1). The deviation from the pattern is thus explained to both Perceval and the reader.

The existence of the familiar motifs by no means makes *The Tale of the Sancgreal* an ordinary romance, and the very familiarity of the controlling theme of the first part of the action enhances the strangeness of the adventures it contains. Within the thematic pattern of Galahad's achievement of knighthood (more ritual than achievement, since Galahad is perfect rather than becomes so) are included the trials of Perceval, Bors, Lancelot, and the unsuccessful knights. These narratives do not contain many familiar motifs, for the world of the Holy Grail is not that of the usual Arthurian romance. Penance rather than prowess is the requirement for adventure, and the adventures themselves tend to be spiritual trials rather than ordinary deeds of arms. When Bors and Perceval are reunited at the end of Bors's initial quest they recount not the deeds they have done but rather "ayther told other of their temptacions" (xvi.17).

Nevertheless, the reader has no difficulty in following the meaning of the actions, for even in Malory's version, where the explanations are drastically condensed, each dream, adventure, and temptation is clearly explained in exhausting allegorical detail, and even the most inattentive reader must realize he has moved from the realistic world of *Sir Tristram* to a world of symbolism. The symbol that unites and defines the action is that of armor, as used in St. Paul's famous allegory (Ephesians 6), where the good Christian is advised to "put on the armor of God."[7] Most of the preliminary adventures are concerned in one way or another with the armor of God as opposed to the false arms of this world. Thus Galahad comes to Arthur's court with neither sword nor shield, and he is supplied with both by supernatural means, first the sword with which he begins his knightly life in the tournament, and then the shield that he obtains just before he abolishes the evil custom at the Castle of Maidens. Lancelot, on the other hand, begins his adventures in his ordinary earthly arms. He straightway loses both his armor and his horse (xiii.18-20), and he must do penance before new arms are given to him by a holy hermit. Perceval likewise begins with a trust in earthly arms, and he is determined to be avenged on Galahad for unhorsing him, but he then loses his horse completely. He is thus deprived of the symbol essential to earthly chivalry ("What is a knyght but whan he is on horseback?" asks Gawain in *Sir Tristram*; x.48) but far less important to the celestial knights, who customarily enter boats (the symbol of their withdrawal from secular life) to journey on their quests. Perceval, still unregenerate, accepts a new horse from the devil (unbeknownst), and he is almost carried off to perdition (xiv.6). After his strange adventure with the lion and serpent he is subjected to a sexual temptation, to which he nearly succumbs (xiv.8-9) and bitterly penitent he stabs himself in the thigh with his sword, symbolically becoming a eunuch for the Lord.

Bors is not deprived of his arms, because he begins as a penitent, trusting not in his armor but in his faith. He dons a penitential scarlet coat, which thus covers his usual armorial device, and adopts a diet of bread and water (xiv.6). He therefore has one real adventure. (Only the penitent encounter adventures; Gawain and Ector find none at all; xiv.1.) He abolishes an ill custom, and then he successfully passes a test of his chastity and the much more difficult test of refusing to strike back when attacked by his brother (xiv.14). His success in these temptations is more important than the abolition of an ill custom; when he has succeeded, he is qualified to join Perceval, whom he meets on the strange boat where, as they say, "We lak nothynge but Sir Galahad, the good knyght" (xvi.17).

Their wish is soon answered, for Galahad now completes the theme of the achievement of full knighthood that brackets the lesser Grail knights' quests, and he joins Perceval and Bors on the boat. "A," says Bors, "if sir Launcelot, your fadir, were here . . . then we fayled nothynge" (xvii.2). But Lancelot, though he is one of the four best (xiv.1), remains a knight of this world and cannot achieve full fellowship with the other Grail knights. As soon as he has done penance and has acquired new armor, he takes up his old ways: he avenges himself on the knight who took his horse; then he comes to a tournament where he sees that the black knights, who are fighting the white, are being put to the worse, and he determines to "helpe there the wayker party in incresyng of his shevalry" (xv.5). In worldly terms, this is exactly what he should do: after the shame of losing his armor and horse, he should reestablish his knighthood by a preliminary duel (his joust with the horse thief), a triumph in a tournament (which he now enters), and a quest. But the pattern is broken; for the first time in his life Lancelot is defeated in a tournament. The standards of earthly chivalry do not apply in the quest of the Grail, in which worldly codes and mortal armor are of no avail.

Lancelot learns better. When he next encounters a knight who kills his horse and passes on, he "thanked God of hys adventure" (xv.6). Galahad then gives him a new horse, on which he is able to approach the Grail Castle. There, still trusting in worldly arms, he begins to draw his sword on the lions who guard the gate, and a voice speaks: "O, man of evylle feyth and poure byleue! Wherefore trustist thou more on thy harneyse than in thy Maker? For He myght more avayle the than thyne armour, in what service that thou arte sette in" (xvii.14). He sheathes his sword and, trusting in the Lord rather than his armor, he passes unharmed into Castle Corbenic, where he is allowed to see the Grail. But again he falls back on his earthly code of chivalry. Though he knows he is forbidden to enter the sanctuary of the Grail, he goes in to help the aged priest when it seems that the burden of the chalice is too great for the old man. The impulse to help the weak is admirable in earthly terms: "Fayre Fadir, Jesu Cryste," says Lancelot, "ne take hit for no synne if I helpe the good man whych hath grete nede of helpe" (xvii.15). But earthly generosity has no place here. A blinding light strikes Lancelot down, and his Grail quest is ended.

The three who achieve the quest trust not in earthly armor nor in the code it symbolizes. Instead they follow St. Paul's advice to take up the sword of the spirit and the shield of faith. The first adventure to follow the union of the three Grail knights is Galahad's achievement of a new sword to replace the one he had used in the adventures that preceded the Grail quest proper, which begins when Perceval, Bors, and Galahad have all successfully completed the adventures that prove their worthiness of the quest. With this sword, the three knights free a prisoner, Hernox, and then, with Perceval's sister, abolish an evil custom. Now, however, the evil custom is abolished not by martial deeds but by the piety of Perceval's sister, who gives her blood and thus sacrifices her own life in order that another may live.

When the Grail knights next meet, after Galahad has spent some time with Lancelot, Galahad again has divine accoutrements: a strange white knight gives him the horse that carries him to the Grail Castle of Corbenic (xvii.14). Galahad's preliminary adventures, those which customarily precede an important action, are now purely spiritual. He cures Mordrains, stills the Well of Lust, and saves a sinner from Purgatory (xvii.18). At the Grail Castle he mends the broken sword that had wounded Joseph in the thigh. The Grail appears. Galahad and his companions cure the Maimed King and depart with the Grail for Sarras, where Galahad cures the lame, is briefly imprisoned, and assumes the throne. He dies, borne off to Heaven by a multitude of angels, and a hand removes the Grail from the earth (xvii.21-23). This is the realm of miracles, with the motifs and thematic patterns reminiscent more of the life of Christ than of Arthurian knights.

Those who succeed in the Grail quest are indeed those who pattern themselves on Christ and turn aside from the ways of this world. The Grail knights realize that they must arm themselves with the spiritual armor described by St. Paul because, as they learn from the hermit-expositors, even their apparently earthly adventures are spiritual. Each of the hermits' explanations seems to echo St. Paul's words:

Put on the whole armor of God so that you can stand against the wiles of the devil.

For we struggle not against flesh and blood but against principalities and powers, against the rulers of the dark places of this world, against spiritual evil in high places. (Ephesians 6:11-12)

In the French *Queste* there is a strong suggestion that not only does the Grail quest reflect the spiritual life, but the spiritual life—the meditative life of the hermits—in its turn reflects the deeds of the Grail knights. The hermit priests repeatedly are said to "put on the armor of the Lord" when they don their vestments for Mass, as if they in their armor are engaged in their own quest. The extension of the symbol of armor to the priests reinforces the suggestion that the life of the Grail knights is an allegorical representation of the ideal monastic life and that Galahad and his companions are the fictional realization of the common medieval, but perhaps especially Cistercian, idea that the contemplative is a soldier of God.[8] This is indeed the case: the Grail knights battling the powers of darkness, the hermit-priests in the armor of the Lord, and the Cistercian author of the *Queste* are all *milites domini*, like Timothy, enduring hardness as good soldiers of Christ (2 Timothy 2:3).

By Malory's time this allegorizing of the knightly quest was a commonplace. Siegfried Wenzel has shown the existence of a distinct late medieval genre that is built on this theme, the "pilgrimage of life," which includes such works as Deguilleville's *Pélinerage de vie humaine*, Olivier de la Marche's *Le chevalier délibéré*, and Stephen Hawes's *Example of Virtue*.[9] The works in this genre are characterized by the use of the quest as the main theme, the allegorical use of armor, the hero's battles against the temptations of the world, and a number of other details familiar to readers of the *Queste del Saint Graal*—such as Deguilleville's use of a boat to symbolize the religious life, which seems to be its meaning in the *Queste*. The resemblances between the *Queste* and Deguilleville's *Pélinerage* are probably due to the fact that both stem ultimately from the work of St. Bernard, the great Cistercian, and because the *Queste* is also, as Wenzel characterizes Deguilleville's *Pélinerage*, "anchored in the tradition of monastic spirituality."[10]

However, Wenzel shows that the later works in this genre, such as Olivier de la Marche's *Le chevalier délibéré*, while retaining the conventions of the earlier pilgrimages, exhibit a marked change in tone and emphasis. The later works are notably less monastic in outlook, more "gradualistic" in their spiritual values. Jean de Courcy's *Chemin de Vaillance*, Wenzel tells us (it remains unpublished), is a pilgrimage not to attain the perfect monastic life but to achieve " 'Vaillance,' which only at the end of the Quest turns out to be the heavenly city of the Apocalypse."[11] Likewise, Olivier de la Marche's *Le chevalier délibéré* concerns not so much a rejection of this world as a reconciliation to old age, when the narrator must give up the knightly life and prepare for his end. The contemplative life seems less an alternative to worldly adventure—one to be adopted by a young Galahad or Perceval—than a suitable conclusion to a chivalric career. That is the case of the hero, an aged knight, and of his hermit instructor, who was once a knight-errant well known to the Round Table. It was the case of Olivier de la Marche himself. He had long been an admirer of chivalry and was a participant in such great events as the duel between Lord Scales and the Bastard of Burgundy. By 1486, when he wrote *Le chevalier délibéré*, he was in his seventies and preparing to meet his end.

Malory's *Tale of the Sancgreal* differs from the *Queste del Saint Graal* in much the same way that these later pilgrimages of life differ from Deguilleville's *Pélinerage*. Malory likewise uses the same narrative events as an earlier work, but he also replaces its monastic asceticism with a more secular tone. The Christ-like aspect of Galahad emerges as clearly from Malory's text as from the *Queste*, perhaps more clearly, since Malory's Galahad is even less worldly than the French.[12] Likewise, a good deal of the monastic *contemptus mundi* survives in Malory's tale, and even the suggested parallel between the

Grail knights and the hermits remains in the hermit-priest's donning the "armour of Oure Lorde" to say Mass (only once in Malory; xvii.9). Yet Malory's omission of so much of the hermits' allegorical exposition has the effect of changing the focus of the tale, bringing the action itself more directly to our attention. In the French work the action almost disappears under the weight of moral and allegorical commentary. For example, in both works Lancelot comes upon a hermit whose companion left the cloister to fight for his family's honor against the mighty Earl de Vale. In the French text, the narration of the episode takes about nine pages in all (Sommer, VI, 84-92); it is preceded by a two-page introduction in which Lancelot is recognized and vilified by a squire who upbraids him for his failures. Lancelot is so humiliated by the justness of these accusations that he dares not reply, and he leaves, weeping. Then we have the brief episode of the renegade hermit, which is followed by a six-page lecture on Lancelot's failure, not just in the quest but in his whole life, because of his lust for Guenevere. The episode of the renegade hermit serves merely as an occasion for an extended moralizing attack on Lancelot. In Malory the eleven pages of the French are reduced to two pages: there is no insulting squire preceding the episode, and the hermit's six-page lecture is reduced to one brief paragraph, with no specific mention of any of Lancelot's offenses (xv.1-2). The action itself becomes the focus of attention.

Malory's omission of such moralizing and allegorizing commentary, which provides the principal coherence of the French tale, thus shifts the source of coherence from the hermits to the knights, especially Lancelot, the one knight who appears throughout the entire tale. In both *The Sancgreal* and the *Queste* Lancelot's adventures extend throughout the entire narrative and provide a continuing parallel to Galahad's exploits. However, Malory makes Lancelot even more prominent than he was in the French. He invents a final scene in which Lancelot is brought to the center of our attention after the conclusion of the quest. He thereby creates a bracket for the entire action; we begin and end the tale with our attention upon Lancelot, as if he, rather than Galahad, were the main concern. And within the tale, the reduction in the proportion of commentary to action, as we have seen in the hermit-renegade episode, brings Lancelot's adventures repeatedly to the foreground.

We begin with a scene in which Lancelot is the main character. Because he is the best knight in the world, he is summoned to bestow knighthood on his son Galahad. Then the narrative concentrates on Galahad's first adventures (xiii.9-17). Next Lancelot begins his quest, but the account of his quest is left in suspension while the entire adventure of Perceval is narrated (xiv.1-9). We return then to Lancelot, but again we leave his adventures incomplete while we turn to the account of Gawain and Ector (xvi.1-6) and the complete story of Bors's trials (xvi.6-17). Galahad then triumphs in the tournament, and the earthly adventures are ended. The Grail quest proper then begins for Galahad, Perceval, and Bors, but once more the narrative shifts to Lancelot for the completion of his adventures (xvii.13-17) before the accomplishment of the Grail by Galahad and his companions. When that is finished, Bors returns to the court, where, in the one scene Malory added to the tale, Bors is united with Lancelot. Lancelot's adventures provide the means of uniting the preliminary adventures with the Grail quest proper and, because of the bracket formed by the first and last scene, they lend the tale a sense of completion that is lacking in the French, where Bors's return to the court seems only an anticlimactic device to round off the narrative. The early quest of the Grail knights had been for companionship with one another, and, as we have noted, when the three successful Grail knights meet on the boat, Bors says that if only Sir Lancelot were here, "then we fayled nothyng" (xvii.2). The final scene, in which Bors and Lancelot embrace and swear eternal friendship, suggests a unifying theme, which began with Bors's words at the moment the Grail quest proper began and which is here concluded.

Lancelot had almost as important a role in the French tale as in Malory, but there he served mainly as a foil to Galahad. The French romancer loses no opportunity to heap scorn and humiliation upon Lancelot's earthly chivalry, and his adventures in the *Queste* are a recurring reminder of the sinfulness rejected by his moral betters. Malory's Lancelot clearly retains some of this function, for he does fail to achieve the Grail. Yet Malory removes much of the attack on Lancelot, thus considerably softening the effect of Lancelot's failure, and he adds many passages praising Lancelot, as if to assure his readers that Lancelot's failure in the spiritual quest does not diminish his knightly stature.

For example, in the opening scenes of both the *Queste* and *The Sancgreal* twelve nuns request Lancelot to grant knighthood to Galahad: "We pray you to make hym knyght, for of a more worthyer mannes hand may he nat resceyve the Order of Knyghthode" (xiii.1).

In the *Queste* this praise of Lancelot is a necessary preliminary to the attack that will follow. The reader is reminded that Lancelot is the best so that he will feel more deeply the effect of the announcement that Lancelot is deprived of his honor. As soon as Galahad achieves the adventure of the sword in the stone, a damsel appears to announce that Lancelot is no longer the greatest of knights, and, as if to rub it in a bit, she makes her announcement in a public way carefully calculated to diminish his "worship."

"Ah, Lancelot, how greatly your state has changed since this morning!"
    And when he heard this he said, "Damsel, tell me how."
    "By my faith," she said, "I shall tell you in the hearing of everyone in this place. Yesterday you were the best knight in the world, and he who called you 'Lancelot, the best knight of all,' spoke the truth, for then you were. But he who would say that now would be considered a liar, for there is a better one than you." (Sommer, VI, 11)

Then, to make her point even clearer, she turns to Arthur and tells him that the appearance of the Grail is a great honor for his court, but that it is "not for you, but for another."
    Malory retains the lady's announcement that Lancelot is no longer the best, but then he adds:

"As towchynge unto that," seyde sir Launcelot, "I know well I was never none of the beste."
    "Yes," seyde the damesell," that were ye, and ar yet, of ony synfull man of the worlde. And, sir kynge, Nascien the eremeyte sendeth the worde that the shall befalle the grettyst worship that ever befelle kynge in Bretayne." (xiii.5)

This is the direct opposite of the lady's message in the *Queste*, where the whole point of the division between earthly and celestial chivalry is the irreconcilable opposition between good and evil, with all the glory in the spiritual and only lust and shame in the earthly. That opposition is missing from Malory's "gradualistic" version; the spiritual is the greater but not the only realm of the good and glorious. In this version, the Grail reflects honor on the court for its own sake, and Lancelot remains the best of earthly (therefore necessarily sinful) knights, different not only in degree but almost in kind from the celestial and sinless Galahad, who, as we have noted, is an even more abstract and unearthly figure in Malory's *Sancgreal* than he is in the *Queste*. No doubt Malory's Lancelot would be a greater knight if he could succeed in the Grail, but, as Malory repeatedly assures us, his failure in the spiritual quest by no means diminishes his earthly glory. In Malory's version the hermits and recluses, even while advising Lancelot to turn away from the world, almost invariably add, "Thou haste nat thy pere of any synfull erthly man" (xv.6).

Moreover, Malory makes two notable additions which serve to diminish considerably the dimensions of Lancelot's failure: the first is the nature of Lancelot's Grail vow. When Lancelot confesses to the hermit that his battles have been mainly for the queen's sake and not for God's, the hermit administers an oath:

"Sir, I woll counceyle you," seyde the ermyte, "yf ye shall ensure me by youre knyghthode ye shall no more com in the quenys felyship as much as ye may forbere."
And than sir Launcelot promysed hym that he nolde, by the faythe of hys body. (xiii.20)

"As much as ye may forbere" seems curiously equivocal compared to the unqualified and stern words of the hermit in the French version:

"Then I require of you," said the good man, "that you promise me that you will never transgress against your Creator by doing mortal sin with the queen or any other woman nor in any other matter that might offend Him but rather that you will guard against this with all your power."
And he swore to do so like a loyal knight. (Sommer, VI, 48)

The Lancelot of the Vulgate clearly breaks this vow when he returns to his old love for the queen. Malory's Lancelot keeps his vow; he does avoid the queen's company as much as he can. His problem is that he cannot forbear it, for love, as Malory explains in *Lancelot and Guenevere*, is too powerful to suffer restraint. Lancelot nevertheless does his best, and that is all that Malory's hermit requires.

Even more striking is Malory's addition of a prophecy assuring us that despite his failure in the Grail quest, Lancelot will die a right holy man, as Galahad does; a hermit tells Gawain that Lancelot has at least forsaken sin in this quest: "And nere were that he ys nat stable, but by hys thoughte he ys lyckly to turne agayne, he sholde be nexte to encheve hit sauff sir Galahad his sonne; but God knowith hys thought and hys unstablenesse. And yett shall he dye ryght an holy man, and no doute he hath no felow of none erthly synfull man lyvyng" (xvi.5). As Vinaver notes, "The suggestion that Lancelot 'shall dye ryght an holy man' is as strange in the context of the Grail story as it is typical of M."[13] Yet it is true that Lancelot will die a holy man, and though it is out of keeping with the spirit of the thirteenth-century *Queste*, it is in the spirit of later works like the *Chemin de vaillance*, in which one achieves grace by knightly deeds, by striving, as Lancelot promises in his Grail vow, "to sew knyghthode and to do fetys of armys" (xiii.20).

Such additions clearly ameliorate the role of Lancelot and his worldly knighthood in *The Sancgreal*. Nevertheless, Lancelot emerges fourth-best from the Grail quest. He does have some success, more than any other earthly knight save Bors, but that is the main problem. Galahad and Perceval are purely celestial knights, so pure that they must die when the Grail quest is complete, for they cannot return to the world. Their success in Malory's tale can hardly diminish Lancelot's stature. Bors is another matter. He is an earthly knight, of Lancelot's own kin, and his one sin against perfect virginity was his affair with King Brandegoris's daughter (xii.9), a parallel to Lancelot's one sin against his perfect love for Guenevere. Bors does return to the court, and his return serves as a visible reminder that Lancelot could have succeeded if he had only been "stable."

Yet Malory manages to diminish the effect of Bors's success by adding that final scene which brings Lancelot back to the center of the action and provides a bracketing structure both for the entire tale (which, as we have noted, begins and ends with our attention on Lancelot) and for the Grail quest proper (which begins with Bors's wishing Lancelot were with the Grail knights and ends with the union of Bors, the only surviving Grail knight, with Lancelot). In Malory's version Bors returns to the court, bringing Lancelot a final greeting from Galahad and a warning to "remember of thys unsiker world."

Then sir Launcelot toke syr Bors in hys armes and seyde, "Cousyn, ye are ryght wellcome to me! For all that ever I may do for you and yours, ye shall fynd my poure body redy atte all tymes whyle the spyryte is in hit, and that I promyse you feythfully, and never to fayle. And wete ye well, gentyl cousyn sir Bors, ye and I shall never departe in sundir whylis our lyvis may laste."

"Sir," seyde he, "as ye woll, so woll I." (xvii.23)

Our final view of Lancelot in *The Sancgreal* is thus not of his separation from the three who succeed but of his union with the only surviving Grail knight. More subtly, we are shown the reestablishment of the earthly order of knighthood, for it seems almost as if Bors's success in the Grail quest has been rewarded with Lancelot's friendship in the same way other questing knights in earlier tales have been rewarded. Lancelot welcomes Bors back into the court, and he takes the initiative in offering Bors his friendship. Bors's meek reply—"As ye woll, so woll I"—is emblematic of his resumption of a position subordinate to Lancelot, a position that he faithfully maintains in the tales that follow.

None of these changes negate the essential import of the tale that Malory inherited from the authors of the *Queste*. Bors remains Lancelot's superior in matters of the spirit. Lancelot is still subjected to extreme forms of penance because of the vanity and sin of his previous life, and he still emerges from the quest as one who could not slough off the Old Law of earthly chivalry and steadfastly embrace the New Law of the spirit. Instead, Malory's changes complicate the tale. For all its allegorical complexity and skill, the *Queste del Saint Graal* is morally very simple, with the spirit on one hand, the flesh on the other, and the reader left with no doubts about which is to be preferred and what the effects of that choice must be. This is perhaps natural enough in an allegory of the monastic life, in which the claims of the world are of concern only as threats to spiritual perfection. Malory, like Milton, was less concerned with the problems of a fugitive and cloistered virtue than with the moral difficulties of this world, in which both the spirit and the flesh have their necessary roles. Certainly Malory would not deny the values of the *Queste*, and to die "ryght an holy man" was indeed devoutly to be wished. But Malory's ideal spiritual quest was much more that of the *Chemin de vaillance*, the "worshipful way" that Lancelot follows and thereby achieves the Heavenly City by way of earthly knighthood.

Malory's Grail quest is thus part of a continuum of adventures rather than a sharp break with the Round Table's past. Many critics today would still agree with Edward Strachey, who believed that "the severence between good and evil that has been declared through the Sancgreal cannot be closed again"; the old chivalry has been discredited and must now die.[14] That is indeed the case in the *Queste del Saint Graal*. But in Malory's version the quest becomes an Arthurian adventure as well as a spiritual one, and earthly worship remains a positive value.[15] Moreover, the hermits' prophecy that Lancelot will die a holy man serves notice that *The Sancgreal* marks not the end of Lancelot's greatness but the beginning of his movement toward a new greatness. The full meaning of Malory's *Sancgreal* is thus to be found not within its own limits but in the larger narrative structure, which is most clearly defined by the following *Book of Sir Lancelot and Guenevere*.

11

The Book of
Sir Lancelot and Guenevere

The *Book of Sir Lancelot and Guenevere* is of crucial importance to our understanding both of the overall structure of the *Morte Darthur* and of the place of *The Tale of the Sancgreal* within this larger economy. That overall structure is more important and more obvious to the reader in this part of the book than in its earlier sections, for Malory's method of organizing the last three tales is his most skillfull realization of the potentialities of the prose cycle as a literary form. In the first part of the *Morte Darthur*, in *The Tale of King Arthur* and *Arthur and Lucius*, Malory uses the cycle as a means of organizing diverse materials into a coherent and balanced whole. In this final section he uses the cyclic form as a means of carrying the theme from one tale to another, so that although each tale remains an independent unit, each is also clearly a part of a thematic and historic development that comprehends all three, and an important part of our understanding of any one tale is dependent upon our recognizing its relation to the others. *Lancelot and Guenevere*, which is sometimes regarded as a flaw in the larger structure of the *Morte Darthur*, is Malory's principal means of defining the structural function of his cyclic form. *The Sancgreal* and *The Death of Arthur* are necessary parts of the history; *Lancelot and Guenevere* is Malory's own invention, necessary to his thematic modification of that history.

This is not immediately obvious because, as we have seen, there are two cyclic structures in the *Morte Darthur*. One is the historical three-part structure. From the standpoint of history all Arthurian cycles are tripartite, for all tell the story of the birth, life, and death of Arthur and the accompanying rise, flowering, and fall of the Round Table. The *Morte Darthur* is no exception. The first four tales (*King Arthur, Arthur and Lucius, Sir Lancelot, Gareth*) describe the rise of the Round Table; the flowering is described in *Sir Tristram*, where the new stage is marked by a shift in the time scheme; and the fall is told in the last three tales (*The Sancgreal, Lancelot and Guenevere, The Death of Arthur*). Alongside this historical structure is the thematic scheme defined by the two tales of Lancelot, which establish a much different organization, with a brief historical introduction (*King Arthur, Arthur and Lucius*) and conclusion (*The Death of Arthur*) and the long thematically organized central section that begins with *Sir Lancelot* and ends with *Lancelot and Guenevere*. This central section has a pyramidal structure, of which *Sir Tristram* is the apex, with the secular chivalry of Gareth on one side, balanced by the spiritual chivalry of Galahad on the other, and with the tales of Lancelot bracketing the whole. The three middle tales are all proof-of-knighthood stories, with Lancelot providing the measure of knighthood in each, knighting Gareth at the beginning of *The Tale of Sir Gareth*, bringing Tristram to the Round Table in the central tale, and welcoming Bors back into the Round Table at the end of *The Sancgreal*.

The structure has an aesthetic value in itself, but it is also important to the development of Malory's overall concern with his presentation of chivalry. In this structure, *The Sancgreal*, which initiates the downward movement in the historical scheme, is only one in a series of adventures. Malory's interlacing of the beginning of the Grail quest with the end of *Sir Tristram* (the begetting of Galahad precedes the conclusion of Tristram's adventure with Palomides) as well as the use of the Grail-like motif of healing at the end of *Lancelot and Guevevere* firmly places *The Sancgreal* in the context of worldly chivalry, an assurance that earthly knighthood retains its value even after the introduction of the spiritual chivalry of the Grail. Nothing could have been further from the intent of the French author of the *Queste*; from his standpoint, the Round Table's failure in the Grail quest must lead directly to its downfall. By interposing *Lancelot and Guenevere* between the Grail quest and the fall, Malory breaks that direct connection and shows Lancelot rising from his failure in the quest to an even higher degree of worship.

Malory's tale is therefore hardly "regressive."[1] The opening chapters of the *Mort Artu* more nearly deserve this criticism, though it would be unfair, since some form of regression is obviously necessary to that tale. Lancelot must return to his old love for Guenevere, and characters such as Gawain and Gaheriet (Gareth) must be brought back into the foreground as a preparation for the roles they will play in the final catastrophe. Most important, the world of Arthurian chivalry must be reestablished and its virtues reasserted. Earthly chivalry had been so debased in the *Queste* that we must again be brought to admire Arthur and Lancelot so that we can understand that the final catastrophe is tragic rather than merely just retribution. One has the feeling that all this was a congenial task for the author of the *Mort Artu*, for he was more compassionate than the author of the *Queste* and he clearly admired his heroes even as he condemned them.

If Malory's tale seems more regressive than the French, it is because he developed the admiration for Arthur and Lancelot that all but the most ascetic readers of the *Mort Artu* must have felt into an integral part of his narrative. To the two episodes that he drew from the first part of the French work—"The Fair Maid of Astolat" and "The Poisoned Apple," which would have been sufficient to reestablish Lancelot's worldly virtue, if that had been Malory's only purpose—he adds "The Great Tournament" (apparently his own invention), "The Knight of the Cart" (drawn from the prose *Lancelot*), and "The Healing of Sir Urry" (probably also his own invention).[2] These extend the reassertion of chivalric values necessary to the history into an independent tale that ends with Lancelot in an even higher position than he formerly held, capable now of a Grail-like healing, despite (from the standpoint of his history)—because of (from the standpoint of theme)—the love for Guenevere that caused his failure in the Grail quest.

To achieve the healing of Sir Urry, the supreme test of his knighthood, Lancelot must reestablish himself as the paragon of earthly chivalry. He had emerged from the Grail quest in a somewhat ambiguous position, still the greatest of earthly knights but now the lowest of the Grail knights. Because he had been faithful to Guenevere, he could not remain "stable" in the quest for the Grail. Ever his privy thoughts had been on her. At the beginning of *Lancelot and Guenevere*, partly because he tries to remain faithful to his Grail vows ("Madam, I was but late in that queste, and wyte you well, madam, hit may not be yet lyghtly forgotyn"; xviii.1), he attempts to stay away from the queen, and she therefore believes him faithless to her and orders him out of her presence. Lancelot is, in short, at the lowest point of his career—returned from a quest in which he partially failed and now scorned by his lady. In the ensuing tale we see him rise to the highest point by means of the one virtue incompatible with the Grail quest, his faithfulness to his lady.

To win this worship Lancelot must undergo the proof-of-knighthood so frequently employed in the long center section of the *Morte Darthur*. Like Gareth and La Cote, he must demonstrate his loyalty by enduring his lady's unfair criticism, and he must learn to be guided by her commands; he is wounded in the tournament at Winchester because he disregards Guenevere's warnings, triumphs in the Great Tournament because he follows her advice. He must prove his faithfulness to her by resisting sexual temptations, as he had in the previous *Noble Tale of Sir Lancelot*; here he resists the offers of the Maid of Astolat and of the lady who holds him prisoner in the "Knight of the Cart" episode. He must also demonstrate his prowess in duels, with Mador and Mellyagaunce, and in the two tournaments. Finally, having proven himself worthy of his lady and demonstrated his prowess, he is qualified to undertake the culminating test, the healing of Sir Urry, which establishes Lancelot once more as "the best knight of the world."

These themes and motifs are those we have so often seen before, and they are organized in the simple and balanced structure that Malory preferred. The narrative begins and ends with tests, Guenevere's ordering Lancelot from the court and Lancelot's healing of Sir Urry, in both of which humility is a dominant concern. The duel with Mador de la Porte near the beginning of the tale has its parallel in the duel with Mellyagaunce near the end, and the two duels thereby create a second bracket within the "moral tests" provided by Guenevere and Urry. Within this bracket, the pattern of major episodes is tournament-temptation, temptation-tournament. The tournament at Winchester, in which Lancelot is badly wounded because he failed to heed Guenevere's warnings, is followed by the Maid of Astolat's insistent offer of herself to Lancelot. Though Lancelot resists the temptation, this leads to another separation from Guenevere, parallel to that in "The Poisoned Apple." But Lancelot and Guenevere are reconciled, and this ends the first half of the tale.

The conclusion of this first half is marked by a minor tournament in which Sir Lavyne, the Maid's brother, does so well that all remark that he will be made a member of the Round Table come next Pentecost. Sir Lavyne's role is much larger in *Lancelot and Guenevere* than it was in the *Mort Artu*, and he serves a number of functions: he is the young aspirant whom Lancelot guides to a place at the Round Table, necessary to the full reassertion of his preeminent knighthood. Lavyne is also the emblem of Lancelot's blamelessness in the Maid of Astolat affair, the proof of his continuing good relations with the Maid's family (and hence an assurance of Lancelot's innocence in that affair). Finally, Lavyne's participation in this tournament and the subsequent prediction that he will join the Round Table provide the bracket that binds the second part of the action to the first; the whole tale ends at Pentecost with another minor tournament in which the prediction is fulfilled: Sir Lavyne does so well that he is indeed made a knight of the Round Table.

The second half of the tale (almost exactly proportionate to the first—nineteen folios in the first, twenty in the second) repeats, with variation, the motifs of the first half. Again there is a tournament, but this time Lancelot follows Guenevere's advice and does not fight against his kindred, and this time, though Lancelot is again disguised (since he is still proving himself), he wears not the red sleeve of the Maid of Astolat but the gold sleeve of Guenevere. The tournament serves to reestablish Lancelot as the unquestioning servant of his lady. It also provides a means of bringing Gareth to the forefront of the action; he appears as the knight second only to Lancelot, and he is elaborately praised by Bors and Lancelot (xviii.19).

Then follows the abduction of Guenevere. Lancelot rescues the queen and, as further proof of his submission to his lady, he spares the evil Mellyagaunce. Lancelot spends the night with the queen, but the traces of blood he leaves on the bed allow Mellyagaunce to accuse Guenevere of adultery, and Lancelot must fight him again on her behalf. The treacherous Mellyagaunce plays upon Lancelot's trust ("For ever a man of worshyp and proues dredis but lytell of perels, for they wene that every man be as they bene"; xix.7). Lancelot is made captive and held in a cave, this time by a lady who will supply him with arms only if he grants her his love. Lancelot passes the test and returns to save Guenevere from the stake for the second time in this tale. He fights Mellyagaunce and, at her command, kills him—a sign not of her cruelty, for Mellyagaunce deserves to die, but of Lancelot's perfect submission to the will of his lady. This final proof of Lancelot's prowess and love qualifies him for the culminating adventure, the healing of Sir Urry.

Though there are problems of interpreting this episode, its function is clear. It gives proof that Lancelot is the best of knights and provides a kind of summarizing conclusion for the whole middle section of the *Morte Darthur*. The 110 knights who try and fail to heal Sir Urry are each named, frequently with allusions to the preceding tales in which they appeared, and sometimes with allusions to tales that have not been told—such as Gawain's begetting of Florence and Lovell on Sir Brandelys's sister, or the relation between Lancelot and Sir Severause le Brewse, whom the Lady of the Lake made friends. We hear of Gareth "that was of verray knyghthod worth all the brethirn," of the begetting of Tors, of the virtue of Lamerok, of the peerless Sir Perceval and Galahad who excelled "in holy dedis," "but they dyed in the queste of the Sangreall"; we are told how Sir Bors begat Helayne le Blank, what knights Lancelot overcame when he was wearing Kay's arms, and we learn the details of Tristram's death and of Sir Bellengerus's revenge upon King Mark. All this, and more, serves both as a grand summary of Arthurian adventure and as the best possible proof that Lancelot's healing of Sir Urry does indeed establish him as the greatest knight in all the world. There have been many previous tests in the book, and conventionally a hero's success in an adventure is preceded by the failures of others, which serve as a foil to set off the achievement. But none is on so grand a scale as this, the culminating adventure of the Round Table.

It is furthermore a Grail-like adventure, a divine healing of the sort that only Galahad has heretofore performed. Only Lancelot himself, early in his career, had achieved anything like it, in his healing of Melyot de Logres in *A Noble Tale of Sir Lancelot* (vi.14), an episode that helps reinforce the parallel between the two tales of Lancelot. But that healing is a much lower accomplishment than this, and it came long before the advent of the Grail and its accompanying condemnation of Lancelot's earthly chivalry. That Lancelot, whose love of Guenevere had prevented his achieving the Grail, should achieve this healing after reestablishing his faithful love of Guenevere seems a sign of divine approval. It is surely a sign that Malory did not make a simple equation between the sin of lust and the fall of the Round Table. Lancelot is a sinful man; but the sinless men, Perceval and Galahad, "dyed in the queste of the Sangreall," and we are once again in a world where all are sinful. Even Bors has now resumed his secondary position; he is among those who try and fail to heal Sir Urry.

Yet, when Lancelot succeeds, he "wepte, as he had bene a chylde that had bene betyn." Malory's statement is simple, probably commonplace (the same expression appears in Chaucer's *Miller's Tale*, v. 3759), but it has great force, and critics have offered a variety of explanations for Lancelot's tears. Robert Lumiansky argues that Lancelot weeps from sheer relief: he feared to undertake the test because he thought he would fail and thereby reveal to the king his adulterous relation with Guenevere.[3] P. E. Tucker explains that Lancelot is reluctant to undertake the test because of his humble awareness of his own unworthiness, and he weeps because of his humility.[4] Or Lancelot may cry like a child because, as Edmund Riess believes, he now "understands something of what he would have been if it had not been for his instability and earthly love."[5] Or he may weep for the reason adduced by C. S. Lewis: pure joy at what God has allowed him to perform.[6] I suspect that there is some validity in all these explanations. But I think the main reason Lancelot weeps is to express Malory's own sadness that this, his favorite hero's greatest adventure, must also be his last.

Around this whole tale clings a sense of finality. It contains the last tournaments, the last quests, the last happy union of Lancelot and Guenevere, and the last scenes in which the Round Table still exists in a time when "he that was curteyse, trew, and faytheful to hys frynde was that tyme cherysshed" (xviii.24). The long list of knights who try and fail to cure Urry's wounds provides a summary of all that has gone before and conveys the sense that the whole series of preceding adventures is focused upon this moment. *The Tale of the Sancgreal* does indeed mark a turning point in history, a break with the past, but *The Book of Sir Lancelot and Guenevere* is the emotional climax of the central section and conveys a true sense of an ending. At the conclusion of *The Sancgreal* when Lancelot and Bors agree to be friends in the future, that future seems unlimited. At the end of *Lancelot and Guenevere* Lancelot has clearly reached the pinnacle of his career; anything more would be anticlimax. Malory is aware of this ("I leve here of this tale and overlepe grete bookis of syr Launcelot"), and the reader, because of the summarizing of the whole book that preceded Lancelot's achievement, is also aware that a glorious period has come to an end. The sympathetic reader must surely feel some touch of sadness at this, and one wonders if Malory did not intend to show that Lancelot felt it as well.

The mixed emotional quality of this final scene, its sadness and joy, reflects the combination of tragic and comic elements throughout the whole of *Lancelot and Guenevere*. Thus far I have considered this tale only from the standpoint of theme, and the thematic movement is essentially comic, progressing steadily upward from the lowest point in Lancelot's career to the highest, his triumphant healing of Sir Urry. This comic movement does dominate the tone of the tale. But if we shift our perspective and consider the tale from the standpoint of the historical framework, we recognize that much of the action of *Lancelot and Guenevere* is shaped by the tragic, downward movement that begins in *The Sancgreal* and culminates in the final catastrophe of *The Death of Arthur*.

Lancelot and Guenevere begins with a clear statement of the heedlessness of Lancelot's love for the queen ("they lovid togydirs more hotter than ever they dud toforehand") and of the dangers the lovers face from "Sir Aggravayne, sir Gawainis brothir, for ever he was opynne-mowthid" (xviii.1). And the tale ends with the statement that "Every day and nyght sir Aggravayne, sir Gawainis brothir, awayted quene Gwenyver and sir Launcelot to put hem both to a rebuke and a shame." Within the ominous bracket of these allusions to Agravain, we see the dangerous development of Lancelot's love for Guenevere as it becomes ever more open and culpable. Lumiansky has shown that the whole tale has a structure of growing suspense, as we move closer to the moment when Arthur is made publicly aware of the adultery.[7] Lumiansky notes that this suspense, which mounts as we anticipate Arthur's discovery, is accompanied by the increasing culpability of the lovers, symbolized by the duels that Lancelot fights on the queen's behalf: first he fights Sir Mador to defend her from a charge of which she is completely blameless. Next he fights and kills Sir Mellyagaunce to defend her from a charge of which she is only technically innocent (since she has been accused of adultery with one of the wounded knights rather than with Lancelot). In the next tale Lancelot again saves Guenevere from the stake, although this time she is clearly guilty, and in the process he kills the blameless and unarmed Gareth. By this point the adultery has become public knowledge and the fellowship of the Round Table is broken as a result.

The main subject of this tale, the love of Lancelot and Guenevere, also has differing, even contradictory, aspects when we consider it from the opposing standpoints of history and theme. So far as the historical structure is concerned, Lancelot and Guenevere's affair is sinful and blameworthy. Much of the hermits' commentaries in *The Sancgreal* is devoted to detailed explanations of exactly how sinful their love is, and clearly this love affair is one of the most important causes of the final tragedy. It is not surprising that critics intent upon tracing a consistent tragic movement in the final tales should find that in Lancelot and Guenevere this love turns into simple and shocking lust.

Yet, from the standpoint of theme, Lancelot's love of Guenevere is a positive virtue, a necessary part of the perfect chivalry that is rewarded in "The Healing of Sir Urry." To this extent, *Lancelot and Guenevere* is a kind of anti-Grail, a proof that just as the Grail reverses the code of chivalry so that the first shall be last, so the code of the Grail can be reversed, with the knight who was last becoming the first by means of worldly love and prowess. In place of the hermits' lectures on the evils of earthly love Malory includes two emphatic and extended defenses of human love. Both are Malory's own inventions, and each is characterized by a passion and lyricism that lends it special force in this usually restrained narrative.

The first is Elaine's stout refusal to reject human love. When she is on her deathbed, dying for the love of Lancelot, "hir ghostly fadir bade hir leve such thoughtes." She replies,

"Why sholde I leve such thoughtes? Am I nat an erthely woman? And all the while the brethe ys in my body I may complayne me, for my belyve ys that I do none offence, though I love an erthely man, unto God, for He fourmed me thereto, and all maner of good love comyth of God. And other than good love loved I never sir Launcelot du Lake. And I take God to recorde, I loved never none but hym, nor never shall, of erthely creature; and a clene maydyn I am for hym and for all othir. And sitthyn hit ys the sufferaunce of God that I shall dye for so noble a knyght, I beseche The, hyghe Fadir of Hevyn, have mercy uppon me and my soule, and uppon myne unnumerable paynys that I suffir may be alygeaunce of parte of my synnes. For, Swete Lorde Jesu," seyde the fayre maydyn, "I take God to recorde I was never to The grete offenser nother ayenste Thy lawis but that I loved thys noble knyght, sir Launcelot, oute of mesure. And of myself, Good Lorde, I had no myght to withstonde the fervent love, where fore I have my deth!" (xviii.19)

The immediate function of this passage—remarkable because it casts Malory in the unusual role of a theoretician of love—is to explain and to excuse Elaine's conduct. But it also helps explain and excuse Lancelot's conduct. Elaine's question, "Am I nat an erthely woman?" may seem to echo Criseyde's "I nam nat religious," but there is no Chaucerian irony in Elaine's words. Galahad and Perceval are dead, and the earthly life must go on, however much the Grail hermits might wish that all the world were a monastery.

Love, which is natural to earthly creatures, is the gift of God. It must be love for a single individual (to love several, as we are told a number of times over, is not love but lechery). It offends against God's law only when it is excessive, "oute of mesure." But even this sort of *démesure*, a sin both in courtly and religious terms, comes by "the sufferaunce of God," for love is irresistible: "of myself, Good Lorde, I had no myght to withstonde the fervent love." The hermits of the Grail, and some modern critics, would reply that of course one can withstand sin, especially the sin of lust, by total withdrawal from this sinful world. But the hermits of the Grail are absent from this scene, and Malory—and perhaps his reader—is not willing to take that easy solution. The tragedy of Elaine is that she is the victim of passion rather than its agent; the force of love is greater than she, and we must pity rather than condemn her.

Lancelot is likewise the victim of passion rather than its willingly sinful agent. In the Grail quest he confesses to the hermit that he loved the queen "unmesurebly and oute of mesure longe" (xiii.20), but, like Elaine, he is powerless and cannot forbear the queen's company. Sir Bors realizes this; after he meets the Fair Elaine, " 'God wolde, fayre cousyn,' seyde sir Bors, 'that ye cowde love her, but as to that I may nat nother dare nat counceyle you' " (xviii.16). Bors knows that Lancelot is as incapable of loving Elaine as she is of ceasing to love him.

Lancelot himself explains this to Guenevere and Arthur when they have read Elaine's letter. Guenevere tells Lancelot he should have shown the maid more kindness, but he explains that love is beyond rational control:

"I love nat for to be constrayned to love, for love muste only aryse of the harte selff, and nat by none constraynte."
"That is trouth, sir," seyde the kynge, "and with many knyghtes love is fre in hymselffe, and never woll be bonde; for where he ys bonden he lowsith hymselff." (xviii.20)

Love, as Chaucer's Franklin had said (*Franklin's Tale*, vv. 761-762), can be neither constrained nor restrained.

In her defense of love Elaine specifies that hers is "good love" and that she dies a "clene maydyn," though that is no fault of her own. In Malory's second extended discussion of love in this tale he takes care that his readers should not assume that unrequited love is the only form of virtuous love. As he prepares for the most passionate scene between Lancelot and Guenevere, the assignation at Mellyagaunce's castle, Malory inserts his famous passage on the lusty month of May, in which he defines "virtuous love." This passage is well known to every reader, but given the widespread critical suspicion that Malory depicts these lovers as victims of lust rather than exemplars of love, it may be a good idea to quote again Malory's unequivocal statement: "And therefore all ye that be lovers, calle unto your remembraunce the monethe of May, lyke as did quene Gwenyver, for whom I here make a little mencion, that whyle she lyved she was a trewe lover and therefore she had a good ende" (xviii.25). The emphatic insistence that Guenevere was a "trewe lover" is, as we have noted, set within a discussion of "old love," love in the days of King Arthur, a past so distant that adultery can be at least partially excused.

However, the insistence that Guenevere is a good lover also helps to relieve any doubts we may have after Guenevere's imperious, not to say shrewish, behavior toward Lancelot in the earlier parts of the tale. Her ordering Lancelot out of her presence at the beginning of the tale seems excessive, but it is a necessary trial for Lancelot. He must demonstrate his humility in his relations with Guenevere, with his fellow knights (he admits that pride led to his jousting with Bors; xviii.16), and finally with God, to whom he humbly bows and prays that he be allowed to cure Sir Urry. Lancelot's humility is the most obvious aspect of that final episode, and it culminates the recurring concern with humility that helps unite the earlier adventures.

Lancelot shows loyalty to his lady as well as obedience to her commands in the adventures that precede the healing. He is separated from Guenevere by her own command in "The Poisoned Apple." He is separated from her again—and again she unfairly blames him—in "The Fair Maid." And he is separated from her for a final time when she is kidnapped by Mellyagaunce in "The Knight of the Cart," in which Lancelot is so humbly loyal to Guenevere that the life and death of Mellyagaunce depends upon her whim. All this may seem excessive to a modern reader, but it is Lancelot's perfect loyalty even to his lady's unreasonable demands that qualifies him as the best knight in the world, able to touch and cure Sir Urry's wounds.

All this would have horrified the saintly hermits of the Grail. Yet even the Grail adventure was dependent on Lancelot's loyalty to his love for Guenevere. The quest could be achieved only if he fathered the Grail knight upon that other Elaine, the daughter of King Pelles. The means of bringing that about was Lancelot's love for Guenevere. Lancelot's affair with Pelles's daughter was a sin against his love for

Guenevere and a consequence of his earthly devotion to the queen that prevents his own attainment of the Grail, but it is a necessary sin, as we have noted, in the redemptive history of the Grail. Likewise, the love for Guenevere that caused Lancelot's failure in the Grail quest is part of the perfect knighthood that enables him to cure Sir Urry and that finally motivates his entering the hermitage to die "ryght an holy man" as the Grail hermit had prophesied. Lancelot's earthly love is the theme that holds the whole last part of the *Morte Darthur* together—a recurrent concern in the Grail quest, the main subject of *Lancelot and Guenevere*, and in *The Death of Arthur* the immediate cause both of the fall of the Round Table and of Lancelot's own salvation.

12

The Death of Arthur

The last tale of the *Morte Darthur* presents the convergence of the historical forces that produce the great anger "that stynted nat tylle the floure of chyvalry of alle the worlde was destroyed and slayne" (xx.1), and the narrative method becomes more historical than thematic. The movement of the action is tragic, as we see Lancelot, who was at the height of his career at the end of *Lancelot and Guenevere*, plunged into misery, and the tone becomes one of mourning, tears, pity, and distress. The historical tragedy that began in *The Sancgreal* here reaches its conclusion. Yet the tone of *The Death of Arthur* is also one of forgiveness, of final joy, and it shows the ultimate triumph of virtue over vice, if not in the world at large at least in the protagonists themselves. Arthur, Gawain, Guenevere, and Lancelot all bear part of the guilt for the tragic fall of the Round Table, yet all four are forgiven and we see each for the last time not as a sinful and flawed tragic figure but as an exemplar of virtue finally rewarded for faithfulness to love or chivalry. Though Lancelot is plunged into misery, he rises to the joy of Heaven. This movement is part of the thematic comedy that continues throughout the final three tales, the overall rise of Lancelot from the failure of his Grail quest to the triumph of his end and the affirmation of the values for which he stands. The double movement of Lancelot's fortunes within this tale is a recapitulation of the simultaneous comedy and tragedy that informs the whole last section of the *Morte Darthur*.

As in each of the final tales, the figure of Lancelot provides the main coherence. The narration begins with Lancelot, Arthur, and the Round Table still abiding in prosperity. The treachery of Agravain and Mordred sets the forces of tragedy in motion; Lancelot must flee (xx.4-6), Guenevere is sentenced to die at the stake, and Lancelot rescues her, accidentally killing Gareth as he does so (xx. 8). This unfortunate act earns him the implacable hatred of Gawain and brings on the first war between Lancelot and Arthur. The war is temporarily settled when Lancelot returns Guenevere to Arthur and is exiled from England. This brings Lancelot to his lowest point in the tale, a victim, as he says, of Fortune. Arthur remains in relative prosperity even during the siege of Benwick that follows (xx.18-22). His tragic fall begins with Mordred's betrayal. Lancelot is left in Benwick, while Arthur returns to England, where both he and Gawain are killed, the Round Table is destroyed, and Guenevere flees to a nunnery. Only then, after the complete narration of Arthur's fall, do we return to the story of Lancelot, who comes back to England to begin the comic movement from the "povre estat" upward to the highest point, borne up by countless angels to Heaven, where, we assume, he still abides in prosperity.

Consequently, although *The Death of Arthur* is indeed a "most piteous" and tragic tale, it is a very unusual example of that genre. Perhaps most unusual in a fifteenth-century tragedy is the absence, in the story of Arthur's fall, of any reference to Fortune, the force that invariably appears in and defines the genre of late medieval tragedy. Malory mentions Fortune only once in the entire tale, and then only in reference to Lancelot's fall. No doubt all the characters are in Fortune's power, but Malory makes almost nothing of this. His French source, the *Mort Artu*, makes a great deal indeed of the role of Fortune. For example, in the *Mort Artu* Arthur's dream of Fortune is not just a comment on the action, as in the analogous alliterative *Morte Arthure*; it is a symbol of the tragic movement of the entire work. Arthur recognizes this: "A, Fortune! Contrary and varying creature, the most disloyal thing that might be in this world, why were you so courteous and friendly to me if you were to sell it to me so dearly in the end? You who were once my mother have become my step-mother, and to make me die of grief you have brought Death with you, so that you have shamed me in two ways at once, through my friends and through my land" (p. 221). He returns to this theme when he is dying: "Girflet, Fortune, who has been my mother until this but has now become my step-mother, makes me spend the rest of my life in grief, bitterness, and sorrow" (p. 247). Fortune has done as she threatened in Arthur's dream, and in the *Mort Artu* the final battle is the realization of the symbolism of that dream.

Although Malory knew both the dream of Fortune in the *Mort Artu* and the much more elaborate account in the alliterative *Morte Arthure*, he turns for his version to the stanzaic *Morte Arthur* and thus reduces the dream to a brief presage of coming disaster:[1] Arthur dreams that he is seated on a great wheel, above hideous black water in which are all manner of beasts and serpents. The wheel turns, he falls among the beasts, and he awakes crying "Helpe! Helpe!" (xxi.3). There is no Dame Fortune to turn the wheel and no direct hint that Fortune controls the events of Arthur's last days.

Certainly this does not remove Fortune completely from the work. Though she does not appear in Arthur's dream, her wheel does, and in this context only the most obtuse fifteenth-century reader could have missed its implications. Likewise, although Fortune is mentioned only once in the tale, this occurs in Lancelot's speech after his banishment from England, which marks the moment when the fellowship of the Round Table is broken forever, and the reader must recognize that Arthur's situation as well as Lancelot's is due to the workings of Fortune. Finally, when Lancelot describes himself as a victim of Fortune, he cites as previous examples Hector and Alexander, who are, like Arthur, among the Nine Worthies. In later medieval literature the Nine Worthies are common *exempla* of the workings of Fortune (they so appear in the alliterative *Morte Arthure*), and the mention of two of the pagan Worthies in this context must surely have reminded many of Malory's readers of the first and greatest of the Christian Worthies, as Caxton calls Arthur in his preface to this book.

The implications are clear and probably intentional: Arthur is a tragic figure. Malory could hardly have presented him in any other light. However, it is also clear that Malory makes as little as possible of Fortune's power over Arthur. By Malory's time the older, morally neutral idea of the tragedy of Fortune (a fall, deserved or not) was developing toward the more modern idea that the tragic hero, because of some flaw, bears responsibility for his own fall. This is already the case in the *Mort Artu*, where the fall is a punishment for sin, and by the middle of the fifteenth century it was true of an increasing number of tragedies of Fortune.[2] By avoiding any direct mention of Fortune in relation to Arthur, Malory provides as little occasion as possible for suggesting these associations to his readers. Instead, he makes Lance-

lot the focus of the tragedy, and though he omits every mention of
Fortune that he found in the *Mort Artu* he invents that speech in
which Lancelot blames Fortune for his fall.

Lancelot's lament on Fortune comes very early in the tale, well
before Arthur's last battle. Apparently we are to see Arthur as the victim of Lancelot's tragedy, with Lancelot as the scapegoat for Arthur's
fall. Lancelot can bear the blame, for unlike Arthur, whose history
required a sudden fall and death, Lancelot's history allowed time for
amendment of life, for the comic upward movement that redeems him
in our eyes as well as God's. Of course, even Lancelot bears little guilt.
Malory spreads the blame so widely that little is left for Lancelot:
Gawain and Guenevere claim they are to blame; Mordred and
Agravain are indeed guilty of initiating the disaster; and blind destiny,
the English people, even the adder, are among the causes of the final
catastrophe.

Arthur alone remains relatively blameless. Malory even removes,
as much as possible, Mordred from his role as agent of divine retribution for Arthur's incest. This is, of course, a major force in the historical tragedy. In *The Tale of King Arthur* Merlin had foretold that
Mordred would kill Arthur as a punishment for his incest, and Mordred does exactly that. In the *Mort Artu* the reader is clearly reminded
of this. When Arthur learns of Mordred's rebellion, he says: "Ah,
Mordred, now you make me recognize that you were the serpent that I
once saw issue from my belly and that burned my land and attacked
me. But never did a father do as much to his son as I shall do to you,
for I shall kill you with my two hands" (p. 211). And at exactly the
moment the mortal blows are exchanged, we are told "Thus the father
killed the son, and the son mortally wounded the father" (p. 245).
Malory mentions in passing that Mordred was made regent of England
because "syr Mordred was kynge Arthurs son" (xx.19), but he never
refers to the earlier prophecy, and the only mention of Mordred's sinful engendering is in a context designed to emphasize Mordred's incestuous longings rather than Arthur's. Mordred "Toke quene Gwenyver, and sayde playnly that he wolde wedde her (which was his unclys
wyff and his fadirs wyff)" (xxi.1).

However, our impression of Arthur as the victim of Fortune rather
than the sinful agent of his own destruction arises mainly from the
action itself. In the *Mort Artu* Arthur is the ordinary sort of late medieval tragic hero, blinded by pride and heedlessly rushing to his own
doom. The dying Gawain begs him to send for Lancelot's help in the

coming battle with Mordred, but Arthur steadfastly refuses to do so. After Gawain has died, he appears to Arthur in a dream, and again he begs him to avoid the coming battle.

Sir Gawain said, weeping: "Sire, avoid fighting Mordred; if you fight him, you will die or be mortally wounded."

"Certainly," said the king, "I shall indeed fight him, even if I must die for it, for I would be a coward if I did not defend my land against a traitor." (P. 225)

Arthur receives further warnings, and Mordred himself offers to negotiate. Arthur rejects Mordred's offer and ignores the warnings. When the archbishop begs him to delay the battle, "the king swore by the soul of his father Utherpendragon that he would never turn back" (p. 228). Even when the archbishop shows Arthur the stone that Merlin erected to prophesy the king's defeat, his pride will not allow him to turn back.

"Sire," said King Arthur, "I see enough that, if I had not come so far forward, I would turn back, whatever desire I had had until now. But now may Jesus Christ help us, for I shall never leave here until Our Lord has given the victory to me or to Mordred; and if it turns out badly for me, that will be through my sin and my excess, for I have a greater number of good knights than Mordred has." (P. 229)

Arthur's army is badly outnumbered (p. 230), but he is too blinded by pride to recognize this. Too late he realizes that he should have taken Gawain's advice and sent for Lancelot, "For I know well if I had asked him he would have come willingly and courteously" (p. 240). Neither the Arthur of the *Mort Artu* nor its reader is left in any doubt about the king's responsibility for his own fall.

Malory's version is altogether different. In the beginning of the tale Arthur is the headstrong king of the *Mort Artu*, determined to avenge himself upon Lancelot. But his anger is soon tempered; he is eager to forgive Guenevere and take her back to end the first campaign against Lancelot, and he invades Benwick only because Gawain forces him to. He also does all he can to avoid the last battle. When the dead Gawain appears to Arthur and warns him to delay the battle until Lancelot arrives with reinforcements, Arthur immediately sets about arranging a truce. He, not Mordred, offers to negotiate, and he is willing to grant Mordred the most generous terms in order to avoid the battle in which he knows the flower of chivalry will be destroyed.

That final battle takes place not because of Arthur's blind pride but because of blind chance—the adder that glides forward just at the

moment when Arthur and Mordred are about to settle their differences peaceably:

Ryght so cam oute an addir of a lytyll hethe-buysshe, and hit stange a
knyght in the foote. And so whan the knyght felte hym so stonge, he
loked downe and saw the addir; and anone he drew hys swerde to sle
the addir, and thought none othir harme. And whan the oste on bothe
partyes saw that swerde drawyn, than they blewe beamys, trumpettis,
and hornys, and shoutted grymly, and so bothe ostis dressid hem
togydirs. And kynge Arthur toke hys horse and seyde, "Alas, this
unhappy day!" And so rode to hys party, and sir Mordred in lyke
wyse. (xxi.4)

"Unhappy" has the meaning "ill fortune," and it recurs throughout
this tale; but it also means "miserable" and "unlucky," for it is a more
ambiguous and less exact term than "Fortune." Clearly the fall of the
Round Table is predestined by history, by Providence or Fortune.
Those two "unhappy knights" Mordred and Agravain are the immediate agents of the tragic fall, and Arthur's incest, the feud between the
houses of Pellinor and Lot, and the love of Lancelot and Guenevere
are the ultimate causes. But one cannot escape the feeling that save for
a series of unhappy accidents the catastrophe might have been
avoided: if Lancelot had not accidentally killed Gareth, if the English
people, beyond Arthur's control, had not proved fickle at just that
moment, if the adder had not glided forward when it did—all might
have ended differently. The *ifs* are of course illusory; the book had to
end this way, but the recurring suggestion of accident in Malory's version clearly implies that Arthur is helplessly and innocently caught in
forces beyond his or anyone's control.

Nevertheless, Arthur does bear part of the blame for the tragic fall
of the Round Table. Therefore, for Arthur, as for all of his protagonists, Malory provides a form of forgiveness, and our last view of the
king is one that suggests divine approval. Malory's most striking
addition to the history of Arthur is the prophecy of Arthur's return.
The *Morte Darthur* has so powerfully shaped our own ideas of
Arthurian history that many readers believe the prediction of Arthur's
return is an inevitable part of the story of his death.

Yet som men say in many partys of Inglonde that kynge Arthure ys
nat dede but had by the wyll of oure Lorde Jesu into another place;
and men say that he shall com agayne, and he shall wynne the Holy
Crosse. Yet I woll nat say that hit shall be so, but rather I wolde sey:
here in thys world he chaunged hys lyff. And many men say that there
ys wrytten upon the tumbe thys:
    Hic iacet Arthurus; rex quondam rexque futurus. (xxi.6)

There is nothing like this in any other version of Arthur's death known to Malory. The manuscript of the alliterative *Morte Arthure* ends with that inscription which "men say" is on Arthur's tomb, but this was added in a later hand and has nothing to do with the poem itself, which ends with Arthur dead and the survivors weeping in despair. Likewise, in the stanzaic *Morte Arthur*, Arthur says he will go "a little stounde / Into the Vale of Avaloun" (vv. 3514-16), but there is no hint of his return. In that poem, as in the *Mort Artu* and Hardyng's *Chronicle*, any allusion to Arthur's survival would have weakened the tragic effect at which the authors aimed. Malory seems determined to do just that, to undercut the tragedy by the suggestion that "Arthur by the wylle of oure Lorde Jesu" has "chaunged hys lyff." Malory's point is not that Arthur will return ("I woll nat say that hit shall be so") but that his death is marked by divine approval for the good deeds of his life, which clearly outweigh his human defects.

Malory suggests that the same is true of each of his other characters. Even Gawain, who of the four major characters comes nearest to being the direct agent of the downfall of the Round Table and who is clearly the least virtuous, is rehabilitated in death. Gawain confesses his guilt to Arthur in his dying speech: "Thorow me and my pryde ye have al thys shame and disease, and had that noble knyght, sir Launcelot, ben with you, as he was and wolde have ben, thys unhappy war had never begun" (xxi.2). Then Gawain makes amends for his sins. He writes a letter to Lancelot, "flour of al noble knyghtes that ever I harde of or saw be my dayes," and he explains that he alone is responsible for his own death. He begs Lancelot to come to England and pray for his soul and help defeat that false traitor Mordred.

Lancelot does come to England, and he prays for three days at Gawain's tomb. Gawain thus received Lancelot's forgiveness, and perhaps the reader's as well. He seems clearly to have had God's forgiveness, for after his death he is allowed to appear to Arthur in a dream in which he warns the king to avoid the coming battle with Mordred (advice which, as we have noted, Arthur does his best to take). This is significant, since it means that our last view of Gawain is of a good knight doing his duty by his king. But more significant is the fact that God allows Gawain to return from death in this manner because of the chivalric deeds he achieved while he was living. Gawain appears to Arthur accompanied by a great crowd of ladies. He explains, "Al thes be ladyes for whom I have foughten for, whan I was man lyvynge. And all thes ar tho that I did batayle for in right-euous quarrels, and God hath gyvyn hem that grace, at their grete prayer, bycause I ded batayle for them for their ryght, that they shulde brynge me hydder unto you" (xxi.3). Gawain, as we know, did many unrighteous battles as well, but apparently his good deeds outweight his evil, and chivalry avails even in Heaven.

So perhaps does earthly love. We have already remarked that passage in which we learn that Guenevere is destined to have a "good end" because she was a "trewe lover." There is obviously a difficulty here, since her acts as a true lover created the conditions that brought about the fall of the Round Table. She is aware of this and takes the veil to atone for her ill deeds. Like Gawain, she confesses her sin. When Lancelot comes to the nunnery, she tells her fellow nuns, "Thorow thys same man and me hath al thys warre be wrought, and the deth of the most nobelest knyghtes of the worlde, for thorow oure love that we have loved togydir is my moste noble lorde slayne. Therefore, sir Launcelot, wyte thou will I am sette in suche a plyght to gete my soul hele" (xxi.9). That she does get her soul "hele" is shown by two passages that Malory invented—Guenevere's gift of prophecy, whereby she foretells her own death (xxi.11), and the miraculous vision that announces her death to Lancelot with the divine command that she be buried next to Arthur. Just as our last view of Gawain is of the good knight doing his duty by his king, so our last view of Guenevere is of the good wife, at last reunited with her husband.

Again Malory's version is much different from the French. In the *Mort Artu*, as in most versions of the last days of the Round Table, Guenevere enters the nunnery not out of any sense of penitence but because she fears for her safety. She thinks Mordred will kill her if he wins the last battle, and Arthur will kill her if he wins. She spends a sleepless night, "badly frightened, for she could see no escape anywhere" (p. 217), and she finally decides to flee to a nunnery: "Thus the queen remained there with the nuns because of the fear that she had of King Arthur and of Mordred" (p. 219). As the author of the alliterative *Morte Arthure* tells it, "She kaires to Caerlion and caught her a veil / Askes there the habit in the honour of Crist / And alle for falsede and fraud and fere of her lord!" (vv. 3916-18).

Malory's Guenevere is a more admirable character, truly repentent for her sin and yet a "trewe lover." By her good example she brings Lancelot to salvation. And, though she must renounce any possibility of happiness with Lancelot, we are shown in her death scene that she still loves him, knows the power of her love, and therefore dares not look upon him. "Wherfore the quene sayd in heryng of hem al, 'I beseche Almyghty God that I may never have power to see syr Launcelot wyth my worldly eyen!' " (xxi.11). Lancelot has become a temptation rather than a joy to her, but this is because her love for him remains true, and she has a good end.

Finally, Lancelot is absolved from blame and has the holy death that the Grail hermit prophesied for him. Lancelot, as we have noted, is the one explicitly tragic figure in *The Death of Arthur*; he himself tells us this in his speech of farewell to the "Moste nobelyst Crysten realme, whom I have loved aboven all othir realmys": "But Fortune is so varyaunte and the wheele so mutable that there is no constant abydyng. And that may be preved by many old cronycles as Noble Ector of Troy and Alysaunder the myghty conquerour and many mo other; when they were moste in theyr royalté, they alyght passying lowe. And so faryth hit by me" (xx.17). Unlike the usual tragic hero, a Hector or Alexander, Lancelot has suffered neither death nor loss of wealth and prosperity. He remains the king of Benwick, a knight of such prowess that even Gawain with his supernatural strength cannot avail against him. Lancelot is brought passing low by being deprived of his lady and his king. The measure of his tragic fall is the measure of his virtue, for it is only his loyalty to Arthur and to Guenevere that leads him to regard his situation as tragic.

Likewise, his loyalty, the main source of his "worship" throughout the *Morte Darthur*, underlies his movement upward from this low position to the joy and solace that he attains in the comic plot that brackets the tragic story of Arthur's death. Lancelot never wavers in his loyalty to Arthur, even during their wars. He refuses to fight against the king even when he is besieged at Joyous Garde and Arthur unrelentingly attacks him: " 'God defende me,' seyde sir Launcelot, 'that ever I shulde encounter with the moste noble kynge that made me knyght' " (xx.11). Later, during the same campaign, when Bors has struck down Arthur, he draws his sword and asks Lancelot,

"Sir, shall I make an ende of thys warre?" (For he mente to have slayne hym.)

"Nat so hardy," seyde sir Launcelot, "uppon payne of thy hede, that thou touch hym no more! For I woll never see that moste noble knyge that made me knyght nother slayne nor shamed." (xx.13)

During the siege of Benwick, Lancelot does all in his power to avoid shedding the blood of Arthur or his knights, restraining his own men and steadfastly refusing to return evil for evil. He fights Gawain only when he is forced to, and he will not slay him despite Gawain's insulting refusal to surrender. His patience changes Arthur's attitude, and henceforth the king bitterly regrets the war that has come between them. Lancelot spares Gawain and begs Arthur to lift the siege:

"And therefore, my lorde Arthur, remembir you of olde kyndenes, and howsomever I fare, Jesu be your gyde in all placis."
    "Now, alas!" seyde the kynge, "that ever thys unhappy warre began! For ever he forbearyth me in all placis, and in lyke wyse my kynne, and that ys sene well thys day, what curteysye he shewed my neveawe, sir Gawayne!" (xx.22)

When Gawain writes to Lancelot, absolving him of any blame in his death and telling him of Mordred's treachery, Lancelot momentarily despairs, but Ector reminds him of his duty to the king. Lancelot thanks him—"for ever ye woll my worshyp" (xxi.8). He realizes that his "worship" depends on his loyalty, despite the trials to which he is subjected by Arthur in the sieges of Joyous Garde and Benwick. He immediately sets out for England, eager to serve the king once more.

Lancelot also remains true to Guenevere, and his faithful love for the queen, which prevented his achieving the Grail, becomes the means of his salvation. Guenevere truly repents of her love for Lancelot, and she takes the veil to atone for that sin. Lancelot enters the religious life not because he forsakes his earthly love but because he remains true to it. When he meets Guenevere for the last time, she urges him to remain in the world and take a wife. Lancelot, for the first time in his life, cannot obey his lady, because to do so would be to forsake his love:

"Well, madame," seyde he, "ye say as hit pleasith you, for yet wyste ye me never false of my promyse. And God deffende but that I shulde forsake the worlde as ye have done! For in the queste of the Sankgreall I had that tyme forsakyn the vanytees of the worlde, had nat youre love bene . . . And therefore, lady, sythen ye have taken you to perfeccion, I must nedys take me to perfection, of ryght. For I take recorde of God, in you I have had myn erthly joye, and yf I had founden you now so dysposed, I had caste me to have had you into myn owne royame. But sythen I fynde you thus desposed, I ensure you faythfully, I wyl ever take me to penaunce and praye whyle my lyf lasteth, yf that I may fynde ony heremyte, other graye or whyte, that wyl receyve me. Wherefore, madame, I praye you kysse me, and never no more."
    "Nay," seyde the quene, "that shal I never do, but abstayne you from such workes." (xxi.10)

One wonders what the Grail hermits would make of this sort of vocation. It is, to say the least, a curiously worldly way of renouncing the

world. And this must surely be Malory's purpose—to provide a means
for Lancelot to renounce the world, as the history requires, without
renouncing his faithful love for the queen.

Lancelot remains loyal to his chivalric ideals even in and beyond his
religious retreat. His last wish is that he be buried at the Joyous Garde.
Though he repents of so worldly a vow, like a good knight he remains
true to it: "bycause of brekyng of myn avowe, I praye you al, lede me
thyder" (xxi.12). Likewise, almost the last deed in his life is his taking
Guenevere's body to lie next to Arthur's, thus finally proving loyal
both to his lady and his king. When Guenevere is buried, Lancelot
swoons, and a fellow hermit upbraids him:

"Ye dysplese God with suche maner of sorow-makyng."
    "Truly," seyd syr Launcelot, "I trust I do not dysplese God, for he
knoweth myn entente; . . . my sorrow may never have ende. For whan
I remember of hir beaulté and of hir noblesse, that was bothe with
hyr kyng and wyth hyr, so when I sawe his corps and hir corps so lye
togyders, truly myn herte wold not serve to susteyne my careful
body. Also whan I remember how by my defaute and myn orgule
and my pryde that they were bothe layed ful lowe, that were pereles
that ever was lyvyng of Cristen people, wyt you wel," sayd syr
Launcelot, "this remembred, of their kyndenes and myn unkyndenes,
sanke so to myn herte that I myght not susteyne myself." So the
French book maketh mencyon. (xxi.11)

The speech is, of course, Malory's own invention, the last of the series
of confessions—by Gawain, by Guenevere, and now by Lancelot. The
earlier French author would not have presented a Lancelot still as concerned with the things of this world ("whan I remember of hir beaulté
and of hir noblesse"). Malory's Lancelot remains essentially a chivalric
knight, and he thus has a good end. He is borne to Heaven, as the
hermit bishop says, by "mo aungellis than ever I sawe men in one
day," and he dies in the unmistakable odor of sanctity, "wyth the
swetist savor aboute hym that ever they felte" (xxi.12). His soul goes
to heaven, but his body is returned to the Joyous Garde.

This is the end of the history of the Round Table. But Malory's
book does not end here. The suggestion that Lancelot remains a true
knight even in the saintly last days now becomes explicit in the new
conclusion that Malory provides for the whole story of King Arthur.
These final pages are of great thematic importance to the work, but
they are frequently ignored by critics who concentrate only on the
"plot" and who have therefore emphasized since Strachey's day their
conviction that the book ends with Lancelot and his fellowship "once

knights but now hermit priests doing bodily all manner of penance."[3] From this point of view the book does seem to end, as Charles Moorman writes, "with the burial of the chivalric ideal."[4] That is true of works such as the *Mort Artu*, but not of Malory's *Morte Darthur*, which ends with a powerful definition and celebration of the chivalric ideal and a clear statement that chivalry survives even the death of Lancelot.

Throughout the last pages of the *Morte Darthur* we witness the slow gathering of the surviving knights of the Round Table. In the *Mort Artu* and the stanzaic *Morte Arthur*, the surviving knights gather to end their days in penance at the hermitage. In the *Morte Darthur* the gathering serves a different purpose. The last of the knights to come to the hermitage is Sir Ector, who arrives immediately after Lancelot's death and delivers his moving tribute to the dead hero:

"Ah Launcelot!" he sayd, "thou were hede of al Crysten knyghtes! And now I dare say," sayd sir Ector, "thou sir Launcelot, there thou lyest, that thou were never matched of erthely knyghtes hande. And thou were the curtest knyght that ever bare shelde! And thou were the truest frend to thy lovar that ever bestrade hors, and thou were the trewest lover, of a synful man, that ever loved woman, and thou were the kyndest man that ever strake wyth swerde, and thou were the goodlyest persone that ever cam emonge prees of knyghtes, and thou was the mekest man and the jentyllest that ever ete in halle emonge ladyes, and thou were the sternest knyght to thy mortal foo that ever put spere in the reeste." (xxi.13)

The speech is a powerful reassertion of the virtues that Lancelot exemplified throughout his earthly life, and because Lancelot achieved his saintly end by remaining a true knight, Ector's threnody is by no means incongruent with Lancelot's holy death.

Nevertheless, holiness is of no concern in Ector's speech. Malory apparently wants his readers' last view of Lancelot to be not of the repentant hermit but of the perfect worldly knight. Ector ignores Lancelot's years in the hermitage certainly not because he fails to admire them but because they are finally not essential to Lancelot's greatness. The world has had many good hermits but only one great Lancelot, and in Ector's speech Malory defines exactly the nature of Lancelot's greatness.

This would merely heighten the sense of tragic loss if Lancelot were the last knight to live by the code of chivalry. However, Malory's final addition to his story assures us that chivalry survives even the death of Lancelot. The knights who gather at the hermitage form the last of the groups of four of which Malory is so fond, and they carry on the life of chivalry:

Somme Englysshe books maken mencyon that they wente never oute of Englond after the deth of Syr Launcelot—but that was but favour of makers. For the Frensshe boke maketh mencyon—and is auctorised—that syr Bors, syr Ector, syr Blamour, and syr Bleoberis wente into the Holy Lande, thereas Jesu Cryst was quicke and deed. And anone as they had stablysshed their londes, for, the book saith, so syr Launcelot commaunded them for to do or ever he passyd oute of thys world, these foure knyghtes dyd many batayles upon the myscreauntes, or Turkes. And there they dyed upon a Good Fryday, for Goddes sake. (xxi.13)

Of course, the French books mention no such thing, and Malory's insistence upon written authority for this passage, as usual, merely conceals his own invention. In no other French or English version do Arthur's knights leave the hermitage to carry on the chivalric life in this manner.

Lancelot's companions may have been purified by their stay in the hermitage, since they now fight exclusively against the "myscreauntes, or Turkes," but they follow the chivalric way nevertheless, earning worldly rewards ("stablysshed their landes") and dying in a manner that, as we have seen, many a fifteenth-century knight in both life and fiction would have wished. Malory is so intent upon emphasizing for his readers that the history of the Round Table does not end in despair or penance that he forgets, or perhaps simply does not care, that Bors, Blamour, and Bleoberis have taken religious vows. The author of the *Queste del Saint Graal* would not have made such a mistake; since Bors is to return to the world at the end of the *Queste* its author carefully specifies that when Bors stayed at the hermitage with Perceval he did not adopt "religious clothyng": "He chonged never hys secular clothyng, for that he purposed hym to go agayne into the realme of Logrus" (xviii.23). Malory includes that in his *Tale of the Sancgreal* just as he includes in his *Death of Arthur* the fact that when Bors comes to Lancelot's hermitage, "He preyed the Bysshop that he myght be in the same sewte. And so there was an habyte put upon hym, and there he lyved in prayers and fastyng" (xxi.10). But so far as Malory is concerned, this is of no importance compared to Bors's loyalty to Lancelot's dying command that he continue the worshipful way of knighthood in the world.

The last paragraphs of the *Morte Darthur* epitomize Malory's method of dealing with the problems raised by his inherited history. He retains the historical facts and the consequent tragic pattern they suggest, just as he retains the fact that Bors takes religious vows. Then he modifies their effects by additions such as Bors's leaving the hermitage to carry on the chivalric life. The result is not a coherent pat-

tern of tragedy but rather what Stephen Miko calls a "tragic emul-
sion," in which the elements of tragedy are held in suspension, never
quite coming together to produce a tragic effect.[5] They are held apart
by the thematic, essentially comic elements that prevent the historical
pattern from coalescing. Consequently, the end is neither completely
tragic nor purely comic. As Edmund Reiss writes, we are left in doubt
whether to be "wholly delighted or thoroughly disenhearted by what
has happened."[6] That doubt can never by completely resolved, for it is
this mixture of joy and sorrow that lends the conclusion of the *Morte
Darthur* its peculiar force and beauty. Perhaps, after all, Caxton was
right; he best characterized this complex book when he humbly
beseeched the noble lords and ladies of his audience "That they take
the honest actes in their remembraunce, and to folowe the same;
wherein they shall fynde many joyous and playsaunt hystoryes and
noble and renomned actes of humanyté, gentylnesse, and chyvalryes.
For herein may be seen noble chyvalrye, curtoyse, humanyté, frendly-
nesse, hardynesse, love, frendshyp, cowardyse, murdre, hate, vertue,
and synne. Doo after the good and leve the evyl, and it shal bringe
you to good fame and renommee."

Notes

Bibliography

Index

Notes

ABBREVIATIONS

ALMA	*Arthurian Literature in the Middle Ages: A Collaborative History*, ed. Roger S. Loomis (Oxford, 1959)
Essays on Malory	*Essays on Malory*, ed. J. A. W. Bennett (Oxford, 1963)
Malory's Originality	*Malory's Originality: A Critical Study of "Le Morte Darthur*," ed. Robert M. Lumiansky (Baltimore, Md., 1964)
Vinaver, *Works*	*The Works of Sir Thomas Malory*, ed. Eugène Vinaver, 2d ed. (Oxford, 1967), 3 vols. (continuous pagination)

In the notes, as in the text, primary works that are quoted or discussed are cited by short title; full bibliographical references are included in the Bibliography.

1 MALORY AND THE PROSE CYCLES

1. George Saintsbury, *The English Novel* (London, 1913), p. 25.

2. For a brief discussion and references see my "Sir Thomas Malory's *Le Morte Darthur*," in *Critical Approaches to Six Major English Works*, ed. Robert M. Lumiansky and Herschel Baker (Philadelphia, 1968), pp. 81-131. See also Derek Brewer, "The Present Study of Malory," in *Arthurian Romance: Seven Essays*, ed. D. D. R. Owen (a reprint of *Forum for Modern Language Study*, 6 [1970]), pp. 83-97. A full and well-annotated bibliography is available in Elizabeth Pochada's *Arthurian Propaganda: "Le Morte Darthur" as an Historical Ideal of Life* (Chapel Hill, N. C., 1971); a complete listing is in R. H. Wilson, "IX. Malory and Caxton," in Albert E. Hartung, *A Manual of the Writings in Middle English*, III (New Haven, 1972).

3. Malory's knowledge of these romances is thoroughly discussed in the essays in *Malory's Originality* and in the commentaries in the third volume of Vinaver, *Works*. See also R. H. Wilson, "Malory's Early Knowledge of Arthurian Romance," *Texas Studies in English*, 29 (1950), 33-50, in which Wilson shows how well read in romance Malory was before he began his writing.

4. Quoted by Eugène Vinaver in *The Rise of Romance* (Oxford, 1971), p. 54.

5. The hint of cyclic structure appears in Chrétien's *Yvain* (vv. 3563-3898), where we are told that Lancelot is absent from the court because he is off rescuing the queen in the adventure narrated in *Le chevalier de la charette*. See Pierre Le Gentil, "The Work of Robert Boron and the *Didot Perceval*," in *ALMA*, pp. 251-262.

6. On the editions see Jean Frappier, "The Vulgate Cycle," in *ALMA*, p. 317. Even neoclassicists such as Jean Chapelain admired *Lancelot*. In his *Opuscles critiques*, ed. Alfred C. Hunter, Société des textes français modernes (Paris, 1936), p. 215, the "father of the unities" writes: "Si Aristote revenait et qu'il se mit en tête de trouver une matière d'art póetique en *Lancelot*, je ne doute point qu'il n'y réussît aussi bien qu'en *l'Iliade* et *l'Odyssey*." On the later popularity of Arthurian romance see Frappier, "Les romans de la Table ronde et les lettres en France au xvie siècle," in *Amor cortois et Table ronde* (Geneva, 1973), pp. 265-281.

7. See the discussion in Frappier, "The Vulgate Cycle."

8. For the student of Malory the best study remains Eugène Vivaver, *Le roman de Tristan et Iseut dans l'œuvre de Thomas Malory* (Paris, 1925), though for a more recent bibliography one should also see Vinaver's "The Prose *Tristan*," in *ALMA*, pp. 339-347.

9. For a full discussion of the manuscripts see Löseth, *Tristan*.

10. See Fanni Bogdanow, "The *Suite du Merlin* and the Post-Vulgate *Roman du Graal*," in *ALMA*, pp. 325-335, and *The Romance of the Grail* (Manchester, 1966).

11. See María Rosa Lida de Malkiel, "Arthurian Literature in Spain and Portugal," in *ALMA*, pp. 406-418.

12. Henry J. Chaytor, *From Script to Print: An Introduction to Medieval Vernacular Literature* (Cambridge, 1945), p. 85.

13. See Cedric E. Pickford, *L'évolution du roman arthurien en prose vers la fin du moyen âge d'après le manuscrit 112 du fonds français de la Bibliothèque nationale* (Paris, 1960), pp. 212-213.

14. See Eugène Vinaver, "On Art and Nature: A Letter to C. S. Lewis," in *Essays on Malory*. p. 36.

15. The three versions are *Arthour and Merlin* (early fourteenth-century verse), Lovelich's *Merlin* (verse, about 1425), and the prose *Merlin* (about 1450).

16. Vinaver, *Works*, p. 1449.

17. Fragment 103 has "si comme nous deviseron cha devant"; 99 omits the reference. See Löseth, *Tristan*, p. 111, n. xl.

18. See R. H. Wilson, "How Many Books Did Malory Write?" *Texas Studies in English*, 30 (1951), esp. pp. 10-12; Robert M. Lumiansky, "The Question of Unity in Malory's *Morte Darthur*," *Tulane Studies in English*, 5 (1959), 29-39.

2 FIFTEENTH-CENTURY PROSE ROMANCE

1. Alex R. Myers, *The Household of Edward IV: The Black Book and the Ordinance of 1478* (Manchester, 1959), esp. pp. 1-5; Norman F. Blake, *Caxton and His World* (London, 1969), pp. 65-70.

2. Georges Doutrepont, *La littérature française à la cour des ducs de Bourgogne: Philippe le Hardi—Jean sans Peur—Philippe le Bon—Charles le Temeraire* (Paris, 1909), pp. 18-19.

3. Ibid., p. 19.

4. Ibid., p. 176.

5. Quoted by Henry S. Bennett in *Chaucer and the Fifteenth Century* (Oxford, 1947), p. 206; Bennett offers a full refutation of this once common position. See also Blake, *Caxton and His World*, esp. pp. 64-78.

6. Henry L. D. Ward, *Catalogue of Romances in the Department of Manuscripts in the British Museum* (London, 1883), I, 341.

7. Ibid., p. 358.

8. *The Scholemaster* (written 1570), in *Elizabethan Critical Essays*, ed. George Gregory Smith (Oxford, 1904), I, 4.

9. *An Apology for Poetry* (written about 1583), in Smith, *Elizabethan Critical Essays*, I, 188.

10. Rosamund Tuve, *Allegorical Imagery: Some Mediaeval Books and Their Posterity* (Princeton, 1966), pp. 335-446.

11. Even this must be qualified in England, where chroniclers like Hardyng still used verse.

12. Léon Gautier, *Les épopées francaises: Etude sur les origines et l'histoire de la littérature nationale*, 2d ed. (Paris, 1878), I, 484.

13. Paul Meyer, *Alexandre le grand dans la littérature française du moyen âge* (Paris, 1886), II, 300-329; George Cary, *The Medieval Alexander*, ed. D. J. A. Ross (Cambridge, 1956), pp. 228-233.

14. See the full survey of this movement in Georges Doutrepont, *Les mises en prose des épopées et des romans chevaleresques du xive au xve siècle* (Brussels, 1939).

15. Gautier, *Les épopées*, p. 490.

16. Quoted in Henry J. Chaytor, *From Script to Print: An Introduction to Medieval Vernacular Literature* (Cambridge, 1945), p. 88.

17. Ward, *Catalogue*, pp. 64, 130.

18. Cedric E. Pickford, "Miscellaneous French Prose Romances," in *ALMA*, pp. 350-352.

19. See Edmund G. Gardner, *Arthurian Legend in Italian Literature* (London, 1930).

20. See W. J. Entwhistle, *Arthurian Legends in the Literatures of the Spanish Peninsula* (London, 1925); María Rosa Lida de Malkiel, "Arthurian Literature in Spain and Portugal," in *ALMA*, pp. 406-418.

21. Hendricus Sparnaay, "The Dutch Romances," in *ALMA*, pp. 443-453.

22. Pickford, "Miscellaneous French Prose Romances," p. 335.

23. For descriptions of these manuscripts see Fanni Bogdanow, *The Romance of the Grail* (Manchester, 1966), pp. 277-279 (esp. descriptions of MSS B.N. frs. 758, 2440); Löseth, *Tristan*.

24. Henry S. Bennett, *The Pastons and Their England*, rev. ed. (Cambridge, 1927), pp. 102-103.

25. Caxton, *Godeffroy of Boloyne*, p. 2.

26. Caxton, *Charles the Grete*, p. 1.

27. Doutrepont, *Les mises en prose*, p. 402.

28. Quoted in Doutrepont, *La littérature française*, p. 505.

29. Cary, *Medieval Alexander*, p. 229.

30. Elisabeth of Nassau-Saarbrücken may be an earlier example.

31. *Charles the Grete*, p. 2. Note that Caxton classes his "book of the most noble & victoryous kyng Arthur" with *Charles the Grete*. See Blake, *Caxton and His World*, p. 110.

32. Doutrepont, *Les mises en prose*, pp. 485, 600, 618; see also Jeanne Lods, *Le roman de Perceforest: Origines, composition, caractères, valeur et influence* (Geneva, 1951), pp. 21-22.

33. Wauquelin's preface to his *Belle Hélène* is quoted in Doutrepont, *Les mises en prose*, p. 388.

34. Cary, *Medieval Alexander*, p. 246.

35. *Les épopées françaises*, I, 499.

36. See Bibliography, s.v. "Gonnot, Michel."

37. Quoted in Cedric E. Pickford, *L'évolution du roman arthurien en prose vers la fin du moyen âge d'àpres le manuscrit 112 du fonds français de la Bibliothèque nationale* (Paris, 1960), p. 210.

38. Pickford, "Miscellaneous French Prose Romances," p. 355.

39. Pickford, *L'evolution*, p. 291.

40. Ibid., p. 293.

41. Ibid., p. 213; Pickford notes (p. 292) that Malory condenses far more freely than Gonnot, whose technique resembles Caxton's more than Malory's.

42. Ibid., p. 109.

43. Ibid., pp. 181, 185.

44. Quoted in ibid., p. 210.

45. James Boyd, *Ulrich Fuetrer's Parzifal: Material and Sources* (Oxford, 1936), p. 1.

46. Ibid., p. 2.

47. Karl Otto Brogsitter, *Artusepik* (Stuttgart, 1965), p. 118; see also Pickford, *L'évolution*, pp. 186-201.

48. For a recent discussion of the difficult problem of the order of composition of the tales, see Toshiyuki Takamiya, " 'Wade,' 'Dryvande,' and 'Gotelak'—Three Notes on the Order of Composition of the *Morte Darthur*," *Studies in English Literature* (The Literary Society of Japan), English no., 1974, pp. 131-148.

49. Vinaver, *Works*, p. 1275.

50. Thomas C. Rumble, " 'The Tale of Tristram': Development by Analogy," in *Malory's Originality*, pp. 118-183.

51. Thomas L. Wright, " 'The Tale of King Arthur': Foreshadowings and Beginnings," in *Malory's Originality*, esp. pp. 18-21.

52. Richard Stansby's edition (1634) was reprinted by Thomas Wright, ed., *The Most Famous and Ancient History of Prince Arthur, etc.* (London, 1858). Stansby deleted Caxton's division into books and divided the work into three parts (*Arthur to Gareth; Tristram; Sancgreal* to end). He retained Caxton's chapter divisions but numbered them consecutively throughout each part. He also modernized the language.

3 TECHNIQUES OF ADAPTATION:
THE TALE OF KING ARTHUR AND *ARTHUR AND LUCIUS*

1. Quoted and translated in Ralph C. Williams, *The Theory of Heroic Epic in Sixteenth-Century Italy* (Baltimore, Md., 1917), p. 9; a fuller discussion of this point is in my "Sir Thomas Malory's *Le Morte Darthur*," in *Critical Approaches to Six Major English Works: "Beowulf" through "Paradise Lost*," ed. Robert M. Lumiansky and Herschel Baker (Philadelphia, 1968), pp. 81-131.

2. Vinaver, *Works*, p. lvii.

3. R. H. Wilson, "Malory's Early Knowledge of Arthurian Romance," *Texas Studies in English*, 29 (1950), 33-50.

4. On the possible influence of *Sir Gawain* see Vinaver, *Works*, p. 1435, n. 305.6-308.14; of *Sir Orfeo*, p. 1472, n. 493.35-494.5.

5. William Matthews, *The Ill-Framed Knight: A Skeptical Inquiry into the Identity of Sir Thomas Malory* (Berkeley, 1966), pp. 75-115, a valuable discussion of Malory's relation to English romance, especially northern.

6. "Tristram" appears in one French manuscript; see Vinaver, *Works*, p. 1469. Both "Tristrem" and "Tristram" are used in English; see Robert W. Ackerman, *An Index of the Arthurian Names in Middle English*, Stanford University Publications, University ser., Language and Literature, 10 (1952).

7. Vinaver prints "sir Gromersom Erioure," clearly an error for "Gromer Somer Ioure." See R. H. Wilson, "Addenda on Malory's Minor Characters," *Journal of English and Germanic Philology*, 55 (1956), 567-587.

8. Vinaver believes that this character is identical with Melyon de Tartre; see *Works*, p. 1612, n. 1148.16-17.

9. Malory's knowledge of the Vulgate *Merlin* is shown most clearly by the anger of Arthur's knights, who would have slain the Roman ambassadors had not Arthur stopped them. Mary E. Dichmann (" 'The Tale of King Arthur and the Emperor Lucius': The Rise of Lancelot," in *Malory's Originality*, pp. 70-71) cites this as evidence that Malory knew Wace. But it seems clearly based on the Vulgate (Sommer, II, 424). See Wilson, "Malory's Early Knowledge."

10. For a full discussion see Edward D. Kennedy, "Malory's Use of Hardyng's *Chronicle*," *Notes and Queries*, 16 (1969), 169-170. The coronation of Arthur also occurs in *Ly myreur des histoires* by Jean d'Outremeuse, but Kennedy adduces other details from Hardyng's work to establish the fact that Malory drew on the *Chronicle*.

11. Robert W. Ackerman, "English Rimed and Prose Romances," in *ALMA*, p. 481.

12. Dieter Mehl, *The Middle English Romances of the Thirteenth and Fourteenth Centuries* (London, 1969), esp. pp. 22-38.

13. See *Romance of Horn*, II, 1-2, 107-121.

14. *Ywain and Gawain*, p. xvii.

15. See *Romance of Horn*, II, 15-16, on Horn as a model courtier; *King Ponthus*, pp. xlvi-xlix, for a discussion of *Ponthus et la belle Sidoine* as a courtesy book.

16. *Romance of Horn*, II, 7-8.

17. Ibid., pp. 113-114.

18. See *Floris and Blancheflour*, p. 20; *Amis and Amiloun*, "Introduction," which contains a thorough discussion of the various versions. The many manuscripts of both the French and English versions of *Amis and Amiloun* render any exact comparison impossible. My estimate is based on the versions printed by Eugen Kölbing.

19. See *Kyng Alisaunder*, II, 28-40.

20. Helaine Newstead notes that even the admired battle scenes are subordinated to the main theme ("2. Arthurian Legends," in J. Burke Severs, *A Manual of the Writings in Middle English: The Romances* [New Haven, 1967], p. 74). The work is, of course, fragmentary.

21. Cf. James Boyd, *Ulrich Füetrer's "Parzifal": Materials and Sources* (Oxford, 1936), p. 2; Cedric E. Pickford, *L'évolution du roman arthurien en prose vers la fin du moyen âge d'après le manuscrit 112 du fonds français de la Bibliothèque nationale* (Paris, 1960), p. 89.

22. Matthews, *Ill-Framed Knight*, p. 102, shows that Malory knew these works, and the fact that he reveals this knowledge indicates that he at least remembered and probably liked them.

23. Vinaver, *Works*, p. 1369. See also Dichmann, " 'The Tale of King

Arthur and the Emperor Lucius' "; the discussions in William Matthews, *The Tragedy of Arthur: A Study of the Alliterative "Morte Arthure"* (Berkeley, 1960), pp. 172-177; idem, *Ill-Framed Knight.*

24. Matthews, *Ill-Framed Knight,* p. 176.

25. Vinaver, *Works,* p. lxviii.

26. Ibid.

27. A full discussion of *Arthour and Merlin* is forthcoming in the second volume of G. D. Macrae-Gibson's EETS edition. See Eugen Kölbing's edition and the review by K. D. Bülbring in *Englische Studien,* 16 (1892), 251ff.

28. Vinaver, *Works,* p. lxviii.

29. *Amis and Amiloun,* p. xcvii; *Floris and Blancheflour,* p. 24.

30. Wilson, "Malory's Early Knowledge."

31. Vinaver, *Works,* pp. 1290-91, n. 25.27-26.15. G. D. Macrae-Gibson has pointed out to me in a personal communication that the manuscript quoted by Sommer (II, 111), B.N. fr. 105, has "*x roys et un duc*" and that this caused "*il rois Carados briebras de al terre destraigorre,* in some variant form of his name, to be divided into a king Brangore of Strangore and a king Carados in the version underlying both *AM* and Malory." See G. D. Macrae-Gibson, *Of Arthour and of Merlin,* vol. II (EETS, forthcoming), "Commentary," note to line 3405.

32. See R. H. Wilson, "The Rebellion of the Kings in Malory and the Cambridge *Suite du Merlin.*" *Texas Studies in English,* 31 (1952), 17.

33. Although I am inclined to think the author of *Arthour and Merlin* independently changed the treasure episode, G. D. Macrae-Gibson argues cogently that a common manuscript version may underlie both episodes. He notes that in Malory's version Arthur apparently has no prior knowledge of the treasure, whereas in *Arthour and Merlin* Arthur seems to know of it already—"Who told þe of mi tresour?" Such inconsistency is below the author's usual level of skill and, given the Malory correspondence, may therefore indicate the common use of a defective version that omitted the earlier reference to this treasure. See Macrae-Gibson, *Of Arthour and of Merlin,* vol. II, "Introduction," section called "Source and Treatment of Source."

34. Vinaver, *Works,* p. 1275.

35. D. S. Brewer, "Form in the *Morte Darthur,*" *Medium Aevum,* 21 (1952), 17.

36. C. S. Lewis, *The Allegory of Love,* rev. ed. (Oxford, 1936), p. 300: Malory "often leaves his separate stories unfinished or else, if he finishes them, fails to interlock them at all (so that they drop away from the rest of the book as independent organisms)."

37. C. S. Lewis, "The English Prose *Morte,*" in *Essays on Malory,* p. 27.

38. Stephen Knight, *The Structure of Sir Thomas Malory's Arthuriad,* Australian Humanities Research Council, monograph 14 (Sidney, 1969), argues that differing structural principles apply to the various parts of Malory's book, though his conclusions differ from mine.

4 THEMATIC INVENTION:
A NOBLE TALE OF SIR LANCELOT

1. C. S. Lewis, "The 'Morte Darthur' " (review of Vinaver's *Works, Times Literary Supplement,* June 7, 1947), reprinted in *Studies in Medieval and Renaissance Literature,* ed. Walter Hooper (Cambridge, 1966), p. 110.

2. Ibid., p. 107.

3. William Matthews, *The Tragedy of Arthur: A Study of the Alliterative "Morte Arthure"* (Berkeley, 1960), pp. 32-67.

4. Larry D. Benson, *Art and Tradition in Sir Gawain and the Green Knight* (New Brunswick, N.J.), pp. 3-55.

5. G. L. Kittredge, *A Study of Gawain and the Green Knight* (Cambridge, Mass., 1916), esp. pp. 85-89.

6. *Awntyrs of Arthur*, pp. 18-29.

7. *Degrevant*, pp. lxii-lxxii.

8. J. Burke Severs, *A Manual of the Writings in Middle English: The Romances* (New Haven, Conn., 1967), pp. 13-16.

9. Chestre, *Sir Launfal*, pp. 24-31.

10. Helaine Newstead, "2. Arthurian Legends," in Severs, *Manual*, pp. 50-51.

11. Paul J. Ketrick, *The Relation of "Golagros and Gawane" to the Old French "Perceval"* (Washington, D.C., 1931); R. E. Bennett, "The Sources of the *Jeaste of Syr Gawayne*," *Journal of English and Germanic Philology*, 33 (1934), 57-63.

12. Kittredge, *Study of Sir Gawain*, pp. 118-125; R. W. Ackerman, "English Rimed and Prose Romances," in *ALMA*, pp. 501-505; Edwin Greenlaw, "The Vows of Baldwin," *PMLA*, 21 (1906), 575-636.

13. *Eger and Grime*, pp. 151-157; *The Squyr of Lowe Degre*, pp. xxv-xlvi.

14. Vinaver, *Works*, p. 1363, n. 175.30-35.

15. Henry S. Bennett, *Chaucer and the Fifteenth Century* (Oxford, 1947), p. 201.

16. Morton W. Bloomfield, *Essays and Explorations* (Cambridge, Mass., 1970), pp. 97-128.

17. Per Nykrog, "Two Creators of Narrative Form in Twelfth Century France: Gautier d'Arras—Chrétien de Troyes," *Speculum* 48 (1973), 258-276.

18. George Kane, *Middle English Literature: A Critical Study of the Romances, the Religious Lyrics, "Piers Plowman"* (London, 1951), pp. 48-49.

19. Christian Gellinek, "*The Romance of Horn*: A Structural Survey," *Neuephilologische Mitteilungen*, 66 (1965), 330-333, offers an analysis differing in some ways from the following.

20. Albert E. Hartung, "Narrative Technique, Characterization, and the Sources in Malory's 'Tale of Sir Lancelot,'" *Studies in Philology*, 70 (1973), 253-268; see also Robert M. Lumiansky, "'The Tale of Lancelot': Prelude to Adultery," in *Malory's Originality*, pp. 91-98.

21. Ackerman, "English Rimed and Prose Romances," p. 500.

22. Tomoni Kato, *A Concordance to the Works of Sir Thomas Malory* (Tokyo, 1974): the word *paramour* in its various forms (e.g., *paramoure, peramour*) appears twenty-eight times in the *Morte Darthur*. It is almost always used of evil temptresses such as Morgan la Fay, of casual lovers, or of untrue lovers. The exceptions are morally neutral cases such as Andred's lady (ix.20) and the King of the Hundred Knights and the Queen of Northgales (x.60), and those cases where the word is used as the opposite of "wife" (vii.35, xviii.19-20); Morgan uses the word of Lancelot (ix.41) and Palomides declares that he loves Isode "paramoures" (x.53). The only real exception is the use of the word to describe Launceor and Columbe in *The Tale of King Arthur* (ii.7). The phrase "trewe love" is used only as a general term or in reference to Launceor and Columbe and Lancelot and Guenevere, and the word "lover" is restricted to admirable characters except for one use in *The*

Tale of King Arthur, where Morgan is said to have a "lover" (ii.11). The fact that the exceptions to Malory's general usage of both "paramour" and "lover" appear only in *The Tale of King Arthur* provides a further indication that this is an early work.

23. E.g., Sommer, IV, 357-358; V, 146-147.

24. Vinaver, *Works*, p. 1410, characterizes *Sir Lancelot* as "this puzzling work."

5 THE TALE OF SIR GARETH

1. See E. Brugger, "Der schöne Feigling in der arthurischen Literatur," *Zeitschrift für romanische Philologie*, 61 (1941), 63 (1943), 65 (1949), 67 (1951); William H. Schofield, *Studies on the Libeus Desconus*, Harvard Studies in Philology and Literature, 4 (Boston, 1895).

2. R. H. Wilson, "The Fair Unknown in Malory," *PMLA*, 58 (1943), 2-21.

3. *Lybeaus Desconus*, p. 48.

4. Eugène Vinaver, "A Romance of Gaheriet," *Medium Aevum*, 1 (1932), 157-167; idem, *Works*, pp. 1427-1434.

5. Vinaver, *Works*, p. 1428.

6. Thomas L. Wright, "Originality and Purpose in Malory's 'Tale of King Arthur,'" Ph.D. diss., Tulane University, 1960, pp. 279-284, cited by Wilfred L. Guerin, " 'The Tale of the Death of Arthur': Catastrophe and Resolution," in *Malory's Originality*, pp. 103-104; the whole of Guerin's discussion is valuable.

7. Roger S. Loomis, "Malory's Beaumains," *PMLA*, 54 (1939), 656-668.

8. Guerin, " 'Tale of the Death of Arthur,' " p. 106.

9. Vinaver, *Works*, p. 1432, n. 1.

10. Henry Weber, *Metrical Romances of the Thirteenth, Fourteenth, and Fifteenth Centuries* (Edinburgh, 1810), III, 363-364. Since writing this chapter I have had a chance to read Claude Luttrell, *The Creation of the First Arthurian Romance* (Evanston, Ill., 1974). Luttrell considers, in app. B, "The Relation of *Sir Gareth* to Ipomedon II," and concludes: "*Sir Gareth* goes back to a source close to Ipomedon II, from which that source may indeed in turn have been derived" (p. 268). As my discussion shows, I suspect the relation may be more direct.

11. L. Lengert, "Die schottische Romanze Roswall and Lillian," *Englische Studien*, 17 (1892), 358-364; Charles Henry Carter, "Ipomedon: An Illustration of Romance Origin," in *Haverford Essays: Studies in Modern Literature Prepared by Some Former Pupils of Francis B. Gummere in Honor of the Completion of the Twentieth Year of His Teaching in Haverford College* (Haverford, Pa., 1909), p. 345.

12. Carter, "*Ipomedon*," pp. 237-270.

13. This summarizes the last part of the romance (vv. 6300ff). In the early part we have been told how Ipomadon, disguised, comes to the court of the Lady of Calabria, falls in love with her, but pretends he is a worthless and lazy young man. Disguised, he takes part in a three-day tournament and wins her love; then he leaves, to return at the point where this summary begins.

14. Murray A. Potter, *Sohrab and Rustem: The Epic Theme of a Combat between Father and Son* (London, 1902), p. 207.

15. Jesse L. Weston, *The Three Days' Tournament* (London, 1902).

16. In which Sir Valentine's knights threaten to hang the hero.

17. Hence the use of disguise by knights (such as Lancelot) engaged in reestablishing their merits: the name must be concealed until its bearer has again proved he is worthy of it.

18. The Red Knight's strength increases every day until noon (vii.17); this is one of Gawain's traits (cf.xx.21) and thus suggests a relation between Gareth's two main duels.

6   THE BOOK OF SIR TRISTRAM

1. E. K. Chambers, *Sir Thomas Malory*, English Association Pamphlet, 51 (London, 1922), p. 41.

2. As Vinaver writes (*Works*, p. 1446), "The prose version, with its clear-cut division of characters into heroes and villains, and the natural tendency to make the heroes happy and the villains miserable was much after his own heart." The exact version of the *Tristan* used by Malory remains unknown. See Thomas C. Rumble, " 'The Tale of Tristram': Development by Analogy," in *Malory's Originality*, pp. 118-183; Eugène Vinaver, *Le roman de Tristan et Iseut dans l'œuvre de Thomas Malory* (Paris, 1925), and *Works*, pp. 1443-1533, on which I am most dependent.

3. Cf. François Remigereau, "Tristan, 'Maître de venerie,' dans la tradition anglaise et dans le roman de Tristan," *Romania*, 58 (1932), 218-237; Vinaver, *Works*, p. 1510, n. 682.26-683.4. Malory adds an even more extensive account of Tristram's invention of the terms of hunting in viii.3: "Wherefore, as me seemeth, all jantyllmen that beryth olde armys ought of right to honoure sir Tristrams . . . unto the Day of Dome."

4. Vinaver suggests that "amen" is an ironical scribal addition (*Works*, p. 1510, n. 683.4). I would agree with D. C. Muecke, "Some Notes on Vinaver's *Malory*," *Modern Language Review*, 70 (1955), 327: "The *amen* is exactly what one would expect from Malory himself."

5. See Vinaver, *Works*, p. 1478, n. 540.28-36.

6. So we learn in *Sir Tristram*, x.25. Later he is listed among the knights who attempt to cure Sir Urry (xix.11). This sort of inconsistency sometimes bothers modern readers, to whom it seems evidence of carelessness. More likely it is an indication that thematic appropriateness (the mention of Dinadan's death at this point in the narrative) is more important to Malory than consistency.

7. Vinaver, *Works*, p. 1501, n. 643.23-25.

8. P. J. C. Field, *Romance and Chronicle: A Study of Malory's Prose Style* (London, 1971), pp. 124-125, contains a brief discussion with examples. Cf. Shakespeare, *Henry IV, Part I*, act 3, sc. 1: "Swear me, Kate, like a lady as thou art, a good mouth-filling oath."

9. For a discussion of this technique, see Rumble, " 'Tale of Tristram.' "

10. Vinaver, *Works*, p. 1450, n. 425.11-13 (Isode's desire that Palomides be baptized); p. 1452, n. 717.10-19 (the reference to his baptism in the Red City adventure); p. 1532, n. 840.16-845.9 (Tristram's fight with Palomides and his conversion). See also p. 1452, n. 738.22-25. In adding all this Malory did confuse the issue slightly by saying, in the Red City adventure, that the achievement of the Beste Glatisant is also (in addition to the seven battles) a condition of Palomides' baptism. Apparently he intended this, then thought better of it, for Palomides rides off after the questing beast in the final lines of the tale. The theme of the Saracen seeking baptism may have been suggested by Priamus in

Arthur and Lucius, though it is fairly common; or Malory may have known that in the prose *Tristan*, after Tristan's death, Palomides is baptized, becomes a member of the Round Table, undertakes the quest of the Grail, and is treacherously killed by Gawain and Agravain (Löseth, *Tristan*, pp. 396-400).

11. The contrast between Mark and Arthur is heightened by the similarities. Lamerok explains that he took the horn (intended to reveal Guenevere's adultery to Arthur) to Cornwall to reveal Isode's adultery to Mark, "And hit were to do again, so wolde I do, for I had lever stryff and debate felle in Kyng Markys courte rather than in kynge Arthurs courte, for the honoure of both courtes be nat lyke" (viii.38). According to Rumble, " 'Tale of Tristram,' " p. 182, this is Malory's own invention.

12. The influence worked both ways. See James D. Bruce, *The Evolution of Arthurian Romance* (Baltimore, Md., 1923), I, 484, for the influence of the legend of Tristan on Lancelot.

13. Vinaver, *Works*, p. 1513, n. 698.22-700.8.

14. In the French version, edited by Cedric E. Pickford, *"Alexandre l'Orphelin": A Prose Tale of the Fifteenth Century* (Manchester, 1951), Alexander is killed by Helyas le Roux; see Vinaver, *Works*, pp. 1497-1500.

15. Vinaver, *Works*, p. 1528, n. 810.1-20.

16. We have already been assured that his triumph is but temporary, since Alexander's son, Bellengerus le Breuse, finally kills Mark. This episode, invented by Malory, is recalled in the passage in which we are told how Tristram was killed by Mark "as he sate harpyng afore hys lady": "And thys sir Bellynger revenged the deth of his fadir, sir Alysaundir, and sir Trystram, for he slew kyng Mark" (xix.11). Vinaver argues that Breunys sanz Pité is identical with the Brown Knight without Pity whom Gareth kills (*Works*, pp. 1440-41, n. 355.14-24). This is obviously not the case, though it is equally obvious that Breunys probably suggested the name and character of the Brown Knight.

17. Rumble, " 'Tale of Tristram,' " pp. 180-181.

18. Vinaver, *Works*, p. 1446.

7 FIFTEENTH-CENTURY CHIVALRY

1. As in La Sale, *Jehan de Saintré*, p. 109.

2. The phrase is W. P. Ker's, quoted by H. R. Patch, "Chaucer and Medieval Romance," in *Essays in Memory of Barrett Wendell* (Cambridge, Mass., 1926), p. 107. Patch is aware that not all romances fit this definition, though even today the assumption is common in discussions of medieval romance. A good recent discussion of the romance mode is in Pamela Gradon, *Form and Style in Early English Literature* (London, 1971), pp. 212-272.

3. Martín de Riquer, *Cavalleria fra realtà e litteratura nel quattrocento* (Bari, 1971), p. 5.

4. R. W. Chambers, *On the Continuity of English Prose from Alfred to More and His School*, EETS, 191a (London, 1932), p. cxxxix.

5. Arthur B. Ferguson, *The Indian Summer of English Chivalry: Studies in the Decline and Transformation of Chivalric Idealism* (Durham, N.C., 1960); Johan Huizinga, *The Waning of the Middle Ages*, trans. F. Hopman (London, 1924). For a somewhat earlier period, see also John Barnie, *War in Medieval English Society: Social Values and the Hundred Years War, 1337-1399* (London, 1974).

6. Henry S. Bennett, *Chaucer and the Fifteenth Century* (Oxford, 1947), p. 200.

7. Edmund Reiss, *Sir Thomas Malory* (New York, 1966), p. 19.

8. This interpretation was first advanced in the "Introduction" to *Le Morte Darthur*, ed. Edward Strachey (London, 1868). For a full treatment from this point of view see Vinaver's introduction to the final tale in *Works*, pp. 1615-26; Charles Moorman, *"The Book of Kyng Arthur": The Unity of Malory's "Morte Darthur"* (Lexington, Ky., 1965); and Moorman's more recent *Kings and Captains: Variations on a Heroic Theme* (Lexington, Ky., 1971), esp. pp. 162-165.

9. Elizabeth Pochada, *Arthurian Propaganda: "Le Morte Darthur" as an Historical View of Life* (Chapel Hill, N.C., 1971), p. 60.

10. See Jacques Levron's excellent introduction to his reduced edition of Léon Gautier's *Chivalry*, trans. D. C. Dunning (New York, 1965). For the older view, note the use of the word "progress" in the chapter titles in Charles Mills, *History of Chivalry; or, Knighthood and Its Times* (Philadelphia, 1824): e.g., "The Progress of Chivalry in Great Britain." Mills believes that chivalry began to wane after Henry V, but he notes that Caxton greatly exaggerated and that there were many in the period "worthy to have been the paladins of Charlemagne, the knights of the Round Table" (p. 161). The eighteenth-century writer Jean Baptiste de la Curne de Sainte-Palaye in his *Mémoires sur l'ancienne chevalerie*, rev. ed. (Paris, 1826), ranks Francis I, Henry VIII's companion on the Field of the Cloth of Gold, among the most illustrious of "les models et les protecteurs de la Chevalerie." Vulson, in his *Vray théâtre d'honnevr* (published 1648), regards Good King René of Anjou, whom some modern historians of chivalry unjustly dismiss as a buffoon, as one "dont la virtue heroïque rendra sa nom venerable jusque la fin du monde." Andrew Favine (André Favyn), in his *Theatre of Honour and Knighthood* (London, 1623; a translation from the French), drew his accounts of chivalric deeds—with but one exception—from the sixteenth century. Basil Willey, "Lord Herbert of Cherbury: A Spiritual Quixote of the Seventeenth Century," *Essays and Studies by Members of the English Association*, 27 (1941), 24, describes the seventeenth century as "the declining years of chivalry." Edmund Burke perhaps exaggerated when he said, in his famous comment on the French Revolution, "The Age of Chivalry is dead," but Walter Scott seemed to believe that the Highlanders who supported the Pretender in the eighteeenth century still carried on some of the chivalric tradition.

11. Gautier, *Chivalry*, p. 28.

12. Ibid., p. 30.

13. Gustave Cohen, *Histoire de la chevalerie en France au moyen âge* (Paris, 1949), p. 202.

14. Sidney Painter, *French Chivalry: Chivalric Ideals and Practices in Medieval France* (Baltimore, 1940); Richard W. Barber, *The Knight and Chivalry* (London, 1970). Barber's is the best recent history of chivalry; it contains an excellent bibliography, and his ideas have helped shape my own.

15. Painter, *French Chivalry*, p. 92.

16. Kenneth B. McFarlane, *The Nobility of the Later Middle Ages: The Ford Lecture for 1953 and Related Studies* (Oxford, 1973), p. 114.

17. Painter, *French Chivalry*, p. 142; Barnie, *War in Medieval English Society*, pp. 56-96.

18. Huizinga, *Waning of the Middle Ages*, p. 244: "We might venture the paradox that the Middle Ages knew only applied art."

19. Ferguson, *Indian Summer*, p. 137.

20. Quoted and translated in William H. Schofield, *Chivalry in English Literature: Chaucer, Malory, Spenser, and Shakespeare* (Cambridge, Mass., 1912), pp. 5-6.

21. Quoted in Daniel Poirion, *Le poète et le prince: L'évolution du lyrisme courtois de Guillaume de Machaut à Charles d'Orléans* (Grenoble, 1965), pp. 31-32.

22. The change, however, was gradual, and the fifteenth-century system was "a refinement, and not a degeneration of an earlier feudal system" (William Huse Dunham, Jr., *Lord Hasting's Indentured Retainers, 1461-1483, Transactions of the Connecticut Academy of Arts and Sciences*, 39 [1955] 1). Though the founding of the *gendarmerie* in France is sometimes thought to have marked the end of the old feudal army, McFarlane says that the composition of Henry VIII's army was not significantly different from that of Edward III (*Nobility of the Later Middle Ages*, p. 162). See also Michael E. Powicke, *Military Obligation in Medieval England: A Study in Liberty and Duty* (Oxford, 1962): "One thing is clear: the feudal lords retained and possibly increased their leadership in matters of war" (p. 213). The last attempt at a general feudal levy was in 1385, but Powicke records many later examples of lords summoning their retainers.

23. See Vincent J. Scattergood, *Politics and Poetry in the Fifteenth Century* (London, 1971), pp. 270-271.

24. Apparently the word "gentleman" was first used in its modern, class-defining sense in the early fifteenth century. See A. W. Reid, "Chivalry and the Idea of a Gentleman," in *Chivalry: A Series of Studies to Illustrate Its Historical Significance and Civilizing Influence, by Members of King's College, London* (London, 1928), esp. pp. 208-210; Ferguson, *Indian Summer*, p. 12.

25. Kenneth B. McFarlane, "Bastard Feudalism," *Bulletin of the Institute of Historical Research*, 20 (1945), 161-180; Dunham, *Lord Hasting's Indentured Retainers*.

26. Pochada's *Arthurian Propaganda* is the fullest treatment of Malory's *Morte Darthur* in relation to contemporary political thought; as is apparent, I am not always in agreement with her position.

27. A sample contract is printed in *English Historical Documents, 1327-1485*, ed. Alex R. Myers (London, 1969), p. 1126. See also the documents printed in Dunham, *Lord Hasting's Indentured Retainers*.

28. Scattergood, *Politics and Poetry*, p. 308. See also the letter quoted in Henry S. Bennett, *The Pastons and Their England* (Cambridge, 1927), p. 14: "Sundry folk have said to me that they think verily . . . while the world is as it is, you can never live in peace until you have his [duke of Suffolk's] good lordship."

29. Warkworth, *Chronicle*. This comment is Warkworth's explanation of the people's readiness to accept Henry in 1471. After the accession of Edward IV in 1461 a stanza was added to Lydgate's "Verses on the Kings of England" urging the reader to "rejoice with mirth, for now the good times are come." See James Gardiner, ed., *The Historical Collections of a Citizen of London in the Fifteenth Century*, Camden Society (London, 1876).

30. These verses, written in 1453 after the murder of Charles's friend the duke of Suffolk, are quoted and discussed in Enid McLeod, *Charles of Orléans: Prince and Poet* (London, 1969), pp. 326-327. Charles had a considerable interest in chivalry; he founded his own chivalric order, the Order of the

Gamail, and for his "high renown" and "valor" he was made a member of the Order of the Golden Fleece (Toison d'or); p. 251.

31. Raymond L. Kilgour, *The Decline of Chivalry as Shown in the French Literature of the Late Middle Ages* (Cambridge, Mass., 1937).

32. The first nineteen chapters of book vi of the *Policraticus* are on this subject. See *The Stateman's Book of John of Salisbury*, trans. John Dickinson (New York, 1927).

33. Chrétien, *Yvain*, vv. 31-33.

34. Preface to vol. I.

35. Eugène Vinaver, *Malory* (Oxford, 1929), p. 56. In a note Vinaver observes that "Spenser's letter to Sir Walter Raleigh also contains some obvious analogies with Caxton's Preface, doubtless due to deliberate imitation." One might add other works, such as Sir William Segar's *Honour, Military and Ciuill*, for the idea was widespread.

36. E. K. Chambers, *The Elizabethan Stage* (Oxford, 1923), I, 139-148.

37. Quoted by Gerald R. Owst in *Literature and Pulpit in Medieval England*, 2d ed. (Oxford, 1961), p. 332.

38. Owst, *Literature and Pulpit*, pp. 331-332.

39. Ibid.

40. See Roger S. Loomis, "Edward I, Arthurian Enthusiast," *Speculum*, 28 (1953), 114-127; Owst, *Literature and Pulpit*, p. 332; for Guérin see *De Berenger au lonc cul*, trans. in Larry D. Benson and Theodore M. Andersson, *The Literary Context of Chaucer's Fabliaux* (Indianapolis, 1971).

41. Owst, *Literature and Pulpit*, p. 332. Peter of Blois wrote of the knights of the twelfth century: "Non ferro sed vino, non lanceis sed caseis, non ensibus sed utribus, non hastibus sed verubus onerantur." Chap. 5 of Painter's *French Chivalry* is an excellent survey of criticisms of chivalry.

42. Freeman is quoted along with a number of other nineteenth-century historians in F. J. C. Hearnshaw, "Chivalry: Its Place in History," in Prestage, *Chivalry*, p. 30. Plummer is quoted in McFarlane, "Bastard Feudalism."

43. See Caxton's preface to *The Book of the Ordre of Chyvalry:* "Read Froissart. And also behold that noble king Henry V and the captains under him . . . and many others whose names shine gloriously by their virtuous noblesse and acts that they did in honor of the order of chivalry."

44. Painter, *French Chivalry*, p. 61.

45. See Walter Scott, *Essay on Chivalry* (London, 1816). Schofield, *Chivalry in English Literature*, likewise defines chivalry as a spirit rather than an institution.

46. Painter, *Chivalry*, p. 1.

47. Richard Grafton, *Chronicle*, II, 4. Warkworth also gives a circumstantial account of the sentence for the degrading of Grey (*Chronicle*, pp. 36-39), which was to have been a formal ceremony, complete with the king's cook striking off his spurs. However, the full degradation ceremony was evidently not carried out. See Rosamund J. Mitchell, *Sir John Tiptoft, 1427-1470* (London, 1938), pp. 96-99.

48. See E. F. Jacob, "The Beginnings of Medieval Chivalry," in Prestage, *Chivalry*, pp. 37-55.

49. Moorman, *Kings and Captains*, pp. 163-164.

50. Chandos Herald, *Le prince noir*, vv. 71-72; Christine de Pisan, *Livres des fais et bonnes meurs du sage roy Charles V*, pp. 115-116; Hardyng, *Chronicle*, p. 125.

51. Lydgate, *Fall of Princes*, vv. 2738-39; *Knyghthode and Bataile*, vv. 404-

405. See Ferguson's chapter "Chivalry and the Commonwealth" in *Indian Summer*, pp. 104-141.

52. See Harold Arthur, Viscount Dillon, "On a MS. Collection of Ordinances of Chivalry, Belonging to Lord Hastings," *Archeologia*, 57 (2d ser., 7) (1901), 68; on Grey's degradation see n. 47 above.

53. "Le vingtiesme quilz ne devoiēt prandre ne toucher nulle Dame ne damoiselle proposant quilz leussēt cōquise de force darmes si elle ny prenoit plaisir et que elle y fut consentante." This is a variant recorded only in the Morgan Library copy of *La forme quon tenoit des tournoys et assemblees au temps du roy uterpendragon et du roy artus*, ed. Edouard Sandoz: "Tourneys in the Arthurian Tradition," *Speculum*, 19 (1944), 402.

54. Dillon, "Ordinances": the herald is charged "to help wydows and maidens, and in cas be that any man wold doo them wrong or forse or disherite them of their lyflode . . . that you do help them."

55. Quoted in Schofield, *Chivalry in English Literature*, p. 120. For the original see Berners, *Boke of Saint Albans*, p. ai recto and verso. Sir William Segar, *Honour Military and Ciuill*, maintains the most commendable nobility is "mixture of auncient noble blood with vertue" (p.113). When Malory addresses the reader on Tristram's invention of the terms of hunting, he likewise specifies ancient noble blood: "all jantyllmen that beryth olde armys" (viii.3).

56. Quoted in Ferguson, *Indian Summer*, p. 11.

57. Chastelain, *Chronique de J. de Lalain*, p. 11. This was a common formula. Of course, nobles sometimes acted like commoners. Edward IV was not above engaging in trade; see *The Chronicles of the White Rose of York*, p. 177. And commoners, or at least rich merchants, prized the trappings of nobility; Gregory reports in his *Chronicle of London* that at the coronation of King Edward's wife Elizabeth five London Aldermen were among the knights of the Bath that were then made (p. 228). Likewise, men of means (40 pounds or more per annum) were compelled to accept knighthood or pay a fine.

58. Francis H. Cripps-Day, *The History of the Tournament in England and in France* (London, 1918), app. 6, p. xliii; See P. E. Tucker, "Chivalry in the Morte,' " in *Essays on Malory*, pp. 64-103.

59. Hardyng, *Chronicle*, p. 125; Vulson, *Vray théâtre*, preface to vol. I: "Mon principal but est de bannir l'oysiueté et la molesse ou les pluspart de Gentilshommes se plongent."

60. "The manner of making knights after the custom of England, in time of peace, and at the coronation, that is to say, knightes of the Bath," in James Gairdner, ed., *Three Fifteenth Century Chronicles with Historical Memoranda By John Stowe, the Antiquary*, Camden Society (London, 1880), pp. 106-113; "the king says, 'Be ye a good knyght,' kissyng him" (p. 112). In another version, printed in Dillon, "Ordinances," app. C, there is no kiss and the words are the familiar French formula, *Soyez bon chevalere* (p. 69).

61. Gairdner, *Three Fifteenth Century Chronicles*, p. 112. The custom was still observed in the seventeenth century, and Lord Herbert of Cherbury tells how a lady removed the lace from his robe; see Willey, "Lord Herbert," p. 24.

62. *Pageant of the Birth, life, and Death of Richard Beauchamp*, plate 9.

63. Haye, *Gilbert of the Haye's Prose Manuscript*, II, 13, 40.

64. William Segar, *Honour, Military and Ciuill*, p. 49.

65. D. W. Robertson, "The Concept of Courtly Love as an Impediment to the Understanding of Medieval Texts," in *The Meaning of Courtly Love*, ed. Francis X. Newman (Albany, N. Y., 1968), p. 17.

66. John F. Benton, "The Court of Champagne as a Literary Center," *Speculum*, 36 (1961), 551-591; "Clio and Venus: An Historical View of Courtly

Love," in Newman, *Meaning of Courtly Love*, pp. 19-42. The Newman volume is reviewed in detail by Jean Frappier, *Amour cortois et Table ronde* (Geneva, 1973), pp. 61-96.

67. Henry duke of Lancaster, *Le livre de seyntz medicines*, pp. 22-23, 77-78; the discussion in Barnie, *War in Medieval English Society*, pp. 61-65; *The Book of the Knight of La Tour-Landry*, p. 175. Such warnings against "false love" were commonplace (and underlie Malory's own discussion of "good love"): cf. Christine de Pisan, *Epistre au dieu d'amours*, in *Œuvres poétiques*, vol. II, and the translation by Thomas Hoccleve, "The Letter of Cupid," in *The Minor Poems*, ed. Frederick J. Furnivall and I. Gollancz, rev. Jerome Mitchell and A. I. Doyle, Early English Text Society, extra ser., 61, 73 (London, 1970). The problem was as old as courtly love itself; see Stephen Manning, "Game and Earnest in Middle English and Provençal Love Lyrics," *Comparative Literature*, 18 (1966), 225-241.

68. Chastelain, in his *Chronique de J. de Lalain*, depicts little Jacques's father instructing him in the seven deadly sins, each of which can be remedied by a courtly virtue, and the father's catechism is actually a brief art of love.

69. Lord Scales, for example, is depicted by the heralds and chivalric chroniclers as a model of bravery and honor, and nothing is said about the facts reported by the Milanese ambassador to the duke of Milan: "Once when he was staying with the duke of Burgundy, in 1476, he told the duke, Charles the Rash, that he would be delighted to join his war against the Swiss by taking his place in the line of battle. 'But hearing . . . that the enemy was near at hand and they expected to meet them, he asked leave to depart, saying he was sorry he could not stay . . . the duke laughed about it to me, saying, he has gone because he is afraid' " (Mitchell, *John Tiptoft*, pp. 104-105).

70. See Theodor Straub, "Die Gründung des Pariser Minnehofs von 1400," *Zeitschrift für romanische Philologie*, 77 (1961), 1-14; Arthur Piaget, "La cour amoreuse dite de Charles VI," *Romania*, 20 (1891), 417-454. Straub shows that the founding could not have been as elaborate as the records claim, since many of the participants were not even in Paris at the time. Yet the records are early, written within the lifetimes of those listed as participants, and at the very least those who were listed as members could not have objected. A passage from Guillebert de Metz, describing the notable persons of Paris in 1407, mentions the Prince of Love, the main officer of the court; see William A. Neilson, *The Origins and Sources of the "Court of Love,"* Harvard Studies and Notes in Philology and Literature, 6 (Boston, 1899), p. 252. Neilson provides a valuable survey of the tradition and a just discussion of the Paris Court of Love. See also Paul Remy, "Les 'cours d'amours': legende et realité," *Revue de l'université de Bruxelles*, 7 (1954-55), 179-198.

71. Charles Poitvin, "La charte de la Cour d'amour," *Bulletin de l'Académie royale des science, des lettres, et des beaux-arts de Belgique*, 3d ser., 12 (1886), 210.

72. Arthur Piaget, "Un manuscrit de la cour amoreuse de Charles VI," *Romania*, 31 (1902), 597-603.

73. Leopold Deslisle, review of *Choix des testaments tournaisiens anterieurs au xvie siècle*, by A. de la Grange, *Journal des savants*, June 1898, pp. 340-342. Poetic appeals were directed to Pierre, asking for his decision in difficult questions of love. See Neilson, *Origins and Sources*, p. 252.

74. Cf. *Epistre au dieu d'amours*, vv. 225-244 (in *Œuvres poétiques*, vol. II), which praises the knights Hutin de Vermeilles and Othe de Granson. The poem *Le dit de la rose* (also in vol. II) summarizes Christine's position in the controversy over the *Roman de la rose* and seems to have been inspired by the

example of Boucicaut and the Paris Court of Love (II, x-xi). Hutin also appears as an expert on love in the *Cent ballades.*

75. François de Gelis, *Histoire critique des Jeux floraux despuis leur origine jusqu'à leur transformation en Académie (1323-1694)* (Toulouse, 1912).

76. De Gelis, *Histoire,* pp. 31, 33. De Gelis suggests that for "amour" we read "poésie."

77. See Horace Walpole's comment, cited in Frederick S. Shears, *Froissart: Chronicler and Poet* (London, 1930), p. 213, n.

78. Brantôme, *Vies des dames illustres françaises et étrangères,* pp. 340-341.

79. *Vies des dames galantes,* in *Oeuvres,* IX, 390; the incident provided (indirectly) the source of Schiller's ballad *Der Handschuh.*

80. See Gervase Mathew, "Ideals of Knighthood in Late Fourteenth-Century England," in *Studies in Medieval History Presented to F. M. Powicke,* ed. R. W. Hunt et al. (Oxford, 1948), pp. 354-362; Mathew notes that English romances are generally more moral than earlier French romances, but the same could be said of fifteenth-century French romances.

81. Warwick did, however, play the role of courtly lover to his wife, to whom he wrote a poem in which he begged for his lady's mercy and swore to be her humble servitor. He was apparently sincere. See Henry Noble Mac-Cracken, "The Earl of Warwick's *Virelai,*" *PMLA,* 22 (1907), 597-607.

82. The same Burgundian knights who applauded Jacques de Lalaing's perfect knighthood were equally delighted by the *Cent nouvelles nouvelles* (once attributed to Antoine de la Sale). There is an excellent discussion of fifteenth-century attitudes toward courtly love in Poirion, *Le poète et le prince:* Poirion considers the problem of sincerity and concludes that at least in the court of Réne d'Anjou (father-in-law of Henry VI), "Le Roi René et son entourage semblent vraiment pris pat leur rêve" (p. 52).

8   KNIGHTHOOD IN LIFE AND LITERATURE

1. For a study of William's life see Sidney Painter, *William Marshall: Knight-Errant, Baron, and Regent of England* (Baltimore, Md., 1933).

2. Painter, *William Marshall,* p. 30; Painter also notes that "apparently the ladies and romancers had not yet had their way with the tournaments . . . Only in the case of the tournament at Joigni does the *Histoire* mention the presence of ladies . . . William and the other pure lovers of battle were still in control of the cult of chivalry" (p. 59).

3. *L'histoire de Guillaume le Maréchal,* vv. 7209-32.

4. Painter, *William Marshall,* pp. 40-41; *L'histoire,* vv. 3381-3424. The count of captives is kept by Wigain, Young King Henry's clerk; this has not yet become the business of heralds.

5. *L'histoire,* vv. 18578ff.

6. *Histoire du bon chevalier Bayart,* pp. 62-64.

7. See the anecdote recounted in Painter, *William Marshall,* p. 22.

8. Ulrich von Lichtenstein, *Frauendienst,* ed. Reinhold Bechstein, Deutsche Dichtungen des Mittelalters, 6-7 (Leipzig, 1888). Recent scholarship has questioned Ulrich's veracity. See J. W. Thomas, trans., *Ulrich von Lichtenstein's "Service of Ladies"* (Chapel Hill, N.C., 1969), esp. pp. 12-22. Thomas argues that the work is mainly fictional and humorous. However, it is difficult to imagine a thirteenth-century German noble making himself the butt of his own joke.

9. As specified in the rules written by Tiptoft in 1466, the *Ordinances for Justes and Tournaments*.

10. As specified in the challenge of Pierre de Massé, printed in Harold Arthur, Viscount Dillon, "On a MS. Collection of Ordinances of Chivalry, Belonging to Lord Hastings," *Archeologia*, 57 (2d ser., 7) (1901), 36.

11. In Samuel Bentley, ed., *Excerpta Historica; or, Illustrations of English History* (London, 1833), pp. 242-243, there is a transcript of an account of Lord Scales's expenses at the tournament to celebrate the marriage of Prince Richard in 1477, and of Scales's complaint at the size of the fees.

12. La Marche, *Mémoires*, III, 48, n. 3. The reasons for the Bastard's journey were diplomatic as well as chivalric; hence this huge outlay.

13. As an example see "Miei sirventes voulh far de ls reis amdos," ed. and trans. in Frederick Goldin, *Lyrics of the Troubadours and Trouvères* (Garden City, N.Y., 1973), pp. 232-235.

14. Alcius Ledieu, *Un compagnon de Jeanne d'Arc: Etienne Vignoles* (Paris, 1889), p. 83.

15. Dillon, "Ordinances," app. D.

16. Chandos Herald, *Le prince noire*, p. x.

17. Sidney Painter, *French Chivalry: Chivalric Ideals and Practices in Mediaeval France* (Baltimore, Md., 1940), pp. 155-156; Charles Mills, *History of Chivalry; or, Knighthood and Its Times* (Philadelphia, 1826), p. 96, gives several examples of churchmen's teachings on the damnation of those who were killed in tournaments and quotes the story of Matthew Paris concerning Roger de Toeny, who appeared to his brother after death and explained that he was burning in Hell: "Vae, vae mihi, quare unquam torneamenta exercui, et ea tanto studio dilexi?"

18. Gerald R. Owst, *Literature and Pulpit in Medieval England*, 2d ed. (Oxford, 1961), p. 355. By the time Bromyard was writing the Church had already softened its position. Richard W. Barber, *The Knight and Chivalry* (London, 1970), notes that tournaments were frequently held at the papal court at Avignon in the fourteenth century: "By 1471 they appeared in St. Peter's Square itself, and in 1565 the chief feature of the celebration to mark the completion of the Vatican Belvedere was a great tournament" (p. 187). For an account of that tournament and a survey of Italian tournaments in the fifteenth and sixteenth centuries see Mario Tosi, *Il torneo di Belvedere in Vaticano e i tornei in Italia nel cinquecento* (Rome, 1945). The Church's objection to earlier tournaments was based on the general licentiousness of behavior at them as well as their violence, for they were not the solemn and ceremonial affairs that they later became; the anonymous author of *La clef d'amours* advises the prospective lover to frequent tournaments, which are well stocked with available damsels (see *The Comedy of Eros: Medieval French Guides to the Art of Love* trans. Norman R. Shapiro [Urbana, Ill., 1971]), pp. 21-22. The advice is an adaptation to medieval times of Ovid's advice (in the *Ars amatoria*) that young Roman men should frequent the gladatorial games, but it applied nevertheless. See Giulio Ferrerio, *Storia ed analisi degli antichi romanzi di cavalleria e dei poemi romanzeschi d'Italia* (Milan, 1828), II, 110, plate 20; the ladies watching the jousting knights in this illustration of a thirteenth-century manuscript indecently expose themselves, leaving no doubt as to what the fighting is all about. It could well serve as an illustration for the *Lai du Lecheor*; see Per Nykrog, *Les fabliaux* (Copenhagen, 1957), pp. 182-183.

19. Joseph Strutt, *Sports and Pastimes of the English People*, ed. J. Charles

Cox (London, 1903), bk. iii, chap. 1, sec. 19. William of Newburgh says that tournaments were first held in England in 1135-1136, but as late as 1179, according to Matthew Paris, youthful nobles such as Young King Henry were in the habit of crossing the Channel to participate in "conflictibus Gallicis."

20. Barber, *Knight and Chivalry*, p. 295.

21. Two marks was about a week's pay for a landless knight; in the year 1198, according to *The Chronicle of Jocelin of Brakelond*, ed. L. C. Jane (New York, 1966), the abbot, whose own knights simply refused to answer King Richard's feudal call, hired in their place four knights "and gave them at once thirty-six marks for their expenses for forty days" (p. 135).

22. Nicholas Upton, *De studio militari*, ed. F. P. Bernard (Oxford, 1931); quoted by Arthur B. Ferguson, *The Indian Summer of English Chivalry: Studies in the Decline and Transformation of Chivalric Idealism* (Durham, N.C., 1960), p. 14. Strutt, *Sports and Pastimes* (bk. iii, chap. 1, sec. 22) quotes from MS Harley 69 an act of Parliament in the reign of Henry V Regulating tournaments "at the request of all the nobility of England." The history of the English tournament is best treated by Dietrich Sandberger, *Studien über das Rittertum in England, vornehmlich während des 14. Jahrhunderts* (Berlin, 1937), pp. 15-75, for the earlier period, and, for the later, by Sidney Anglo, *The Great Tournament Roll of Westminster* (Oxford, 1968), pp. 19-73.

23. Francis H. Cripps-Day, *The History of the Tournament in England and in France* (London, 1918), app. 6, p. xliii.

24. See E. K. Chambers, *Sir Henry Lee: An Elizabethan Portrait* (Oxford, 1936), pp. 129-130.

25. Roger S. Loomis, "Arthurian Influence in Sport and Spectacle," in *ALMA*, pp. 553-559.

26. On Edward III's determination to imitate Arthur's Round Table (though the Garter lost the direct association), see Adam of Murimath, *Continuatio chronicarum*, ed. E. M. Thompson, Rolls ser. (London, 1889), pp. 155-156, 231-232. The correspondence between King Henry IV and the Seneschal of Hainault concerning his challenge in 1408 states that the Order of the Garter was founded in imitation of the Round Table, and both Henry and the Seneschal assume that Garter knights are bound by that precedent: British Museum MS Add. 21370, fols. 1-4 recto; the letters are printed from "MS No. 8417, in the Royal Library at Paris" in George Frederick Beltz, *Memorials of the Most Noble Order of the Garter* (London, 1841), pp. 403-407.

27. *La forme quon tenoit des tournoys et assemblees au temps du roy Uterpendragon et du roy Artus*, ed. Edouard Sandoz, "Tourneys in the Arthurian Tradition," *Speculum*, 19 (1944), 389-420. See also Ruth H. Cline, "The Influence of Romances on Tournaments of the Middle Ages," *Speculum*, 20 (1945), 204-211.

28. On "triumph" see Cripps-Day, *History of the Tournament*, p. 17. The usage is based on the supposed relation of the tournament to Roman triumphs. Malory uses "play his pageant" at x.74 and 79, which Vinaver glosses as "do his part." In *Pageant of the Birth . . . Earl of Warwick* the word "pageant" refers to the illustrations, which are the main feature of the book.

29. Robert C. Clephan, *The Tournament: Its Periods and Phases* (London, 1919), p. 78.

30. In Bentley, *Excerpta Historica*, pp. 223-239, there is an account by an English herald of this affair.

31. *Des anciens tournois et faictz d'armes*, p. 197, in Bernard Prost, ed., *Traités du duel judiciare: Relations de pas d'armes et tournois* (Paris, 1872).

32. Martín de Riquer, *Cavalleria fra realtà e litteratura nel quattrocento* (Bari, 1970), pp. 43-70.

33. The story is told in Bowar's continuation (written about 1449) of Johannis de Fordun, *Scotichronicon genuinum*, ed. Thomas Hearne (Oxford, 1722), IV, 1123-24. After Sir Piers had his two front teeth knocked out, he complained that Sir William had better armor. William, hearing this, offered to ride six new courses—for a prize of 200 pounds—provided that the two opponents were equal in all respects. Sir Piers agreed, whereupon William, who had lost an eye at Otterburne, demanded that Piers should have one eye put out. This began a general brawl which King Richard, laughing, brought to an end.

34. Riquer, *Cavalleria*, pp. 43-47.

35. Chastelain, *Chronique de J. de Lalain*, p. 81.

36. Ibid., pp. 103-185; the adventures described in the next paragraph are found on pp. 186-212.

37. In his *Excerpta Historica*, Bentley prints the orders specifying that a scaffold is to be erected so that the king "may have sight of the battle" between John Halton, appellant, and Robert Norreys, defendant.

38. *Petit Jehan de Saintré*, pp. 69-82. The episode is summarized in Riquer, *Cavalleria*, pp. 69-78.

39. There are many accounts of this duel, which is mentioned, usually at length, by almost every English chronicler of the time. The fullest and best account is that of Thomas Whiting, the Chester Herald, who carried Scales's challenge to Burgundy and kept the official record; see Bentley, *Excerpta Historica*, pp. 171-212. Sidney Anglo, *The Great Tournament Roll*, p. 33, n. 2, characterizes the fight as a "fiasco," but contemporaries found it satisfying. The Bastard's horse was killed when the jousters collided, and this cut short the first day's fight, for he hotly refused the offer of a new mount.

40. Gregory, *Chronicle of London*, p. 236.

41. Bentley, *Excerpta Historica*, p. 209.

42. Ibid., p. 211.

43. Scales was fighting with Thomas Hansard at the tourney held to celebrate the marriage of Edward's son Richard. The account is published in William H. Black, ed., *Illustrations of the Ancient State of Chivalry Preserved in the Ashmolean Museum*, Roxburghe Club (London, 1840), p. 38.

44. *Paston Letters*, p. 539.

45. Quoted by Johan Huizinga, "The Political and Military Significance of Chivalry in the Late Middle Ages," in *Men and Ideas*, trans. James S. Holmes and Hans van Marle (New York, 1959), p. 199. Huizinga also quotes a Burgundian chronicler's praise of Henry V: "He maintained the discipline of chivalry well, as the Romans did formerly" (p. 198).

46. William Segar, *Honour, Military and Ciuill*, p. 202.

47. For a full account of Tiptoft's life and works, see Rosamund J. Mitchell, *Sir John Tiptoft, 1427-1470* (London, 1938). The quotation is from Thomas Fuller's *History of the Worthies of England*, ed. P. A. Nuttall (London, 1840).

48. The work exists in several versions (of which two are listed in the Bibliography). In Sir John Harrington's *Nugae antiquae* (London, 1779), vol. III, the *Ordinances* are printed as they were commanded in 4 Eliza. (1562) "to be observed and kept in all manner of Justes of Peaces Royall within this realme of England." They provide for the prizes, "Reserving alwaies to the Queene and to the ladyes present, the attribution and gifte of the prize, after the manner and forme accustomed."

49. "Le conte de Volcestre tint lieu de connestable et estoit accompagne du mareschal d'Angleterre, st sçavoit bien faire son office" (La Marche, *Mémoires*, III, 50).

50. Bentley, *Excerpta Historica*, pp. 189-190.

51. This is now Pierpont Morgan MS 775; it was analyzed and partially printed in Dillon, "Ordinances." For a full account see Curt F. Buhler, "Sir John Paston's Grete Boke, a Fifteenth-Century 'Best Seller,' " *Modern Language Notes*, 56 (1941), 345-351. Bühler's comparison of Astley's manuscript to the Lansdowne Manuscript (see Cripps-Day, *History of the Tournament*, app., for an analysis) and to Sir John Paston's "Grete Boke" shows the popularity of chivalric ordinances and accounts of contemporary chivalric deeds. Some, judging from the number of manuscript copies, were more popular than many romances.

52. The challenges for the fights with Massé and Boyle are included in Astley's manuscript. Cripps-Day believed that Astley killed Boyle as well as Massé and that he was "not improbably a bully like the expert duellists of later days" (*History of the Tournament*, p. 96). On Boyle's career see Riquer, *Cavalleria*, pp. 180-188,

53. Martín de Riquer, *Lletres de batalla: Cartells de deseiximents i capitols de passos d'armes* (Barcelona, 1963), I, 60.

54. Robert Fabyan's is the best (at least the most amusing) of the many accounts of this duel. As it shows, one did not have to be noble to fight in a judicial duel, though the degrading conditions imposed on the thief Thomas Whitehorn and his defendant in 1456 seem to show that the low-born were discouraged from appealing to arms; see Gregory's *Chronicle of London*, pp. 199-202.

55. Printed as an appendix in Cripps-Day, *History of the Tournament*; there are many manuscript versions of this ordinance, in both French and English.

56. This is not far off the mark. J. G. Bellamy, *The Law of Treason in England in the Later Middle Ages* (Cambridge, 1970), pp. 109-116, explains that Richard II attempted to broaden the scope of the laws of treason. The murderers of John Imperial of Genoa were convicted of treason in 1397, since the victim had been given a safe conduct as an ambassador (p. 135). Sir Patryse is presumably also under royal protection, though no ambassador, since as a foreign knight he would have been granted a safe conduct by the king.

57. George Neilson, *Trial by Combat* (Glasgow, 1890), pp. 205-206.

58. *The True Travels, Adventures, and Observations of Captain John Smith*, in *The General Historie of Virginia, New England, and the Summer Isles, etc.* (Glasgow, 1907), II, 128-130. The fifteenth-century German knight, Georg von Ehingen, also fought a formal single combat against a Saracen, whom he killed and who was then beheaded. See Georg von Ehingen, *Diary*, trans. Malcolm Letts (London, 1929).

59. Basil Willey, "Lord Herbert of Cherbury: A Spiritual Quixote of the Seventeenth Century," *Essays and Studies by Members of the English Association*, 27 (1941), 25. See *The Life of Lord Herbert of Cherbury, Written by Himself*, ed. Horace Walpole (London, 1770).

60. A *Latin Life of John Smith*, by Henry Wharton, trans. Laura Planyi-Striker (Chapel Hill, N.C., 1957), which was written in 1685, narrates Smith's jousts in an even more heroic and romantic style than Smith's own account and provides, Planyi-Striker argues, proof of contemporary belief in Smith's adventures. Everett M. Emerson, in *Captain John Smith* (New York, 1972), p. 94, quotes Phillip L. Barbour (writing in 1963): "Nothing Smith wrote has yet been found to be a lie."

61. Quoted in Willey, "Lord Herbert of Cherbury," p. 22.

62. Ibid.

63. Maurice H. Kean, *The Laws of War in the Middle Ages* (London, 1965), pp. 54-59.

64. Neilson notes that the last judicial duel was fought between Adam Bruntfield and James Carmichael in 1597; Carmichael was slain (*Trial by Combat*, p. 307). The duel of chivalry survived longer, and one was fought in 1631; see Clephan, *Tournament*, p. 167. On the attempts to abolish the trial by combat see Neilson, *Trial by Combat*, pp. 327-331.

65. For a full account of Spanish knights-errant see Riquer, *Cavalleria*, pp. 79-213, and *Caballeros andantes españoles* (Madrid, 1967).

66. Riquer, *Cavalleria*, p. 211.

67. Ibid., pp. 303-307.

68. Joseph A. Vaeth, *"Tirant lo Blanch": A Study of Its Authorship, Principal Sources and Historical Setting* (New York, 1918). The resemblances between Tirant and Beauchamp are very general.

69. I am assuming that Malory was an older man when he began his work (as was Martorell). William Matthews, *The Ill-Framed Knight: A Skeptical Inquiry into the Identity of Sir Thomas Malory* (Berkeley, 1966), has shown that we can no longer be sure exactly who Malory was. Not all scholars are convinced by Matthews' argument; see esp. P. J. C. Field, "Sir Thomas Malory, M.P.," *Bulletin of the Institute of Historical Research*, 47 (1974), 24-35. Nevertheless, Matthews has cast real doubt on the previous identification of our author, and we cannot be sure whether he was old when he wrote, like Martorell, or young, like Antoine de la Sale, who did not die until the end of the century.

70. In the manuscripts analyzed by Cripps-Day, in the appendixes to his *History of the Tournament*, see Lansdowne MS 285, item 39; Harley MS 69, items 11, 12, 15.

71. Brantôme, *Oeuvres*, I, 340; Brantôme's authority is the work by the legalist Paris de Puteo, *Duello, libro de re, imperatori, principi, etc.* (Venice, 1521).

72. Froissart, *Chroniques*, IV. See Brererton's translation, pp. 373-381.

73. Riquer, *Cavalleria*, pp. 82-144.

74. P. G. Evans, "A Spanish Knight in Flesh and Blood: A Study of the Chivalric Spirit of Suero de Quiñones," *Hispania*, 15 (1932), 141-152.

75. Clephan, *Tournament*, pp. 57-60.

76. For an account of this and René's other tourneys, see Marie-Louyse de Garnier des Garets, *Un artisan de la renaissance française au xve siècle: Le roi René, 1409-1480* (Paris, 1946), pp. 143-146. For René's *Traicté de la forme et devis d'ung tournay* see Cripps-Day, *History of the Tournament*, app. 7, and *Traité de la form et devis d'un tournoi*, ed. Edmond Pogne (Paris, 1946). Antoine de la Sale in his *Des anciens tournois* remarks on the presence of Suffolk and many other English knights; see Prost, *Traitiés du duel judiciaire*, p. 216.

77. Clephan, *Tournament*, pp. 71-73; Marche, *Mémoires*, I, chap. 18.

78. Johan Huizinga, *The Waning of the Middle Ages*, trans. F. Hopman (London, 1924), p. 83.

79. Chastelain, *Chronique de J. de Lalain*, pp. 216-281.

80. "Comme chevalliers errans querans leurs aventures, ainsi que jadis firent les chevaliers de la Table Ronde" (*Pas d'armes de Sandricourt*, ed. A. Vaysièrre [Paris, 1874]); quoted in Cripps-Day, *History of the Tournament*, p. 89.

81. *Paston Letters*, p. 396.

82. Black, *Illustrations of the Ancient State of Chivalry*, p. 37.

83. Clephan, *Tournament*, pp. 82, 84. For references to the affair at Richmond see Viscount Dillon, "Tilting in Tudor Times," *Archaeological Journal*, 55 (2d ser., 5) (1898), 299.

84. A contemporary English account (probably by a herald) is in Bentley, *Excerpta Historica*, pp. 223-239.

85. Edmund Reiss, *Sir Thomas Malory* (New York, 1966), p. 194, n. 10: "T. W. Williams has suggested that in the late 1460's Malory may have gone to Bruges and there have come into contact with Caxton to whom he gave a copy of his romance (*Sir Thomas Malory and the Morte Darthur* [Bristol, 1909])." As Reiss puts it, "The idea is, if nothing else, certainly pleasant to think about."

86. MS Harley 69, item 3, in Cripps-Day, *History of the Tournament*, app. 6.

87. For these sixteenth-century tournaments see Clephan, *Tournament*, pp. 114-115, 123-124, 125-126; F. Warre Cornish, *Chivalry*, 2d ed. (London, 1908), p. 108.

88. Sir John Fortescue, *De laudibus legum Anglie*, ed. S. B. Chrimes (Cambridge, 1942), pp. 2-3. The prevalence of unrecorded jousts may be indicated by an edict of Henry V, reconfirmed in 9 Henry VI, designed to preserve the tranquility of the masters and scholars of Cambridge University, forbidding "Torneamenta aliqua, Aventure, Juste, seu hujusmodi hastiludia" within five miles of Cambridge. (*Rotuli Parliamentorum ut et Petitiones, et placita in Parliamento* [London, 1767], V, 426.)

89. Riquer, *Cavalleria*, p. 6.

9   THE REALISM OF FIFTEENTH-CENTURY ROMANCE

1. C. S. Lewis, *English Literature in the Sixteenth Century, Excluding Drama* (Oxford, 1954), p. 103.

2. C. O. Parsons, "A Scottish 'Father of Courtesy' and Malory," *Speculum*, 20, (1945), 51-64.

3. Nellie S. Aurner, "Sir Thomas Malory—Historian?" *PMLA*, 48 (1933), 360-391. She suggests many parallels, such as the possibility that Malory's Tristram was modeled on the duke of Orléans. On the relation of *Arthur and Lucius* to Henry V's campaigns, see Vinaver, *Works*, pp. 1396-98, and William Matthews, "Where was Siesa-Sessoyne?" *Speculum*, 49 (1974), 680-686; Matthews casts considerable doubt on Vinaver's hypothesis.

4. William Matthews, *The Ill-Framed Knight: A Skeptical Inquiry into the Identity of Sir Thomas Malory* (Berkeley, 1966).

5. The author was John Rous, and the work was probably written between 1485 and 1490 (*Pageant*, p. iii). In the following text the numbers are references to the plates in the edition, cited in the Bibliography.

6. Printed in app. 5 of Francis H. Cripps-Day, *The History of the Tournament in England and in France* (London, 1918).

7. Eugène Vinaver, *Malory* (Oxford, 1929), pp. 3-4.

8. For a full survey see B. J. Whiting, "The Vows of the Heron," *Speculum*, 20 (1945), 261-278.

9. Oliver de la Marche's account is printed as an appendix to Chastelain's *Chronique de J. de Lalain*, pp. 393-448.

10. Kenneth H. Vickers, *Humphrey, Duke of Gloucester: A Biography* (London, 1907), pp. 155-167. It is clear that Gloucester did not intend to fight.

11. Johan Huizinga, *The Waning of the Middle Ages*, trans. F. Hopman (London, 1924), pp. 96-98.

12. The challenge is printed in Alex R. Meyers, ed., *English Historical Documents, 1327-1485* (London, 1969), p. 1127; see Jonathan Blow, "Nibley Green: The Last Private Battle Fought in England," *History Today*, 2 (1962), 598-610.

13. When Bohemian ambassadors came to Edward IV's court in 1466 they brought their jousting equipment, evidently assuming this was an ordinary part of an embassy, though Edward refused them permission to joust (Meyers, *English Historical Documents*, p. 1169). See also Richard W. Barber's chapter "The Prince and Chivalry" in *The Knight and Chivalry* (London, 1970), pp. 293-304.

14. Jocelyne G. Russell, *The Field of the Cloth of Gold* (Oxford, 1969); see also Sidney Anglo, *Spectacle, Pageantry, and Early Tudor Policy* (Oxford, 1969).

15. Johan Huizinga, "The Political and Military Significance of Chivalry in the Later Middle Ages," in *Men and Ideas: History, the Middle Ages, the Renaissance*, trans. James S. Holmes and Hans van Marle (New York, 1959), p. 197.

16. Boccaccio had criticized John for allowing himself to be captured. Lydgate, *Fall of Princes*, 9.3169-3202, heaps scorn on "Bochas" for knowing so little of chivalry. King John's captivity was praiseworthy, for when his followers fled, "Laud of King Iohan was that he abood; / In that he quit him lik a manli knight."

17. Raymond L. Kilgour, *The Decline of Chivalry as Shown in the French Literature of the Late Middle Ages* (Cambridge, Mass., 1927), observes that Charles le Téméraire "possessed just enough chivalry to spoil his policy and just enough policy to spoil his chivalry" (p. 295).

18. Robert L. McKie, *King James IV of Scotland: A Brief Survey of His Life and Times* (Edinburgh, 1958), studies the material and concludes that the promise of the crusade rather than the queen's appeal was the main motive of James's action. On James's fondness for jousting and his admiration for King Arthur, see John Leslie, *Historie of Scotland*, trans. James Dalrymple, ed. E. G. Cody and William Murison, Scottish Texts Society (Edinburgh, 1895), II, 128. On the queen's appeal see Robert Lindsay of Pittscottie, *The Histories and Chronicles of Scotland*, ed. Æ. J. G. MacKay, Scottish Texts Society (Edinburgh, 1899), I, 254: "The queen of France wrait ane lufe letter to the king of Scotland, callit him hir lufe schawand him that sche had sufferit mekill . . . Scho beleiffit suirlie that he wald recompence hir againe witht sum of his knyghtlie support . . . to that effect scho send him ane ringe of hir finger witht xxiij thowsand frinche crownis to mak his expensis."

19. McKie, *James IV*, p. 273.

20. See Leslie, *Historie of Scotland*, II, 146. Leslie wrote in the late sixteenth century.

21. Fabyan, *Chronicles:* "I cease for Paynfull it were to rede, and more paynfull & sorrowfull to here that the feythe of Cryste shulde in so vyle maner be dyspysed" (p. 628).

22. Samuel Bentley, ed., *Excerpta Historica; or, Illustrations of English History* (London, 1833), p. 208.

23. Bentley, *Excerpta Historica*, p. 391. They were licensed to preach for two years beginning in July 1467.

24. Matthews, *Ill-Framed Knight*, II, 99-100, n.

25. Monstrelet, *Chronicles*, pp. 232-233.

26. E. K. Chambers, *Sir Henry Lee: An Elizabethan Portrait* (Oxford, 1936), pp. 135-144; Frances A. Yates, "Elizabethan Chivalry: The Romance of the Accession Day Tilts," *Journal of the Warburg and Courtauld Institutes*, 20 (1957), 21, says that Lee probably represented the hermit in Ramón Lull's *Order of Chivalry* (trans. by Caxton as *The Book of the Ordre of Chyvalry*).

27. "Occupy the time of your ages and feebleness of body in ghostly chivalry of deeds of arms spiritual" (Scrope, *Epistle of Othea*, p. 121).

28. Monstrelet, *Chronicles*, I, 634.

29. Alcius Ledieu, *Un compagnon de Jeanne d'Arc: Etienne Vignoles* (Paris, 1889). La Hire was something of a wit. Celebrated for his ferocity, he was of the opinion that "Guerre sanz feux ne vaut rien, non plus qu'andouilles sans moutarde."

30. *Chronicles of the White Rose of York*, p. 209. Scales's hair shirt was hung up before the image of the Holy Virgin in the Carmelite Friary at Doncaster.

31. Rosamund J. Mitchell, *Sir John Tiptoft, 1427-1470* (London, 1938), pp. 142-143.

32. This is discussed in Alice Morgan, " 'Honour and Right' in *Arthur of Little Britain*," Harvard English Studies, 5 (1974), 371-384. See also John Barnie, *War in Medieval English Society: Social Values and the Hundred Years War, 1337-1399* (London, 1974), pp. 68-71, on the practical aspects of chivalry.

33. C. S. Lewis, "The English Prose *Morte*," in *Essays on Malory*, p. 12.

34. "The Buke of Knychthede," in Haye, *Gilbert of the Haye's Prose Manuscript*, II, 13, 14-15, 69. The translation was made in 1456.

35. Vinaver, *Malory*, p. 110.

36. William H. Schofield, *Chivalry in English Literature: Chaucer, Malory, Spenser, and Shakespeare* (Cambridge, Mass., 1912), pp. 76-77.

37. E. K. Chambers, *English Literature at the Close of the Middle Ages* (Oxford, 1945), p. 197.

38. La Sale, *Little John of Saintré*, trans. Irvine Gray, p. 20.

39. Schofield, *Chivalry in English Literature*, p. 76.

40. *Paston Letters*, p. 128.

41. Ibid., p. 396.

42. A list of his books is printed in ibid., pp. 517-518.

43. Ibid., p. 539.

44. An example of how present experiences shape one's attitudes toward the past is provided by *The Book of Honour and Armes*, attributed to Sir William Segar. The author barely mentions Sir Tristram and Sir Lancelot, and he mentions Arthur not at all, for "by means of writers that have added unto their acts many untruths, their prowess and enterprise are holden as fables." In 1602 Segar published his *Honour, Military and Ciuill*, book iii of which is in effect a new edition of *Honour and Armes* with one significant change: Arthur now figures prominently throughout, and customs that in *Honour and Armes* were simply called very ancient are now called usages of "about the year of Christ 500 near which time king Arthur reigned in England" (p. 53). Segar writes that some hold Arthur and his deeds but fables, "Yet whoso shall consider enterprises of later time achieved by private persons may be easily induced to think that a great part of praise written of that mighty monarch

may reasonably receive belief" (p. 55). The "private persons" to whom he refers are *"Hernando Cortez* and *Pisarro* in our own time" and the great English captains and voyagers such as Sir Francis Drake. In the decade between the publication of *Honour and Armes* and the writing of *Honour, Military and Ciuill* Richard Hakluyt's *Voyages* (1598-1600) had appeared.

10   *THE TALE OF THE SANCGREAL*

1. Jean Frappier, "The Vulgate Cycle," in *ALMA*, p. 313. William Leckie, of the University of Toronto, is now working on the "historical" aspects of the prose romances. In recent lectures he has argued convincingly for the influence of Joachimite ideas of universal history on the Vulgate romances, especially the *Queste del Saint Graal*.

2. Albert Pauphilet, *Etudes sur la Queste del Saint Graal* (Paris, 1921).

3. *La mort le roi Artu*, pp. xix-xxix.

4. Karl J. Höltgen, "König Arthur und Fortuna," *Anglia*, 75 (1957), 35-54.

5. Valerie Lagorio, "The Evolving Legend of Joseph of Glastonbury," *Speculum*, 46 (1971), 209-231.

6. The modern interpretation of Malory begins in the "Introduction" to Edward Strachey's editon of *Le Morte d'Arthur* (London, 1868).

7. Pauphilet, in his *Etudes*, discusses this at length. The allegorizations in *The Epistle of Othea* are frequently based on the same idea.

8. Pauphilet, *Etudes*, p. 62; Vinaver, *Works*, p. 1576, with references.

9. Siegfried Wenzel, "The Pilgrimage of Life as a Late Medieval Genre," *Mediaeval Studies*, 35 (1973), 370-388.

10. Wenzel, "Pilgrimage of Life," p. 384; on the relation of the spirituality of the *Queste* to St. Bernard of Clairvaux, see Etienne Gilson, *Les idées et les lettres* (Paris, 1932), pp. 62-64.

11. Wenzel, "Pilgrimage of Life," p. 384.

12. Charles Moorman, " 'The Tale of the Sancgreal': Human Frailty," in *Malory's Originality*, p. 196.

13. Vinaver, *Works*, p. 1464.

14. Strachey, *Le Morte d'Arthur*, p. xii.

15. See Vinaver's discussion in *Works*, p. 1535.

11   *THE BOOK OF SIR LANCELOT AND GUENEVERE*

1. Edmund Reiss, *Sir Thomas Malory* (New York, 1966), p. 159, labels *Lancelot and Guenevere* "the pause that regresses."

2. P. E. Tucker, "A Source for the Healing of Sir Urry," *Modern Language Review*, 48 (1955), 490-492, suggests that Malory based the episode on an adventure in the Vulgate *Lancelot*, but if that is the source Malory drew from, it supplied little more than the general idea.

3. Robert M. Lumiansky, " 'The Tale of Lancelot and Guenevere': Suspense," in *Malory's Originality*, p. 231.

4. Tucker, "Source," p. 492.

5. Reiss, *Malory*, p. 172.

6. C. S. Lewis, "The English Prose *Morte*," in *Essays on Malory*, p. 20.

7. Lumiansky, " 'Lancelot and Guenevere,' " pp. 205-232.

12 *THE DEATH OF ARTHUR*

1. Throughout *The Death of Arthur* Malory depends more upon the stanzaic *Morte Arthur* than upon the *Mort Artu* for the organization of his narrative, and the English poem provides at least a partial precedent for his relatively "nontragic" treatment. For full discussions of Malory's use of the English poem see Vinaver's commentary and notes and Wilfred L. Guerin, " 'The Tale of the Death of Arthur': Catastrophe and Resolution," in *Malory's Originality*, pp. 233-274.

2. See Willard Farnham, *The Medieval Heritage of Elizabethan Drama* (Berkeley, 1936).

3. Edward Strachey, *Le Morte d'Arthur* (London, 1868), p. xii.

4. Charles Moorman, "Malory's Tragic Knights," *Mediaeval Studies*, 27 (1965), 126.

5. Stephen J. Miko, "Malory and the Chivalric Order," *Medium Aevum*, 35 (1966), 214.

6. Edmund Reiss, *Sir Thomas Malory* (New York, 1966), p. 191.

Bibliography

This bibliography includes only primary works that are quoted or discussed in the texts. Literary works mentioned only in passing are not listed, and most historical documents that are quoted only once or twice have also been omitted (and bibliographical details supplied in the notes). Where appropriate, French originals of English works are listed in brackets. I have also frequently listed modern English translations of literary works in foreign languages, though the translations of passages quoted in the text are my own.

All quotations from Malory are from *The Works of Sir Thomas Malory*, ed. Eugène Vinaver (Oxford, 1967), 3 vols. The one-volume edition occasionally mentioned in the text is Vinaver's *Works of Sir Thomas Malory*, Oxford Standard Authors, 2d ed. (London, 1971). The Winchester Manuscript is cited from the microfilm copy in the Library of Congress.

The following abbreviations are used:
CFMA   Classiques français du moyen âge.
EETS   Early English Text Society (e.s. = Extra Series).
SATF   Société des anciens textes français.
SHF   Société de l'histoire de France.
STS   Scottish Texts Society.

Items are alphabetized by author or first principal word in the title; that is, *La*, *King*, *Sir*, and similar words are ignored. Short titles used in the text precede full titles.

Alisaunder: Kyng Alisaunder, ed. Geoffrey V. Smithers, EETS, 227, 237 (London, 1952-1957).

Alliterative *Morte Arthure*, in *King Arthur's Death: The Middle English Stanzaic "Morte Arthur" and Alliterative "Morte Arthure,"* ed. Larry D. Benson (Indianapolis, 1974).

Amis and Amiloun, ed. MacEdward Leach, EETS, 203 (London, 1937). [See also (for sources) Eugen Kölbing, *Amis und Amiloun zugleich mit der altfranzözischen Quelle, nebst einer Beilage Amicus ok Amílius Rímur*, Altenglische Bibliothek, 2 (Heilbronn, 1884).]

Arthour and Merlin: Of Arthour and of Merlin, ed. G. D. Macrae-Gibson, EETS, 268 (London, 1973). [See also (for apparatus) *Arthour and Merlin, nach der Auchinleck-HS.*, ed. Eugen Kölbing, Altenglische Bibliothek, 4 (Leipzig, 1890).]

Arthur of Little Britain: John Bourchier, Lord Berners, *The History of the Valiant Knight, Arthur of Little Britain: A Romance of Chivalry*, ed. E. V. Utterson (London, 1814).

Avowing of Arthur: The Avowynge of King Arthur, Sir Gawan, Sir Kay, and Sir Bawdewyn of Bretan, in *Middle English Metrical Romances*, ed. W. H. French and C. B. Hale (New York, 1930).

Awntyrs of Arthur: The Awntyrs off Arthure at the Terne Wathelyne, ed. Robert J. Gates (Philadelphia, 1969).

Bayard: La très joyeus, plaisante, et récréative histoire du gentil seigneur de Bayard, ed. J. Roman, SHF (Paris, 1878). [See also the same editor's *Histoire du bon chevalier Bayart d'après le Loyal Serviteur et d'autres auteurs contemporains* (Paris, 1882). *The Story of Bayard, the Good Knight without Fear and without Reproach*, trans. Kenneth Hare (London, 1911).]

Berners, Dame Juliana, *The Boke of Saint Albans*, with an introduction by William Blades (London, 1899).

Bevis of Hampton: The Romance of Sir Beves of Hamtoun, ed. Eugen Kölbing, 3 vols., EETS, e.s., 46, 48, 65 (London, 1885-1894). [*Der anglonormannische Boeve de Haumtone*, ed. Albert Stimmung (Halle, 1899).]

Book of the Knight of La Tour-Landry: see Tour-Landry, Knight of the.

Boucicaut: *Le livre des faicts du mareschal de Boucicaut*, in *Collection complète des mémoirs relatifs à l'histoire de France*, ed. Claude B. Petitot (Paris, 1825), VI, 375-513; VII, 1-234.

Brantôme: Pierre de Bourdeille, Seigneur de Brantôme, *Œuvres complètes*, ed. Ludovic Lalanne, SHF (Paris, 1864-1882), 11 vols. [For a translation of the *Vies des dames galantes* see A. R. Allison, trans., *Lives of Fair and Gallant Ladies* (London, 1922).]

————, *Vies des dames illustres françaises et étrangères*, ed. Louis Moland (Paris, 1868).

Carl of Carlisle: Syre Gawene and the Carl of Carlyle, ed. R. W. Ackerman, University of Michigan Contributions in Modern Philology, 8 (Ann Arbor, 1947).

Caxton, William, *Charles the Grete: The Lyf of the Noble and Crysten Prince, Charles the Grete*, ed. Sidney J. H. Herrtage, EETS, 36-37 (London, 1880-1881).

————, *Godeffroy of Boloyne*, ed. Mary N. Colvin, EETS, e.s., 64 (London, 1893).

————, *The History of Jason*, ed. John Munro, EETS, e.s., 111 (London, 1913).

————, *The Book of the Ordre of Chyvalry*, ed. Alfred T. P. Byles, EETS, 168 (London, 1926).

————, *Paris and Vienne*, ed. MacEdward Leach, EETS, 234 (London, 1957).

Cent ballades, by Jean le Seneschal et al., ed. Gaston Raynaud, SATF (Paris, 1901).

Chandos Herald, *The Life of the Black Prince*, ed. and trans. Mildred K. Pope and Eleanor C. Lodge (Oxford, 1910). [See also *Le prince noir: Poème du heraut d'armes Chandos*, ed. Francisque-Michel (London, 1883).]

Chastelain, Georges, *Chronique de J. de Lalain: Chronique du bon chevalier Messire Jacques de Lalain, frère et compagnon de l'ordre de la Toison d'or,* in *Collection des chroniques nationales françaises,* 41, ed. J. A. Buchon (Paris, 1825).

Chaucer: *The Works of Geoffrey Chaucer,* ed. F. N. Robinson, 2d ed. (Boston, 1957).

Chestre, Thomas, *Sir Launfal,* ed. A. J. Bliss (London, 1960).

Chrétien de Troyes, *Erec et Enide,* ed. Mario Roques, CFMA (Paris, 1952).

———, *Lancelot: Le chevalier de la charette,* ed. Mario Roques, CFMA (Paris, 1958).

———, *Yvain (le chevalier au lion),* ed. Thomas B. W. Reid, 2d ed. (Manchester, 1948). [For English versions of this and Chrétien's other romances see W. W. Comfort, trans., *Arthurian Romances,* Everyman's Library (London, 1914).]

Christine de Pisan, *Livre des fais et bonnes meurs du sage roy Charles V,* ed. S. Solente, SHF (Paris, 1936-1940), 2 vols.

———, *Oeuvres poétiques,* ed. Maurice Roy (Paris, 1886-1890), 2 vols.

Chronicles of the White Rose of York: A Series of Historical Fragments . . . Relating to the Reign of Edward IV (London, 1845).

Courcy, Jean de, *Chemin de Vaillance* (unpublished manuscript summarized by Siegfried Wenzel, in "The Pilgrimage of Life as a Late Medieval Genre," *Mediaeval Studies,* 35 [1973], 370-388).

Degare: Sire Degarre, ed. Gustav Schleich, Englische Textbibliothek, 19 (Heidelberg, 1929).

Degrevant: The Romance of Sir Degrevant: A Parellel Text Edition, ed. L. F. Casson, EETS 221 (London, 1949).

Eger and Grime: A Parallel-Text Edition of the Huntingdon-Laing Versions of the Romance, ed. James R. Caldwell, Harvard Studies in Comparative Literature, 9 (Cambridge, Mass., 1933).

Estoire del Saint Graal: see Sommer, *Vulgate Version.*

Estoire de Merlin: see Sommer, *Vulgate Version.*

Fabyan, Robert, *The New Chronicles of England and France,* ed. Henry Ellis (London, 1811).

Floris and Blancheflour, ed. Albert B. Taylor (Oxford, 1927). [See also the more recent edition, *Floris and Blauncheflur,* ed. Franciscus Catharina De Vries (Groningen, 1966), and the French version, *Flor et Blancheflor,* ed. M. M. Pelan, 2d ed. (Paris, 1956).]

Froissart, Jean, *Chroniques,* in *Oeuvres de Froissart,* ed. Kervyn de Lettenhove (Brussels, 1867-1877), 25 vols. [*Froissart's Chronicles,* trans. Geoffrey Brereton, Penguin Classics (Baltimore, Md., 1968).]

Fuetrer, Ulrich, *Buch der Abenteuer.* This has never been published as a whole, though most of the parts are in print. The most important are *Die Gralepen,* ed. Kurt Nyholm, Deutsche Texte des Mittelalters, 57 (Berlin, 1964); *Merlin und Seifrid de Ardemont,* ed. Friedrich Panzer (Tübingen, 1902); and *Persebein,* ed. Renate Munz (Tübingen, 1964).

———, *Die Prosaroman von Lantzelot,* ed. Arthur Peter (Tübingen, 1885).

Gawain and the Carl of Carlisle, ed. Auvo Kurvinen, Annales Academiae Scientiarum Fennicae, B 71.2 (Helsinki, 1951).

Gawain and the Green Knight, ed. J. R. R. Tolkien and E. V. Gordon, 2d ed., rev. Norman Davis (Oxford, 1967).

Gest of Sir Gawain: The Jeaste of Syr Gawayne, in Frederic Madden, ed., *Syr Gawayne,* Bannatyne Club, 61 (London, 1838).

Golagros and Gawain: The Knightly Tale of Golagros and Gawane, in F. J. Amours, ed., *Scottish Alliterative Poems in Riming Stanzas,* STS (Edinburgh, 1892-1897).

Gonnot, Michel, *Le livre de Lancelot*, analyzed in Cedric E. Pickford, *L'évolution du roman arthurien en prose vers la fin du moyen âge d'après le
manuscrit 112 du fonds français de la Bibliothèque nationale* (Paris,
1960). Only parts have been printed: *Die Abenteuer Gawains, Ywains
and Le Morholts mit den drei Jungfrauen*, ed. Heinrik O. Sommer, *Bei-
hefte zur Zeitschrift für romanische Philologie*, 47 (Halle, 1913); *Erec:
Roman arthurien en prose*, ed. Cedric E. Pickford, 2d ed. rev. (Geneva,
1968).

Grafton, Richard: *Richard Grafton's Chronicle: or, History of England* (London, 1809), 2 vols.

Gregory, William, *Chronicle of London*, in *The Historical Collections of a
Citizen of London in the Fifteenth Century*, ed. James Gairdner, Camden
Society (London, 1876).

Grene Knight, in *Bishop Percy's Folio Manuscript*, ed. John W. Hales and
Frederick J. Furnivall, rev. I. Gollancz (London, 1905-1910), vol. II.

Guillaume le Maréchal: L'histoire de Guillaume le Maréchal, ed. Paul Meyer,
SHF (Paris, 1891-1901), 3 vols. [Contains a full summary in modern
French.]

*Guy of Warwick: The Romance of Guy of Warwick: The Second or Fifteenth-
Century Version*, ed. Julius Zupitza, EETS, e.s., 25-26 (London, 1875-
1876); *The Romance of Guy of Warwick*, ed. Julius Zupitza, EETS, e.s.,
42, 49, 59 (London, 1883-1891); *Guy of Warwick, nach Coplands Druck*,
ed. Gustav Schleich, Palaestra, 139 (Leipzig, 1923). [*Gui de Warewik*, ed.
Alfred Ewert (Paris, 1929-1933), 2 vols.]

Hardyng, *Chronicle: The Chronicle of John Hardyng*, ed. Henry Ellis (London, 1812).

Havelok: The Lay of Havelok the Dane, ed. W. W. Skeat, rev. ed., EETS,
e.s., 4 (Oxford, 1902). [*Le lai d'Havelok*, ed. A. Bell, Publications of the
University of Manchester, French ser., 4 (Manchester, 1925).]

Haye: *Gilbert of the Haye's Prose Manuscript (A.D. 1456)*, ed. J. H. Steven-
son, STS (Edinburgh, 1901-1914), 2 vols.

Henry, duke of Lancaster, *Le livre de seyntz medicines*, ed. Emile J. Arnould,
Anglo-Norman Texts, 2 (Oxford, 1940).

Horn: King Horn, ed. Joseph Hall (Oxford, 1901).

Horn et Rigmel: The Romance of Horn, ed. Mildred K. Pope, Anglo-Norman
Texts, 9-10 (Oxford, 1955-1964), 2 vols.

Hugh of Rutland: Hué de Rötelande, *Ipomedon*, ed. Eugen Kölbing and E.
Koschwitz (Breslau, 1899).

Ipomadon [English]: *Hué de Rötelande's "Ipomedon" in drei englischen Bear-
beitungen*, ed. Eugen Kölbing (Breslau, 1899). [The stanzaic *Ipomadon*
("Ipomadon A") is on pp. 3-256, the couplet *Lyfe of Ipomydon* ("Ipomadon B") on pp. 257-322, and the prose *King Ipomedon* ("Ipomadon C")
on pp. 323-358.]

*Joseph of Arimathie: Otherwise Called the Romance of the Seint Graal or
Holy Grail*, ed. W. W. Skeat, EETS, 44 (London, 1871).

*Knyghthode and Bataile: A XVth Century Verse Paraphrase of Flavius Vege-
tius Renatus' "De re militari,"* ed. R. Dyboski and Z. M. Arend, EETS,
201 (London, 1936).

Lancelot of the Laik, ed. W. W. Skeat, rev. ed., EETS, 6 (London, 1870).

Landeval: see Chestre, Thomas, *Sir Launfal*, appendix.

La Sale: see Sale, Antoine de la.

Launfal: see Chestre, Thomas, *Sir Launfal*.

Lindsay, Sir David, *Squyer Meldrum*, ed. James Kinsley, Nelson's Medieval and Renaissance Library (London, 1959).

Löseth, *Tristan*: see Prose *Tristan*.

Lovelich, Henry, *The History of the Holy Grail*, ed. Frederick J. Furnivall, EETS, e.s., 20, 24, 28, 30 (London, 1874-1878), 95 (ed. D. Kempe) (London, 1934).

――――, *Merlin*, ed. Ernst A. Koch, EETS, e.s., 93, 112, 185 (London, 1904-1932).

Lybeaus Desconus, ed. Maldwyn Mills, EETS, 261 (London, 1969). [Renaut de Beaujeu, *Li biaus descouneüs (Le bel inconnu)*, ed. G. P. Williams, CFMA (Paris, 1929).]

Lydgate, John, *The Fall of Princes*, ed. Henry Bergen, EETS, 121-124 (London, 1924-1927).

――――, *The Minor Poems of John Lydgate*, ed. Henry N. MacCracken, EETS, e.s., 107, 192 (London, 1911-1934).

Mannyng, *Chronicle: The Story of England by Robert Manning of Brunne*, ed. Frederick J. Furnivall, Rolls Series (London, 1887), 2 vols.

Marche, Olivier de la, *Le chevalier délibéré*, ed. E. Morgan (Washington, 1945). [*The Resolved Gentleman*, trans. Lewis Lewkanor (London, 1594).]

――――, *Mémoires*, ed. Henri Beaune and J. d'Arbaumont, SHF (Paris, 1883-1888), 4 vols.

Martorell, Johonet, *Tirant lo Blanc*, ed. Martín de Riquer (Barcelona, 1947). [For a detailed English summary see Joseph A. Vaeth, *Tirant lo Blanch: A Study of Its Authorship, Principal Sources, and Historical Setting* (New York, 1918).]

Monstrelet, *Chronicles: The Chronicles of Enguerrand de Monstrelet*, trans. Thomas Johnes (London, 1840), 2 vols. [*La chronique en deux livres avec pièces justificatives, 1400-1440*, ed. L. Döuet-d'Arcq, SHF (Paris, 1857-1862), 2 vols.]

Mort Artu: La mort le roi Artu, ed. Jean Frappier, Textes litteraires français (Paris, 1956). [*The Death of King Arthur*, trans. James Cable, Penguin Classics (Baltimore, Md., 1971).]

Orfeo: Sir Orfeo, ed. A. J. Bliss, 2d ed. (Oxford, 1966).

Pageant of the Birth, Life, and Death of Richard Beauchamp, Earl of Warwick, K.G. (1389-1439), ed. Viscount Dillon and W. H. St. John Hope (London, 1914).

Paston Letters and Papers of the Fifteenth Century, ed. Norman Davis (Oxford, 1971), vol. I. [See also *The Paston Letters*, ed. James Gairdner (London, 1904), 6 vols.]

Perlesvaus: Le haut livre du Graal, Perlesvaus, ed. William A. Nitze and Thomas Jenkins, Modern Philology Monographs (Chicago, 1937). [*The High History of the Holy Grail*, trans. Sebastian Evans (London, 1903).]

Petit Jehan de Saintré: See Sale, Antoine de la.

Ponthus and Sidoine: King Ponthus, ed. Frank J. Mather, PMLA 12 (1897). [*Ponthus et la belle Sidoine*, ed. C. Dalbanne and E. Droz (Lyons, 1926).]

Prose *Lancelot*: see Sommer, *Vulgate Version*.

Prose *Merlin*: "Merlin": A Prose Romance, ed. Henry B. Wheatley, EETS, 10, 21, 36, 112 (London, 1895 [2d ed.], 1877 [2d ed.], 1869, 1899).

Prose *Tristan: Le roman de Tristan en prose*, ed. Renée L. Curtis (Munich, 1963), vol. I. [Since only part of this edition has been published, see Eilert Löseth, *Le roman en prose de Tristan, le roman de Palamède et la compil-

ation de Rusticien de Pise: Analyse critique d'après les manuscrits de Paris (Paris, 1891).]

Queste del Saint Graal: see Sommer, *Vulgate Version.* [*The Quest of the Holy Grail,* trans. Pauline M. Matarasso, Penguin Classics (Baltimore, Md., 1969).]

Richard the Lion-Hearted: Der mittelenglische Versroman über Richard Löwenherz, ed. Karl Brunner, Wiener Beiträge zur englischen Philologie, 42 (Vienna, 1913).

Romance of Horn: see *Horn et Rigmel.*

Roman du Graal: see Fanni Bogdanow, *The Romance of the Grail* (Manchester, 1966).

Russell, John, *The Boke of Nurture Folowynge Englondis Gise,* in *The Babees Book: Meals and Manners in Olden Time,* ed. Frederick J. Furnivall, EETS, 32 (London, 1868).

Sale, Antoine de la, *Jehan de Saintré,* ed. Jean Misrahi and C. A. Knudsen, Textes litteraires français, 117 (Geneva, 1965). [*Little John of Saintré,* trans. Irvine Gray (London, 1931).]

Scrope, Stephen, *The Epistle of Othea, Translated from the French Text of Christine de Pisan,* ed. Curt F. Buhler, EETS, 264 (London, 1970).

Segar, William [attr.], *The Booke of Honor and Armes* (London, 1590).

———, *Honour, Military and Ciuill* (London, 1602).

Sommer: Sommer, Heinrich Oskar, *The Vulgate Version of the Arthurian Romances* (Washington, D.C., 1908-1916), I: *Lestoire del Saint Graal;* II: *Lestoire de Merlin;* III-V: *Lancelot;* VI: *Les Adventures ou la Queste del Saint Graal, La Mort le Roi Artus;* VII: *Supplement: Le Livre d'artus.*

Squyr of Lowe Degre, ed. William E. Mead (Boston, 1904).

Stanzaic Morte Arthur, in *King Arthur's Death: The Middle English Stanzaic "Morte Arthur" and Alliterative "Morte Arthure,"* ed. Larry D. Benson (Indianapolis, 1974).

Suite du Merlin [Huth *Merlin*]: *Merlin, roman en prose du xiiie siècle,* ed. Gaston Paris and Jacob Ulrich, SATF (Paris, 1866), 2 vols.

Thomas of Britainy, *Fragments du Tristan de Thomas,* ed. B. H. Wind (Leiden, 1950).

Three Kings' Sons (English from the French), ed. Frederick J. Furnivall, EETS, e.s., 67 (London, 1895).

Tiptoft, John, Earl of Worcester, *The Book of Noblesse,* in Rosamund J. Mitchell, *John Tiptoft (1427-1470)* (London, 1938), pp. 226-237.

———, *Ordinances for Justes and Tournaments,* in Francis H. Cripps-Day, *The History of the Tournament in England and in France* ([London], 1918), app. 4. [Another version in Francis Douce, "On the Peaceable Justes or Tiltings of the Middle Ages," *Archeologica,* 17 (1814), 290-296.]

Tour-Landry, Knight of La: *The Book of the Knight of La Tour-Landry,* ed. Thomas Wright, EETS, 33, rev. ed. (London, 1906).

Tristrem: Sir Tristrem, ed. G. P. McNeill, STS, 8 (Edinburgh, 1886).

Turk and Gawain: The Turke and Gowin in *Bishop Percy's Folio Manuscript,* ed. John W. Hales and Frederick J. Furnivall, rev. I. Gollancz (London, 1905-1910), vol. I.

Vulgate Cycle: see Sommer, *Vulgate Version.*

Vulson: Marc Wlson de la Columbière, *Vray théâtre d'honnevr et de la chevalerie* (Paris, 1648), 2 vols.

Warkworth, John, *A Chronicle of the First Thirteen Years of the Reign of King Edward IV,* ed. James O. Halliwell, Camden Society (London, 1839).

Wedding of Sir Gawain: The Weddynge of Sir Gawen and Dame Ragnell, ed.
    Laura Summer, Smith College Studies in Modern Languages, 4 (1924).
William the Marshal: see *Guillaume le Maréchal.*
Ywain and Gawain, ed Albert B. Friedman and Norman T. Harrington,
    EETS, 254 (London, 1964). [For French Version see Chrétien de Troyes,
    Yvain.]

Index

285